Communicative Action

Communicative Action

Essays on Jürgen Habermas's
The Theory of Communicative Action

Edited by
Axel Honneth and Hans Joas

Translated by
Jeremy Gaines and Doris L. Jones

The MIT Press, Cambridge, Massachusetts

First MIT Press edition, 1991
This English translation © Polity Press 1991
First published as *Kommunikatives Handeln: Beiträge zu Jürgen Habermas' 'Theorie des kommunkiativen Handelns',* Introduction and chapters 1, 6, 7, 11 © Suhrkamp Verlag, Frankfurt/Main 1986; chapter 4 © *The American Journal of Sociology* (1985/6). Otherwise each chapter is the copyright of the individual author.

Printed and bound in Great Britain.

Library of Congress Cataloging-in-Publication Data

Kommunikatives Handeln. English.
    Communicative action: essays on Jürgen Habermas's Theory of communicative action/ edited by Axel Honneth and Hans Joas: translated by Jeremy Gaines and Doris L. Jones— 1st MIT Press ed.
    p.   cm.—(Studies in contemporary German social thought)
    Translation of: Kommunikatives Handeln.
    Includes bibliographical references.
    ISBN 0–262–08196–2
    1. Habermas, Jürgen. Theories des kommunikativen Handelns.   2. Sociology— Philosophy.   3. Communication—Philosophy.   4. Rationalism.   5. Social interaction.
I. Honneth, Axel, 1949–   .   II. Joas, Hans, 1948–   .   III. Title.   IV. Series.
HM24.H323K6513   1990
301'.01—dc20   90–6125
                                                                                    CIP

Contents

Publishers' Note

All the contributions in this volume have been translated from German, except those by Jeffrey Alexander and Thomas McCarthy, which are published here in their original English versions.

On the Contributors

Jeffrey Alexander, born 1947, is Professor of Sociology at the University of California in Los Angeles. His publications include *Theoretical Logic in Sociology*, 4 vols (Berkeley, 1981–3); *Twenty Lectures. Sociological Theory after 1945*, (New York, 1987).

Johann Pall Arnason, born 1940 in Dalvik, Iceland, has been teaching sociology at La Trobe University in Melbourne since 1978. His publications include *Von Marcuse zu Marx* (Neuwied, 1971); *Zwischen Natur und Gesellschaft* (Cologne, 1976), *Praxis und Interpretation* (Frankfurt, 1988).

Johannes Berger, born 1939, is Professor of Sociology at the University of Mannheim. His publications include (with V. Bader and others) *Krise und Kapitalismus bei Marx*, 3 vols (Frankfurt, 1975); (with V. Bader) *Einführung in die Gesellschaftstheorie* (Frankfurt, 1980). He has written extensively on political economy and research on the labour market.

Günter Dux, born 1930, is Professor of Sociology at the University of Freiburg. His present interest can best be described under the heading of 'history and cognition'. His publications include *Strukturwandel der Legitimation* (Freiburg, 1976); *Rechtssoziologie* (Stuttgart, 1978); *Die Logik der Weltbilder, Sinnstrukturen im Wandel der Geschichte*, 2nd edn. (Frankfurt, 1985); *Die Zeit in der Geschichte* (Frankfurt, 1989).

Axel Honneth, born 1949 in Essen, teaches philosophy at the J.W. Goethe University in Frankfurt. His publications include (with Hans Joas) *Social Action and Human Nature*, (Cambridge, 1988); *Kritik der Macht. Reflexionsstufen einer kritischen Gesellschaftstheorie* (Frankfurt, 1985, English language edn., Cambridge, MA, 1991); *Die zerrissene Welt des Sozialen. Sozialphilosophische Aufsätze* (Frankfurt, 1990).

Hans Joas, born 1948 in Munich, is Professor of Sociology at the Free University Berlin. His publications include *Die gegenwärtige Lage der soziologischen Rollentheorie* (Frankfurt, 1973–8); *G. H. Mead. A Contemporary Reexamination* (Cambridge, 1985); (with Axel Honneth) *Social Action and Human Nature* (Cambridge, 1988); (with Michael Bochow) *Wissenschaft und Karriere* (Frankfurt, 1987). He has published extensively on sociological theory and research on education.

Hans-Peter Krüger, born 1954 in Potsdam, gained his doctorate in 1979 at the Humboldt University in East Berlin with a thesis on *Heroismus und Arbeit in der Entstehungsgeschichte der Hegelschen Philosophie 1788–1803*. He has been a member of the 'Institut für Theorie, Geschichte und Organisation der Wissenschaft' attached to the GDR Academy of Sciences since 1982. His publications include: *Kritik der kommunikativen Vernunft* (Berlin/GDR, 1990).

Thomas McCarthy, born 1940, is Professor of Philosophy at Northwestern University in Evanston, Illinois. He is the author of the book *The Critical Theory of Jürgen Habermas* (Cambridge, MA, 1978), as well as of numerous articles on epistemology and critical theory. He is also the translator of several books written by Habermas, and editor of the series *Contemporary German Social Thought* (Cambridge, MA).

Herbert Schnädelbach, born 1936 in Altenburg, Thuringia, has been Professor of Philosophy, especially Social Philosophy, at the University of Hamburg since 1978. Publications include *Erfahrung, Begründung und Reflexion, Versuch über den Positivismus* (Frankfurt, 1971); *Geschichtsphilosophie nach Hegel* (Freiburg/Munich, 1974); *Reflexion und Diskurs* (Frankfurt, 1977); *Philosophie in Deutschland 1831–1933* (Frankfurt, 1983); (with E. Martens) *Philosophie. Ein Grundkurs* (Reinbek bei Hamburg, 1985). He has contributed to numerous journals, collected volumes and reference work.

Martin Seel, born 1954 in Ludwigshafen am Rhein, is Research Assistant in Philosophy at the University of Constance. His publications include *Die Kunst der Entzweiung. Zum Begriff der ästhetischen Rationalität* (Frankfurt, 1985).

Charles Taylor, born 1931 in Montreal, is Professor of Political Philosophy at the McGill University in Montreal. His publications include *The Explanation of Behavior* (London, 1964); *Hegel* (Cambridge, 1975); *Hegel and Modern Society* (Cambridge, 1979); *Philosophical Papers I and II* (Cambridge, 1985); *Sources of the Self. The Making of the Modern Identity* (Cambridge, 1989), and numerous articles.

Introduction

Axel Honneth and Hans Joas

In 1981, Jürgen Habermas published his 'Theory of Communicative Action' as a two-volume book (English language edn, Boston, 1984 and 1987). He thus brought to a provisional conclusion the intellectual efforts of twenty years of reflexion and research. The basic idea informing it, namely that an indestructible moment of communicative rationality is anchored in the social form of human life, is defended in this book by means of a contemporary philosophy of language and science, and is used as the foundation for a comprehensive social theory. As is often the case in Habermas's writings, systematic argumentation and the close scrutiny of theoretical traditions are closely intertwined here. The theories of Weber, Mead, Durkheim and Parsons, as well as Marxism (albeit more in the background), provide the system of reference within which the basic ideas for a theory of society are historically justified and at the same time tested by argument.

As soon as the book appeared, it attracted widespread attention which, given the difficulties which it presented to the reader, is indeed surprising. The first published reactions to it, however, fell embarrassingly short of the complexity and richness of the book; the most common criticism, usually voiced ironically, was that it was a hopelessly idealistic undertaking, although such reviews neither discussed the book in any depth nor gave a fair account of it. It was not long, however, before a more serious-minded discussion of the book began, and this has continued unabated ever since and, to a remarkable degree, is being carried on at the international level. It would hardly be an exaggeration to say that Habermas's writings as a whole and this book in particular have become a focal point of international debate on theory in the social sciences – and with good reason. There can be few other authors who, in terms of systematic argumentation and knowledge of intellectual history, thematic breadth and the drive to diagnose the present, are so capable of drawing together the most diverse areas and issues of discussion. Indeed, anyone participating in debate today with nothing at all to say about this great figure excludes him/herself from the ranks of serious theorists.

It is our impression that the discussion has focused increasingly on four thematic complexes and the intrinsic links between them. These four themes are: firstly, the question of a meaningful concept of the *rationality* of actions, persons or forms of life; secondly, the problem of an appropriate *theory of action*; thirdly, the question of the connection between individual actions, in other words, the problem commonly treated in sociology as that of defining a concept of *social order*; fourthly, the *diagnosis of contemporary society* – in other words, analysis of the principal present trends and crises. Habermas's proposed solutions to these problems cannot be reconstructed adequately here. Roughly speaking, he seeks firstly to defend a concept of communicative rationality by means of a specific conception of 'validity claims intrinsic to speech', in order to resist instrumentalistic reductions of rationality as well as those fashionable slogans which put the blame on reason. Secondly, his theory of action is characterized by dichotomously juxtaposing communicative action and instrumental or strategic action. Thirdly, at the level of a theory of social order, Habermas introduces two concepts: the concept of 'lifeworld' and that of 'system', which is derived from functionalism; a wide-ranging exposition is devoted to the historical process in which these two types of order factually separate out. Fourthly, this pair of concepts is also at the heart of Habermas's diagnosis of contemporary society, which above all emphasizes the danger to the lifeworld posed by system imperatives, but at the same time warns against withdrawing the rationality of systemic mechanisms from the domain of the state and the economy.

Given the time that has now passed since its original publication, it would appear possible and fruitful to take preliminary stock of the discussion surrounding the contribution which *The Theory of Communicative Action* makes to philosophy and the social sciences. This is the task which the present collection of articles has set itself. It contains some previously published contributions to the discussion, but most of the chapters were written especially for this book. The principle that guided us in selecting or requesting contributions was whether the respective author was able – despite concentration on specific weaknesses, real or apparent, in Habermas's theoretical edifice – to keep sight of the overall structure. One disadvantage of this approach is that no attempt is made to have the relevant expert communities conduct the equally necessary examination of Habermas's interpretations of the sociological classics. Only a few of the contributions to this volume include even marginal comments correcting Habermas's interpretations of Weber, Mead, Durkheim, Parsons and Marx.

The volume starts off with three essays devoted to Habermas's suggestions for a solution to the issue of rationality. Herbert Schnädelbach, Charles Taylor and Martin Seel critically examine from different perspectives the approach that Habermas uses to distinguish between different validity claims intrinsic to speech in an attempt to reconstruct three aspects of the rationality of action. Herbert Schädelbach's essay is one of the first detailed publications on *The Theory of Communicative Action*. After providing a summary of the work that is as concise as it is skilled in handling the material, Schnädelbach concentrates on a critique of three of Habermas's propositions. He doubts that a theory of rationality can be supported by reference to the quality of action-related knowledge, as Habermas suggests with his cognitivist approach. Next, he questions the internal relationship Habermas establishes between understanding and evaluating linguistic utterances. Finally he criticizes – as do other authors in this book – the ambiguous use Habermas makes of the concept of lifeworld: Habermas initially introduces this from the participant's perspective, only then to change perspective and transform it into the subject of a distanced analysis. Schnädelbach summarizes these doubts by questioning whether Habermas has actually succeeded in justifying the normative premises of his projected social theory.

At the beginning of his essay, Charles Taylor, who became well known in Germany chiefly through his masterly book on Hegel, develops the foundations for a 'theory of communicative action' from a 'dialogue theory' of language. His criticism is initially directed at the assumption of the possibility of ethical formalism. Taylor maintains that the strict separation between questions of justice and questions of the good life, which Habermas proposes in his discourse ethics, cannot be made, because every formal or procedural criterion of justice is, for its part, already invariably included in a comprehensive understanding of the good life. This argument is then expanded into a general criticism of the material appropriateness and normative desirability of Habermas's differentiation between three aspects of rationality. In the process, Taylor aims to develop an expanded concept of rationality which breaks any formalist confines.

Martin Seel's contribution takes up this line of Taylor's argument in a sense, but gives it a creative twist. He begins by demonstrating an interreferential connection between the three dimensions of rationality distinguished, and attempts to show that all specialized argumentation necessarily includes assumptions about the validity domains thus excluded. If this is true, the manner in which switches are made from one form of argument to another would be the substantive problem facing a comprehensive theory of rationality. The surprising chain of thoughts with which Seel concludes his essay aims to go some way towards providing such a solution. He proposes that 'communicative rationality' be understood precisely as that situational faculty for judgement which helps to accomplish 'rationally' the constant switch between the validity domains.

The middle section of the volume, i.e. the contributions by Alexander, Dux, Joas, McCarthy and Krüger, focuses on the fundamental theoretical questions of social theory. Jeffrey Alexander is a young American sociologist who attracted widespread attention with his ambitious four-volume work, *Theoretical Logic in Sociology*. His contribution deserves attention as a confrontation between this neo-Parsonian approach and that taken by Habermas. Alexander places Habermas in the tradition of Critical

Theory, but thinks him distinct from it both because of the insistence on explicit justifications being given for the normative referential framework and because of his willingness to consider a wide spectrum of empirical-theoretical traditions. He agrees emphatically with Habermas's critique of Weber's instrumentalist reductions, but discerns a contradiction between this criticism and Habermas's own critical theory. His main criticism is that Habermas does not really elaborate a theory of society on the basis of a non-instrumentalist concept of action, but instead creates an action-theoretic residual category of non-communicative action, and thus, in the style of Critical Theory, ultimately submits a largely non-normative description of modern life.

Günter Dux concentrates on the question of the (phylogenetic) origin of norms. He bases his approach on the idea that Habermas's distinction between action, on the one hand, and discourse relieved of action functions, on the other, has to situate the development of norms in discourses and not in action, which is usually guided by interests. He attempts to verify this in a critical discussion of Habermas's remarks on the historical reconstruction of early societies; this approach is based on the assumption that weak points in the historical reconstruction are indicative of deficiencies in systematic thought. Dux's criticism of Habermas, which draws on interesting anthropological material, concludes with the allusion to an alternative concept to help explain the genesis of norms.

In his essay, Hans Joas seeks initially to demonstrate the relative narrowness of the action theory proposed by Habermas and to raise the question whether the concept of communicative action can do justice to the tasks of the sociological theory of action, the richness of intellectual history and the phenomenal breadth of action as a topic. In a second step, he attempts to show that precisely this constricted action-theoretical approach and a problematical understanding of the logical status of action theory compel Habermas to resort to (untenable) functionalist constructs. The obverse side of this reliance on functionalism is the introduction of the 'lifeworld' concept, which Joas does not find convincing. He disputes the idea that the concept of the lifeworld, which Habermas deployed in communication theory, and to which he also gives an epistemological thrust, can at the same time be construed in terms of a theory of social order. If 'system' and 'lifeworld' are thus extremely problematic concepts in Habermas's theoretical edifice, doubts also arise about his diagnosis of contemporary society, since it utilizes these concepts.

Thomas McCarthy concentrates solely on the distinction between 'system' and 'lifeworld', which certainly represents the core of the concept of society as developed by Habermas. As the title of his essay suggests, McCarthy sets out to justify his suggestion that, by adopting the functionalist concept of system, Habermas succumbs to the seduction of a tradition in the social sciences which can be criticized precisely by means of Habermas's own original approach. McCarthy pursues a theoretical, methodological and normative line of argument, attempting to delineate an action-theoretical alternative to the systems-theoretical analysis of formal organizations; in support of this criticism he cites the political sphere of late capitalism as an example, and finally justifies the suspicion that a systems-theoretical concept of politics makes it necessary to sacrifice a radical model of democracy.

Hans-Peter Krüger, a remarkable young philosopher from the GDR, analyses Habermas's work critically on the basis of a stance which relies on Hegel, historical materialism and Soviet psycho-linguistic traditions. He develops interesting arguments to refute Habermas's critique of Marx and to make a case for the potential afforded by a scholarly tradition of studying language so far completely ignored by Habermas. The issue which forms the core of his work, however, is the question whether the 'theory of communicative action' can ever overcome the alleged dualism of systems and action theory, or whether this problem needs to be formulated differently. By raising the prospect of a 'new mode of communication for society as a whole', Krüger shows briefly how this could be achieved and what consequences this would have for social theory.

While all the essays mentioned so far deal primarily with the fundamental theoretical assumptions of Habermas's book, Johannes Berger makes the implications of its diagnosis of contemporary society the focus of his essay. The rigid allocation of the two types of action, 'communicative' and 'strategic', to distinct domains is, as Berger sees it, the central problem involved in Habermas's fundamental premises; the consequences for the diagnosis of contemporary society become especially clear in the dangers lurking in the phrase 'colonization of the lifeworld'. In effect, this concentrates attention on the intrusion of systemic imperatives into the lifeworld. On the one hand, this makes it easy to overlook the possibility of internal crises in the political or economic domain of action. On the other, it also does not seem at all to take into account the possibility of an intrusion of lifeworld orientations into the spheres of purposive-rational action.

Many of the contributions assembled in this volume are based on possible alternatives to Habermas's theory. This prospect becomes most evident in the last contribution, the essay by Johann P. Arnason. He wishes to pursue the insights of *Dialectic of Enlightenment* in a productive way by adopting that interpretation of human socialization which takes a 'logic of domination' as its guideline. Arnason's first criticism is that Habermas fails to consider either the intrinsic dynamics of the state or the global interdependence of the capitalist economic system. He then relates these empirical criticisms to Habermas's basic assumptions, applying the critique of the systems-theoretical interpretation of the polity and economy, which actually hinders the comprehensive analysis both of the way in which social power functions and of the constitutive role played by exchange value. The implications of this criticism for the theory of action become clear in the next step: only if the concept of strategic action as such is more strongly differentiated can phenomena of social conflict such as war and competition be recognized as constitutive dimensions of human socialization. In a final step, Arnason sketches the conclusions to be drawn from his criticisms for a theory of modernity. Modernity would have to be analysed not as a homogeneous 'project', but as a 'field of tension' between the competing interpretations of Enlightenment and Romanticism, if it is to be perceived in the referential framework of a theory of society.

Our volume concludes with an extensive reply by Jürgen Habermas, not only to the commentaries on his work presented here, but also to many of the critical discussions published on his book to date. We wish to express our gratitude for his cooperation.

1 The Transformation of Critical Theory

Herbert Schnädelbach

The adage that books have a fate of their own has proved to be true once again in the case of Jürgen Habermas's *The Theory of Communicative Action* (*TCA*). What was to be expected did of course happen: an attempt was made to intercept an important book before it reached its readers and, by making suitable commentaries, to lay down the shape its reception should take. Among these were some overhasty classifications in terms of politics or intellectual history intended to ensure that readers would not be irritated by the fact that the book was unusual. Habermas's book was written 'for those who have a professional interest in the foundations of social theory' (*TCA*, vol. I, p. xlii) but unfortunately this cannot be said of the early reviewers; other interests were sometimes stronger. What is annoying about this is the danger of polarization it entails, a situation hostile to a factual discussion. The following is an attempt to avoid following that path; I wish to address critically those questions which would probably be of interest for a philosophical journal, yet without either claiming to provide an exhaustive account or merely giving a simple definition in terms of the 'pros and cons' of the theory.

Habermas's book has repeatedly been called opaque, his train of thought convoluted and full of detours, although the author himself repeatedly sets out charts offering an overview and giving pointers for initial orientation. The origin of these charges is probably to be found in the fact that the overall project is situated at the intersecting point between two sets of distinctions which are normally treated respectfully as opposites, namely that between 'philosophy and social theory, on the one hand, and between theory and the history of theory, on the other. With regard to the second distinction, Habermas endeavoured in his *Knowledge and Human Interests* (*KHI*) to develop theory further, using means drawn precisely from the history of theory, and to present the systematic theses, put forward in his inaugural lecture of the same name via the medium of a critical hermeneutics, of important precursors in theory. By contrast, the separation of the reconstructive excursus on the classics (cf. *TCA*, vol. I, p. xl) from the argumentative intermediate observations and the summarizing conclusion has the advantage of not overburdening the one with the other.

The author thus gains room for manoeuvre on both flanks. He no longer has to carry the critical exegesis of existing theories so far that in the light of it his own project appears convincing; and conversely, lines of argumentation then become possible for which no interpretative proof is available. Yet he is persuaded that the interlinking of theory and the history of theory must be retained, although this is not only justified in immanent philosophical terms, namely by referring, for example, to the well-known hermeneutic arguments. Rather, his approach points to the unique interconnection of philosophy and social theory, which is where he takes up the project of Critical Theory. Habermas brings the two disciplines together in such a manner that they change. 'The theory of communicative action is not a metatheory, but the beginning of a social theory concerned to validate its own critical standards' (*TCA*, vol. I, p. xxxix). Whereas in *Knowledge and Human Interests* we can still read that 'philosophy is preserved in science as critique' (*KHI*, p. 63), and 'Outside of critique, however, philosophy retains no rights', the 'theory of rationality' is now the 'point' upon which 'philosophy in its postmetaphysical, post-Hegelian form is converging' (*TCA*, vol. I, p. 2), and this in full awareness of the fact that the 'critique of ideology' (*KHI*, loc. cit.) does not suffice to generate critical standards for social theory. This theory of rationality is, however, at the same time no longer possible in the form of a purely philosophical theory, as was traditionally claimed with reference to 'Reason'.

'Rationality' cannot be explicated without an investigation of what is actually experienced as a rational life or is claimed to be such (cf. *TCA*, vol. I, p. xli), and this, in turn, requires a social theory which is more than merely sociology as practised today (ibid., p. 5ff.). For such a social theory must at least be conscious of the fact that lived rationality is the result of the implementation of certain concepts of rationality in the lifeworld in the course of processes of rationalization. A social theory oriented toward the problem of rationality cannot, in order words, dispense with the instructive immersion in social history and the conceptual endeavours in explication normally expected of philosophy. In addition, it must also secure its own history, because it is not, for the reasons given above, merely linked externally to its object: as the consciousness of lived rationality – without which rationality cannot be lived – it is simultaneously a part of rationality.

Social theory as a critical theory of modernity, and philosophy as the theory of rationality, are thus dependent on one another. The theory of rationality is expected to provide the 'critical standards' for the social theory, whereas the theory of a modernity understood as the result of social rationalization wishes to extricate the traditional philosophy of reason from the ghetto of purely conceptual immanence (cf. ibid., pp. 273ff.), and to force it to form itself anew in the field of formal universal pragmatics. The concept of 'communicative rationality' is the middle term here, and it is to this that the title of the book refers – the concept is intended to permit a linking of a theory of rationality and social theory in such a way that 'a conceptualization of the social-life context that is tailored to the paradoxes of modernity' (ibid., p. xl) becomes possible. One can from this vantage point then understand the structure of a theory of communicative action characterized by 'a theory of communicative action that places understanding in language, as the medium for coordinating action, at the focal point of interest' (ibid., p. 274; cf. also pp. 86 and 94ff.).

It is significant that this theory thinks of communication and action as a unity, without reducing the one to the other (cf., for example, ibid., pp. 100ff.). The concept of 'communicative rationality' avails itself as a link connecting the two, a concept which is introduced and justified at three levels in the Introduction (cf. ibid., p. 7). At the metatheoretical level, an attempt is made to show that every comprehensive understanding of communication and action must refer to the theme of rationality and that this can also be demonstrated using the 'sociological concepts of action current today' (ibid.). With respect to methodology, Habermas proposes that an internal connection obtains between the concept of a sociology that understands meaning (*sinnverstehend*) and the problematics of rationality for the simple reason that communicative actions always require an interpretation that at least attempts to be rational (cf. ibid., pp. 105ff., in particular p. 116). And, finally, empirico-theoretical deliberations on the modernization of societies are intended to show that this process can be adequately understood only as a process of rationalization.

The major chapter on Max Weber subsequently has the function both of correcting any interpretations which reduce social rationalization to the implementation of purposive rationality and of preparing the ground for a more powerful alternative. It relies on the notion of elaborating the conceptual distinction between instrumental and communicative action – the central area of Habermas's thought since his essays on 'Labour and Interaction' – in such a manner that it can be applied in the context of social theory. 'Intermediate Reflections' in the first volume is dedicated to this end. Yet the author interweaves two chapters on the history of theory before embarking on the application of that distinction.

The critique of Critical Theory is intended to highlight the aporias in which a critical theory of modernity necessarily entangles itself if informed solely by Weber's model of rationalization. It also outlines the absolute necessity of transforming Critical Theory from the standpoint of communicative rationality, and endeavours to pinpoint an initial basis for this in Adorno's work. The chapter on Mead and Durkheim, by contrast, is intended to shield this transformation against any suspicion of its merely being theoretical pie-in-the-sky. It demonstrates that the 'paradigm shift' in social theory from purposive rational action to communicative action had already taken place in the work of these two major thinkers and that what they developed needs to be integrated into the Weberian discussion of rationalization in order to initiate a critical theory of modernity.

This integration is undertaken in a systematic form in the 'Intermediate Reflections: System and Lifeworld' in the second volume (*TCA*, vol. II, pp. 113–98). The pair of concepts used in the title is to be understood to represent terms in social theory which correlate to the difference in action theory between purposive rational action and communicative action. 'Life-world' is expressly introduced as a 'correlate to processes of reaching understanding'; 'subjects acting communicatively always come to an understanding in the horizon of a lifeworld' (*TCA*, vol. I, p. 70). In Habermas's usage, however, the concept of 'system' implicitly corresponds as a type to 'purposive action', for societies can be experienced only as systems and then observed from a third-person perspective to the extent that

> action oriented to success can be freed from the imperatives of an understanding that is to be communicatively renewed over and over again and can be at least partially uncoupled from action oriented to reaching understanding. This makes possible a societal institutionalization of purposive-rational action for general-ized goals, for example, the formation of subsystems, controlled through money and power, for rational economics and rational administration. (*TCA*, vol. I, p. 72; cf. also in particular vol. II, pp. 117ff.)

The problem of the relation between system and lifeworld, which according to the author is not solved either by Max Weber or by Critical Theory, makes a two-level social theory necessary, one that embraces both system and lifeworld (cf. *TCA*, vol. II, p. 119), a social theory which conceives of the tension-laden difference between the two as the product of history, yet which can understand itself only as critical social theory if it is able to provide a systematic account of the genetic and normative primacy of communicative action and of the lifeworld as the social counterpart of such a history (cf. *TCA*, vol. I, p. 279). The chapter on Parsons serves to put the demand made by the history of theory for a concrete systematic 'two-level concept of society which links the aspects of lifeworld and system' into practice, and leads into the 'Concluding Reflections', which, by combining the results of the systematic investigations into the history of social theory, sketch the project of a Critical Theory transformed into a theory of modernity.

Following this cursory overall survey of the issues tackled in the book and of its main thesis and structure, I wish now to move on to a separate discussion of individual complexes of problems which should be decisive for the book's reception in philosophy. The key terms 'rationality', 'com-municative action', 'lifeworld' and 'Critical Theory' serve to illustrate the areas addressed.

In a 'preliminary specification' the author situates the concept of 'rational-ity' at the point where two fundamental distinctions intersect and at the same time creates a 'cognitivist version' (*TCA*, vol. I, p. 10) of the concept.

The two distinctions concern the dispositional and non-dispositional as well as the descriptive and normative usages of 'rational' as a predicate. We use the term in a dispositional form if we attribute it to person; if we refer by it to actions and utterances (of the widest variety; cf. ibid., pp. 14–15), then we use it non-dispositionally. Now Habermas asserts that whenever we speak of the ' "rationality" of a stimulated response, or the "rationality" of a system's change in state' – and one could add to this talking about the rationality of institutional rules that do not arise intentionally – we use the word in a 'derived' or 'metaphorical' sense. We must ask here whether there really are compelling reasons to link the non-dispositional meaning of 'rationality' in the substantive sense back to the dispositional meaning. Or, to put it differently, what compels us to ascribe all the phenomena which we term rational to the competence of subjects capable of language and action?

The significance of such a form of introducing the argument for theory's underlying stategy has been obvious since the debate with Luhmann. The intention is to reduce the systemic rationality championed by systems theorists to systemic functionality, and to use the remaining, additional meaning of 'rationality' as the basis for a 'critique of functionalist reason'. However, this leaves the question open of whether the context in which Habermas chooses to introduce 'rational' does not over-prejudice the discussion. Analytically speaking, numerous plausible reasons can be cited for 'rationality' belonging to 'person-action-language'; and much historical evidence is available to suggest that the society's character as a system – the reason why systems theory has enjoyed such a boom – arises in contexts of action. The sceptic will nevertheless doubt whether this genesis can be completely referred back to the disposition for rationality among subjects capable of language and action. It is perhaps clear that this way of introducing 'rationality' into the argument is linked to the thesis of the primacy of communicative rationality over purposive rationality, and we should not doubt that Habermas has a number of arguments independent of this at his disposal with which to buttress the thesis. The systems theorist will question all the same – just as Luhmann actually did in his replies to Habermas – whether the non-dispositional form of rationality which the systems theorist interprets in terms of systems theory has to be referred back to people's dispositions. To the extent that such rationality can be interpreted as the actualization of dispositions – and even this is far from self-evident – the systems theorist will refer it back precisely to systemic dispositions. It is not the object here to question the accuracy of Habermas's conceptualization of rationality in principle, but rather to indicate that it can be truly justified only in the course of the overall project – and this, after all, attempts via immanent critique to go beyond systems theory.

With respect to the distinction in dimension drawn between 'descriptive' and 'normative', Habermas assumes that the concept of 'rationality', if used in a descriptive-theoretical sense, is always also 'substantive in normative terms' (cf. ibid., p. xl). The question here is whether that which is intuitively obvious can at the same time be proven to exist in principle. We certainly always also use 'rational' as an evaluative, indeed as a normative predicate. Bennett has shown in his *Rationality: An Essay towards an Analysis* (1964) that when analysing 'rational' one can study at close quarters our institutions and the conceptual weaponry implemented in the relevant empirical knowledge without making use of the normative connotations of the predicate. Yet, even if one feels these connotations to be essential, the question still remains whether the normativity of the rational is something which affects the observer or can rather be situated fully on the 'side of the object' in the sense that one talks of normativity here only with respect to its signifying regulations for the behaviour, or orientation for action, of the persons observed or of social systems (cf. the theses in *TCA*, vol. I, pp. 114ff.). The neo-historicism and neo-relativism of followers of the later Wittgenstein (cf., for example, B. R. Wilson (ed.), *Rationality*, Oxford, 1970) thrive on this difference. The programme for a universal pragmatics, as it is developed further in the first 'Intermediate Reflections', can also be interpreted as the attempt to block off this escape route and to stabilize anew the inseverable interconnection of rationality and normativity – which was regarded as a matter of course by German Idealism and Critical Theory – by means of a theory of validity claims linked to communicative action. Yet here again the theory as a whole has to bear the burden of providing proof for the exposed position created by the intuitive conceptual explanation.

The implicit normativism in the way in which the concepts are introduced is made clear by the following statement: 'We can summarize the above as follows: Rationality is understood to be a disposition of speaking and acting subjects that is expressed in modes of behavior for which there are good reasons or grounds. This means that rational expressions admit of objective evaluation' (*TCA*, vol. I, p. 22). 'Good reasons' and 'objective' are to be understood here to mean that both are not exhausted in what people hold to be good or objective when arguing with one another about something claimed rationally. This corresponds to the systematic linking of rationality and 'knowledge' (ibid., p. 8), i.e. the 'cognitivist version' of rationality (cf. ibid., p. 10), which Habermas admittedly expands without actually abandoning it. Habermas may well 'presuppose this concept of knowledge without further clarification, for rationality has less to do with the possession of knowledge than with how speaking and acting subjects *acquire and use knowledge*' (ibid., p. 8). However, the fact that at least the intuitive understanding of rationality quite definitely does depend on the quality of the knowledge used by subjects capable of language and action would suggest that the opposite holds true. The further explanations in the Introduction show that Habermas operates with a very elastic concept of knowledge which does not mean much more than 'the consciousness of . . . ' or (put traditionally) the reflexive possession of means of orientation which are then followed by speech and action. This is not altered by 'knowledge', understood in this way, being determined more closely at a later stage – by validity claims which are purportedly linked to it – for this at best leaves us with determinate claims to knowledge. If this step is indeed meant thus, then the question remains against which standards one can measure whether judgements are good or the assessment objective, both of which are, going by the quotation, essential components of rationality.

How seriously should we then take the cognitivism in the theory of rationality, given that Habermas tends towards a cognitivist position in ethics as well (cf. ibid., p. 19)? Behind this question lurks the controversy whether reason must be defined as a capacity for knowledge and thus via a constitutive reference to truth or not. (It is a well-known fact that, for Kant, the domain of reason is greater than that of knowledge to the extent that it is at the same time the origin of transcendental appearance and, as practical reason, is one of the grounds determining will; Hegel is of a different opinion.) I would like to suggest giving up cognitivism in the theory of rationality, that is, avoiding weighing it down with a theorem of knowledge. We can, after all, also classify utterances and actions as rational if the estimations on which they are based prove to be erroneous, whereas cognitivism is not able to do so, given that it binds reason to knowledge and truth: in its eyes, anything erroneous, all lies and all deception must be irrational.

The question of whether or not certain validity claims are substantively linked to the rational is, however, not touched by this proposal. One can give up cognitivism without having to contest that rational utterances or actions as a rule purport to follow good reasons and stand the test of an objective assessment. The standards for this cannot be sought in the truth of the knowledge involved, but in the rules of consensus formation through argumentation. This is indeed the approach taken by Habermas:

> Thus the rationality proper to the communicative practice of everyday life points to the practice of argumentation as a court of appeal that makes it possible to continue communicative action with other means when disagreements can no longer be repaired with everyday routines and yet are not to be settled by the direct or strategic use of force. For this reason I believe that the concept of communicative rationality, which refers to an unclarified systematic interconnection of universal validity claims, can be adequately explicated only in terms of a theory of argumentation. (*TCA*, vol. I, pp. 18–19)

It is therefore somewhat misleading of Habermas in turn to term his conviction 'according to which practical questions can in principle be settled by way of argumentation' a 'cognitivist position' (*TCA*, vol. I, p. 19). One can either understand this solely against the background of his consensus theory of truth – for what could 'cognitivism' mean without referring substantively to truth? – or as a figure of speech which could better be replaced by 'rationalist position'. The rationality incorporated in everyday communicative practice can adequately be characterized with the aid of validity claims which one considers can be decided by means of argument; yet, as a theorist of rationality, one does not need to take a stance on the quality of such claims, i.e. on whether they can be decided effectively in argument and what the results of this would be: the mere existence of a 'reflexive medium' (cf. ibid., p. 20) suffices.

Habermas sharply contests precisely this in his discussion of Skjervheim (cf. *TCA*, vol. I, p. 113ff.). He maintains in the section on understanding meaning in the social sciences that the interpreter of speech acts oriented toward reaching understanding 'must bring to mind the reasons with which a speaker would if necessary and under suitable conditions defend its [an expression's] validity . . . [and] is himself drawn into the process of defending validity claims' (ibid., p. 115).

Habermas continues:

> For reasons are of such a nature that they cannot be described in the attitude of a third person, that is, without reactions of affirmation or negation or abstention. The interpreter would not have understood what a 'reason' is if he did not reconstruct it with its claim to provide grounds: that is, if he did not give it a *rational interpretation* in Max Weber's sense. The *description* of reasons demands *eo ipso* an *evaluation*, even when the one providing the description feels that he is not at the moment in a position to judge their soundness. One can understand reasons only to the extent that one understands *why* they are or are not sound, or why in a given case a decision as to whether reasons are good or bad is not (yet) possible. An interpreter cannot, therefore, interpret expressions connected through criticizable validity claims with a potential of reasons (and thus represent knowledge) without taking a position on them. And he cannot take a position without applying his *own* standards of judgment, at any rate standards that he has made his own. (*TCA*, vol. I, pp. 115–16)

This lengthy quotation demonstrates clearly how staunchly Habermas defends his normativist and cognitivist position in the theory of communicative rationality; it perhaps also shows that we have to do here with the foundations of Critical Theory as a whole. Only if Habermas can show that communicative action is fundamental to all other types and structures of action and that thematizing such communicative action necessarily compels the theorist to adopt a position in the light of his/her own standards has he proved that every exhaustive theory of communicative action *must* take the shape of Critical Theory; if such a proof should not be forthcoming, then this would not be the case. Yet neither the passage quoted, nor the context in which it appears, suffices to bear the burden of such a proof. It is unclear why the person who brings to mind the reasons for action and attempts to interpret them rationally is 'drawn into the process of defending validity claims'; to interpret something *rationally*, i.e. on the basis of reasons. This is not the same as interpreting that it *is* rational. Incidentally, Habermas expressly allows that the third person may 'react by abstaining' to the reasons for that which s/he observes and precisely this reaction is in the Weberian version the principle of value freedom. In Schütz's work, the difference between social experience and experience in the social sciences consists precisely in such an *epoché*, i.e. in that methodological interruption of communicative co-action which makes observation and understanding in the social sciences possible in the first place. Why then does Habermas claim that one 'can understand reasons only to the extent that one understands why they are sound'?

The reason for this is to be found in how he construes communicative action in the 'First Intermediate Reflections', where he attempts to create an inseverable composite of the meaning and validity of speech acts, which is then retained in the theory of communicative action even after the integration of a pragmaticist interpretation of 'understanding in language as the medium for coordinating action' (*TCA*, vol. I, p. 274). This is intended to provide a 'formal-pragmatic concept of interaction among speaking and acting subjects, interaction that is mediated through acts of reaching understanding' (ibid., p. 276). Neither analytic action theory nor intentionalist semantics offers a suitable basis in this context, for their field of inquiry is too restricted (cf. ibid., pp. 335ff.). Habermas as a consequence takes up communication theory following in the footsteps of Karl Bühler, and links this to a '*theory of the use of meaning*' (ibid., p. 374, German edn), which admittedly has to be expanded to include certain dimensions in order to cover all aspects of processes of understanding reached through language (cf. ibid., pp. 276ff.).

However, certain difficulties arise at this juncture. First of all, it is questionable whether the 'theory of the use of meaning' (in the singular) really exists. After all, Wittgenstein says, 'For a large class of cases – though not for all – in which we employ the word "meaning" it can be defined thus: the meaning of a word is its use in language' (*Philosophical Investigations*, tr. G. E. M. Anscombe, Oxford, 1958, p. 20e). I, at any rate, am not aware of any theory which has really succeeded in itself reconstructing all linguistic meaning from the ways in which words are used, although some claim to do so. Probably for this reason Habermas does not trust one of these 'theories of the use of meaning' alone (cf. his self-critical remarks in this context, *TCA*, vol. I, pp. 335ff.), but at the same time resorts to 'truth semantics' in the shape devised by 'Frege, and developed through the early Wittgenstein to Davidson and Dummett' (ibid., p. 276) in order, after expanding this to include non-cognitive validity claims, then to insert it into the foundations of his theory of communicative action (cf. ibid., pp. 277ff.). The advantage of this is that he subsequently no longer has to take all conceivable uses of a word into consideration, but rather only those with which validity claims are raised. 'Not all illocutionary acts are constitutive for communicative action, but only those with which speakers connect criticizable validity claims' (ibid., p. 305). Conversely, according to this theory one can understand only those word usages with which validity claims are raised. According to Davidson et al., one understands a sentence when one knows its truth conditions, in other words, when one knows under which conditions it would be true. In its formal-pragmatic elaboration, this amounts to the proposition that one understands linguistic utterances of all types and can make them the basis for coordinating action only if one knows what validity claims are raised by them and under what conditions they can be considered to be justified in terms of argumentation. Habermas wishes thus to transfer the 'internal connection between the *meaning* of a linguistic expression and the *validity* of a sentence formed with its help' (ibid., p. 277) into the theory of communicative action.

The problems involved can be addressed by focusing on the question of the role played by validity claims in communicative understanding. In Davidson's work, at any rate, there is *no* demand that someone who understands a sentence by knowing its truth conditions should in any manner adopt a position on whether these truth conditions are fulfilled or not. Is it then really compelling to include the third-person observer, the interpreter or theorist of communicative action in the critical analysis of the justification of validity claims raised in communicative actions and to maintain that s/he must, in order even to be able to understand her/his object, her/himself adopt a position with regard to her/his own value standards? There is usually no place for such analyses in the first place in lifeworlds that have not become problematic or colonized; in such cases, the social scientist is not compelled by the object to bring her/his own standards to bear. If, however, a discursive situation arises and the communicative actors proceed to thematize and discuss the validity claims they have raised, then it is even less clear why the observer and interpreter, who precisely *does not* participate, should be able to understand all this only by participating in it *after all*. (And risking evaluative or normative judgements of her/his own – thereby entering into the discourse – would be to do exactly this.) To paraphrase Davidson, s/he can understand the situation if s/he knows under which conditions the validity claims raised *could* be considered to have been redeemed in discourse, i.e. if s/he knows what the consensus then reached *would look like*. Habermas states that '*we understand a speech act when we know what makes it acceptable*' (*TCA*, vol. I, p. 297), but in order to understand it he does not have already to possess convictions with respect to what is to be understood actually being already inherent in such a consensus.

It would seem that Habermas has not really demontrated the internal connection between describing and evaluating reasons in his 'First Intermediate Reflections'. The basis for Habermas's normativism – which proves that his project is indeed a critical theory – is not to be found in his universal or formal pragmatics; it is quite definitely to be sought in his material convictions on the relation between 'subject' and 'object' in social theory as a whole, i.e. in his theory of the relation between communicative action and lifeworld.

I have already mentioned the proposition that communicative rationality has genetic and normative primacy over other systems of rationality. It is my contention that Habermas has succeeded in lending this proposition sufficient evidential strength and that his formal-pragmatic foundation of the theory of communicative action is so designed that it permits its linking to empirical pragmatics and a two-level social theory, that is, one which is geared toward the levels of both action and system. The issue of normativity is then decided by whether or not the normative primacy of communicative rationality necessarily also extends to the theorist of rationality or to the social theorist. In Habermas's project, the concept of lifeworld plays a· key role in this context. On the one hand, it is intended in such a way 'that we can see the points of connection for social theory within the theory of communicative action' (*TCA*, vol. I. p. 337). On the other, it serves to enable the linking of formal and empirical pragmatics by representing that mutual, communicative background knowledge without which the communicative use of words cannot be fully grasped as their meaning (cf. ibid., pp. 335ff.). Both functions are connected in such a manner that the second makes the first possible: if the formal theoreticization of communicative action did not point *ipso facto* to a consensus already having been reached empirically, then there would be no conceptual necessity to make the transition from a theory of communicative action to social theory.

The concept of lifeworld as used by Habermas – it is brought into play as the concept complementing that of 'communicative action' – leads to certain difficulties to the extent that it embraces various, highly different motifs. Habermas merges the theoretical traditions of Husserl and Schütz, Wittgenstein and Searle with socio-theoretical deliberations on the relation between interactions structured, on the one hand, by communicative rationality and, on the other, by purposive rationality, as if it were obvious that the concept of 'lifeworld' covered all of this. To put it succinctly, I do not see how it is supposed to be possible to reinterpret in a formal-pragmatic sense this philosophically-loaded term which originated in phenomenology, and then to insert it into social theory in such a manner as to enable one to speak of the 'colonization of the lifeworld', using 'lifeworld' in a non-equivocal sense. I need not remind anyone that in the thought of Husserl and Schütz 'lifeworld' is a concept taken from epistemology developed in the context of a transcendental philosophy or phenomenology. This ties the concept to the first person singular of the researcher, or to the plural of a community of researchers, who, in reflecting on the 'conditions of possibility' of their knowledge, encounter an insurmountable horizon of their possibilities for understanding and knowledge; here 'lifeworld' designates an a priori, which, for all its substantive content, is never quite objectifiable. Habermas tries to rid himself of the connotations this concept has for a philosophy of consciousness by linking what was meant by the concept to Moore's and Wittgenstein's 'common sense certainties' (cf. *TCA*, vol. I, pp. 336ff.) and reinterpreting it in terms of a theory of communicative action. He is, to my mind, able to do so only by forgoing any strict compliance with the first-person perspective. The insurmountability of 'my own respective' lifeworld, which I become aware of via a transcendental approach, becomes a more general thesis on the existence of a background knowledge that cannot be rendered problematic and which plays a role in *all* communication. This leaves the terrain wide open for a two-level conception which allows one to conceive of 'societies *simultaneously* as systems and lifeworlds' (*TCA*, vol. II, p. 118) and, one should add, both are obviously seen from a third-person perspective.

I believe Habermas's concept of lifeworld faces the following dilemma. On the one hand, he wishes to create space in which to deploy the concept for social theory and not just epistemologically by uncoupling it from the context in which it was originally developed, namely phenomenology and a philosophy of consciousness. On the other, it is precisely this new use which is supposed to permit one to join Mead and Durkheim in conceiving of society 'from the perspective of acting subjects as the *lifeworld of a social group*' (ibid., p. 117). On the one hand, the intention is to avoid what Albrecht Wellmer terms 'hermeneutic idealism' (cf. ibid., pp. 119ff.), although I myself hold that this exists only when observers believe they can see everything to do with society (including things foreign to them) only from the perspective of their own particular lifeworld; this may merely be to split definitional hairs. On the other, the object is to retain the 'perspective of acting subjects' which first enables things social to be thematized 'from within', i.e. by means of understanding their meaning. However, if one changes the concept of lifeworld in the way Habermas does, then all that remains is the perspective of the participant seen from the perspective of the observer – or, to put it loosely, the first person in the third person. One is then concentrating on the *observing participant*, and it is easy subsequently to move on to a two-level model of society which no longer poses any problems of perspective. The price to be paid is, however, that the lifeworld is reduced to the everyday world – an everyday world which has already always been understood – of the observers taking part in it, and which, if viewed from the perspective of the third person, can be considered the embodiment of their sensory and motivational resources.

If one transposes this dilemma back on to the theory of communicative action, where Habermas introduced 'lifeworld' as a complementary concept, then the problem of the perspective adopted leads us back again to the question of whether or not the genetic and normative primacy of communicative action necessarily always refers also to the theorist who thematizes communicative action. If one believes that it does, then this means that every theorist of communicative action already always participates in the lifeworld which is the complement to that which s/he thematizes. Even if one may not wish to term this idealism, it amounts at any rate to the universal perspectivism of the observer's own lifeworld, for s/he can in principle never cast off the perspective of observer. The normativism inherent in the thesis that the observer must also always adopt a position similar to that of a participant with regard to the validity claims raised in communicative action if s/he is able to understand it in the first place would then be secured – at the price of relativism. (This is relativism, for meaning and validity of linguistic utterances are thus bound back to the lifeworldly 'background of an implicit knowledge' which 'participants normally regard as trivial and obvious' (*TCA*, vol. I, p. 336), and the observer her/himself is inalienably one of them.) If alternatively one extricates the possible observer fully from the role of participant, be it by means of a consistent change of perspective or the fiction of an *epoché* already effected, this would perhaps bring about a general conceptual network independent of persons and participants, with which one could then study social action from the two-fold point of view of system and communicatively experienced everyday world. Yet, such an approach would not imply that the person who used it would her/himself be subject to the validity claims which might have been applied in the subject-matter studied.

To summarize: I propose that it suffices to abide by the difference in types between purposive-rational and communicative action when developing the difference between system and lifeworld, and not to weigh this difference down with the problem of the perspectives of the first and third persons and their relation to one another. The theory of communicative action is itself fertile enough to provide the justification for such a two-level concept of society and to press ahead with it. Yet to forgo such an elaboration of perspectives leads to the problem of whether and in what sense this concept can then still be called 'critical'.

Habermas's 'theory of communicative action' understands itself as a new definition of the possibilities and tasks of critical theory. The critique of Critical Theory, which is exemplary in its clarity (cf. *TCA*, vol. I, pp. 339ff.), should not just be taken as simple distantiation, but rather as the attempt to create the necessary space for a repetition of a 'critique of instrumental reason' (Horkheimer) as the critique of functionalist reason. This occurs, to put it briefly, both by pinpointing the limits of a paradigm based in a philosophy of consciousness, an approach to which the whole issue of alienation has remained bound at least since Lukács, and by proposing that in their critique of instrumental reason Horkheimer and Adorno had already resorted to another concept of reason without, however, thereby having the necessary conceptual means at their disposal with which to provide foundations for it (cf. ibid., pp. 373ff.). This diagnosis is more than adequate.

The theory of communicative action claims, as quoted above, to be the 'beginning of a social theory concerned to validate its own critical standards' (*TCA*, vol. I, p. xxxix). Habermas noticed at an early date how problematical the normative foundations of the older Critical Theory were, and that it was able to 'secure its normative foundations only in a philosophy of history' (*TCA*, vol. II, p. 382). His Frankfurt inaugural lecture of 1965, 'Knowledge and Human Interests', should today be read as a document in which he emphatically formulates a programme which is brought to temporary completion by the two volumes of *TCA*. At that time, the idea of searching for the normative foundations of Critical Theory in language was launched, and Habermas has ever since, and through his ongoing contact with Karl-Otto Apel, tenaciously attempted to elaborate this: *The Theory of Communicative Action* is the result. This is not the place to go into the individual steps involved. It is also hardly fruitful to argue with the author about the changes which the original plan has since undergone. (At the time, certain 'orthodox' Frankfurt School disciples already bemoaned Habermas's 'destruction' of Critical Theory.) The characterization of the normative foundations themselves would, however, seem to have undergone an important shift. In the inaugural lecture we read that with the structure of language 'maturity (is) already posited for us. Maturity is the only idea which we dispose over in the sense of the tradition of philosophy' (*Technik und Wissenschaft als 'Ideologie'*, Frankfurt, 1968). By contrast, Habermas now formulates the position as follows: 'Reaching understanding is the inherent telos of human speech' (*TCA*, vol.

I, p. 287), i.e. nowadays, a normative concept of reaching understanding intended to justify the critical side of a theory of society has replaced maturity (cf. ibid., pp. 307ff.).

I am not prepared to adopt the all too frequently aired interpretation, according to which this change is some resignative or conservative turn. Habermas has undoubtedly only drawn the obvious conclusions from the difficulty of effectively differentiating between practical and emancipatory interests in knowledge; for this reason he probably later operates only with the distinction between instrumental and communicative action, which he subsequently subdivides even further (cf. *TCA*, vol. I, pp. 319ff.). The normative concept of reaching understanding then suffices in order to distinguish between freedom and repression in the practical domain, which is then specified more closely as the domain of communicative action. Habermas has remained true to himself when he asserts that 'the ideas of reconciliation and freedom . . . can in fact be developed by means of the concept of communicative rationality' (*TCA*, vol. II, pp. 1–2).

Critical opinion varies widely on the issue of whether Habermas's project furthers Critical Theory or not, indeed whether it even is Critical Theory. Whereas one reviewer is concerned about the 'affirmation of social and political structures' for which one could gain 'space' only if one were not to share the 'prejudice for a theory which is supposedly critique', he also speaks of a theory 'which, owing to its point of departure, can only be a theory critical of modern society' (Klaus Hartmann in *Die Welt*, 26 February 1982). Another accuses the author of 'a depotentiation of Critical Theory' (Stefan Breuer in *Leviathan*, 1 (1982), pp. 132ff.). Anyone who feared that a critical theory of society could only take the shape of a condemnation of the present, with appropriate political conclusions being drawn, should perhaps allow these fears to be allayed by Habermas: 'We would not be able to ascertain the rational internal structure of action oriented to reaching understanding if we did not already have before us – in fragmentary and distorted form, to be sure – the existing forms of a reason that has to rely on being symbolically embodied and historically situated' (*TCA*, vol. I, p. xli; cf. also vol. II, pp. 400ff.). Just as Critical Theory, following Marx, always referred to the freedom and equality of all human beings, and this was purportedly incorporated, at least in the form of a claim, into bourgeois society and drew its critical energy from this source, so Habermas attempts to use a normative concept of reaching understanding founded in communicative action itself as the basis for his 'critique of given relations of reaching understanding' and the paradoxes and aberrations of Modernity. (Whether one can derive all this from Marx's theory of value, as Breuer maintains, would first have to be demonstrated.) Certain readers will forever suspect Habermas of conservatism because, like all hermeneuticians, he always respects reason, which is thus already a given in his rule-reconstructing procedures. And the other camp will be suspicious of the fact that he nevertheless understands himself as a *critical* hermeneutician. It is perhaps best to disregard such labels as 'left' and 'right' and to remind oneself of the original meaning of 'critique'.

Critical thought, as a differentiating way of thinking that opposes all dogmatism, is not only the opposite of affirmation, but also of negation. Critical Theory does not wish to relinquish passing *judgement* on its object, but it is precisely this that the neo-conservatives also do not want – they simply judge *differently*. The dispute on Critical Theory cannot, in other words, take up the contrast between affirmative and negative judgements, but can consider only the question whether a theory of society can contain judgements in the first place.

A Critical Theory is not worthy of its name if it does not endeavour to provide an account of the dimensions and standards of its judgements, something Habermas quite conscientiously undertakes to do. He essentially conceives of critique as *immanent*, and this is developed following 'the Marxian model. It is *critical* both of contemporary social sciences and of the social reality they are supposed to grasp' (*TCA*, vol. II, p. 375). The expansive chapters on the history of theory are devoted to an immanent critique of classical outlines for a theory of society. Here, the intention is to measure the outlines in respectively different constellations against their own premises and claims and to ascertain the deficits and still latent potential of these theories. (Interpreters of Weber, Mead, Durkheim, Parsons, Horkheimer and Adorno will, in future, pay close attention to these passages.) Habermas describes the meaning to be attached to an immanent critique of society within a 'theory of capitalist modernization developed by means of a theory of communicative action' (ibid., p. 375) as follows:

> It is critical of the reality of developed societies inasmuch as they do not make full use of the learning potential culturally available to them, but deliver themselves over to an uncontrolled growth of complexity. As we have seen, this increasing system complexity encroaches upon nonrenewable supplies like a quasi-natural force; not only does it outflank traditional forms of life, it attacks the communicative infrastructure of largely rationalized lifeworlds. (loc. cit.)

The general theory of such 'communicative infrastructures' is, however, the theory of communicative action, which 'clarifies the normative foundations of a critical theory of society' (ibid., pp. 396–7).

The theory of communicative action will, however, succeed in effecting such a clarification only if it does not stop short at reconstructing 'the communicative infrastructure of largely rationalized lifeworlds' in terms of its value-free nature. Even if it contrasts its reconstruction with what the infrastructure has been turned into by the 'colonization of the lifeworld', this need not force it to move to the level of critique, for it could nevertheless refrain from passing judgement. Immanent critique must precisely also be *critique* if the label 'immanent critique' is not to be misleading. Habermas claims nothing less than that his project could form the basis for critique in the emphatic sense.

> The theory of communicative action is meant to provide an alternative to the philosophy of history on which earlier critical theory still relied, but which is no longer tenable . . . Social theory need no longer ascertain the normative contents of bourgeois culture, of art and of philosophical thought in an indirect way, that

is, by way of a critique of ideology. With the concept of a communicative reason ingrained in the use of language oriented to reaching understanding, it again expects from philosophy that it take on systematic tasks. The social sciences can enter into a cooperative relation with a philosophy that has taken up the task of working on a theory of rationality. (*TCA*, vol. II, p. 397)

The question whether Habermas has really succeeded in clarifying the 'normative foundations of a critical theory of society' will, in the final instance, be decided by whether the philosophy cooperating with it is really able to provide justifications for 'that moment of unconditionality that, with criticizable validity claims, is built into the conditions of processes of consensus formation' (ibid., p. 399). Habermas would like to believe that it can: in the form of a 'feeder' and free of 'foundationalist claims' (ibid., p. 399). At this point I see myself again confirmed in my sceptical assessment of Habermas's normativism above all by methodological considerations. Irrespective of how one may judge the details of the project Habermas develops, I do not in principle see in what way a reconstructive philosophy with merely hypothetical validity claims (cf. ibid., pp. 399ff.) is supposed to be suited to generating that 'moment of unconditionality' without which 'normative foundations' are simply not to be had. The alternative would be hermeneutics as a practical philosophy *free* of any claim to unconditionality, and all the relativist consequences this entails. It may indeed be the case that communicative action always involves unconditional claims being made, but this does not qualify it to provide the foundations for Critical Theory. To do so, it would itself have to be open to critical assessment. In other words, the theorist would have unconditionally to provide the unconditional standards for critique from the outset and s/he will never be able to derive these from the subject-matter via hypothetical rule reconstruction. It is no coincidence that Karl-Otto Apel staunchly retains his transcendental philosophy. Critical unconditionality without foundationalism – this is the aim Habermas has set himself; doubts are in order whether he has reached it.

2   Language and Society

Charles Taylor

In what follows I wish to comment in two distinct steps on *The Theory of Communicative Action*. The book is exceptionally rich and dense, and I cannot, therefore, claim to provide an exhaustive interpretation. As a first step, however, I would like at least to attempt to interpret one of the main arguments running through the book; as a second step I shall present the elements of a critique.

The area on which I wish to focus could be called the turn taken by the theory of society in the light of a philosophy of language. I shall endeavour in the first section of this essay to portray this turn by reconstructing the central arguments involved. In the second section I shall question whether other central elements in Habermas's theory accord with the concept in the manner in which I have reconstructed it.

If I understand Habermas correctly, he assumes that language must be comprehended in terms of the structures of discourse. We could take as our motto Hölderlin's phrase, 'Since we have conversed we are.' The roots of this central theme of Habermas's approach are to be found in the work of Herder and Humboldt. Habermas attempts to understand society from the vantage point of language. In other words, society is to be explained by referring to the structures of discourse.

I shall now try to divide Habermas's theory into four approaches, each of which relies logically on the others. This subdivision serves to aid my own understanding and may also have the advantage of explaining the relation between this theory and other conceptions which contradict one or the other of the approaches.

1   The fundamentalist approach: language develops and renews itself in discourse. We acquire the ability to speak only as a party to discourse. I have a command of a certain vocabulary, for example, only because I have

learnt, together with other people, to use the words. I can admittedly later invent new and unique expressions, but only against the background of a common language; and there is no guarantee that these new coinages are meaningful. When assuming that I have generated a new meaning I must at least impute to others the *ability* to understand my ideas.

I need not develop this thesis any further. It has become commonplace in philosophy, and followers of Wittgenstein are its leading representatives. It would be useful, however, to outline briefly the consequences it has for a theory of society: any atomistic conception of society in the tradition of Hobbes and Locke which explains social order in terms of the actions of and agreements between indivduals becomes unacceptable. By contrast, the individual's particular projects and plans are drawn from the sum of what has been handed down by the linguistic community of which s/he is a member. S/he first proceeds the way 'one' proceeds and only subsequently can s/he find formulations for truly individual intentions. The notion of a self-centred individual presupposes the community and consequently a framework of customs and norms within which s/he acts. Social theory cannot exclusively take the individual into account, but must also consider this framework of common customs and norms.

2   The complementarity between structure and practice. A language can be understood as a structure or as a code. This structure is normative for speech acts. Yet, the relation between structure and act is not one-sided in that the former exists only because it is continually renewed in linguistic practice. In other words, a reciprocal relationship obtains between structure and practice or, to use Saussure's terms, between 'langue' and 'parole', preventing the one side of the relation being reduced to the other. We do not create the structure in our respective speech acts, for these presuppose the existence of that code; but the structure survives only in those acts and reproduces itself in them – thus persisting in the form of ceaseless mutation. As a consequence, any monist theory of language, be it structuralist or intentionalist in nature, such as in Grice's work, is in principle inadequate.

One would think that it would have been obvious to apply this structure/practice principle to a theory of society. Yet, it has in reality always been neglected. Most thinkers, such as Hegel and Herder, defended the first, fundamentalist approach, namely the originality of community, and thus paid a certain amount of attention to the S/P principle. However, the principle more or less went overboard in the reception of the fundamentalist approach in French sociology, from Saint-Simon and Comte to Durkheim. Durkheim therefore offers us a non-atomistic theory of society, stating that there are non-reducible 'faits sociaux', without, however, paying any heed to the second approach, namely the S/P princple.

If I understand Habermas's thesis correctly, then he believes that whoever ignores this principle invariably misinterprets the primacy of society by having to interpret the latter in the context of a philosophy of consciousness. A society's norms and customs would accordingly inevitably appear simply to have been impressed on individuals in the course of socialization. A theory of internalization that is used in order to attempt to explain how the individual's consciousness is influenced in such a manner that 'les représentations collectives' continue to exert a force through each and every individual. In this way, the theory remains bound to the classical tradition of an epistemological model of subject and object.[1]

If one is, however, prepared to understand language from the standpoint of discourse and society from that of language, then it immediately transpires that such a sociological approach as that just outlined is completely inadequate. Social tradition can continue to exert an influence through individuals only to the extent that it is continually renewed by them – like all structures, it continues to exist by virtue of practice. And in the course of this it necessarily undergoes changes, be it as the result of creative achievements and deliberate innovations or owing to the pressure of ecological, economic or political conditions, or even, ultimately, owing to some unclassified event.

Whatever the case, just as there can be no appropriate theory of language which takes only either structures or speech acts into consideration, so too a theory of society must be formed on complementary levels. Society can be construed as a system or as a structure and the actions of the participants explained in such terms. However, we cannot avoid also explaining them from the perspective of the actors themselves, because we must take their innovative practice into account; it would otherwise be impossible to understand the system or the structure itself. Yet, if one wishes to explain something from the perspective of the participants, then this includes engaging in direct acts of understanding. The S/P principle thus secures a hermeneutic dimension for any appropriate theory of society.[2]

3 Background knowledge. The consequence of the S/P principle just mentioned is reinforced if one takes the significance of background knowledge into account. Linguistic practice, as I have said, applies the code by simultaneously recreating it. All too frequently, however, the assumption is then made that this code already exists completely, as it were as a stock of ready expressions that one needs only call up in order to use them in speech. However, like all practice, linguistic practice moves not only in the framework of a ready-made code, but also draws on a background knowledge, namely the horizon of our implicit know-how and pre-understanding. This engenders the possibility of innovative expressions which are invented in the course of speech and articulate for the first time part of this implicit understanding.

The same is true of society: there are always customs which are already laid down and norms already articulated; these are used and at the same time renewed in the course of practice. That practice, however, relies on a never exhausted background which can simultaneously be the source of innovative statements and articulations.[3] (Wittgenstein, in particular, has emphasized the inexhaustibility of this background when discussing what it means to follow a rule.)

This has significant consequences for a theory of society. We have already noted that this theory must be developed on at least two levels in order to do justice to the polarity of structure and practice. An explanation at the structural level must always be supplemented by reference to contexts of action. And at this point it becomes clear that the role played by the dimension of practice is of even greater importance. Action refers not only to the system of explicit norms and rules of a form of life, but also always to a background which can generate new norms. However, these new behavioural norms bring with them a change in that form of life. One behaves with reference to a rule otherwise than against the horizon of a background understanding. This can have important consequences. Thus, for example, repressed or subconscious contradictions take an unpredictable shape as soon as our hitherto implicit pre-understanding is given a public platform.

Furthermore, articulation is in itself not some unproblematical process whose contents are already determined by the background. There are always many ways of rendering our pre-understanding explicit. As a result, articulating action plays a significant role; one frequently argues about the appropriate terms in which to formulate our background knowledge. I shall return to this under (4) below.

As I see it at present, the S/P principle has two consequences for social theory that both go beyond merely reinforcing the thesis already put forward in (2) above.

(a) Firstly, it becomes apparent that if we develop our theory from the perspective of the observer, then its positioning is problematical. In order to be able to explain the actions of the participants in a form of life from our perspective, we often have to articulate elements of their background understanding which for them remain implicit. We utilize formulations in the explanation which we provide 'from without' – were they to be adopted by the participants, they would probably trigger off great changes and would be highly controversial. The reifying metatheory could with a clear conscience convince itself that it had 'really' discovered the underlying structure in the same manner as the physicists found theirs with the aid of atomic theory. However, this interpretation becomes problematical the minute we take the position of background knowledge seriously. The question arises how we can legitimate *our* explanation for *their* background knowledge. I contend that here we have an implicit reference to a counterfactual state: our explanation is supposed to be accurate because the participants, if they were to understand themselves well and all false consciousness were to be eliminated, would articulate themselves in this way.

(b) It can be clearly shown by referring to the meaning of background knowledge that all fashionable attempts to explain society by means of a computer model must invariably fail. A computer programme is completely formalized: transitions from one state to another must occur on the basis of formal characteristics. This is Alan Turing's brilliant insight: it must be possible to transpose a mathematical question which can be answered in one of two ways on to a mechanical device. The mechanical programme offers a criterion precisely because a merely formal proof is supposed to be based only on formal properties and must therefore fully renounce any use of background knowledge. If, by contrast, we follow a proof only intuitively, then we can always make use of our pre-understanding. If we were, however, to transpose this proof on to a computer programme, then we would be *certain* that it was correct in formal terms.[4]

It follows that it is nonsensical to conceive of a form of life as being modelled after a computer programme intended to direct actions. In real action there is always and necessarily a component that is not yet formulated. Transitions which are purely formal in nature play only a limited role; they admittedly exist, and they crop up increasingly in highly developed societies.[5] Nevertheless, human practice is structured in such a manner that a form of life which was comprised solely of such formal links would in principle be impossible. It would thus be a quite meaningless task to try and conceptualize such a form of life in a theory.

4 The complementarity of 'I' and 'We'. Such linguistic practice as both uses and simultaneously innovates the code, 'initially', and 'usually' involves participating in a discourse. In discourse *we* talk about something. This means, however, that the matter in hand exists not just for me and for you, but for us. When we first engage in discourse we open up a common referential space, as it were. What is of interest then is the relation between this We-stance and the I-perspectives of the participants.

We participate in a common space. Our attention, both mine and yours, is focused on the matter in hand; we ignore the fact that this space is produced and maintained at once by speech acts we both use. I am usually, without noticing this, moving on the basis of mutual practice in that space, a space common to us, however, owing to your and my actions; I must have an implicit understanding of these. In other words, I must be capable of finding my own individual contribution to this space again, for otherwise I would no longer be able to participate in it.

This can be made clear if we take the case of our literally sharing a mutual orientation towards a space. We have to know how the different locations relate to one another spatially, and we must also be able to find our own way in this landscape. The language we use as a consequence requires two different types of referential expressions, namely both geographical descriptions and deictic expressions such as 'here' and 'there' that can be used only from the perspective of the speaker. If these two forms of expression are not interlinked – in other words, when we have lost the ability to connect them with one another and are consequently no longer capable of making identifying statements that connect expressions of these two types – then we have lost our way.[6]

The central role of 'I' as a self-referential expression (and Habermas elucidates this) stems from the above.[7] It cannot fail as a referential expression. Yet, this does not help us at all if we do not connect and interlink it with expressions drawn from the common space. For the term is meant to serve our finding ourselves again as constitutive participants in this space.

There is thus a complementary relationship between the We-perspective and the I-perspective in discourse. The former is earlier in origin, in that language is founded in discourse and the discourse therefore necessarily creates a common space. However, the I-perspective must equally enter into every discourse if the speaker is to be able to take part in constituting it, which in turn means that the We-perspective by no means simply arises from the accumulation of individual I-perspectives, because these cannot precede the former. Nevertheless, in the normal case of adult participants, the We-perspective itself requires an at least implicit understanding of the I-perspective. The adult implicitly already always understands the difference between 'I' and 'We' as well as the way in which they interlock.

The adult, needless to say, achieves such an understanding only by an ontogenetic process – Piaget's phase of 'egocentricism' – in the first stages of which the two levels are not yet marked off from one another. Yet, normal communication between adults requires precisely this differentiation and interlinking of the two levels.[8]

This conception of the structure of discourse can serve to enable us to understand the specificity of social action. As I have said, the code is both deployed and innovated in the course of linguistic practice. This practice 'initially' and 'usually' approximates a discourse: the participants act from a We-perspective. *We* follow the rules, *we* carry out the ritual and *we* apply the norms: an African tribe's ritual dance is a good example of this. However, the We-perspective is jeopardized if we no longer understand the 'common space' of norms in the same way. 'I' and 'We' then no longer bear the correct relation to one another. Here, the I-perspectives are explicitly expressed and the 'We' may then be the subject of a dispute or dissolve.

If we wish to recover that common 'We', then a process of reaching consensus must ensue. We cannot, however, construe this process to be the attempt to synthesize 'I'-perspectives which are completely independent of one another. Rather, our study of the structure of discourse has shown us that the perspective of the 'We' is of prior origin. We must reach a new consensus in order to repair the damage to this perspective. Yet, each individual rupture is itself embedded in overarching 'We'-perspectives. We always share other norms which are not yet contested and a common background knowledge. This stock of overarching common properties in principle allows us to hope that we can generate a new 'We'-perspective.

It is at this juncture that the highly original and interesting theory of rationality which Habermas develops comes to bear. Here, reason is not understood monologically, but rather as a perfection of this process of reaching understanding in such a way that the ruptures in the commonly shared 'We' are supposedly repaired. By dint of the fact that we have to do here with ruptures in our common understanding, which are in turn bridged by more deeply rooted common properties, it makes sense to repair such ruptures in the commonly shared horizon. This, however, implies that we must search for 'reasons' within this horizon acceptable to *all* if we are to bring about a new consensus on the matter in dispute.

The ideal of a process of reaching understanding motivated solely by reason follows from this, a process aimed at fully recreating the ruptured consensus. According to Habermas, this is the appropriate basis for our ideal of rationality.

I have attempted to reconstruct Habermas's speech act theory of society. The structures of discourse are intended to aid us in understanding society as a whole. I divided the central plank of the theory into four approaches, which I should like to summarize here in three theses: (a) with the first approach we assert the primacy of society over the actors involved; (b) the second and third approaches cause us to stress the irreducible complementarity of structure and/or system as well as practice and/or action; (c) with the fourth approach we claim finally that practice involves a complex I/We polarity. One acts from a We-position, which can stand the strain of friction because it is nurtured by the perspectives of the individual subjects. The mutuality of 'We' then has to be recreated via a process of reaching understanding. It is the nature of this process which determines a degree of perfection which we call rationality. According to Habermas's theory of human development, the need for understanding increases as merely symbolic, non-reflexive We-positions are overcome.[9]

I hope that my reconstruction at least does justice to the main seams in Jürgen Habermas's very rich and complex theory. The theory strikes me as exceptionally original, fertile and convincing in two respects. Firstly, it enables a transformation of social theory which takes into account that the structure of human action resembles that of discourse. Secondly, it provides the basis for a new understanding of political crisis in late capitalist societies. According to Habermas, we are confronted today not only by system theory's intellectual repression of the discursive structure of social life, but also by the real repression of processes of reaching understanding in favour of systemic forms of integration such as the market or the bureaucratic state, which to a certain extent function behind the backs of the participants and achieve their ends by means of steering mechanisms. This is the origin of both the widespread current experience of a loss of freedom and the related experience of a loss of meaning. These experiences are not, as some would believe, an irreparable result of the process of modernization *per se*. Rather, they do not ineluctably arise owing to the dissolution of older world views, be they of a religious or metaphysical nature. If such world views were by contrast to be replaced by free and non-dominative processes of understanding, then people today would be able to imbue life in society with a meaning once more. It is the domination of meaningless mechanisms which therefore creates the experience of meaninglessness.[10]

Habermas's theory thus opens up profitable and fruitful perspectives both from theoretical and normative viewpoints. Yet, it is, to my mind, also impaired by a severe weakness. This weakness can be described in various ways. The central problem, to my mind, is that the concept of reaching rational understanding is developed using a merely *formal* ethics of rationality. I would like to contrast such a formal ethics with a 'substantialist' ethics. Aristotle's philosophy could provide us with a paradigm for this: his ethics proceeds from a concept of the good life. Kant is the most important representative of formal conceptions, arguing that we should determine the good life not in terms of its contents, namely as a form of life to be realized. Rather, we determine what is correct on the basis of the procedure we adopt to decide what we should do. It is this procedure which is supposedly rational. It is then rationality as the perfection of the procedure, i.e. procedural rationality, which is the fundamental concept and not, as in Aristotle's work, the good life.

Now there are indeed important reasons which speak in favour of a procedural ethics: it avoids the major epistemological problems inherent in any determination of the good life and it would appear to be more open to a radical concept of freedom than is a substantialist ethics. Habermas would, furthermore, appear to set great store by a third reason, namely that only a formal ethics can fully distance itself from all specific cultural forms of life. A substantialist ethics, by contrast, which is informed by a concept of the good life, is always more closely bound to the ideals and values of a particular culture and therefore more or less seals itself off from all other cultures. In certain respects, Aristotle's ethics is bound up with the polis of classical antiquity. Today, however, slavery and the lower, degraded position of women – both of which obtained in the societies of the day – are politically and morally unacceptable. One could thus be forgiven for thinking that the only ethics which is really universal must be formal in nature.

These are strong reasons in favour of designing a formal ethics. However, I hold a purely procedural ethics to be inconsistent. Even Kant, I believe, returned to a substantialist ethics. The weaknesses of a formal ethics become apparent the minute one turns to the radical questions of justification.

As an actor, I can always ask the question why I should actually proceed according to a particular norm, namely rationally. Why should this be a norm that I cannot deny? This is a question which one can only answer, to use my own terminology, with 'strong valuations'. Kant, for example, answers it with his concept of a rational being for whom dignity is befitting. As a consequence, his ethics in the final instance refers to a substantialist concept: as we *are* rational beings, we should act in line with this, as it is our nature. We should respect reason both in ourselves and in others.

Habermas, however, wishes to limit himself to a purely proceduralist ethics. We strive, according to his underlying principle, to reach rational understanding. We should endeavour to replace non-rational mechanisms of action coordination by rational forms of reaching understanding. Yet this demand is also confronted by the question why I should strive for this. Let us accept that such a norm is structurally based in the situation of human speech (as is assumed by universal pragmatics) and that rational understanding is the appropriate manner of overcoming disturbances in the mutuality of a 'We' (as is maintained by the theory of communicative action) – I nevertheless also have other aims, other interests. Why then should I prefer rational understanding? Why should precisely this aim occupy a special position?

Attempts at justification, such as are derived from the structure of the situation of speech by a discursive ethics,[11] do not suffice in the case of such radical questions. The fact that I should argue with the aim of achieving domination-free understanding may admittedly be structurally implied by the logic of discourse. If, in other words, I attempt to assert my own interests irrespective of all the objections other participants to the conversation raise, then I certainly violate the logic of the discourse. But why should I not do this? Why should I not attempt to reach my desired goal at the cost of being slightly inconsistent?

The fitting answer to this question is to be found only at another level. I must be able to show why it is I attach a value to rational understanding so great that it *should* be preferred to all other purposes. In which case, reaching understanding comprises one *purpose* among others, one which can lay claim to primacy only owing to a substantialist concept of human life.

Habermas's description of the contemporary situation in late capitalist society – he advocates that we must defend ourselves against the technicization of the lifeworld,[12] in order to create the space for processes of reaching rational understanding – requires different and stronger justifications. His analysis is bereft of any foundations if coupled to a merely procedural ethics. It is none the less very convincing for us as contemporaries, yet this is only because we implicitly share a concept of humankind which allocates a central position to discourse and reaching rational understanding. We still presuppose, even if only in an implicit and opaque manner, that humankind is defined in the old way as *zoon echon logon*, as a talking animal. In order, however, to meet the demands we make, we must completely reinterpret this definition in the framework of our modern understanding of ourselves. The first steps for such a reinterpretation are to be found, I believe, in Herder's and Humboldt's theories of language. Perhaps I overestimate these theories; nevertheless, it seems to me indisputable that a similarly substantialist theory is also necessary in the case of such a reinterpretation – and a purely procedural ethics thus radically misses its goal.

The inadequacy of a procedural ethics can also be viewed from another angle. A fundamental principle of the type comprised by the norm of rational understanding cannot decide all questions of strong valuation. Admittedly, this principle is different from Kant's basic principle, which is frequently claimed to be of no use for decisions on moral questions. Habermas's concept of rationality is clearly bound up with social implications precisely because it is no longer monological – the principle of reaching rational understanding seems to be incompatible with authoritarian conditions or exploitation. There are, however, other questions which affect our form of life: ecological questions, for example, demand strong valuations which cannot be decided solely by resorting to a procedural

principle. Such problems require substantialist determinations of what constitutes the good life.

Habermas is forced to make a strict distinction between questions of
these two orders in order to defend his conception of a procedural ethics.
Only those questions which can be decided on the basis of a criterion of
universal processes of reaching rational understanding are in his eyes
actually moral questions; there is, he avers, another type of question which
refers to our understanding of the good life. Such questions are, he admits,
no less important, for humankind's existence involves the wish to attain the
goal of a life which has turned out 'well' or 'has more or less succeeded'.
He immediately adds that these questions are rather more *clinical* than
moral.[13]

It is, however, exceptionally difficult to defend this distinction. On the
one hand, it starkly contradicts our usual moral consciousness. From the
viewpoint of our normal conception it would seem bizarre to define our
form of life as simply a question of health and thus to uncouple it completely from the moral dimension – or at least from the dimension of
strong valuations. Yet it is even harder to defend the distinction if we
consider that reaching rational understanding must also, as already mentioned, be construed as a purpose which is able to constitute the source for
important ideals for our lives. Reasonableness is also a virtue which we
attempt to realize in our own form of life; the same holds just as true for
the openness towards other cultures so valued today as it does for that
shown towards such virtues of selflessness as serve universal understanding. In the typical case a person is willing to unite these virtues with other
virtues which are not connected with some form of charity: virtues such as,
for example, that of self-development, authenticity, sincerity or thankful-
ness. We have to do here with a central area of moral problems which
focuses on weighing up the often mutually competing claims of the different virtues against one another and bringing about a uniform, consistent
form of life. Questions of precisely such a kind belong at the centre of
moral life; it would therefore be completely arbitrary and unfounded
simply to exclude this whole area by adhering to the false thesis that only
virtues oriented toward charity have a moral character. If this were not the
attempt merely to avoid unavoidable questions, than it would be nothing
more than a meaningless gesture.

Thirdly, the two types of virtues are linked with one another. The fact
that we should prefer rational understanding to norm-free steering
mechanisms is closely bound up with our understanding of human dignity
which, in turn, is inseparable from certain concepts of self-development
and self-obligation.

The overall attempt to draw a sharp line between questions of justice and
questions of the good life is, from the outset, falsely construed. It is the
unhappy consequence of the underlying decision to opt for a procedural
ethics.[14]

An even more important consequence is the fundamental distinction
between three dimensions of rationality which Habermas borrows from
Weber's theory of modernity and unreservedly incorporates into his own

theory. In earlier times, questions of factual truth, normative rightness and personal authenticity were often inextricably bound up with one another. Normative questions, for example, were solved, as they were in the Platonic tradition, by deploying a concept of cosmological order. What we today regard as questions of personal authenticity – types of questions such as how I can best realize myself – would have been meaningless to our ancestors, for such questions were not yet distinguished from those as to whether something was normatively right.

It is obvious that modernity has led to a relative differentiation of the three areas. Sciences, or at least the natural sciences, now exist which are value-free; questions of personal realization have, as mentioned, been accorded a separate status. Yet some theorists have gone still further and asserted that modernity has separated three independent domains of rationality off from one another, that is, three areas in which questions are solved on the basis of respectively different justifying reasons and criteria.

This thesis rests on two prior assertions: firstly, that modernity does indeed increasingly treat questions of truth, rightness and authenticity as though each applied in a logically independent sphere of its own; and secondly, that this is factually correct, in other words, that modern differentiation constitutes progress by taking into account the logical structure of these questions in their respective particularity more effectively than the traditional interlinking of the different dimensions of validity involved. Habermas proceeds from both assertions.[15] The close connection that obtains between these assumptions and the fundamental decision to adopt a procedural ethics is clearly visible here: it would indeed be possible to solve questions of a purely formal ethics quite independently of questions of factual truth.

In my opinion, both strands of the proposition are, as I have already adumbrated above, open to question. For our practical reason does not in fact proceed formally by ascertaining what our duties are on the basis of a procedural criterion. Rather, we initially recognize differing purposes of life or virtues, among which reasonableness, justice and charity play a central role; and we strive to merge them all at the correct point and in an appropriate relation to one another in this one life which we have. Our deliberations when weighing up these purposes, justifying them or assessing their relative importance can be considered neither factually nor in principle to be a process of reflexion that addresses questions of objective truth only indirectly. Quite the opposite is true: our deliberations on those purposes to which we *should* accord recognition are inextricably linked to those considerations on what we as humans *are*. As a consequence, questions of morals are closely tied to theories of human motivations;[16] the same concepts appear in both types of investigations.

The strict demarcation of truth from rightness can thus not be retained in such a form. And an overselective singling out of that third dimension, namely authenticity, would be just as distorting in the picture it would give. If questions of personal realization are severed from considerations of truth and universal rightness, then this opens up a realm of pure subjectivism. This is certainly *one* of the paths chosen by some of the representatives of modernity, but it is itself hotly contested and can by no means be depicted as *the* path of modernity – and whether it is the *best* path is also a moot point. Habermas rightly views modern art as a domain in which, above all, questions of authenticity are thematized. If, however, we regard this complex as a completely isolated domain, then we must consider contemporary art to be a project primarily concerned with self-presentation. This is highly questionable, for there is an important current in modern art which opposes precisely such a subjectivism by attempting to uncover something that is not merely subjective.

If this critique holds true then either rationality as the fundamental ethical principle must be supplemented, or an expanded concept of rationality must be introduced. Such an expanded concept would also include substantialist criteria – one aspect would be that one could broach one's own moral situation without any distortion thereof. Language would thus also possess the function of disclosing the morality involved and would not just serve to enable understanding to be reached. Or rather it would make it possible to reach understanding only to the extent that it would disclose what our situation was without any distortion.

I believe that such a conception of language (and of rationality) is already inherent in my reconstruction of the fourth approach. If we wish to remove the friction in the common properties of the 'We' by means of an overarching background consensus, then we must try to articulate what in our form of life is both good and has proved itself in intersubjective terms.

This last observation offers a means with which to summarize my criticism of *The Theory of Communicative Action*. A discourse theory of language has enormous, beneficial consequences for a theory of society in both theoretical and politico-moral terms. Yet the benefits are partially gambled away by opting for both a procedural ethics and the distinction this entails between three logically independent dimensions of rationality. As a result, the notion of practical reason is distorted; in particular, the central role language plays as a means of disclosing new terrain remains hidden. Language as such is situated in a separate domain of rationality: in its expressive dimension it solely serves a knowledge of self and the presentation of self, and contributes nothing to determining what is normatively right.

If I am correct, then this limitation is a severe mistake. Language plays an indispensable role as an expressive medium in the overall domain of practical reason. We express our moral ends and our understanding of ourselves as humans by at the same time understanding and justifying our ends: we articulate the implicit understanding which comprises the background of our social norms, customs and institutions, and which is closely bound up with our understanding of moral ends.

Furthermore, language plays a constitutive role with regard to these ends, norms and customs: it is only through their articulation in language that our norms and purposes can also be changed. Yet language effects this only by disclosure, i.e. by lending expression to a part of our pre-understanding of these ends and norms either affirmatively or critically.

This whole dimension of disclosure through language is left untouched by a theory of society geared towards a proceduralist ethics. As a consequence, the ingenious theory of disclosure in turn risks sacrificing the most important achievements it has made, namely its transformation of social theory and its political diagnosis of contemporary society.[17]

3 The Two Meanings of 'Communicative' Rationality: Remarks on Habermas's Critique of a Plural Concept of Reason

Martin Seel

A Literal and Metaphorical Name

The 'Theory of Communicative Action' is, among other things, a theory of various forms of rationality, and the differences between these are constitutive for the existence of a 'communicative' reason. Given this underlying critique of reason, Habermas's analyses face a dual task. They have to highlight the *intrinsic* meaning of the theoretical-instrumental, the moral-practical and the aesthetic-expressive forms of rationality, as well as elucidating the *interconnection* between these in action oriented to reaching understanding. For it is only both aspects together, namely difference and unity, which distinguish communicative reason from the one-dimensionality characteristic not only of instrumental rationality; *any* form of one-sidedly restricting the plural meaning of validity would have to be understood as a sign of reification, even if in modernity theoretical rationality represents the foremost paradigm for such alienation. This means, however, that plurality, the sheer coexistence of the different dimensions of validity, does not suffice to explain the meaning of communicative reason. Therefore, as Habermas writes at the end of his investigation:

> The mediation of the moments of reason is no less a problem than the separation of the aspects of rationality under which questions of truth, justice and taste were differentiated from one another. The only protection against an empiricist abridgement of the rationality problematic is a steadfast pursuit of the tortuous routes along which science, morality and art communicate *with each other*.[1]

Habermas conspicuously uses primarily metaphorical turns of phrase to describe the 'internal relations'[2] between the different validity spheres he

has distinguished from one another. The unabridged rationality of communication is supposed to be thought of at the same time as 'communication' between the aspects of rationality, and it is the free 'play' of these
which first permits the potentiality of a multi-layered reason to unfold in a
productive fashion.[3] This dual literal and metaphorical meaning given to
the concept of communicative rationality is indicative of a methodological
problem. Given that much of the *Theory of Communicative Action* con-
centrated on elaborating the *difference* between the validity dimensions to
which the participants in interaction have to refer *simultaneously* if they
want to cooperate with each other, an additional problem arises, namely,
that of the *interrelation* of validity claims previously separated from one
another. My question is what the implications for the basic concept of
'communicative rationality' are if the *Theory of Communicative Action* is
read from back to front – in other words, if we begin with the question
concerning the *inter*dependence of the aspects of rationality which are
treated primarily as being *in*dependent.

A Sociological and a Philosophical Consideration

The ambiguity in the main concept Habermas develops has to do, among
other things, with an unclarified relationship between his theory's sociological and philosophical strands. Habermas the sociologist adopts Weber's
theory of the modern separation of value spheres (interpreted as validity
spheres); Habermas the philosopher, however, is not completely convinced
that this separation has become a thorough-going reality. It would seem
worthwhile to me at this juncture to strengthen the standpoint of the
philosopher who wishes to persuade the sociologist that the separability of
value spheres, so crucial in shaping the way industrial societies in this
century view themselves, represents a piece of false consciousness bought
at great cost. Seen thus, both the totalitarian *unification* and the rigid
separation of the capacity for reason would appear to be complementary
ideologies of a modernity in the thrall of the dialectic of Enlightenment. A
differentiated critique of reason must defend itself against these in a war
waged on two fronts. The project undertaken in the *Theory of Communicative Action* expressly takes up this intermediate position. However,
Habermas would make it considerably easier for himself to repel the
counterattacks, be they informed by a scepticism of reason or a dialectics
of reconciliation, if his theory did not, in turn, reproduce within itself the
validity-theoretical ambivalence of irreducible separation, on the one hand,
and necessary interrelation, on the other.

In the everyday world, so Habermas assumes, 'those aspects of rationality are still intimately intertwined as separate out into science, morality and
art, and are then treated as isolated areas';[4] in modern expert cultures, by
contrast, 'reason has disintegrated into its component parts'. This disin-
tegration can, however, be described only as a (not necessarily alienating)
process of rationalization because the value spheres that have separated out

'in the syndromes of the lifeworldly background and in the tradition-dependent hermeneutics of everyday communication'[5] again refer and continue to refer genuinely to each other. In this and other formulations rationality comes to have two faces: its basic types appear to be structurally related, on the one hand, and yet structurally indifferent, on the other. An unambiguous interpretation of this ambiguity – which is itself admittedly one of the phenomena described – can proceed in exactly two ways. It can either deduce the *illusion of their integration within the lifeworld* from the fact of their separation, or derive the *illusion of the specializing separation* of the dimensions of rationality from the factual circumstance of 'communicative' interdependence. Habermas, it seems to me, wants to have it both ways. This is why in his work the lifeworld, on the one hand, appears to be the mere 'background' of a reality divided up among the expert cultures, but on the other, figures as the fertile soil cultivated in communicative action towards which every sifting of the stores of truths contained in such a reality, no matter how 'autonomous' this process may be, necessarily behaves parasitically.[6] In order to eliminate these inconsistencies, the idea of what is then the *relative* autonomy of the validity spheres would, on the one hand, have to be defined more strictly in *inter*relative terms; on the other, this would have to involve sacrificing the regulative assumption of a consensual *integration* of the elements of validity under ideal conditions. The dimensions of truth, which are to be distinguished on the basis of the modes of their respective justification, do not comprise a 'system',[7] since the forms of justification in which a case can be made for theoretical, practical and aesthetic validity are not compatible. Nor are the thus differentiated validity spheres separable from one another, for their argumentational portrayal always draws on presuppositions which can be explained only extrinsically, namely in the medium of a deliberation tuned in to a different form of validity. Even the most liberal discourse cannot completely forgo this dependence on different kinds of validity.

Of course, an approach altered in this way would, in turn, have to meet sociological standards. For, it would have to be able to show that the supposed interdependence of the dimensions of rationality also determines social practice, determining it precisely where the sharply-contoured differentiation of these dimensions was and is raised to the status of a programme.

Speech Acts and Argumentation

The inclination to treat the various dimensions of validity primarily under conditions adjusted for their separability has at the same time to do with the basic language-theoretic assumptions of the *Theory of Communicative Action*. Habermas introduces the substantive concepts of validity in the context of standardized speech acts intended to demonstrate those different aspects of the constitutive reference to validity inherent in speech to which every speech act is more or less explicitly related. This identification and interpretation of the cardinal validity spheres in terms of speech act theory is questionable not only from the standpoint of a theory of language (because it also blurs conceptual differences between the very different kinds of relations to validity of speech oriented towards reaching understanding).[8] Together with the assignment of abstract – not to say, reifying – world-concepts, this interpretation suggests an independence or at least the separability of truth dimensions of equal and simultaneous origin. Yet, according to Habermas's own findings, this has no impact on either the reality of communicative action in the lifeworld nor on the logic of lines of argumentation that thematize validity. On closer examination, the 'intermodal transfer of validity'[9] – which Habermas refers to in order to supplement his argument – proves to be an interargumentative *need* for validity, the addition or dismantling of which can itself not be completely regulated by argumentative procedures. To my mind, it is possible to show (indeed, using some of Habermas's own arguments) that each of these justifications incorporates assumptions and presuppositions which cannot themselves be thematized in validity-critical terms in the respective argumentation. This is true not only in the case of the aesthetic critique (which Habermas has in the meantime conceded),[10] but also for theoretical and practical discourses. The alternation of these modes of justification (and of the pragmatic orientations expressed in them) may be prompted by an external critique intervening in them, but cannot be accomplished by relying on a logic that transcends the bounds of the respective discourse. This being the case, however, the fundamental validity dimensions are, from the outset, *interdependent and yet cannot be integrated*; and they remain thus, even with respect to the specializing negotiation of theoretical, practical or aesthetic validity. A formal-pragmatic theory of meaning and validity can no longer identify the language-constitutive dimensions of rationality as being *independent* of one another, precisely if it does not wish to identify them *with each other* in some false reconcilement.

This is evidenced by the fact that the meaning of validity – the intrinsic logic – of the forms of argumentation distinguished by Habermas is not reflected linearly in the validity that may be claimed with various *utterances*. For one thing, it becomes clear from the concept of expressive 'truthfulness' ('Wahrhaftigkeit') that it is not speech acts, but only modes of *justification* which are paradigmatic for the intended differentiation between types of rationality. Since, as Habermas himself says,[11] it is not possible to argue for the truthfulness of utterances, there can as a consequence also be no form of rationality – of justifiability – 'specialized' in this validity claim. Thus, the construct of 'expressive rationality' used by Habermas is repeatedly divided into forms of non-morally *practical* rationality, on the one hand, and an independent form of *aesthetic* rationality, on the other. Admittedly, the validity of truthfulness plays an important role in both the justification of tenets with regard to the value of the individually and collectively good life as well as the justification of aesthetic judgements, and yet in each instance the role is respectively different. However, this is equally true, again with a differing emphasis involved, for the nexus of theoretical and moral-practical lines of argumentation. As is the case with the 'comprehensibility' of speech acts and symbols, which is to be understood differently in different contexts, so too the status of truthfulness, no matter how it varies, is also a ubiquitous phenomenon in the communicative usage of language and cannot be pruned so severely that it comprises only the root of a specific norm of rationality.[12] The same is true for the regulative claim made by demands and even for the constative mode of assertions. For the claim which can respectively be made using such utterances can be specified to be a claim to rational *justification* only at the level of an analysis of the *forms of argumentation* in which the validity of the utterances can be thematized and negotiated through discussion of reasons and counterreasons, i.e. by means of statements.

In other words, the validity in which the basic types of argumentation are in fact 'specialized' can in no way be depicted in terms of the meaning and comprehensibility of sentences or speech acts, no matter how standardized these may be – unless we always already presuppose this possible reference to argumentation. Explaining the comprehensibility of utterances, which is in various cases and forms related to validity, does not at one fell swoop explain the theoretical, practical and aesthetic justifiability of *statements* which (in their context) raise a respectively different truth claim. However, even if these justifications do not actually refer to presuppositions, they nevertheless necessarily depend on such presuppositions as cannot be directly thematized in the respective procedure of justification. No form of specialization, irrespective of how far it goes, can free justification from this referential structure. 'Expert' specialization consists merely in suppressing any articulation of the different kind of validity inherent in those presuppositions upon which the expert's merely internally sovereign deliberations rest. The *illusion* of specialization, be it thus theoretical, practical or even aesthetic in nature, is always the belief in there being an 'ultimate basis' for one's own (deliberating) action, separating it from the action of the amateurish others. Habermas himself leaves no doubt that there are no such separatist foundations.[13] This being the case, however, any derivation of the theory of argumentation from the basic pillars of speech act theory is somewhat of a misleading manoeuvre.

This consideration has implications for the status of a pragmatic theory of language. If Habermas identifies the validity forms using standardized speech acts, and associates these, in turn, with the basic forms of meaning, he comes closer in method to conventional truth semantics than a pragmatically oriented theory of meaning can afford to be. Yet, precisely a pragmatically informed theory of argumentation cannot dispense with an orientation towards forms and applications of statements, as long as it does not identify the essence of statements (and their truth) with the status of theoretical-descriptive statements (and as long as it does not equate meaning with the statement's meaning). To this extent, the interdependence of the forms of rationality and/or argumentation refers to meaning, validity and justification as factors which also cannot be derived from one explanatory model. Neither the modes in which expressions made in language are *articulated* meaningfully in the contexts in which they arise, nor the modes of *reference to validity* in these forms of expression, nor the possibilities of *argumentation* for the validity of problematized orientations can be dealt with on one and the same methodological level.[14]

Forms of Argumentation

I would like at least to sketch out the assumptions on which the assertion of the basic interdependence of theoretical, practical and aesthetic validity rests. For this purpose I shall make a distinction between the cardinal validity domains that is somewhat different from that employed by Habermas.[15]

Statements are *theoretical* if they are asserted and justified solely with a view to whether they are true. Statements are *practical* which are asserted and justified with a view to granting what is said validity as a reason for action; the practical justification is the justification of a reason. The truth of practical statements consists in giving sufficient or conclusive reasons for the behaviour prescribed or called for in corresponding precepts or recommendations. In the case of aesthetic truth, the decisive conditions of justification have one more level. Statements are *aesthetic* if they are asserted and justified with a view to lending the *object* of these statements validity as a *reason* for adopting world-shaping views. The justification of aesthetic judgements elevates the object of these judgements to the status of an explication of lifeworld experiences. In argumentation for or against the truth of aesthetic statements, a case is made for the significance of experiences and/or the appropriacy of ways of seeing, the essence of which is articulated in major works of art.

Since practical and aesthetic judgements are always value statements, whereas this is only occasionally true of theoretical judgements (which then have a derived meaning), we can, to put it briefly, say that the justification (of the self-sufficient validity) of a sentence is theoretical, whereas the justification (of the motivational validity) of a value statement that is to be established as a reason for action is practical, and the justification (of the explicative validity) of a value statement to be established as a reason for the perception of a 'reason' (of and for lifeworldly experience) is aesthetic. In each of these cases, however, the negotiation on the 'truth' of a proposition, the 'rightness' of an action or the 'authenticity' of a work of art ensues by means of and/or together with the truth of the various kinds of *statements* – together with the acceptability of theoretical, practical or aesthetic judgements.

Even without here going seriously into the justifiability of these judgements (which I, following Habermas, presuppose), it is nevertheless easy to perceive the interconnection, the interdependence, indeed the merely relative autonomy of the respective forms of argumentation mentioned. It would be trivial to point out that practical considerations in one or the other form will have to be supported by a descriptive knowledge of the situations meant or the means to be employed. It would seem clear to me that ethical-practical considerations (which may or may not be moral in the stricter sense) not only have to be supported by more or less aesthetic 'interpretations of needs', but also rest on experiences of life and a form of life which can, if at all, be lent only a controversial expression in aesthetic critique. It can be shown that aesthetic deliberations cannot occur independently of various forms of theoretical and ethical-practical knowledge.[16] It is gradually becoming common knowledge in the philosophy of science that theoretical considerations, even and precisely in instances where they are made in the context of developing a theory, also depend on practical decisions for which theoretical justifications can be forthcoming. By the same token, no theoretical consideration and argumentation is immune to coming up against the limits inherent in the perspectives which constitute the context of inquiry in question. The appropriacy of these perspectives cannot be defended or rejected in theoretical argumentation, but at best again only in aesthetic terms. (Theoretically, I can *appeal* to a different perspective on things only by referring to the untenable *consequences* of the rejected approach.[17]

Even if the above *is* the case, why should it nevertheless not be possible – at least in principle – to alter, indeed to have reasons for altering, the priorities of the argumentation as required? Why should we not be able, for the sake of justification, especially when relieved of the pressure to act and of time pressures, to resort in justification to problematic presuppositions which require a different means of justification from those which gave rise to our original deliberations? An *initial* reply would be: because this ability so to resort at any time is an (ideal) condition pertaining solely to a theoretical inquiry. Consequently, the thought 'of a universe of language that can be explored only in and through argumentation' distorts the structure of argumentation as defined by the model of theoretical argumentation and renders it one-sided.[18] We can admittedly at any time resort – in principle – both in theoretical discourse itself and from the context of practical and aesthetic considerations to the assumptions still to be justified theoretically. These had played a (hitherto) unquestioned role in them. This form of reflexivity in argumentation – which consists in being able at any time to question the assumptions about the world which were the pillars of the deliberation thus far – is genuinely theoretical; it must not be pointed up as the reflexivity of argumentation as such, as is the case in Habermas's work.

Moral contentions cannot be problematized in a manner analogous to theoretical ones. Morally problematic premises cannot be discerned and clarified in the way in which theoretical premises can be made out either inside or outside moral discourses – unless, that is, we were to take a theoretical approach to the practical grounds of morality by treating these as self-sufficient statements (about the quality of maxims and norms), while not imbuing them with the force of reasons that intersubjectively direct action by applying them interpretatively to ethically precarious situations. Treating moral questions and the answers to them (and this also always includes the statements which tentatively or conclusively formulate a moral valuation) as *practical* questions and suggestions means at the same time conducting with the possible formulation of generalizing precepts and norms what Habermas calls an 'application discourse'. In such a discourse, however, the *validity* of modes of behaviour has to be negotiated *together* with the *interpretation* of the situations in which a given moral orientation comes into being and becomes problematic.[19] These situations and the conflicts that arise in them *are* the moral problems which are to be solved by finding a justifiable social regulation thereof. We do not, normally, encounter these moral difficulties through reflexion. The morally controversial situation has to *take place* in the context of lifeworldly, interactive actions and experiences – it must *emerge* from regulative expectations of behaviour clashing – so that we can *posit* its problem to ourselves and the other participants (and so that we can thus resignedly or repressively *avoid* it). Only because Habermas adjusts moral discourse to match its theoretical counterpart can the impression arise that the 'transition' from theoretical to ethical-practical questions can be made at any time by means of a reflexive change in topic. This change in attitude is not simply something at the disposal of argumentation.

At least not in principle. And even assuming that a purely reflexive problematization would be possible here, what immediately comes into view is the *second* delimitation of the possibility of an 'orderly, rationally controlled transition'[20] between the basic kinds of justification. Each of these transitions can be justified only from the vantage point which we *have* now adopted. Moral intervention into theoretical (or other) domains can be justified only in moral terms, and not with respect to the theoretical (or other) interconnections at which the critical intervention is aimed. Here, theoretical problematization is a perfect analogy. Even if such a problematization arises in the context of non-theoretical argumentation, we have to do nevertheless with theoretical grounds that are lent validity within a differently weighted consideration; and even the necessity of this casting-into-question can be justified theoretically only at its respective point of origin, irrespective of how relevant the result of this reflexion will be for the non-theoretical context of justification. The transition, the change in perspective, has to be accomplished; it is often only retrospectively possible to show to what extent the transition was justified and meaningful, namely by turning to the arguments of one kind which, in turn, may be cast into doubt from another rational perspective. This transargumentative move does not itself follow a particular logic; in favourable cases, it follows the logic of the justification which it adheres to at that time.

The two aspects, namely, the structural impossibility of a form of justification which discursively permeates all forms of argumentation, and the pragmatic improbability (mentioned in the example of moral justification) of a purely reflexively informed change in perspective (at least in the non-theoretical domains), also emerge when we consider aesthetic contexts. Not only the transition from theoretical to moral lines of argumentation, but also that from moral and theoretical to aesthetic forms of justification (as well as incidentally from aesthetic to moral) can as a rule not be effected by means of simply resorting reflexively to unconsidered presuppositions. To do so would be to reduce the aesthetic object to an example of non-aesthetic complexes of consideration. The revelatory power of aesthetic arguments in complexes of theoretical and ethical experience cannot be internally plotted in line with some theoretical and practical interest; rather it comes to light in the vast majority of cases when it suddenly breaks from the outside into the conceptions of what was until then a customary practice. Precisely the fact that an aesthetic argument can also, by virtue of being aesthetic, have theoretical or practical consequences, highlights the hurdle which has to be surmounted if this consequence is to be accorded a theoretical or practical impact; we have to decide in each case to 'make the transition' from the aesthetic affirmation of a viewpoint to the discussion of the factual assumptions or the appropriate modes of action which are inherent in or originate in a confirmed aesthetic view.

Habermas writes that 'between the differentiated moments of reason there is now only a formal connection, namely the procedural unity of argumentative grounding.'[21] My theses seek to call attention to the fact that the equation of the unity of reason with the unity of argumentation is not tenable without further qualification, for the formal quality of the unity of modern reason cannot be identified by referring to argumentation as such, but rather in terms of the irreducible interlocking of its forms. This interlocking takes the shape of thoroughly material dependencies (bound to presuppositions of reciprocal content), without it being possible to pinpoint and describe the relationship between these materials within the medium of a unifying philosophical theory. The procedure of reason, and I would agree with Habermas on this point, is left to the reason of its argumentative procedures – yet, without being regulated by the unity of an all-embracing procedure.

Understood thus, the relativity of the underlying validity dimensions does not have relativistic consequences. Aesthetic, practical and theoretical judgements can certainly be made unconditionally (without this unconditionality always implying a claim to universality). The analysis of the corresponding forms of justification elucidates what this signifies. However, the unconditionality of the assertions by means of which various kinds of validity are thematized in a sense also possesses an index of the kinds of argumentation to which claim is laid and thus also of foundations which cannot at the same time be thematized in deliberation. Although such argumentation is thus not exhaustive, but only partial, it is not relativist as long as it is aware that its presuppositions can be subjected to external criticism. It would be relativistic only if insight into the perspectival character of reason itself constituted relativism. This supposed relativism is, however, only the dummy for an alleged fundamentalism. Relativism and fundamentalism converge in the blindness they show to the relativity of the dimensions of validity into which the reason of a non-relative orientation divides itself.

Rationality and Communication

If every form of justification has to make use of assumptions and presuppositions which cannot be grounded in this form of argumentation itself, then what Habermas normatively designates the 'interplay' of truth dimensions is always already in force in depotentiated fashion in every form of justification – albeit not in a normative sense, but rather as the structure of even the most narrow-minded of justifications. The declared belief in the interrelating of aspects of rationality can assume normative status once a certain behaviour towards the relationship of grounding possibilities appears advisable. All talk of an 'interplay' or a 'communication' of metaphorically personalized aspects of rationality foregrounds this behaviour from the outside and in a conspicuously de-dramatizing way – as if we, who find ourselves in this game, could control all its components at one and the same time (or at least in one round).

A reservation of Derrida's can be brought to bear against this scenario. Although it was originally directed against structuralist centrism, it also still strikes at the persistent adherence to a procedural-reflecting unity of a decentred reason. Derrida's criticism was levelled at the notion of a 'justified play' of structure, of truth, of reason.[22] It is directed against the belief that the meanings of our relations to the world are abstractly coordinated according to a uniform scheme, if not (purely metaphysically) via an external authority, then at least (residually metaphysically) in the structure of the linguistic forms of articulation, and thus can in principle also be coordinated in concrete terms at any time. This notion of uniformity, however formalized it may be, plays down the speech-constitutive difference between the relations of meaning and the possibilities for justification. It is on account of this difference that individual forms of articulation first acquire their value as achievements in reaching understanding. We can understand this to mean that a decentred relation to the world has also grown out of the generating logic of a form of securing meaning and testing validity. However, what is noteworthy here is precisely the price Derrida pays for such an – exaggerating – use of this argument. In Derrida's case, the concept of play is implanted, for its part, in the authority of a comprehensive countermetaphor that opposes the optical and acoustic metaphors of knowledge used not only by the Enlightenment; the metaphorical cognition of the limitless 'game' of linguistic signs is intended to designate as metaphysical the whole (precritical and post-Kantian) tradition of the theory of truth and reason. The vaccine against the false whole is lauded as a vitamin that protects one against the utter passion for truth. The game of truth (against untruth) is reinterpreted to be the truth of the game (which stupefyingly transcends the polarity of the reference to truth).

This twist, which totalizes the metaphorics of game/play without any longer allowing rules which function as the original elements of a game – as is common in pre-postmodern understanding – immediately strips the reference to game once more of the critical thrust it once had *vis-à-vis* the idea of a regulatable whole. A game without rules, to put it in Wittgenstein's terms, is a game without sense. A game without sense, however, is an empty fiction. The truth *of* the game, if it is such to begin with, cannot exist without an interplay of, if not *the* truth, at any rate of categorially different *truths*. This game which can as a whole not be regulated by means of its constituent, regulatable elements, however, is nothing other than a non-metaphysical modern metaphor for reason.[23]

The purpose of this brief excursus on the modern/postmodern predominance of game metaphors was to imbue the normative meaning of the 'interplay' of the forms of rationality with a sense above all suspicion. Habermas's desired designation of a determinate relationship (or, more precisely, of a determinate behaviour toward the relationship) of validity dimensions can, in my opinion, apply only to the capacity – which cannot always be exercised playfully or be controlled, in turn, meta-argumentatively – to *change* rational perspectives. A form of behaviour made possible by this capacity – not only in argumentation, but also in everyday action, would not only be *rational*; it would, moreover, be *reasonable*. A multi-dimensional practice oriented toward validity is accordingly reasonable if it at the same time knows how to judge, with respect to the justifications made possible and necessary by it, which form of justification is appropriate at which time and/or when it is imperative to distance oneself critically from a hitherto dominant means of orientation.

This means that the normative thrust of the concept of the interplay of the forms of rationality pertains to a special performance of the *faculty of judgement*. Unlike the arguments and forms of argumentation in which it can also be realized on its own in problematic cases, reason is the capacity for an *interrational* judgement which itself cannot in turn be explained as the form of an excessive logic of argumentation.[24] This special faculty of judgement exercised in the capacity to change rational perspectives must not be equated with the ability to apply intelligently justified or justifiable knowledge. Nor does the reason shown in this capacity for judgement stem from a (philosophical) knowledge which exists alongside insights that can be derived theoretically, practically and aesthetically. The achievements of this faculty of judgement are, in Kant's terms, not 'determinate', but also not 'reflective' in the sense that they seek a (not yet pre-formed) general answer to the respective special problem as to which of the (rational) modes of judgement is to be given priority in the given case at the given point in time. Such a 'reflexion' does not produce results that cannot themselves be stated in the language of theoretical, practical or aesthetic considerations; in it, we encounter the actualization of a knowledge of the limits of knowledge (and ability) toward which every rational process of reaching understanding and of understanding oneself (and of modes of action) is oriented. The 'principle' of this interrational faculty of judgement

– this wisdom of *problematization* which has to link the pace of transitions with the courage to interrupt – is neither the limitation nor the delimitation of the capacity for reason; its principle is liberation from false limitations and equally from false delimitations. This falseness is measured in terms of the forms of unfreedom which stem from forms of blindness to the world, a limitation which goes beyond moral and personal concerns. The libertarian unity of a reason that is not intended to integrate the 'aggregate' of its discursive media into the complex of a 'system' is created in the process of overcoming these limitations; we have to do here with a never-ending process, in that it can never be completed.[25]

It can also be said that the experience of the conditionality of any and every claim to unconditional validity manifests itself together with the insight into the unconditionality of these contrastive conditions in the application of this capacity for judgement. Since the agencies into which modern reason is divided are precisely not cooperatively coordinated and coordinatable, the regulative ideal of a 'balance'[26] between the now separate moments of reason can be nothing other than the occasionally persistent incursions of *critique*. This form of reason, to put it in French terms, comprises a transcendent relationship with the immanent Other of each and every form of rationality, without as a consequence limiting experience and thought metaphysically in the name of an exterritorial Other of reason.

This relationship with the *Other* of each and every justifiable orientation is now visibly related to our dealings with the *Others*. It derives from the interactive relationships in which we acquire the ability to justify, and grows – as it then does – out of communicative dealings with subjects *vis-à-vis* whom we represent the validity of our assumptions and the soundness of our reasons. The constitutive perspectival character of reason cannot be thought of without at the same time conceiving of a plurality of subjects who depend on coordinating their actions in language. To this extent, the (metaphorical) interaction of the forms of rationality are grounded on a (literally) interactive practice which, for its part, must be described as reasonable precisely in such instances as where it is possible to react in such practice to contrasting validity claims in the manner described. However, nothing additionally revealing has been said about the essence of this relation to validity if it is then defined – as Habermas does – in terms of consensus theory, namely as a fundamental communicative relationship. The intersubjective validity of reasons is certainly a problem of communication in many cases, but this does not in turn make it 'communicative' itself. This means that although the structural and normative constitution of rationality rests on the *factuality* of communicative action, it cannot itself be understood as being actual 'communicative' reason – other than in the *figurative* meaning of the world.[27]

To summarize, the dual meaning of a concept of the 'communicative side' to reason can be explained as follows. Whereas the underlying forms of rationality *are* always already structurally coordinated, the normative characteristic of an action that is rational in the narrower sense resides in its *accomplishing* the coordination of the various rational orientations in a specific way (even if the corresponding practices *are* always already more or less reasonably coordinated in institutional structures). The cooperative mode of action-coordination, hinted at under the heading of communicative interaction in Habermas's work, can, it seems to me, be explained only by referring to the irreversible and equally unreconcilable interdependence of the forms of rationality and dimensions of truth. If one expressly reads the *Theory of communicative action* 'backwards', namely beginning with the problem of the 'interplay' of the aspects of rationality, one will find that it is not a key concept of communication which accentuates the particular quality of comprehensive rationality. Rather, the opposite holds true: a redefined concept of rationality accentuates the particular quality of the validity-related, cooperative rationality of action. The metaphorical meaning of 'communicative rationality' appears to be the basic concept involved, whereas its literal meaning seems to be a merely coordinated concept. In other words, it is not a normatively charged concept of communication that provides an explanation for the unabridged contents of reason; rather an unabridged (plural, non-integral and yet non-separatist) concept of reason explains the key meaning of communication oriented to reaching an understanding. The fact that reason is situated in communication does not justify labelling reason as itself communicative.

4 Habermas and Critical Theory: Beyond the Marxian Dilemma?

Jeffrey Alexander

Every critical social theory is faced with the problem of constituting its grounds for critique. Of course, even empirical, 'positive' theory contains an ideological dimension, but because its main ambition is explanatory rather than evaluative it can – indeed, must – leave this normative source implicit and diffuse. For Critical Theory, the situation is quite different. It is explicitly political, seeking to draw readers toward a normative position and often to a political stance. Because this is so, its grounds for moral judgement are explicitly called into question.

There seem to be three ways that the grounds for a critical theory can be constituted. The first is through relativism: 'I criticize society because it violates my principles.' The sources of critique are presented as subjective, as emerging from personal convictions. Here is the 'humanistic' position that became so popular in the non-Marxist critical sociology of the late 1960s and early 1970s, the 'self-reflexive' sociology that eschews the binding character of objectivity and calls upon the theorist to be forthright about his/her own personal values.

In intellectual and political terms, however, this relativist position has seemed unsatisfactory. Critical theorists have usually sought a position that at least appears to be more objective and, hence, less challengeable. The alternative strategy has been to seek an immanent critique, to try to demonstrate that the critical standard grows naturally and inevitably out of the conditions of the society against which the critique is aimed. Two kinds of immanent justification have been offered, the objective and the subjective. Marx is the great exemplar of the former. The communist demands of the proletariat, he insisted, grow not from the head of this or that philosopher or from some free-floating idealistic hope, but from the concrete conditions of real social life. While the dominant thrust of capitalist society is irrational, a more rational form of social organization can, in fact, be gleaned from the actual social conditions of capitalism, from its objectivity, its cosmopolitanism, its universalism and the egalitarian cooperation it forces upon its working class. Hegel represents the exemplar of the alternative approach, seeking an immanent justification in a subjective, idealist form. In his *Phenomenology of the Spirit* he laid out a developmental sequence that was simultaneously logical, psychological, and historical, and he argued that the sources for moving beyond each stage would inevitably be discovered in the experienced inadequacies (illogic, frustrations, social tensions) of each state itself. For both Marx and Hegel, then, an appropriate standard of critical reason was immanent at every historical stage.

The tradition of twentieth-century theory associated with the Frankfurt school of Marxism, initiated by Horkheimer and Adorno and associated most famously with the political theories of Herbert Marcuse, must be credited with making this issue of critical justification completely explicit. Rather than Marxist or Hegelian, it called itself quite simply 'Critical Theory', and it explicitly adopted the transcendent criterion of 'rationality' as the basis for its anti-capitalist critique. This position clearly followed the normative path; the Frankfurt school found only moral bankruptcy in objectivist theories like those of the orthodox Marx. But since the Frankfurt Marxists had abandoned Hegel's faith in God, they had no firm basis for their own moral criticism. Though they postulated an immanent rationality, their work became mystical and arbitrary when they tried to define rationality's source. Perhaps inevitably, this source came to be associated with the prerogative of intellectuals. With this development the universalistic ambition of this Frankfurt Marxist criticism came to seem more and more particularistic. It became an increasingly serious problem in the 1960s, when Marcuse defended critical reason by opposing 'pure tolerance' and at least appeared to apologize for revolutionary coercion in Western societies in a manner that paralleled Fanon's defence of it in the Third World.

It is in the context of this historical and theoretical juncture that Jürgen Habermas's work must be understood. Habermas is a radical, but he is not a revolutionary. Whereas Marcuse celebrated the excesses of the 1960s, Habermas was appalled by them, and he earned the permanent contempt of some German student radicals for his public opposition. As a left-wing humanist and democrat, Habermas has always been acutely aware of the theoretical and political degeneration of Critical Theory. In his 'Reply to My Critics', many of whom were orthodox representatives of the critical school, Habermas insists ('Universal Pragmatics' in Thompson and Held (eds), *Habermas: Critical Debates*, London, 1982, p. 222) that 'revolutionary self-confidence and theoretical self-certainty are gone'. To regain them, Critical Theory must find a way to justify its standard of immanent rationality. This is what Habermas set out to do.

To restore universality to critical rationality and to cleanse the critical tradition of its elitism, Habermas seeks to return to key aspects of Marx's original strategy. He does this not by embracing an objectivist criterion, for he maintains the moral tone of the 'Western Marxist' tradition. Rather, he returns to Marx in the sense of embracing empirical social science and empirically based philosophy. Earlier generations of the Frankfurt school attacked social science as inevitably 'positive', bourgeois and conservative. In contrast, Habermas embraces the most advanced empirical theorizing of his day. As Marx sought to turn political economy against itself in the name of socialism, so Habermas seeks to demonstrate that the empirical processes illuminated by contemporary theories – processes there for all to see – carry inside themselves the potential for critique and transcendence of the status quo.

Over the last fifteen years there have been three traditions of empirical social theory upon which Habermas has drawn. Perhaps the least remarked upon by either Habermas or his interpreters is the Parsonian.[1] Habermas began teaching about Parsons in the early 1960s and, though rarely footnoted, Parsonian themes like systems, pattern-variables and the centrality of socialization permeate his thought. Only in the 1980s has Habermas made this debt explicit, as his work has taken a formidable Parsonian turn. He remarks in the second volume of *The Theory of Communicative Action* (*TCA*, p. 199) that, while interest in Parsons's work was 'pushed into the background for a time by hermeneutically and critically oriented approaches to social inquiry, no theory of society can be taken seriously today if it does not at least situate itself with respect to Parsons'. But Habermas does more than simply clarify the relationship; he takes Parsons' work as embodying the highest level of contemporary theoretical work. 'The body of work he left us', Habermas writes, 'is without equal in its level of abstraction and differentiation, its social-theoretical scope and systematic quality, while, at the same time, it draws upon the literature of specialized research.' In fact, he issues a warning to any 'neo-Marxism which wishes simply to bypass Parsons', averring that 'in the history of social science errors of this type are normally quickly corrected' (ibid.).

Habermas sees that Parsons was centrally concerned with the sociological preconditions of universalism, which is, as Hegel clearly saw, perhaps the most crucial dimension of rationality. More recently, Habermas has relied heavily on the historical twist that Parsons gave to the sociology of universalism in his evolutionary theory. Terms like 'learning processes' and 'normative integration' have become central to Habermas's critical vocabulary. In the book of essays that adumbrated the present work, *Communication and the Evolution of Society* (Boston, 1979, p. 120) Habermas wrote: 'I would even defend the thesis that the development of . . . normative structures is the pacemaker of social evolution.' He is aware that this Parsonian theme turns the tables on Marx:

Whereas Marx localized the learning processes important for evolution in the dimension of objectivating thought – of technical and organizational knowledge, of instrumental and strategic action, in short, of productive forces – there are good reasons meanwhile for assuming that learning processes also . . . are deposited in more mature forms of social integration, in new productive rela-

tions, and that these in turn first make possible the introduction of new productive forces. (ibid., p. 98)

The second line of empirical theorizing upon which Habermas has
drawn is Piaget's work on cognitive and moral development. Whereas
Parsons allows Habermas to claim that universalistic and solidary relationships are grounded in the historical development of real societies,
Piaget allows him to argue that universalistic, critical thought is grounded
in the normal development of the human mind. The internal emphasis of
Piaget – the vocabulary of 'interiorization', 'representation', 'generalization' – complements the normative reference of Habermas's critique; it also
clearly articulates with the Freudian vocabulary of Parsons's socialization
theory, upon which Habermas also relies (for his interweaving of these
traditions, see *Communication*, pp. 81–88). Indeed, Habermas uses Piagetian theory to conceptualize a point that Parsons's critics have somehow
seemed unable to grasp: developmental theory conceives socialization as
learning to be rational and autonomous, not dependent and submissive.
Piaget insists that human intelligence moves from the concrete to the
formal and in the process gains a critical distance from and mastery over
the objects in its environment. These are precisely the qualities that allow
Habermas to extend his empirical theorizing about the immanent source of
critical rationality. By the mid-1970s the key terms of Piagetian theory had
been thoroughly incorporated into Habermas's discussion of contemporary
reality. Consciousness is 'decentred' and 'objective'; it 'goes beyond reality' to think the 'possible'; it seeks universal, generalizable principles, 'the
rules behind rules' (compare, e.g. Piaget, *The Principles of Genetic Epistemology* (1972) with Habermas, *Communication*, pp. 69–94). Finally,
Piaget's emphasis on the pragmatic, concrete character of the developmental crises that promote learning allows Habermas to conceptualize the
immanent growth of mental rationality without falling into the trap of
Hegel's idealism.

What Habermas has taken from Parsons and Piaget is not simply a
theory of the empirical development of rationality, but also the notion that
a great deal of rationality is already realized in the world as structured
today. This is the price of buying into empirical theorizing, and it is the
very price that earlier generations of critical theorists were unwilling to
pay. Horkheimer and Adorno learned a great deal from Hegel's *Phenomenology*, but they seem to have stopped learning after his discussion of
the Enlightenment, which Hegel criticized for its mechanistic version of
rationality (*Phenomenology of Spirit*, New York and Oxford, 1977 [1807]:
VI.B.i and II.A). For Horkheimer and Adorno, Western cultural development evidently stopped at that point; hence their equation: Enlightenment
= Capitalism = Instrumental Reason. Hegel, in contrast, believed that the
reigning conception of reason continued to grow (e.g. *Phenomenology*,
VI.C, *passim*) in the course of subsequent Western development. By passing through later phases of expressive, ethical, and eventually religious
experience, the conception of rationality became enriched and multivalent.
Habermas follows Hegel himself rather than the Horkheimer/Adorno

caricature, though he does not follow him to the point of believing that a completely satisfactory 'rationality' is enshrined in the status quo. Having learned from Parsons and Piaget, Habermas can describe how cognitive, expressive and moral rationality have developed in the present day. He can also argue, in the light of his own more critical ambitions, that their theories provide an explanation not only of contemporary society, but of a rational standpoint from which to go beyond it.

But neither Parsons nor Piaget plays a central role in the first volume of Habermas's most systematic work, *The Theory of Communicative Action*. Parsons receives major consideration in the second volume; Piaget is discussed only passingly in both volumes, though his ideas continue to permeate Habermas's theoretical vocabulary. In this book pride of place is given to the third empirical tradition that Habermas uses to remake his critical theory, the speech act theory which derives from ordinary language philosophy. To 'scientific' sociologists, it may seem strange to claim a modern philosophical tradition as an empirical, or at least empirically related theory. But speech act theory and the 'analytic' movement out of which it grew are directed toward the study of empirical processes in a way that is antithetical to the metaphysical traditions of continental philosophy. This contrast, of course, is exactly what attracts Habermas. By developing a theory of 'communicative action', he wants to use speech act theory to extend his empirical analysis of immanent rationality.

Habermas seems to have been drawn to ordinary language analysis under the influence of Karl-Otto Apel. In a major essay published in 1967, *Analytic Philosophy of Language and the Geisteswissenschaften*, Apel demonstrated a convergence between later trends in English, analytic philosophy and the interpretative tradition of German hermeneutics. He demonstrated (*Analytic Philosophy*, p. 37) that the rationalistic, intentionalist bias that had given early analytic philosophy an atomistic and empiricist approach to meaning has been superceded by Wittgenstein's later 'revolution.' Wittgenstein had shown that rather than denoting intended objects, words really denote simply other words. Wittgenstein believed that words are arbitrarily arranged in language games, and that such games must be interpreted from within. In Apel's view (*Analytic Philosophy*, p. 33) this opened the way for reconciling ordinary language theorizing with the 'Geisteswissenschaften' (i.e. cultural studies) tradition.

Habermas then uses post-Wittgensteinian analytic philosophy to root his rationality standard more firmly in immanent, empirical processes, this time in the nature of ordinary language itself. Though he did not pursue the issue at this early point, Habermas (*Knowledge and Human Interests* (Boston, 1971, p. 314)) articulated precisely this connection in his Inaugural Lecture at Frankfurt in 1965: 'The human interest in autonomy and responsibility is not mere fancy, for it can be apprehended a priori. What raises us out of nature is the only thing whose nature we can know: language.'[2] Habermas argues that in ordinary speech actors make implicit claims about the validity of their statements, claims which, at a pinch, they are prepared to justify through argument. On these grounds, he suggests that rationality 'is ingrained in the very structure of action oriented toward reaching understanding' (*TCA*, vol. I, p. 130). Perhaps the most eloquent expression of the peculiar marriage of Hegelianism and empiricism that inspires Habermas's turn to language can be found in an earlier work. 'In action oriented toward reaching understanding', Habermas writes (*Communication*, p. 97), and here he means to include most ordinary language, 'validity claims are "always already" implicitly raised.' It is 'in these validity claims', he goes on to argue, that 'communication theory can locate a gentle but obstinate, a never silent although seldom redeemed claim to reason'.

In his communication theory, Habermas defines rationality as the quality that makes action 'defendable against criticism' (*TCA*, vol. I, p. 16). To be rational, acts must rest upon 'criticizable validity claims' (ibid., p. 15) rather than on unchallengeable authority or physical force. If challenged, then rational actors will cite potentially consensual grounds that justify their statements or actions. In doing so they will be engaging in 'argumentation.' Argumentation is speech that 'thematizes' contested validity claims, explicitly supporting or criticizing them. Ordinary language, Habermas believes, can rest on four kinds of implicit validity claims, each of which, in the ideal speech situation, can be justified through argument. These claims refer to cognitive, moral and expressive dimensions. In instrumental and strategic action (which Habermas also calls teleological), the claim is made for efficiency; the discourse that thematizes this action – though it is rarely, in fact, subject to such argumentation – is empirical. Related to this, but more generalized, is the kind of speech act that Habermas calls the assertive or constative. These are statements of fact. They refer to actions that rest on purely factual claims, and they are ultimately validated by claims to truth in the cognitive sense. The discourse that thematizes this claim Habermas calls theoretical. While both strategic and constative speech acts are located within the cognitive dimension, Habermas differentiates them by suggesting that strategic action is almost never thematized. This is what makes it, in his view, instrumentally rather than communicatively rational – a distinction that, as we will see, plays a central and often problematic role in his understanding. The third distinct mode of action is expressive, referring both to emotional and aesthetic statements. The claim put forward here is not truth, but 'truthfulness', sincerity and authenticity in a subjective sense. The discourse that thematizes this claim Habermas sometimes calls therapeutic and at other times aesthetic. Finally, there is moral action, which invokes neither efficiency, truth nor truthfulness. Its claim is to 'rightness', to a normative context that is legitimate in the sense of reflecting some moral interest common to all concerned. It is practical discourse that thematizes this claim to validity.

This communication theory – to which I will return – takes up sizeable chunks of Habermas' book (see, especially, *TCA*, vol. I, pp. 8–42, 75–101, and 273–337; for the first and most concise statement of this position, see *Communication*, pp. 1–68). Habermas's analysis of Weber takes up another. In view of Habermas's concern with the empirical immanence of rationality and his commitment to communicative argument, Weber certainly seems an appropriate reference. While Habermas has suggested that rational argument is an implicit part of everyday speech, he thinks this has not always been so. Communicative action can be more or less rational, and the further back we go in examining traditional and primitive societies, the less rational it appears. The point about rational communication is that understanding cannot be conceived a priori. It cannot – and here Habermas gives a communicative twist to Parsons's famous pattern-variable dichotomy – be 'normatively ascribed' (*TCA*, vol. I, p. 70); rather, it must be 'communicatively achieved'. Social rationalization, then, can be defined as the elimination of factors that 'prevent conscious settlement of conflicts' (ibid., p. 119). Here lies the significance of Weber. His historical analysis of the cultural and social processes that produced rationalization can be seen as describing the movement toward communciative rationality. Habermas's communication theory leads him to incorporate Weber and, equally important, to correct him.

Although his reading of Weber's corpus is by no means systematic or complete, Habermas presents a sophisticated and original interpretation of certain key sections. In the positive phase of his reading, he focuses on elements of Weber's cultural history which have not yet received sufficient attention, particularly on 'The Social Psychology of World Religions' and 'Religious Rejections of the World' as they relate to *The Protestant Ethic*. His interpretative perspective is unique because it combines his interest in communication with a late Parsonian interest in cultural differentiation. Here he is influenced by Schluchter, whose own work reflects a similar orientation. While Habermas uses the culture/society/personality distinction as an overall framework, he focuses less on differentiation among these three systems than on differentiation among the cognitive, expressive and moral dimensions of cultural life. He suggests that this separation (see Parsons, 'Introduction to Culture and the Social System' in *Theories of Society*, New York, 1961) has allowed processes of justification to occur in more rational, less ascribed ways. Cultural differentiation has meant that objective knowledge, expressive/aesthetic life and morality can increasingly be conceived without reference to an overarching religious cosmos. 'The devout attachment to concrete orders of life secured in tradition', Habermas writes, can 'be superseded in favour of a free orientation to universal principles' (*TCA*, vol. I, p. 213).

Yet, whereas Parsons always felt that Weber had sustained this level of insight throughout the breadth of his work – his only failure having been the occasional resort to 'type atomism' – Habermas sees significant reductionist tendencies also at work. I have suggested that Weber's reductionism emerges forcefully in the historical sociology of precapitalist societies (*The Classical Attempt at Theoretical Synthesis: Max Weber*, Berkeley and Los Angeles, 1983). Habermas, in contrast, historicizes the reductionism, seeing it as emerging only in Weber's work on the transition, from the earlier phases of cultural differentiation to modernity itself. Here Habermas relies too heavily on the Parsonian tradition's reconstruction of Weber's premodern cultural history, rather than examine Weber's writing in its own right. He does so, ironically, because he follows Marx's radically historicist approach to 'the transition', an acceptance that, we will see, eventually creates major difficulties. In a marvellous passage, Habermas suggests (*TCA*, vol. I, p. 217) that there were three paths that Weber could have taken after he had established the rational potential of Western cultural development. First, he could have studied the social movements, like democratic revolutions and socialist movements, which sought to institutionalize such rationality. Second, he could have developed a cultural sociology of this new, more rationalized contemporary order. Third, he could have studied the institutionalization of one subtype of modern rationality, e.g., on purposively rational action. He suggests that Weber took up only the third possibility, concentrating on the origins and operation of instrumental capitalism and bureaucracy. This decision was an unfortunate one because it meant that 'Weber takes into consideration the horizon of possibilities opened up by the modern understanding of the world only to the extent that it serves to explain the core phenomenon he identified in advance' (p. 221). In other words, by focusing only on the purposively rational institutions of capitalism and bureaucracy, Weber drastically narrowed his thinking about the nature of modern understanding, an issue whose possibilities had been genially opened by Weber's analysis of cultural differentiation in the earlier period.

Is there empirical justification for Weber's choice, or did it result from a theoretical mistake? Some of each, in Habermas's view. Certainly 'the institutionalization of purposive-rational entrepreneurial activity is, from a functional point of view, actually of central importance for modern societies' (ibid.). At the same time, however, there has been 'a noticeable and consequential narrowing of the concept of rationality in Weber's action theory' (ibid.).

By exploring the presuppositional reasons behind Weber's narrowed treatment, Habermas offers an extraordinary account of what Weber's cultural sociology of modernity might have been. The pessimism about modernity was, in Habermas's view, as much the result of Weber's inability to understand the sources of continuing rationality as the result of his empirical insight and ideological sensibility. Weber described all the newly autonomous spheres of modern culture – science, art and sexuality, political morality – as doomed to irrationality. The earlier sense of the rationality of these endeavours, or at least their meaningful validity, had come from their connection to overarching religious principles. But with the victory of science over religion, Weber believed, they could no longer be related to any general principles at all. This is just what Habermas contests.[3] Why can these modern cultural spheres not be seen as related to secular rather than religious principles? His point (p. 229) is worth quoting in full.

[Weber's] explanation of the self-destructive pattern of societal rationalization is unsatisfactory because [he] still owes us a demonstration that a moral consciousness guided by principles can survive only in a religious context. He would have to explain why embedding a principled ethic in a salvation religion, why joining moral consciousness to interests in salvation, are just as indispensable for the *preservation* of moral consciousness as, from a genetic standpoint, they undoubtedly were for the *emergence* of this stage of moral consciousness. (original italics)

Weber, in Habermas's opinion, offers no empirical justification for this claim. His research programme, which was supposed 'to make it possible to estimate "the cultural significance of Protestantism in relation to the other plastic elements of modern culture", was never carried through' (ibid.). If it has been, Weber would have had to include the ethical influence on modern culture of humanism and of both philosophical and scientific empiricism. Combined with the influence of Protestantism, these traditions 'flowed into the rationalism of the Enlightenment and promoted a secularized, lay morality in bourgeois strata'. This latter development promoted what Weber claimed was impossible: the emergence of a 'principled ethic that is removed from religious contexts, and through which the bourgeois strata set themselves off from both the clergy and from the common people caught up in naive piety' (p. 230).

Indeed, as we have seen earlier, Habermas himself demonstrates that principled ethics do survive in a postreligious context, that substantive rationality is pervasive in the modern world. To reintroduce this argument, Habermas argues (p. 249) that 'Weber goes too far when he infers from the loss of the substantial unity of reason, a polytheism of gods and demons struggling with one another, with their irreconcilability rooted in a pluralism of incompatible validity claims'. Habermas suggests, to the contrary, that if one looks closely at differentiated cultural life, one can see that there is a 'unity of rationality in the multiplicity of value spheres'. Though each sphere is anchored in concretely different values – hence their immediate irreconcilability – each conceives itself as justifiable via rational argument. Science seeks justification through propositional truth, expressive and artistic life through sincerity and authenticity, morality through its claim to normative rightness. The medium for common understanding between these spheres – the source of their higher reconcilability – is precisely the fact that they make such claims to validity, and they can thematize these claims through rational argumentation. This is not to say that the interrelationship between these spheres is smooth or integrative. There remains 'the problem of where, in the communicative practice of everyday life, "switching stations" have to be brought into operation so that individuals can shift their action orientations from one complex to another' (p. 250).[4]

This is the general argument through which Habermas demonstrates that, in his words, Weber 'does not apply the comprehensive concept of rationality upon which he bases his investigations of cultural tradition' to his own sociology of modern life. He builds a more concrete case for this criticism through his detailed consideration of Weber's approach to modern law. More than any interpreter since Parsons, Habermas sees the absolute centrality of law to Weber's theory of modern society. If Weber is to make a convincing case that purposive-rational action can, indeed, be cut off from higher moral grounding, he must show that the self-regulation and stability of rational systems can be achieved through an equally rational and value-less law. If Weber wants to sustain his narrowed conception of modernity, therefore, he must succeed 'in uncoupling the development of modern law from the fate of moral-practical rationality and conceptualizing it as just a further embodiment of cognitive-instrumental rationality' (p. 242).

Weber accomplishes this by focusing exclusively on how the systematicity, formality and logicality of modern law allow it to be eminently calculable (pp. 254ff.). But Weber is mistaken. While the formal qualities of modern law are functional for instrumental systems like the economy, this says nothing about how such legal structures are constituted in themselves. To understand the latter, it is necessary to see that contemporary law embodies certain kinds of moral justifications. Weber resisted the connection of law and morality on the grounds that it denies what is precisely the major innovation of modern legality, namely its differentiation from any explicit and substantive moral position. Habermas replies, ironically, that this separation can be maintained only be justifying it with reference to a more general abstract moral consciousness.

> The particular accomplishment of the positivization of the legal order consists in *displacing* problems of justification, that is, in relieving the technical administration of the law of such problems over broad expanses – but not in doing away with them. Precisely the post-traditional structure of legal consciousness sharpens the problem of justification into a question of principle that is shifted to the foundations, but not thereby made to disappear. (p. 261)

Habermas lists a whole series of extralegal principles that form the justifying foundation for modern law, characterizing them under the general Piagetian rubric of 'post-conventional' morality: the notion that a compact between free and legal partners makes contractual obligations possible, the concept of the abstract legal subject's general competency, the very distinction between norms and principles, and so forth. This insistence on the substantive foundations of legal rationality leads him, quite rightly in my view, to emphasize the significance of political constitutions, institutions that Weber almost completely ignored. 'The catalog of basic rights contained in bourgeois constitutions', Habermas suggests (p. 261), is one of the 'expressions of this justification that has become structurally necessary'. He criticizes Schluchter for presenting Weber's legal sociology as if it implied such legal principles and for suggesting that these principles supply a link in Weber's work between his theory of positive law and his discussion of the ethic of responsibility. Such principles, Habermas counters, 'are a foreign element within Weber's systematic construction' (p. 438, n. 34).

This completes Habermas's reconstruction of what Weber's cultural sociology of modernity might have looked like if Weber had not unduly narrowed his conception of rationality. To explain the impoverishment of Weber's actual account of the contemporary order, Habermas faults Weber's understanding of social action. Weber, he suggests (p. 280), operated with an intentionalist rather than a linguisitic conception of action. He saw meaning as the result of actors trying to gain the understanding of others in a purposive way. From such an intentionalist perspective, action is rationalizable only in terms of means/ends relations, invoking the criteria of actual effectiveness and empirical truth. Value and emotion-related actions are, then, not rationalizable by definition; it was for this reason that Weber so sharply opposed *Zweck-* to *Wert-rationalität*.

What is the alternative to such an intentionalist, utilitarian view? We have seen it clearly if we have followed Habermas's argument all along. It is the understanding of action as, in the first instance, an act of communication. Action must be conceived on the model of ordinary language, either as carried on through the medium of language or as modelled upon it. For ordinary language, we have seen, is almost always carried on within the restricting framework of implicit modes of validation. Even if it is strategic, therefore, it is subject to some extra-intentional control. It is these moral foundations that provide the basis for rationalization in something other than an instrumental sense.

In light of the matters discussed thus far – they take up nearly the first two-thirds of the book – it may come as a surprise to the reader to learn that there is not much communicative rationality in the modern world after all! Beginning with the fourth section (I will consider the short, but highly interesting third section below), Habermas seems to bring his theoretical enterprise of the first 270 pages to a screeching halt and laboriously to change direction. He now suggests that communicative rationality is actually limited to a very small section of contemporary society called the 'lifeworld'. His definition of this lifeworld is distressingly vague – it certainly differs from Heidegger's and Schutz's – but he does indicate that it is where 'everyday practice' and 'everyday communication' occur. Whereas it had seemed to be his intention in the first two-thirds of his work to suggest that such 'lifeworld' practices as ordinary language are the basis for institutional behaviour, he is now intent on isolating these practices. He portrays them as vulnerable islands of feeling and thought surrounded by hostile oceans of rationalized 'systems'. Systems are defined as organizations of purely strategic actions, organizations that employ a 'functionalist' form of reason that has nothing to do with human norms or concerns. The capitalist economic system, the legal-rational political system, even the modern mass communications system (p. 372), Habermas claims, do not rely on the medium of language, but employ media like money and power (and influence?) in a coercive, anti-communicative way.

At first Habermas speaks of the relation between systems and lifeworld as 'counteracting tendencies' (p. 341). Almost immediately, however, he puts the relation into the stronger, Marxian language of 'contradiction'. 'The contradiction arises', he writes (p. 342), 'between, on the one hand, a rationalization of everyday communication that is tied to the structures of intersubjectivity of the lifeworld, in which language counts as the genuine and irreplaceable medium of reaching an understanding, and, on the other hand, the growing complexity of subsystems of purposive-rational action, in which actions are coordinated through steering media such as money and power.' Soon he is speaking about the 'colonization of the lifeworld' by modern society's rationalized systems: 'An unleashed functionalist reason of systems maintenance disregards and overrides the claim to reason ingrained in communicative sociation and lets the rationalization of the lifeworld run idle' (p. 399).

An abrupt change indeed. If Habermas were to seek to justify this shift in a thoroughgoing way, he would have to go back and refute, point by point, his entire discussion of Weber. In that discussion, he himself developed a systematic argument against an instrumental reading of modern social institutions. It was he who argued against Weber that instrumental rationality was not the only form of rationality to be institutionalized in the modern world, and he pointed directly to political systems and their legal foundations as his foremost examples. Is he not now arguing directly against this earlier stance?

Although Habermas does not try to refute himself, he turns to earlier members of the Frankfurt school to do much the same thing. In the volume's fourth and concluding section 'From Lukács to Adorno: Rationalization as Reification', he presents this strand of Western Marxism as, simultaneously, a reading of Weber and an accurate description of Western society. This Frankfurt tradition, of course, did rely heavily on Weber's work, but its reading of him was precisely the one-sided, instrumentalized version that Habermas warned us against. Armed with the earlier interpretation, we are in a position to say that these Western Marxists picked up on the wrong Weber. By doing so, moreover, they allowed their picture of Western society to become so heavily instrumentalized that they missed the opportunity to root their own alternative vision of rationality in an immanent, empirical way. The latter, of course, is precisely the ambition of *The Theory of Communicative Action*. Yet Habermas applauds them. He uses this earlier generation of Marxists – the criticism of whose very approach to critical theory has been the implicit starting point for his own work – to steer Weber back to Marx. I said earlier that the Frankfurt theorists seemed to stop reading Hegel's *Phenomenology* after his chapters on the Enlightenment. In the earlier parts of his book Habermas used Weber to develop an empirical way to join Hegel in his post-Enlightenment discussion. But after showing us this promised land, Habermas wants to take us back to the desert. To do this, he must distort Weber's understanding of modern rationality as badly as the Frankfurt school distorted Hegel's.

'Capitalism' now becomes a satisfactory way of defining the present era, and Lukács becomes the theorist who succeeded in producing the best definition. Lukács claimed (in 'Reification and the Consciousness of the Proletariat' (1923) in *History and Class Consciousness*, Cambridge, Mass., 1971) that Marx's conception of commodity fetishism, which conceptualized the capitalist world as totally dominated by the instrumental value of exchange, meant much the same thing as Weber's rationalization theory. Habermas welcomes Lukács's convergence thesis and tries to restate commodity fetishism in terms of his own communications theory. He writes (p. 359) that Lukács 'conceives of the reification of lifeworld contexts, which sets in when workers coordinate their interactions by way of the de-linguistified medium of exchange value rather than through norms and values, as the other side of a rationalization of their action orientations'. In other words, (a) Weber demonstrated that modern actions are only purposively rational and that action orientations have been rationalized and do not appeal to values or norms; (b) Lukács showed that the interrelation of workers through an exchange of commodities – the 'de-linguistified medium of exchange' – rested on the same thing; (c) Lukács's conclusion, that the lifeworld of capitalism is reified, is valid. Habermas praises Lukács for showing that in capitalist society association is so instrumental that it can form only systems, not lifeworlds: 'He makes the system-forming effects of sociation established through the medium of exchange value intelligible from the perspective of action theory' (p. 359).

To the degree that the commodity form becomes the form of objectivity and rules the relations of individuals to one another as well as their dealings with external nature and with internal subjective nature, the lifeworld has to become reified and individuals degraded – as systems theory foresees – into an 'environment' for a society that has become external to them, that has abstracted from them and become independent of them. Lukács shares this perspective with Weber. (p. 361)

Does he? Only to the degree that Weber himself is guilty of reducing his presuppositions about action to an instrumental form. Once this has occurred, collective order, be it capitalist or socialist, can hardly be portrayed as anything other than external and coercive (cf. Alexander, *The Antinomies of Classical Thought: Marx and Durkheim*, Berkeley and Los Angeles, 1982). Habermas proves this when he demonstrates that Weber's externalist perspective on the rationality of contemporary political and legal institutions can be challenged dramatically if his conception of action is made more compatible with the multivalent 'communicative' approach of his writing on cultural history. The critical theorists, from Lukács onward, picked up precisely on Weber's theoretical mistake; given their own predispositions, they saw this mistake as a statement of empirical fact.

We might say, then, that there is an empirical error behind Habermas's abrupt reversal. Modern political and economic life are never simply instrumental. They are always coded by deep structures of cultural life. To mistake this is to confuse the fact of differentiation, which allows relative strategic freedom from ascribed value positions, with the absence of moral foundations. Nor are the modern worlds of values, norms and solidarities ever such simple, intimate and intuitive lifeworlds as Habermas describes. They are themselves also systems subject to organization on levels that individuals scarcely intuit. Moreover, they are interpenetrated with cultural and strategic areas of social life through processes which can be analytically reconstructed as exchange.

But there is probably also an ideological source for Habermas's insistence on the modern isolation of the lifeworld. This is the continuing influence on his work of German Idealism (Alexander, 'The Parsons Revival in German Sociology', *Sociological Theory* 2 (1984), pp. 394–412), which has, of course, deeply affected Western Marxism in all of its forms. This tradition is organized around the dichotomy of ideal versus material things, and it has always perceived the threat to posttraditional society to be one of deracination. Habermas follows this tradition. Despite the occasional avowals about the positive character of differentiation in his work, the oppressive and dangerous parts of modern society are almost always portrayed as emerging from rationalized, material systems, whereas the 'good parts' are associated with the personal intimacy of moral life. For those who do not accept the premisses of the Idealist tradition, however, this ideological dichotomy has little intuitive appeal. The problems of modern society have emerged as much from the lifeworlds of intimate relations – from the authoritarian family, religious sect and peer group – as they have from administrative and economic systems. They have been rooted as much in values and norms – in *Volk* culture, racism and submissive beliefs – as in force and coercion. Indeed, in the history of Western societies it has often been the case that a society's 'idealistic' refusal to allow the depersonalization of economic and political life has signalled its decline into irrationality and despair. Indeed, Loader and I argued ('The Cultural Grounds of Rationalization: Sect Democracy versus the Iron Cage', pp. 101–22 in Alexander, *Structure and Meaning: Relinking Classical Sociology* (New York, 1989)) that this was precisely Weber's own critique of the Gesellschaft – Gemeinschaft dichotomy in German social thought.

Finally, it seems to me that Habermas has made an error on the theoretical, presuppositional level itself. This error, moreover, is much like the one he criticized Weber for himself committing. It is a problem in the conception of action – more specifically, in the manner in which his communications theory is conceived. We turn here to the 'Intermediate Reflections' on 'Social Action, Purposive Activity and Communication' which completes the third section of Habermas's book.

In this third section, Habermas offers his own theory of communicative action. The discussion serves two purposes. On the one hand, it supplies the communicative approach to action that Habermas has just finished chastising Weber for being unable to provide. On the other hand, it is a transition to Habermas's argument, which unfolds in the section that follows, about the contradiction between system and lifeworld produced by the instrumentalization of the modern world. These purposes, however, are incompatible.

How can a theory of communicative action buttress and elaborate Habermas's critique of Weber? It can do so by demonstrating (a) that virtually all action assumes communication, (b) that communication assumes some extrastrategic understanding between actors, and (c) that this understanding usually makes an inherent claim to rational justification. As I have suggested earlier, this is just what Habermas argues in the discussions of communication theory that precede the Weber analysis (pp. 8–42, 75–101). In this third section, which is a more technical 'second visit' to communications, Habermas continues to insist that communication involves understanding and that understanding implies rationality (points (b) and (c) above). In this sense, he expands on his critique of Weber's approach. But considered as a whole, this later discussion actually points in quite a different direction. Rather than elaborating on the role of communicative rationality, Habermas now devotes himself to communication's limited domain (*contra* point (a) above). He does so by developing the contrast between communication and instrumental behaviour. In his earlier discussion, he had allowed that strategic, instrumental behaviour, though conducted with reference to justifying criteria like efficiency and effectiveness, is not, in fact, usually subject to thematization and rational argument. The point of that earlier discussion, however, was that most action was so subject. Now, in contrast, it is the purported lack of argumentation in strategic behaviour that preoccupies him. Instead of presenting a theory of communicative action to supplement Weber, he produces a concept of anticommunicative action to supplement the antinormative description of modern life which is to be the focus of his concluding section.

To argue that substantive rationality does not often occur in the principal institutional spheres of contemporary life, as he does in that final section, Habermas must demonstrate that communicative action is sharply bounded. He must show that instrumental-strategic action involves neither shared understanding nor the intent to communicate, which depends on understanding. The attempt so to argue is what the section with which we are presently concerned – section 3 – is all about. Habermas constructs an ideal – typical dichotomy of 'instrumental vs. communicative action', and he overloads this contrast with heavy conflationary baggage. All actions can be distinguished, he insists, according to whether they are oriented to success (i.e. strategic considerations) or oriented to understanding (i.e. communication). If action is oriented to understanding, he maintains, it is motivated by the desire to create a harmonious relation between the actor and his environment: 'In communicative action participants are not primarily oriented to their own individual successes; they puruse their individual goals under the condition that they can harmonize their plans of action on the basis of common situation definitions' (p. 288). To communicate, then, is the same as to agree: 'Reaching understanding is considered to be a process of reaching agreement among speaking and acting subjects' (ibid.). Now, because strategic, instrumental action implies competition and often conflict, it cannot be termed communicative. Habermas describes it as 'the non-communicative employment of knowledge' (p. 10).

This dichotomy does not seem valid. It seems to reflect a theoretical overreaction that conflates empirical, ideological and epistemological issues. First, the distinction has a clear ideological intent. Habermas maintains (p. 398) that 'the utopian perspective of reconciliation and freedom is ingrained in the conditions for the communicative sociation of individuals'. His definition of communication, in other words, is a scarcely concealed translation of the requisites for ideal political democracy. In contrast to strategic action, where force and deception may be used, in communicative action participants are said to pursue their aims 'without reservation in order to arrive at an agreement that will provide the basis for a consensual coordination of individually pursued plans of action' (pp. 295–6). Or again, as Habermas writes at an earlier point (p. 10), 'this concept of communicative rationality carries with it connotations based ultimately on the central experience of the unconstrained, unifying, consensus-bringing force of argumentative speech'.

My point is not that such ideological ambitions are illegitimate. Far from it. Rather I am suggesting that Habermas's desire to achieve such unconstrained and cooperative social relationships is not presented as an evaluative position, but as part of the very definition of his presuppositions about action. 'Communication = agreement' is a wishful equation. Shorn of the ideological hopes placed in it, communication qua communication does not necessitate cooperation. Nor do conflict and strategizing necessarily imply a lack of understanding. Certainly there are some acts, like war and murder, that do not 'depend upon' understanding in the traditional sense. A bomb can be dropped and murder committed against people who do not have the slightest idea what the meaning of this act is for the perpetrator. But even in these physically coercive acts, understanding still plays a vital role. Murder and war are usually carried out within a 'meaningful' perspective because even murderers and soldiers must understand and typify their actions in concrete and particular ways (e.g. Paul Fussell, *The Great War and Modern Memory*, New York, 1975). The issue, then, is not lack of understanding, but lack of reciprocal or mutual understanding. Habermas claims the distinction is an epistemological difference: does knowledge involve understanding? But what is really at stake is an empirical difference: to what degree is understanding mutual and supportive? Interpreting and strategizing are analytically interpenetrated even in war – the type case of dissensus. But clearer illustrations of interpenetration are acts that are not physically coercive, for example, strategic actions like hucksterism and deceit. The success of these actions depends not only on the perpetrator's intricate understanding of the meaning of his victim's actions, but on the victim's understanding of his interlocutor's actions in an 'objectively interpretable' way. Again, what is lacking is not understanding or communcation, but reciprocal understanding and supportive communication.

Actions form an empirically variable continuum in which constant analytic dimensions are given different weights. Understanding is a component of all action, so is strategic consideration. (I have elaborated this analytic approach to strategization and interpretation, relating them to rationality and social institutions, 'Action and Its Environments', pp. 289–318 in Alexander, B. Giesen, R. Munch, and N. Smelser (eds), *The Micro-Macro Link*, Berkeley and Los Angeles, 1987.) Whether action will be cooperative or conflictual depends on how these dimensions are filled in, on what concrete empirical form they take in specific historical situations. We can understand, now, why Habermas goes out of his way to reject an 'analytic' approach to the distinction between understanding and strategizing. 'In identifying strategic action and communicative action types', he writes (p. 286), 'I am assuming that concrete actions can be classified from these points of view. I do not want to use the terms "strategic" and "communicative" only to designate two analytic aspects under which the same action could be described' (see also p. 292).

It is as if Habermas misconstrues the very distinction between cultural and social systems that informed his discussion of Weber. For Parsons these were analytic distinctions, 'culture' referring to the meaningful organization of the symbols which inform human action and 'society' to the actual behaviour of real people. To abstract the 'understanding' of partners in a real interaction is to point toward the analytic dimension of the cultural system. To describe their degree of conflict or cooperation is to refer to issues that result from the organization of the social system itself. In his discussion of communication, it seems, Habermas wants to tie social system processes directly to cultural ones. He erases the analytic distinction by a rhetorical device which occurs throughout his third section. Writing about speech, he is inclined to refer to its 'binding (or bonding) effect' (see, e.g. p. 294). Speech not only binds people to an understanding (through their participation in the cultural system); it also bonds them together in solidarity (through their integration in the social system). In his first systematic elaboration of his communication theory, written in the mid-1970s, this conflation is already apparent. 'I shall speak of the success of a speech act', he wrote (*Communication*, p. 59), 'only when the hearer not only understands the meaning of the sentence uttered, but also actually enters into the relationship intended by the speaker.' But, while meaning is cultural, relationships are social. Success on one level by no means implies success on another.

It is not at all clear that this radical distinction is justified by the very analytic philosophy upon which Habermas draws. The philosopher whose early work had such an influence on Habermas, Karl-Otto Apel, has tried, for example, to support the instrumental/communicative distinction from the perspective of the synthesis of *Geisteswissenschaft* and ordinary language approaches I mentioned earlier.

The notion of pure strategical rationality of interaction between opponents in a game indeed implies reciprocity of rule-following actions and thus implies the equal status of the partners; but it does not imply, but pragmatically presupposes and thus excludes, the notion of coming to agreement about the rules of the game, i.e. of agreements about possible purposes, means and conditions of relevant actions within the game. Now this is the same, I suppose, as the claim that the notion of strategical action excludes and presupposes the notion of coming to agreement about, and thus sharing, the meanings ... of linguistic ... utterances by communication. ('Three Dimensions of Understanding Meaning in Analytic Philosophy: Linguistic Conventions, Intentions and Reference to Things', *Philosophy and Social Criticism*, 7 (1980), 2, pp. 124–5)

This statement actually seems to deny the validity of the dichotomy it ostensibly supports. Apel is acknowledging that strategic, game-playing behaviour relies upon understanding. In noting that such strategic action excludes the possibility of coming to an explicit agreement about rules, he is not denying the existence of such understanding, but classifying the rule-following it implies as conventional and concrete rather than post-conventional and formal. In the Piaget/Kolberg sense, strategic action may be said to 'presuppose' an agreement to follow rules, and, one might add, the ability to understand them, but to exclude the awareness that these rules are constructed by people consciously agreeing to them. The lameness of Apel's 'I suppose' in his final reference to understanding underscores the ambiguity of his point. His earlier work, we recall, was built precisely on his opposition to the antagonism of strategy and understanding. 'Only when we are dealing with psychotics or with people of a very strange culture', he wrote in the important *Analytic Philosophy* (p. 22), 'do we get the idea of doing without an immediate understanding of their motives.' As a general rule, he insisted (ibid., p. 23), 'objective explanation of facts and intersubjective communication about what is to be explained are ... "complementary" aspects of human knowledge.' Even in the later article he cannot avoid this analytic, synthesizing intention. 'A single person', he admits ('Three Dimensions', p. 123), 'could not understand the intentions of his purposive-rational actions (or even the rules of means–ends rationality) without presupposing already the intersubjective, i.e. common, general and, as it were, timeless, meaning that is fixed by the sign-types of a language.'

It is Austin, however, upon whom Habermas draws most strongly for the philosophic justification of his dichotomy between strategic and communicative action. Austin, one of the pioneers of ordinary-language philosophy, developed the contrast between illocutionary and perlocutionary speech acts. Habermas equates illocutionary with communicative and perlocutionary with strategic, suggesting that Austin's dichotomy parallels, explains and supports his own. Two questions immediately present themselves. First, does Habermas's dichotomy fairly capture what Austin meant to do? Second, is Austin's original intention relevant anyway? Without claiming to present an authoritative interpretation of what remains an enormously complex philosophical discussion, I would like to suggest that the answer to the first question is no, but to the second, yes.

It is very important not to forget Austin's original claim that speaking is doing. It was for this reason that he introduced into language philosophy the term 'performative utterances', and it is this notion which formed the background for Austin's famous set of lectures, *How to Do Things with Words* (Cambridge, Mass., 1961, pp. 233–52), which provides the most significant reference for Habermas's work. Austin insists at the outset of these lectures that 'the issuing of the utterance is the performing of an action' (p. 6). In performing speech, actors have intentions, and they want to achieve goals. Because they speak in circumstances, or situations, they must communicate in ways that are appropriate. To do so, their purposive action is thoroughly enmeshed in convention.

If Austin never abandons this basic conception, why does he introduce the distinction between actions that are illocutionary and those that are perlocutionary? Perhaps because he starts from the assumption that most acts are speeches and not simply that most speeches are acts. He wants, therefore, to distinguish, within the rubric of performative utterances, different kinds of acts (see, e.g. ibid., pp. 108, 109 and *passim*). Illocutionary acts refer to utterances, such as informing, ordering, warning and undertaking, that have in themselves – as words enmeshed in conventions –

a certain force. Perlocutionary acts, by contrast, are utterances which by being said bring about or achieve something outside of the speech situation. Thus, an illocutionary act can be captured in the statement 'In saying it I was warning him', whereas a perlocutionary act is described in the statement 'By saying it I convinced him, or surprised him, or got him to stop' (ibid., p. 109). Austin himself remarks that it is the distinction between illocutions and perlocutions which seems likeliest to give trouble' (ibid., p. 109) and his attempt to make the distinction initiated an argument that has by no means subsided. For our purposes, however, certain points seem relatively clear.

While the differences between these categories relate to their intended reference to extra-speech act effects, this is not the same as the distinction that Habermas evokes to separate strategic and communicative action. In the first place, the extra-speech effect of perlocutionary actions depends on a listener's understanding of the content of the speech. This means that strategic action, which Habermas equates with perlocutionary, could not, in fact, succeed without communication and understanding. To establish just such a connection actually seems to be Austin's intention when he first introduces the distinction. There is a sense, he writes (p. 101), in which to perform 'an illocutionary act, may also be to perform an act of another kind'.

> Saying something will often, or even normally, produce certain consequential effects upon the feelings, thoughts, or actions of the audience, of the speaker, or of other persons: and it may be done with the design, intention, or purpose of producing them; and we may then say, thinking of this, that the speaker has performed an action in the nomenclature of which reference is made either only obliquely, or not at all, to the performance of the illocutionary act. We shall call the performance of this kind the performance of a perlocutionary act.

The gist of this statement is that illocutionary and perlocutionary acts can be differentiated only analytically. Illocutionary acts 'normally' have consequential effects on the environment. If these effects are the principal intention of the speaker, if the act of creating understanding is significant to the speaker only as a vehicle for realizing this effect, then this act can be called perlocutionary.

But if strategic or perlocutionary acts are intended by Austin to include understanding, so also are communicative, or illocutionary, acts intended to include strategizing. Whereas Habermas defines communicative understanding as completely divorced from the strategic calculation of effects, Austin defines illocution as a type of performance. 'I must point out', he insists after an initial effort at distinguishing perlocution from illocution, 'that the illocutionary act as distinct from the perlocutionary is connected with the production of effects in a certain sense' (ibid., p. 115). He goes on to emphasize that 'unless a certain effect is achieved, the illocutionary act will not have been happily, successfully performed' (ibid.). True, successful effect is defined here as 'bringing about the understanding of the meaning and of the force of the locution' (ibid., p. 116), rather than as an effect on the environment separated from speech. But Austin insists that in illocution 'an effect must still be achieved'. Illocutionary understanding, then, can never occur without the calculation of effects and the purposive direction of action toward that end.

Because Habermas is an acute reader of texts and himself a splendid philosopher, it is not surprising that one can find in his discussion the implicit recognition that Austin's categories may not, after all, support his own. For example, introducing Austin's statement (which I quoted above) that illocutionary acts 'normally produce certain consequential effects', Habermas (*TCA*, vol. I, p. 289) alters the meaning of this statement by writing that Austin is suggesting that this happens 'sometimes'. And he turns it quite inside out by describing the phenomenon that 'sometimes' occurs as illocution having a role within perlocution rather than vice versa. Then, after developing the argument that he presents as following on Austin's own illocution/perlocution distinction, Habermas suggests that Austin was confused because he did not make the distinction as cleanly and radically as Habermas himself. 'Austin confuses the picture', he suggests (ibid., p. 294), 'by not treating those interactions . . . as different in type.' But was this a confusion on Austin's part or a justified insight? In attempting to justify his own claim, Habermas inadvertently justifies Austin's position. 'Austin did not keep these two cases separate as different types of interaction', he writes (ibid., p. 295), 'because he was inclined to identify acts of communication, that is, acts of reaching understanding, with the interactions coordinated by speech acts.' This was, indeed, exactly Austin's point. Most speech acts are performative, and illocutions certainly are concerned with interactive effects.

It can even be argued that Habermas recognizes, in spite of himself, the validity of Austin's logic, for in the course of criticizing Austin he introduces residual categories that undermine his effort to make a more radical distinction. Describing an actor engaging in different types of illocution, for example, Habermas suggests that the person 'is acting communicatively and cannot at all produce perlocutionary effects *at the same level of interaction*' (ibid., p. 294, original italics). Does this not imply that rather than distinguishing types of actions, one should distinguish among different levels within an action? If illocution and perlocution are simply different levels of a single act, is this not an analytic rather than a concrete distinction? In fact, Habermas later acknowledges the 'problem' of 'distinguishing and identifying in natural situations actions oriented to understanding from actions oriented to success' (ibid., p. 331). The problem seems to be that 'not only do illocutions appear in strategic-action contexts, but perlocutions appear in contexts of communicative action'. In an apparent effort to explain this anomaly, he introduces the notion of 'phases' of the interaction process, trying to convince us that 'strategic *elements* within a use of language oriented to reaching understanding can be distinguished from strategic *actions*' (original italics). Such *ad hoc* reasoning may avoid explicit acknowledgment of the analytical interpenetration of strategy and communication, but it amounts to implicit recognition. In substance if not in form, Habermas's argument resembles the anti-dichotomy position I ascribed to Apel above.

In my discussion thus far I have sketched both a positive and a negative side to Habermas's effort to ground critical rationality in ordinary language. In a positive vein, his insight into the validity claims of ordinary language allows him to see how substantively rational behaviour actually permeates the modern world. This insight allows Habermas not only to transcend the reductionist and ultimately elitist approach of the orthodox Frankfurt school, but also – in combination with the other theoretical traditions that he employs – to move beyond Weber's rationalization theory in a decisive sense. All of this allows him to insert a more critical edge into the normative-evolutionary tradition associated with Parsons. We have just seen, however, that there is also a negative side to Habermas's communication theory; he also uses it, ironically, to reduce the scope of rationality, first by eliminating understanding from strategic action, and second by idealizing understanding in an impractical way. Instead of elaborating the potential of Weberian theory and transcending 'critical' orthodoxy, this negative utilization of language theory undermines Weber's rationalization theory by pushing it back toward orthodox critical theory itself.

However, Habermas's communication theory also, in my view, suffers from quite another problem, even when it embraces rationality in the more acceptable, expanded sense. By considering what might be called the cultural weakness of Habermas's work, I will not only be engaging in one final interpretative criticism; I will, in addition, try to show how his theory's most far-reaching points must be extended in an important way.

From the beginning of his work on communication Habermas has claimed that engaging in communication assumes the capacity for reaching rational agreement. Understanding is identified with agreement, and agreement is identified with 'unconstrained cooperation'. Agreement, understanding, and the lack of constraint add up to rationality. Lack of constraint is a crucial qualification, for it implies that the actors involved in rational communication are fully conscious of what they say and do. (Recall Habermas's statement that rationalization can be defined as the elimination of factors that 'prevent the conscious settlement of conflicts') (*TCA*, vol. I, p. 119). Not only are they free from external material constraints; they are also free from internalized controls that would place the meaning and the origins of their behaviour out of their conscious reach. If they are not depicted as the complete masters of their behaviour, they cannot confidently be described as able to alter it in a manner that can ensure cooperative understanding.

Why does Habermas make this claim and how does he justify it? In the background, of course, there is his commitment to traditional democratic theory about voluntary cooperation: people must be endowed with conscious rationality if their contracts are to be conceived as having been voluntarily entered into. A more direct justification for this insistence comes from Piaget. The point of Piaget's formal-operational stage, and the stage of 'moral consciousness' that Kohlberg associated with it, is that individuals become capable of rethinking the foundations of their actions and are no longer subordinate to socially given meanings as such. In this sense, Piaget is part of the rationalist tradition that starts with Descartes, his contribution having been to revolutionize our understanding of the social and mental background, the learning processes, upon which the rationality of an adult depends.

Habermas shares this rationalist emphasis on conscious activity. His early description of 'thematization', the ability to argue rationally about the foundations of behaviour, strikingly resembles Piaget's. 'Moral consciousness', he writes, 'signifies the ability to make use of interactive competence for *consciously* processing morally relevant conflicts' (*Communication*, p. 88, original italics). What is left unsaid, but remains, in my view, enormously important, is that this conscious thematization does not have a cultural base. It is rooted in the cognitive and moral capacities of actors, capacities that are the result of developmental encounters that have, pragmatically and experientially, changed the objective structure of the self. In this same early discussion, for example, Habermas finds a parallel to his own notion of communicative agreement in Gouldner's theory that reciprocity underlines all interactions. Given his own commitment to the capacity for absolute consciousness, however, Habermas feels compelled to qualify even Gouldner's theory in an anticulturalist way. He insists that Gouldner's expression, 'the norm of reciprocity', is not 'entirely apt'. Why not? Because 'reciprocity is not a norm, but is fixed in the general structures of possible interaction' (ibid., p. 88).

If understanding means unconstrained, conscious, rational agreement, can it be related to systems of signs, to symbols that are patterned by deep structures or codes? It would seem that it cannot, and for this reason, it seems to me, communicative theory has an antagonistic relationship to the theory of culture. This antagonism becomes paramount in the second volume of Habermas's book, where he interprets Durkheim not as the originator of a symbolic sociology that formed a central reference for structuralism and semiotics (Alexander (ed.), *Durkheimian Sociology: Cultural Studies*. Cambridge, 1988), but as a theorist who explained how modernity's 'communicative liquification' of the sacred allows rational discourse. The elements of such an antisemiotic approach can already be seen in the first volume of *TCA*, particularly in the early discussion of the contrast between 'mythical' and 'modern' modes of thought.

Habermas turns to this contrast to demonstrate that his communication theory is not ahistorical, as some Marixist critics have claimed. What he actually succeeds in demonstrating, in my view, is that his theory is overly historicist. He portrays the movement of modern society away from mythical thought in a manner that supports his contention that communicative rationality allows conscious mastery of thought and action. The problem with mythical thought, he believes, is that it fuses, and therefore confuses, the personal world of the actor, the objective world of society, and the subjective world of thought and ideas. Myth, for example, is based on 'the concretistic relation between the meaning of expressions and the states-of-affairs represented [by them]' (*TCA*, vol. I, p. 49). This confusion is clear in magic, where the names of objects are invoked as if they were directly connected to the objects themselves. This confusing intermingling of worlds is also evident in the mythical belief that 'moral failure is conceptually interwoven with physical failure, as is evil with the harmful, and good with the healthy and the advantageous' (ibid., p. 48). The problem with such intermingling is that it prevents the differentiation of self, morality and society upon which all critical thinking is based. 'A linguistically constituted worldview', Habermas writes, 'can be identified with the world-order itself to such an extent that it cannot be perceived *as* an interpretation of the world that is subject to error and open to criticism.' In this sense, 'the concept of the world is dogmatically invested with a specific content' (ibid., pp. 50–1, original italics). Rational rather than mythical communication becomes possible, Habermas believes, only when such mythical intermingling has ended. 'Actors who raise validity claims', he writes (ibid.), 'have to avoid materially prejudicing the relation between language and reality.' Only if this prejudice is avoided can 'the content of a linguistic worldview ... be detached from the assumed world-order itself.' At a later point, Habermas makes this antithesis between rationality and mythical thought even more pointedly. The cultural tradition, he writes (ibid., p. 71), 'must be so far stripped of its dogmatism as to permit in principle that interpretation stored in tradition be placed in question and subjected to critical revision'.

But this antithesis, like several others Habermas has described, is overdrawn. It is true and not true at the same time. There has certainly been an enormous differentiation of culture, society and personality, and it is this differentiation that has allowed consciousness and rationality to emerge in the modern sense. The problem for social theories of modernity, however, is that the arbitrary, unconscious, fused, and, yes, irrational elements of culture have not at the same time disappeared. Language and world view continue to predefine our understanding of the object world before we even begin to subject it to our conscious rationality. Nor can we regard our linguistically-structured world views simply as humanly constructed interpretations, which are therefore transparently open to criticism. Our 'regard' is, ineluctably, conditioned by the preconscious world itself. It follows, then, that there is an inevitable investment of the world of things and the world of ideas with some kind of dogmatic, uncritical status. Modern, rational people continue to infuse values, institutions, and even mundane physical locations with the mystery and awe of the sacred. It is for this reason that physical, social and moral reality is organized into centres and peripheries. Even for modern people, moreover, there continues to be some intermingling of biological and social life. We 'concretize' moral rules by equating their violation with pollution, dividing the 'forces' of morality into the pure and the dangerous. We also concretize abstract relationships by evoking metaphors and other tropes. Finally, there seems to be abundant evidence that moderns still seek to understand the contingency of everyday life in terms of narrative traditions whose simplicity and resistance to change makes them hard to distinguish from myths. My own work on the symbolic dimensions of the American 'Watergate' episode documents this point ('Culture and Political Crisis: "Watergate" and Durkheimian Sociology' in *Durkheimian Sociology: Cultural Studies*).

None of this implies the elimination of rationality in Habermas's sense. What it does mean is that there is much, much more besides. It means that deeply held conceptions of self, nature, society, beauty and goodness continue to structure modern action in a relatively arbitrary way. Yes, these convictions can be thematized and subjected to rational argument, but such demands for justification must proceed within the confines of some given cultural parameters. Rationality, moreover, is not simply the psychological capacity for such arguments. It is itself a system of significations. For rationality to develop it must be invested with cultural power. This is usually done by connecting 'rationality' to the sacred centres of a modern society through mythical stories about the society's 'rational' origins. The Maoist conception of rationality connected its neo-Confucian understanding of value and will with a revolutionary Marxist theory of material inequality as producing change. The French left's conception of rationality is more solidaristic, linking communal notions from Catholicism and the guild tradition with more universalistic principles from the Revolution. American rationality cannot be separated from Commonwealth ideas about republican virtue, Puritan ideas about individual rights, and revolutionary distrust of power. These examples are only suggestive. The relation between rationality and tradition is a complex problem. The ideological complexes of 'Enlightenment' and 'reaction' have ensured, moreover, that the problem has scarcely begun to be understood.[5]

That the relation exists, however, points to a serious weakness not only in Habermas's account of contemporary society, but also in his theory of communicative action itself. We are not faced with a contrast between, on the one hand, constraint through institutional coercion (established via media like money and power) and, on the other, voluntary cooperation freed from constraint altogether. To the extent that cooperation is achieved, it is voluntary only in a very conditional sense (Alexander, 'Formal and Substantive Voluntarism in the Work of Talcott Parsons: A Theoretical and Ideological Reinterpretation', *American Sociological Review*, 43 (1978), pp. 177–98). It is always mediated by cultural constraints outside any single actor's conscious control and, for that matter, by institutionally coercive processes that can never be completely superseded. We are fortunate that rationality has recently become more available for resolving disputes, but it is neither theoretically justifiable nor politically necessary to envision this rationality in a culturally and institutionally free-floating way.

Conclusion: The Marxian Dilemma

In the second volume of *Theoretical Logic in Sociology* (1982), pp. 345–70, I suggest that the most original theorists of twentieth-century Marxism have been caught inside the 'Marxian dilemma'. Faced with Marx's instrumental approach to action and his deterministic understanding of order, these theorists have sought a more normative and subjective theory of action and a more voluntaristic, multi-dimensional theory of order. It is from this desire that the notions of action as 'praxis' and superstructures as 'relatively autonomous' have emerged. But if these theorists were to remain within the Marxist tradition, they could not step entirely outside the boundaries of Marx's thought. To avoid this, they have done two things: first, they have usually introduced some notion of determinism 'in the last instance'; second, they often have left their revisions of Marx so extraordinarily ambiguous that they can be construed only as residual categories. These options form the horns of the Marxist dilemma. In this century, Marxist thought has careened between the Scylla of indeterminacy and the Charybdis of the last instance. The dilemma can be resolved, and a systematic multi-dimensional theory obtained, only by stepping outside Marxism itself.

With the publication of *The Theory of Communicative Action*, Jürgen Habermas intends to do just that. He seems to step outside Marxism and create a new theoretical tradition. In his earlier work, he struggled with the Marxian dilemma, his loyalty eventually leading him down the path of the last instance and indeterminacy. His theory of communication, in contrast, allows him to offer a systematic alternative to the impoverished 'action' of traditional Marxism, and his developmental theory of normative rationality – which brings together Piaget, Parsons and speech theory – allows him to describe social order in a much more rich and complex way. These presuppositional revisions have also allowed him to avoid one of the central ideological embarrassments of twentieth-century Marxism, for he can root his critical perspective in immanent processes that are both empirical and 'rational' at the same time.

My complaint has been that Habermas does not go quite far enough. There remains in his work a strong residue of the *Weltanschauung* of the Frankfurt School. This leads Habermas to reintroduce themes of instrumental rationality and the determination of lifeworlds by material systems (in the last instance to be sure). His multi-dimensional theory is qualified, so much so that at various points his conceptual innovations become ambiguous, and sometimes downright residual, to his analysis of modern society. But if Habermas has not gone far enough for me, he has certainly gone much too far for others. It is far enough to have created a remarkable book, one from which every effort at creating a democratic and critical social theory must certainly learn.

5 Communicative Reason and Interest: On the Reconstruction of the Normative Order in Societies Structured by Egalitarianism or Domination

Günter Dux

Communicative Action and Normative Order

Communicative action, as Habermas understands it, fulfils a three-fold purpose with regard to the social construction and maintenance of the lifeworld. It serves the symbolic constitution and reproduction of common knowledge, convictions and valuations (culture) – the formation of legitimate orders by means of which the communicating parties establish and secure their solidarity (society) and the cultivation of subjects capable of speaking and acting (*The Theory of Communicative Action*, vol. II, pp. 136f.).[1] I am interested here in the communicative structure of society. Habermas claims in this connection that the innermost formative process of social order occurs via action geared to reaching understanding, action which exhibits precisely that quality he ascribes to communicative action in the first place, namely that of coordinating via a consensus the respective, individually pursued plans of action. The salient point of social integration established in this manner is that the interlinking of the interactions which generate the society's normative order does not ensue as a consequence of the negotiated balance of interests in line with the pattern of action oriented to consequences (ibid., p. 275) similarly to the manner in which private subjects coordinate their interests. Rather, how normative order is to be understood is determined by recourse to common convictions at a level of interpretation transcending the pursuit of interests (*TCA*, vol. I, p. 288)[2]. Apparently, communicative action has as its pattern a discourse that is relieved of a function as action. Precisely for this reason Habermas is able to conduct the analysis of communicative action in terms of the self-sufficiency of the illocutionary speech act. In what follows I shall be concerned with a critique of this manner of grasping the formative and reproductive process of society.

Let us first note that even Habermas declares it illusory to think that the integration of society takes place *solely* under premisses of action oriented to achieving understanding. This reservation refers first and foremost to the systemic aspect: functional and non-normative interconnections, which for the most part are also not even perceived by the actors, are always a determining factor (*TCA*, vol. II, pp. 150f.). The reservation refers, on the other hand, to the moral aspect: in terms of its innermost structure, communicative action requires a moral consciousness committed to the equal satisfaction of the interests of all parties concerned. Habermas concedes that discourses based on this aim resemble islands that are threatened with being flooded by the sea of a practice in which the pattern of overcoming action-conflicts via consensus is by no means predominant (*Moralbewußtsein und kommunikatives Handeln* (*MKH*), p. 116). Ultimately and in the final instance, there is also a built-in historical reservation: historically speaking, the general principles of communicative action are indeed to be found in conventional societies; but they are still tied to contexts which inhibit their effectiveness. Communicative action can fully unfold only in the rationalized lifeworld of post-conventional societies. Irrespective of how one wishes to integrate these reservations into the theory of society (simply having them is not saying very much), one thing is certain: the theory of communicative action would not be what it claims to be, namely, a theory which delves into the innermost process of the formation of society, if Habermas were not of the opinion that with communicative action he had uncovered the process which is constitutive for all social formation. It is only because social orders are constituted via communicative action that they are also always legitimate orders – orders, in other words, whose patterns also 'deserve' their validity, i.e. can also be justified over and above their mere recognition (*TCA*, vol. I, pp. 243f.). The legitimacy established in this way via communicative action is thus part of the basic stock of every kind of society to such an extent that Habermas allows social world and legitimate order to merge, even in conceptual terms (ibid., pp. 48f. and *passim*).[3] Communicative action also takes the lead in evolutionary terms; the double differentiation, namely within the lifeworld itself as well as between lifeworld and system, is ultimately attributable to communicative action's historical evolution (*TCA*, vol. II, pp. 153ff.). It is only logical that Habermas then also seeks to substantiate this process, which is fundamental to all sociation, in his reconstruction of the formative process of the history of the species.

The criticism is direct, but unsatisfying. It is direct, because by doubting that society does in fact emerge and maintain itself via a process of this kind of normativity, I am questioning the social-theoretical tenability of Habermas's concept of communicative action as such. In order to allow no room for misunderstandings, I am not doubting that social action is communicative action as such; rather, the problem, as I see it, is the notion that the concept of communicative action is formed according to the pattern of a discourse that is relieved of action. It is simply not self-evident that social orders are the outcome of an action which has transpired by means of a discourse, as is intrinsic to the structure of Habermas's concept of communicative action. If anything, one should expect the opposite to be the case, namely, that such a type of action predominates in the process of establishing social orders as exhibits intrinsic structures which integrate the pursuit of individual interests with the communicative search for consensus in a manner foreign to discourse. This type is unlike that of instrumental action in the domain of the object world, but also different from Habermas's discourse-theoretical concept of action. The criticism is unsatisfying because any linking of the theory back to the social orders suffers, if only on account of the aforementioned reservations, from not clarifying how the theory of communicative action is related to the empirical structures of historical societies. For my intention is to examine the tenability of the theory of communicative action when referring it back to these empirical structures – a move simply indispensable for all scientific inquiry. This will allow me to embed the criticism of communicative action in a reconstruction of the social orders of an early age, and more specifically with a view to that structural element which is of crucial importance: namely, normativity. In pursuing this criticism, I shall adopt a two-pronged approach: I shall first attempt to show that while Habermas moves towards a sociological concept of norms, murky residues of a philosophical preconception nevertheless render the real concept of the formation of the normativity of social orders unclear. The weak points in the historical-genetic reconstruction, and I would hope to have Habermas's agreement here, are, however, always weak points in the understanding of what is reconstructed – and in the current context, that is the understanding of the validity claims made by norms and thus the formation of the specifically human(e) society in the first place. In a second step, I would therefore like to propose an alternative strategy for the reconstruction of society's beginnings which will allow the critique of the philosophical understanding of normative consensus to emerge in their genesis.

The Genesis of the Normative

Reconstruction of the Beginnings

The notion that the social integration of a society takes place via a consensus that is established on a level of interpretation removed from action causes Habermas to inquire into the formation of this primordial normative consensus in the beginnings of that society. In pursuing this question, Habermas adopts Durkheim's assumption that the binding (bonding) force of every society, including that of primeval societies, manifests itself in a collective consciousness which represents the incarnation of the sacred. Durkheim's argumentation appears to be circuitous because it is grounded in his consistently substantialistic way of thinking.[4] Habermas strips the formation of collective consciousness of this emanatistic-substantialistic content by instilling Durkheim's notion that ritual practice is the original part of religion with an historical dynamic. In ritual, a basic normative consensus is established by means of common, mutual identification with the sacred, an agreement which first and foremost serves to create the foundations for the group's identity. Habermas seeks to reconstruct this process by expanding Mead's phylogenetic conception of the formation of symbolically mediated interaction into a three-stage model of development.[5] Instinctual, gesture-mediated interaction at the sub-human stage is followed by a stage of signal language that is already symbolically mediated. Here, action is further regulated and coordinated by means of instincts and/or instinctual residues, but the triggers no longer function in the same manner as with gesture-controlled action. They are replaced by signals that already have the character of symbols, even if propositional, illocutionary and expressive components have not yet differentiated out. It is only then that the stage of speech that is thoroughly structured in terms of grammar follows – and this, together with normed behavioural expectations, merges into the structure of speech-mediated norm-controlled interaction. Habermas situates the signal stage of language formation – in other words, the actual beginning of speech – in the symbolisms of the early rites.

One can see the structural similarities between ritual action and symbolically mediated interaction steered via signals. Paleosymbols have a meaning that is not yet modally differentiated, and, like signals, they possess the power to steer behavior. On the other hand, ritual actions have lost their adaptive function; they serve to establish and maintain a collective identity, on the strength of which the steering of interaction is transferred from a genetic program anchored in the individual organism over to an intersubjectively shared cultural program. (*TCA*, vol. II, p. 55)

This phase is historically plotted in the 'earliest tribal religions,' although it remains an open question how far they have already progressed (*TCA*, vol. II, p. 54). With the formation of this stage something has happened which Habermas considers crucial, namely the justification of that kind of primordial normative consensus from which further development can then ensue. And it does. With the advance of cognitive development, propositional components are differentiated out in the increasingly objectivating attitude the actors take towards the world of perceptible and manipulatable objects. Habermas suspects that at the same time the domains of the sacred and profane separate. Religious symbols now serve merely to secure social integration via the medium of symbolic communication (ibid., p. 54).

Immanent criticism must concentrate on the two main aspects of this reasoning: the formation of rites via the medium of signal language and the justification of normativity from the thus induced and subsequently developed primordial consensus. The latter is of foremost concern to us here.

Rites and the Basis of Religion

Habermas ascribes two functions to the stage of signal language: on the one hand, signals, like children's one-word sentences, serve to make practice more efficient. As distinct from gestures, signals have already become so reflexive that the sender and receiver are conscious of their common meaning. This raises the question whence this reflexivity comes. It touches on the nerve of the problem because subjectivity and collectivity must have been formed at the same time.

Habermas links both processes to the formation of rites. He ascribes socially constitutive meaning to that formation of rites as was made possible by the formation of signals. The normative consensus of a collective identity has been secured by means of rites. This consensus, however, as Habermas himself establishes, cannot have been *achieved* specially only by means of paleosymbolic ritualization; for, that would require the formation of subjects with at least a limited capacity to act prior to that of society. The identity of the members of society, however, can only have been equiprimordial with the identity of the group (*TCA*, vol. II, p. 53). What, then, sets personalization and sociation in motion? There is actually only one answer: 'The identification in common with the sacred' (ibid., p. 53). The identity of the group members as well as the group's identity must have been established simultaneously by means of this identification. However, in order not to have to presuppose with 'identification in common [!] with the sacred', something which then itself requires explanation, Habermas here again seeks to render the process historically dynamic, and transposes it into the formative process itself. Habermas writes of the ritual ceremonial:

> It is a question of variations on one and the same theme, namely, the presence of the sacred, and this in turn is only the form in which the collectivity experiences 'its unity and its personality'. Because the basic normative agreement expressed in communicative action *establishes* and *sustains* the identity of the group, the fact of successful consensus is at the same time its essential content. (*TCA*, vol. II, p. 53).

It is only natural to ask what makes this factor that is actually constitutive for the formation of consensus – the experience of the sacred's presence – into common experience.[6] It would be to go somewhat further should we then impute a substantialistic concept of the sacred to Habermas. However, either 'the presence of the sacred' must bear the weight of providing the explanation, or the process of group formation remains as unexplained as before. Durkheim's reference to the sacred and to society is tautological and remains so. This is attested by his pronouncement that one has to choose between God and society.[7] No explanations are, therefore, given in Durkheim's work either for the concrete historical forms in which religion has presented itself throughout history – in myth, rite, sacrifice, prayer, in short in all of the manifold forms of expression taken by sacrality – which could come up to the standards of an historical-genetic reconstruction. Yet, precisely this is Habermas's intention. Religion, even in the sense of a purportedly substantialistic sacrality, must also be included here.

The deficient grounding of collectivity comes to light at least as clearly, if not more sharply, in the deficient grounding of early subjectivity. For subjectivity and individual identity can be established only at a level of action in which the resistance offered by the outside world – both the natural and the social world – has to be matched. It is only by virtue of this resistance that organic motoricity can become reflexive, a process constitutive for all subjectivity. If the formation of subjectivity and collectivity respectively have for this reason to be kept together, and the two cannot in fact be separated from one another, then the process of the formation of society also has to be located as a whole at the level of action and not transferred to a level of interpretation that is distinct from it.[8] This being the case, it is doubtful whether there is any point in assuming that there is a primordial normative consensus in the first place conducting research into it. And this doubt becomes stronger if one inquires whether norms indeed take shape via consensuses as Habermas believes.

The Consensus Model. The Ideality and Facticity of Imperative Goals

According to Habermas, as we have seen, the primordial consensus takes shape through the agency of a religious paleosymbolism. The binding moment inherent in primordial consensus would thus already be grounded in a prehuman level of cultural interpretations that is removed from that of interaction and the factors determining it. Habermas calls the consensus established in this manner 'normative' – obviously owing to its binding (bonding) effect. Yet what is there about this binding (bonding) effect that merits being called 'normative'? And what does that normativity consist of? In seeking an answer to these questions, we must nevertheless bear in mind that we are moving in an evolutionary field in which 'normativity' or 'the imperative' in the strict sense cannot be expected to occur. The question is therefore simply whether this first form of a consensus to which the binding (bonding) effect is ascribed can be considered to have an evolutionary potential for the further development of normativity as a specifically human form of organization.

What is the basis of the binding (bonding) effect? We will recall that Habermas characterizes the stage of signal language by assuming that behavioural dispositions and behavioural patterns continue to be bound to instincts; only the triggering function is, as it were, absorbed by the ritual symbols. The binding (bonding) effect attributable to the signal in dealings among members of the species is, however, ultimately also the result of the instinctual securing of behavioural standards. Habermas writes:

> It is true that the functional circuits of animal behavior break down at the stage of symbolically mediated interaction; on the other hand, signals remain tied to

dispositions and schemes of behavior. It is because they are embedded in this way that signals have a binding power that is a functional equivalent for the triggering effects of gestures. (*TCA*, vol. II, pp. 30f.)

This means, however, that one cannot actually speak in terms of a 'normative consensus'. For as long as societal interaction is controlled by instincts, it is precisely not normative. This consensus cannot possibly form 'the archaic core of norm consciousness' (*TCA*, vol. II, p. 46); there is not yet anything contained in it which calls for actions. It becomes clear for the first time that the process of norm formation does not take place at the action-relieved level of mere consensus about meanings.

The difficulties of grasping the normative aspect of what norms are and determining what actually distinguishes the binding (bonding) effect of norms also comes to light at the next stage, namely that of a grammatically structured speech and of a normatively controlled interaction in the full sense of the term. Habermas follows Mead's approach. As we will remember, Habermas holds the shift from the imperative – as is to be found in singular interactions not incorporated into groups – to the 'generalized other' as a nexus of order in which every single expectation is systematically connected to every other, and precisely for that reason also borne by all others to be historically dynamic, and he makes it an independent stage of development in the formative process of normativity. Of course, not much is gained by this initially. For this development proves to invoke nothing other than replacing the imperative of one with the imperative of many. However, if we are to believe Habermas, the many are not just so many individuals, but rather individuals fused into a group. The group can thus take the place of the individuals. That does nothing to change the fact that expectations remain arbitrary – if indeed they were arbitrary before. So where does the moment of bindingness come from? Habermas sees it as stemming from internalization at this stage:

We have seen how the authority that is first held by the individual reference person and then passed over to the combined wills of *A* and *B* is built up to the generalized choice of everyone else by way of the social generalization of behavior patterns. This concept makes possible the idea of sanctions behind which there stands the collective will of a social group. This will [*Wille*] remains, to be sure, a *Willkür*, however generalized it might be. The authority of the group consists simply in the fact that it can threaten to carry out sanctions in case interests are violated. This *imperativistic authority* is transformed into *normative authority* through internalization. It is only then that there arises a 'generalized other' that grounds the validity of norms. (*TCA*, vol. II, p. 38)

This interpretation provides food for thought: the factual violence of the organized others acquires that force of imperative validity intrinsic to norms to the extent that it is accepted by and absorbed into the self. This cannot be; nor, one might say, can this even be what Habermas means. For how is external compulsion to acquire a new quality by being internalized, how is it to maintain the consecration of the normative? We must assume that if anything is gained, then it is that external compulsion is joined by a new internal form, combined with a deformation of the self. The answer is plain and simple: internalization creates assent. This is what Habermas is getting at: 'The authority of the "generalized other" differs from authority based only on disposition over means of sanction, in that it rests on assent. When *A* regards the group sanctions *as his own*, as sanctions he directs at himself, he *has* to *presuppose* his assent to the norm whose violation he punishes in this way' (*TCA*, vol. II, p. 38).

Let us return once more to the model: the material substance of the nexus of interaction in which the individuals find themselves is not important; nor can it be by its very nature. What is decisive is that this structure of being the 'organized other', as Mead also occasionally called it,[9] is present in every individual. This happens in the course of internalization; it transforms the imperative into normative authority. And how does the transubstantiation from the factual into the normative occur? By the person who has internalized the generalized other having to grant validity to every sanction as his/her own sanction. However, s/he can do this only by presupposing his/her having assented to the norm. Internalization involves precisely this assent.

One would not be mistaken in assuming that Habermas wants to account for the normative organization of traditional societies by taking this model as a prototype. This organization is characterized by two outstanding features: factually, but (precisely) not only factually, it is shot through with a good measure of violence as soon as state and rulership have emerged. Normatively speaking, but (precisely) not only normatively, such organization is blinkered; for ethical competence does not suffice to cast factual conditions into question in such a way as to be able to exempt the validity of existence as it is (*Ist-Bestand*). If existence as it is is internalized, then this internalization necessarily presents itself as the logical counterpart in development to this blinkeredness. For there can be no doubt that only such blinkeredness as cannot be overcome historically can prompt the actors to allow themselves to be reproached for having presupposed their assent. If they were able to see through the process of internalization, then they could also withhold their assent. Habermas secures his position by making internalization the governing mechanism of goal validity (*Sollgeltung*) in this era, namely the recognition of that principle which, as he sees it, is fundamental for the social world: to move of necessity in a world of legitimately regulated interpersonal relations (*TCA*, vol. I, p. 420).[10] Thus, there is no distress for most of human history, given that validity and legitimacy are established via internalization. For, if the organized network of interactive relationships, even to the extent that this exhibits the character of arbitrariness, changes into a network of legitimated normative relationships by means of internalization, then only irregular violence remains unaccounted for – and even this can to a great degree be made subject to prediction and thus to organization and internalization. Naturally, this does not imply accepting power. From the historical perspective, this is simply to take into consideration a piece of natural history – the ideal imperative has always been latent in history (*TCA*, vol.

II, p. 39), but naturally conditions have not allowed it. However, inevitable though it may be that we try and make sense of the fact that law is legitimate despite the blatant violence that continues to determine it up to the present, internalization cannot be used as a composite of the two without embroiling the argument in contradictions.

Internalization means, if anything, the internalization of already existing orders. If the normativity of the social order in the full sense of the term has been created only by means of internalization, then the real concrete historical order must have been organized by means other than normative procedures and determinants. In fact, it is difficult to posit a constitutive principle underlying the real order of early times which is based on the kind of communicative action defined by Habermas; in which case, however, the question arises: by virtue of which organizing principles did the social orders of early times then in fact emerge? The question as to the real organizing principles involved, however, again yields the question of a normativity which is not geared to the guiding image of a discursive consensus and does not first come about via internalization. For anthropological reasons it would, in fact, seem impossible for specifically humane social orders to have taken shape in a manner other than by normative orders. Internalization, being a norm-constituting principle, points, in other words, to a contradiction in the concept of the norm; as it is, it does not reach the level of actual societal formation.

There is yet a further objection to be made with regard to the internalization of the social order as a means of reaching a consensus by which the individual is prompted to give his blessing to his normatively secured role: in precisely this manner a contradiction is dropped from the concept which must be retained as it is experienced in reality. The conditions of traditional societies founded in domination and asserted by brute force have violated the interests of those subjected to power in so blatant a manner that we have to assume that these violations were also felt. There is, in fact, evidence of this throughout history. Internalization would also integrate these violations along with the internalized order into the person in such a way that they would disappear; for internalization is the mechanism that transforms what is initially foreign into the life-serving qualities of one's own ego. This is obviously not the case. If the conditions of the past were normatively binding, then this held true not only in spite of the objective violence which went into them, but also in spite of the subjectively felt violence. The contradiction in question has to be acknowledged at least with regard to suffering. This is not contradicted by the fact that the social orders of the past were legitimated all the same. For legitimation ensues not by means of internalization, but rather through a cognitively bound rationalization, it renders one speechless in the pursuit of one's own interests, but it does not go so far as to consent internally to their violation.[11]

The aforementioned problems and contradictions presented themselves on the basis of an epistemologically cleansed understanding according to which the reconstruction of the formative process is the method for understanding human forms of life, especially social orders. In pursuing this reconstruction, however, Habermas makes claims that I have called philosophical and which hinder him from approaching the reconstruction process in a manner that is based on real empirical conditions and that would capture the real processes of social formation in early times. I therefore seek, firstly, to take a new point of departure in the reconstruction and, secondly, to portray the formative process in relation to the organizing principles of the food-gathering and hunting societies known to us. What I intend with this venture into empirical data – indispensable for any reconstruction – is to make clear by means of historical evidence that social integration resulted from the pursuit of interests calibrated according to dependence on others at the level of interaction, and not via a level of 'pure interpretations', set off from it, as it were.

Reconstruction from Ontogeny

The Link to the Reduction of Instincts

For anthropologically compelling reasons, the culturation of human beings must have resulted from the early ontogeny of the members of the species. For the dismantling of instinctive behavioural patterns can be offset in early ontogeny only by cultural life-forms.[12] For one thing, there are ethological reasons which suggest that in the process of early culturation behavioural aspects cannot be separated from external aspects, as is the case in Habermas's work. The two are instinctively tied to each other: those triggering characteristics of the external world are incorporated into the genetic code. It is difficult to conceive how the biological mechanism of instinct could have been split in such a manner as to preserve the instinctive behavioural scheme, while replacing the triggers coupled to the external world with symbols.[13] The only tangible theory of evolution to date which has thematized the systematic interlinking of the reduction of instincts and development of cultural life-forms, and attempts to explain this in terms of a retardation and the neoteny of fetal development,[14] also indicates that it is unlikely that Stage I of the culturation process was formed by the continuance of the subhuman, instinctive regulation of behaviour and the new acquisition of symbolically organized triggers. Finally, it is not supported by the evidence presented by our closest relatives. It is precisely the extraordinary plasticity of motoric activity which makes them capable of a virtually unlimited capacity for action[15] – if they were only to manage to build up the necessary cultural structures.

If in the course of reconstruction one examines the real anthropological conditions of the situation at the beginning of the process of cultural development, one finds that the structural measures have to be sought from the start at the level of action, i.e. in real interaction; and thus the preponderance which Habermas ascribes at this stage to the symbolically organized level of interpretation already ceases to apply. This observation is reinforced if one examines the conditions for development arising from ontogeny. For one then sees that social integration must not be sought at the level of interpretation of a ritually established primordial consensus, but rather in the living practice of family relationships.

The Formation of Families, Culturation and Social Integration

If, for anthropologically compelling reasons, the development of the specifically human(e) organization of society must have resulted from early ontogeny, then for equally compelling reasons the mother–child dyad is the relationship in which this formative process must have primarily taken place. This is true of cognitive development; but it is also true above all of affective development.

The formation of the primary family dyad has an evolutionary twist that has a direct and illuminating bearing on the formative process of human(e) societies, for it also lays the foundations for the formation of the conjugal dyad. In light of the ego-development that emerges in the mother–child dyad, the process of separation from the mother can no longer be seen simply as the result of a biological process of maturation; rather it is matched at a reflexive level. The Ego becomes strong in the assertion of self precisely in relation to the Alter, to which it is affectively bound. This makes a reorganization of the affective relationship necessary. The most important thing is to reorganize during the phase of pre-adolescence and adolescence the need for intimacy which had arisen in connection with the mother. Intimacy is by no means a need which has evolved only in modern times, or in Romanticism in particular. It is elemental.[16] And precisely owing to its fundamental nature, it is excellently suited to form a symbiosis with the now genitally centred sexuality, a symbiosis which leads to the emergence of the conjugal dyad. The development of human society, in a word, merged with the development of the family, regardless of how the latter may have been organized in individual cases.[17]

Habermas believed that he had, by preliminarily securing a symbolically-mediated community of solidarity, first to provide the basis for ontogenetic development. This was why he sought to supplement Mead with Durkheim. However, if Mead offers both phylogenetic and ontogenetic explanations and not infrequently alternates them in his line of argumentation, he does so with the intuitive knowledge that ontogenetic insights are best suited to making phylogenetic development understandable.[18] It would, therefore, seem erroneous to me to want to supplement Mead with Durkheim, in that the anthropological basis of the reconstruction is abruptly abandoned. Rather, it is necessary to describe the early phase of the history of the species in terms of ontogeny, in other words, as an advanced stage of the evolutionary process which has begun ontogenetically. If one retains the ontogenetic perspective of development, then the structuring of a symbolically organized world also acquires a different status, to the extent that one leaves it to the level of dealing with reality. Together with familial determinants, this suffices to bring about social integration.

The Dual Aspect in the Structuring of a Symbolically Organized World

The formative process of the species was under pressure from the start to acquire the ability to act. This was possible in only one way: an ego-structure had in the course of these efforts to take shape on the part of the organism, and on the part of the objects, the external world had to be organized so that it would serve one's own life-interests. It has been a source of intense fascination for the field of sociology up to the present day to see how precisely this collision of organism and object-world sets the process of ontogenetic development in motion and develops it further. The formative process of the species is a process of working itself out *vis-à-vis* the external world. However, the latter exhibits a peculiar dual aspect as a consequence of the original societal situation. Given that this process results from ontogeny, interest is geared primarily towards acquiring the ability to act in the form of the ability to interact. However, this means that the initial experiences and structuring achievements on the object side are made with the more competent others. If there is such a thing as the cunningness of reason [The German 'List der Vernunft' is Hegel's expression (translators)], it would be a factor in the social genesis of the structuring process. For the circumstance that the primary object experiences are made with Alter, and that for the 'socially nasciturns' the mother is nature, results in the early structures in the domain of objects being marked off by an unmistakable social stigma which we encounter again everywhere.[19] There is no question that there are also natural objects in the child's field of action from the very beginning, and they increasingly acquire significance. However, the total organization of the object world is at the same time also the medium of organizing the interactive relationship, and it would hardly be possible outside this interactive relationship. This is particularly true of the linguistic structuring of the world. Not only does cognitively processed interaction supply the basic structure for the grammatical structuring of language as well; the entire conceptual organization of the outside world would not be possible if the young member of the species were not to be compelled by others to adhere to every linguistically processed element. If it is impossible to say of an individual that s/he follows a rule, then it is certainly impossible for an individual to establish his/her own rules. Order, and ultimately also the order of nature, can be established solely through communication not only because language is the technical medium of organization, as it were, but above all because the structuring measures can be stabilized only by means of others' expectations.

The dual aspect of the structuring of the lifeworld, therefore, consists on the one hand of the organization of the natural object-world being integrated into the social world; conversely, its organization is a *conditio sine qua non* of social organization, which is to say from the simple, quasi-communicative relationship at the beginning of every biography all the way to active cooperation as adults. In terms of the logic of development, this means that the two have to develop in common, and this in turn signifies, however, that owing to its practical dimension the symbolically organized world – and precisely also the natural outside world – become the most important medium of social integration.

The process is complex, and has serious consequences. Habermas splits the lifeworld in two. The world of religious symbolism is juxtaposed to a world of perceptible and manipulatable objects that is differentiated propositionally. The former has to achieve what the latter cannot achieve owing to its purely technical understanding from the start, namely, to link the behavioural dispositions and driving power to the medium of symbolic communication (*TCA*, vol. II, p. 54). The process of social formation takes on a different shape if one considers that the members of a society have always been tied to each other affectively and are dependent on one another in the practical way they lead their lives; then the world of objects loses its purely technical-manipulative status; the common nature of propositionally differentiated knowledge is the condition for successful interaction; conversely, social integration is not induced by virtue of a purely sacral symbolism, but instead by the immediate practice of leading one's life. The dual aspect in which both domains of the lifeworld present themselves also recurs in rites.

Structure and Instrumentality of Rites

Rites are the expression of the pristine cognitive structure in the structuring of reality. Given the circumstance that patterns of objects and events take shape in a social relationship, the mother being the primary and dominant object in the child's early field of action, both patterns acquire that subjectival basic structure which is to be encountered throughout early ontogeny as well as in primitive societies' view of reality. In the early stages of history people therefore forever see themselves as being dependent on subjective powers, without the latter necessarily being anthropomorphic. Every rite seeks to have an influence on such a power. A large number of rites are obviously instrumental; fertility rites, for example, seek to have a direct influence on regeneration. Other rites are aimed at social conditions, and reorganize these by enervating the power of the origins whence they come. It is this basic cognitive structure of a common world which imbues the rite with its peculiar reflexive quality: the rite is always bound to an interpretative structure and the semantic transformation – both of which are common to all. Every rite contains a myth, in many cases only cryptomorphically. And, invariably, all are affected because they all know they are dependent on it.

Rites therefore have a non-derivative status because they necessarily emerge with the cognitive structure of a symbolically organized world. But they are not the reason which makes this process of symbolic organization possible in its very beginnings and sets it into motion. Rites always build on developed cognitive structures and their being given a reality in interpretation, something which must have already occurred.[20] Without this already advanced development in cognitive as well as affective terms, no rite would have ever come about. Rites have, therefore, from the very beginning, only an affirmative function for a society already constituted by other determinants. Just as rites can therefore hardly be seen as the reason why the process of social formation began in the first place, so too they do not create the primary condition for its normative structure.

The Genesis of Norms

Norms and Interests

The ability to act can be acquired only as the ability to interact on the part of a young member of the species. Interactions, however, are composed structurally via expectations, and more specifically via what are initially protonormative expectations, as these are first expressed as demands.[21] There are anthropologically compelling reasons for this: a creature that does not have a set body of instincts is dependent upon fulfilling his interests reflexively and providing for their gratification. It has to call on the others to take them into account. Empirically, the basis of normatives lies in such demands: norms are requested. In the absence of this request, there are no norms; wherever it is eliminated, there also the norm is eliminated. The requesting expectation, being the basic structure of interaction, constitutes the difference between human(e) and sub-human forms of organization.

Mental Acceptance

In terms of internal structure, imperative demands do not differ from those secured by norms. There is no difference between an acquaintance's expectation that s/he will be aided in an emergency and that of a close relative, as far as the structure of the expectation itself is concerned. In fact, expectations exist as a general rule and demand to be fulfilled, without reference to how they are normatively secured, and even without an awareness thereof.

Nevertheless, it makes a difference in terms of social organization whether expectations have solidifed into norms or not. Expectations become the norm in the full sense of the term only by means of two further factors: (a) their generalization, and (b) in connection with the generalization, the common acceptance that this is what should be done. It is therefore understandable that in the philosophical understanding of the norm the specifically normative aspect of the norm is posited entirely in acceptance.

What is acceptance grounded in? In sociological terms, the question calls for an answer which will surely provoke the charge that it is a false, utilitarian conclusion. Yet, we do not want to be overhasty in adopting the categorial patterns imposed by a past approach to the problem.

The question guiding our investigation concerns how we understand the social orders throughout history with a view to the moral obligations taken on by the actors. We shall assume that actions are moral; the question is in what way. In pursuing this question, however, the very first reason to be mentioned for the normative acceptance of another's expectations is the reflexively generated consciousness of being dependent and reliant on her/him. Dependence and reliance are qualities of reality from the very start, first in the early phase of ontogeny, then in the adult world. They are elemental. Every person is constitutionally made to live together with others, to have affective bonds and to deal communicatively with them. Therefore, in pursuing his/her own needs, s/he cannot see her/himself as an individual at all, nor does s/he. The more close-knit the living community is, the more resolutely Ego has Alter in view. Therefore, Ego necessarily has to account for Alter's interests when already pursuing its own. The recognition of the other in the pursuit of his/her interests is the reflexively generated condition of one's own existence. Every person perceives her/himself as one of the others from the start, namely in terms of their social integration. Mead, it seems to me, had this pragmatic networking in mind. Its immanent reflexivity integrates the individual into the interactive structure of order.[22]

It does not make much sense to me to discredit this strategy for being utilitarian. It appears to be so only in an ethics that is individual in approach and which then has to call for the 'pure normative' as a dichotomous counterpart to the 'purely purposive rationality' of the pursuit of interests. However, what is correct is that precisely with regard to ontogenetic perspective one should proceed from the ego's needs. Without the self-preservation manifest in the need, there would never be any learning process and no structuring of a human(e) lifeworld.

The anthropological point of departure cannot create an organizational reality for itself that is more dense in structure than the norms: the subject in the process of self-formation is forced to claim validity for its needs; this piece of self-preservation is the heritage of natural history under the altered conditions of the anthropological organizational plan. This constitutes the volitional element in the imperative; however, with its own needs it must also recognize those of others because this is the condition of its own existence. It has to want the normative. And it does. But in practice, the link between this acceptance and one's own set of interests is upheld. This is sufficient to provide justifications for any morals. Moreover, asserting one's own interests against those of the other is the condition for any prospering relationship.[23]

Philosophical Preconceptions

Interests and the pursuit of interests are also the object of communicative action. Communicative action is itself thought of as a process in order to determine their appropriacy. Yet, how is this accomplished? That is the question. It does not suffice for a philosophical understanding to confine this question to the level of the pursuit of interests; nor does it suffice for it that interests in the interacting communities of everyday life are by no means allowed to be rooted ego-logically, that every person knows he is existentially dependent on others and as a matter of reason also takes this into account. Philosophical understanding wants to see the question resolved at a different level, the level of interpretations and common convictions. It has reason to do so above all because it draws on an understanding of the normative in which residues of a metaphysical understanding that are no longer recognizable as such stubbornly persist. This residual stock includes the charge that by incorporating the normative into one's own pursuit of interests one ultimately deprives the imperative of its normative thrust; it is therefore absolutely indispensable to the philosophical meaning of the normative that it set itself off from a person's particular interests. Selflessness and self-discipline are connotations which – and this is also true of Habermas's work – induce the structural linking of morals with the stance *vis-à-vis* the sacred: they permit, as Habermas explicitly states, the normative of self-maintenance to be forgotten (*TCA*, vol. II, pp. 49ff.). Really? Or is a philosophical pre-understanding merely making itself felt here, one which in the end conceives of reason in terms of conceptual contents or something like (a non-Kantian) 'pure reason' – which, in other words, does not leave it chained to the gravitational force of empirical subjects, and precisely because of this also claims that the imperative is cleansed of any and all empirical admixtures (ibid., p. 94). There is no question about it: in the justifications he provides for morality Habermas brings the understanding of morals closest to the structure of argumentation of real empirical subjects. Yet, the meaning of 'reason' in this line of argumentation continues to be philosophically charged.[24]

Habermas believes he has reasons for retaining this conception. In the current context we are only indirectly concerned with the question of the justification of morality. Rather, the question that is of interest to us here concerns the kind of morality/normativity to be seen in the social orders we find throughout history. After all, the category of communicative action is also meant to be understood as a sociological category. The reconstructive line of argumentation, however, leaves us no choice but to fix the process of the formation of norms and thus also acceptance of the other or others as an element of validity at the level of interaction, in other words, without assuming at least structural exemption for the pursuit of one's own interests. The other is therefore also not some socially abstract other, in other words, a person who in the normative dimension is initially viewed outside her/his real social dimenstions. This may in the present allow us to pinpoint neatly what moral argumentation consists of (J. Rawls, *A Theory of Justice* (Oxford, 1973) pp. 34ff.). The actual process took a different course. And it is my aim to focus on the immanent normativity of the structures of what actually transpired. Let us therefore examine how the normative process of organization presents itself in the analysis of the orders we come across.

The Equality of Pristine Societies and its Subjugation by Domination

Equality and Normativity

Primeval societies are egalitarian societies.[25] This observation applies despite the instances in which it breaks down and for which we shall have to account. What is the equality of early societies based on?[26] Certainly not on the fact that, as a material principle, equality lay ahead of the formative process in reflexive terms. That would be an absurd idea from the standpoint of the logic of evolution. In terms of developmental logic, equality can be explained only as a process. Its foundation lies in the same interactive powers which every person develops under the conditions of the early hunter-gatherer societies. By the same interactive powers I mean that each person, in pursuing his own interests, is juxtaposed to all relevant others as someone who is dependent on the others just as they are dependent on him. The fact that, in principle, everyone can develop the same interactive powers is, for one thing, a consequence of family organization; but above all of economic organization – unhindered access to the resources necessary to secure subsistence gives each person the same chance to be dependent on others only to the extent that others are also dependent on her/him.

If our analysis is correct, then the basis every norm has in its linkage to the interests of those who establish it is borne out empirically. At the same time, the fate of the second element, namely acceptance, is resolved. For, the fact that equality is recognized by all as a basic normative principle results from every person having initially made an effort ontogenetically to attain a level of ability and interactive powers which ensures him an equal right to participate in social dealings. This happens as a matter of nature and therefore requires no justification. All others do this as well. Primeval societies are characterized by the fact that this developmental goal which each person pursues by nature is also generally achieved. With respect to adults, therefore, each person finds himself as well as the relevant others in the situation of having the same interactive powers. The reflexively substantiated condition for interaction incorporates the structure of interaction as it is. There is not even any intellectual competence that can grant it virtual exemption in order to reflect on the justifications given for it.

It is unique kinds of circumstances which generally allow each person to achieve what s/he is striving for; blinkered, but egalitarian. There is no question that interpretative processes have entered into this process of the formation of equality which these conditions have, in turn, assimilated. Yet, there is also no question that the social principle of equality – *nota bene* as a lifeworld principle – did not evolve in a process in which certain interests were exempted, or that equality was established as a common conviction on the basis of worldviews, in order then to be institutionalized as a social principle of organization. However, this is precisely the structural shape given to such developments in the reconstruction provided by the theory of communicative action.

The process of the formation of equality just described in its volitional and consensual elements finds its permanent confirmation in instances where it breaks down. The first of these would be the individual differentiations of power and prestige which also form in all of the early hunter-gatherer societies. The interactive power of each and every person is primarily – but not only – determined by socio-structural conditions. This is reflected at the level of individual allocations of position and prestige. Those breakdowns in equality which harden into institutions are more serious. This invariably includes the normatively unsecured status of children and the usually lower status of women. Judging from all that has been explained thus far, the reason for this is not difficult to find; children have no, or at least no adequate, interactive powers; they cannot enforce the validity of their real needs because they cannot generate them reflexively. However, in instances where the volitional factor is missing, or if present, lacks interactive power, no norms evolve. The lower status of women is even more revealing for the process of norm formation. Social strategies have largely interfered with any effort to bring women's interactive strength up to the same level as men's. For fathers, mother's brothers or anyone else who had the power to dispose over the children could take advantage of the children's dependency. The purpose of this could vary; two kinds were preferred: on the one hand, control over girls could serve to provide those men authorized to dispose over the children with younger women via exchanges. On the other, a woman allowed herself to be used in order to gain her own labour, that of her future husband or both. There are countless examples of each of the use-options. The effect was the same everywhere: women were put into a position in which they could not set their own claims against those of others; if anything, others had demands on them, the compensation for which was fixed in advance. I do not see that these inconsistencies, which after all are part of the basic normative structure of these societies, can be explained in any way other than by means of those mechanisms of norm and society formation which I have outlined above. The consciousness reflexively generated in the normative, namely the consciousness that one must take the interests of others into account, is filled with empirical content. Such a consciousness already invariably perceives the other in the organically evolved social position in which s/he finds her/himself. The instances of a breakdown in equality take shape via the same mechanism as equality itself. Primitive societies had their own form of positivism.

The most conspicuous contradiction inherent in reconstructively applying the theory of communicative action emerges if we consider the evolution of the developmental stage of state and domination. Habermas believes that the state and domination originate in a moral learning process. Evolutionary progress is expelled from the lifeworld. Morality and law must first be sufficiently developed, and in particular the subjective responsibility for action must have matured, before the ruler can be institutional-

ized as a judge-ruler and thus before the state can emerge. The empirical
assumptions that go into the theory here simply do not hold water. I shall
outline the process only to the extent that the fundamental contradiction to
the theses of the theory of communicative action become apparent.[27]

Subjugation of Equality by Domination

Equality was subjugated by domination. The genesis of domination persists
in tyranny and exploitation, the two forms in which we encounter it in
every case where a mature form of it becomes historically tangible. It can
be probed in two ways: (a) historically, with a view to the largely contingent events which brought it about, and (b) structurally, with a view to the
conditions for the principle behind its morphology which have been realized in historical development – conditions both visible now.

The historical events in the evolution of state and domination

According to all the indications contained in the archaeological and historical material on the early advanced civilizations, domination was the product of a development in which economic and political processes were
closely interwined. Economically, during the millennia following the transition to agricultural production, social stratification ensued which followed the tendency of the agrarian subsistence economy to maximize
minor organic imbalances and to form dependencies. This gave rise to
client groups. Many regard this formation of client groups as the very
beginnings of the foundation of domination. Yet, the economic formation
of client groups still does not indicate how the formation of client groups
led to the evolution of a ruling elite with coercive power over all members
of society; in that case one would have to conceive of the state's formation
itself as a kind of coup d'état. This was opposed, however, by an egalitarian
constitution and the consciousness asserting it.

The actual path into the border territory of organization structured by
domination leads via the fusion of indigenous population groups with
immigrating groups. In the formative phase of all early advanced civilizations one finds influxes of population groups previously not indigenous to
the area. These influxes take place over long periods of time, more or less
in large numbers and more or less peacefully. Gradual infiltration gives the
indigenous upper stratum the chance to integrate the immigrants by making them dependent, and thus as a foreign client group to form the nucleus
of a forced labour group. Conversely, in cases of large-scale migration, the
new arrivals have the chance to make themselves into the dominating
stratum by using the less organized, if not totally unorganized, indigeneous
population. In both cases, a form of organization develops in which the
upper class is in possession of land, the most important means of production, and controls a considerable degree of potential in terms of organized
power.[28] Whether and to what extent the Rubicon of the formation of
domination is already crossed in this manner depends on the concrete
historical circumstances and cannot be ascertained with any certainty in

every case. This is, however, not so important for a sociological interest in knowledge, although it might be desirable to have more accurate information. For, in any case, the path into the border territory of the organization of domination very quickly leads us to its definitive formation: the existing organizational potential in terms of power is always directed outwards in the form of military conquests. Wherever we find domination and state in their initial formation, we find them in this form of outwardly directed warlike organization. And it is only a matter of time before this also determines the internal form taken by the organization and the fate of equality thus sealed. For the outwardly directed organization is, given its power of dominion, necessarily intended to last. In view of the economic imbalances that had preceded it, the organization becomes internally what the state and domination were in every case from the beginning, namely class society and class domination.

If one looks at the historical formative process, then – even if we concede the existence of uncertainties in certain specifics – there hardly remains a way in which we can assume that the state and domination result from a moral learning process. The authority necessary to settle disputes arising from the altered form of human settlement would never have allowed the judge to arise, given such a form of domination. Moreover, there is nothing to indicate the existence of a thoroughly organized juris-diction by the ruler during early times. In Sumeria jurisdiction over prac-tical everyday affairs still rests in the hands of a kind of popular assembly even once a state has evolved.[29] If there was a need for an arbitrating authority, the emergence of domination in any case preceded its being organized on the basis of an advanced morality. Morality had no choice but to come to terms with this development. The legitimatory protection of domination did not pose any problems for it. It is the structural aspect of the formation of domination which is fascinating for sociology.

The structural condition for the emergence of state and domination

In the process of the organization of pristine society, the network of interactive relationships is, as we have seen, formed by means of the interactive powers which each person can achieve under the given condi-tions. The 'given conditions' include the others as well. This is not the struggle of all against all, because each person is thinking about the other and his chances to assert her/himself. But it is also not the form of communicative action which Habermas has in mind, a form in which each person dispenses with his/her interests until s/he has weighed up the interests of all others against them. This form of putting one's own in-terests aside in line with which moral action is supposedly patterned (*TCA*, vol. II, p. 51) is not to be found in real social action or where it has crystallized into an institutional form. There is an effort to push one's own interests through against the other. That is a harsh principle, but one which is moderated under the family conditions of pristine society and with which one can live under the early conditions of securing one's subsistence. Its true severity becomes manifest as a result of settlements and the agricultural form of production, once the conditions conducive to the formation of equal interactive powers have been eliminated. The increase in organizational authority acquired with the new form of production is exploited in the formation of a dominating clique.

Domination, and this is what is decisive for the sociological and above all normative sociological understanding of the process, is created precisely by means of those mechanisms of social formation which were already effective before: on the outside, a freedom of action exists which is not limited by any form of normativity; on the inside, order takes shape from the real balance of power among the society's members. It is the predominant element in the structural formation of the society. In the process, the equality which has already been weakened by economic factors is subjugated organizationally by the formation of a dominating clique. The evolution of domination was not the Fall of Man. It lay at the foundation of a creature organizing itself socially, which by nature has no morals and can be made to adopt such within society only processually. In the interactive relationships of the small collective groups in daily life, the first and foremost being that of the family, morality is the condition for interaction; this is not the case in the overarching organization of state and domination.[30] The internal contradiction characteristic of domination lies in the latter being formed by means of the same, essentially ambivalent strategies as every moral order, while at the same time transgressing against morality. Those who lived at the time were not able to compensate for this contradiction.

The normativity of domination

There is direct evidence to substantiate the view that domination made use of the basic structure of the process of society's formation as such and exploited it for its own purposes – namely, its normativity. Throughout history, domination has been granted validity by the rulers on the basis of their own right to domination. It was normatively tied to the person of the ruler or rulers, just as law in general during this time was tied to the ruler(s). And why? Simply because norms have always been established through the facticity of successfully deployed interactive powers. To be valid means granting such validity as has taken shape in the course of this organic process. The cognitive competence to cast the validity of what had evolved organically into question was lacking. If domination were what Habermas claims it to be, namely, the organizational implementation of a higher plane of morality acquired through insight, and if the law grounded in domination were what Habermas makes it out to be, namely, the expression of a collective group will, then domination would have to have been exercised from the very beginning on the basis of law derived to that effect – in the name of society. However, this was precisely not the case.

Summary

If one wishes to put Habermas's theory of communicative action into concise terms, it can be said that the coordinating achievements in the process of interaction are tied to an insight which is tendentially based in linguistic communication. The structures of communicative action are developed through discourse and not practical interaction. Validity claims are made in which the guarantee for their redemption in argument is assumed by the maker; and they are adhered to because the addressee can convince himself that this guarantee is justified. If he then acts, he acts because he follows his own insight.

The fact that communicative action is characterized by its relieving action (as is expressly emphasized in adopting the analysis of the speech act lock, stock and barrel) harbours a danger, namely, that it will not prove possible to trace its structures in the real social organizations that have gradually taken on institutional form in the course of history. Habermas himself knows very well, of course, that up till now history has not taken a particularly rational course, and that the real structures cannot be described as sedimented communicative reason.

Habermas himself shows some reservations towards the explanatory power of a theory of communicative action. As a whole, he explains, the reproduction of society cannot adequately be traced back to the conditions of communicative action, whereas indeed the symbolic reproduction of a lifeworld derived from an internal perspective can (*TCA*, vol. II, p. 2). The problem lies in the fact that the processes of reaching understanding which determine the real formative process of a thoroughly normative organization are based on a level of symbolic self-communication that is set off from the real pursuit of interests. For it is difficult to grasp the orders we find in history in this manner. Yet Habermas attempts to do so. The reconstruction of the formative species-historical process in terms of the initial conditions in history utilizes the model of communicative action by situating the actually constitutive structuring phase in symbolically mediated self-communication. In the subsequent phase of a society now organized in human terms in the full sense of the term, reproduction of the social order is secured through the internalization of its norms. In the reproduction of society, the individuals act on the basis of their own judgement, even if this came about under the duress of internalization.

If we review the reconstruction by referring to the real historical conditions, then this clearly reveals a contradiction which applies to both the concept of communicative action and the reconstruction of early formative processes. Neither the social order of the hunter-gatherers nor the archaic societies structured in terms of domination can be explained by situating the communicative achievements that serve to relieve action at a level of symbolic self-communication. These become understandable only if the processes of reaching understanding are regarded as still being controlled by interests, and understanding is held to be something reached by incorporating the interactive powers of the interested parties. This structure of interaction by no means refers back to Hobbes's model of a struggle of all against all. For the ego is a socially needy ego; the realism which lies in its reflecting on its social conditionality focuses on its reliance on the others. In this manner, largely egalitarian orders are established in the familial organizations of the hunter-gatherer societies. Yet, domination is also normatively fixed by means of the same interactive mechanism, so that one can really no longer find any basis for communicative action in Habermas's sense in the historical reality of this form of society. Nowhere does the analytical distortion by the normative handicap of communicative action become so clear as in the depiction of the formation of societies structured in terms of domination which is first a moral learning process in the minds of those who are dominated, and only thereafter (!)[31] becomes implemented in the real political form of organization of domination.

6 The Unhappy Marriage of Hermeneutics and Functionalism

Hans Joas

The thematic breadth of Jürgen Habermas's work is extraordinary, and his theoretical undertaking has been progressing with a high degree of internal coherence. In *The Theory of Communicative Action*, Habermas has attempted to use his impressive intellectual tools and the results of his theoretical endeavour to produce a systematic work which both clarifies highly abstract fundamental theoretical questions and offers handy formulae that give a diagnosis of the present era. The work's scope and the diversity of the problems treated in it make it difficult for anyone who wants to enter into dialogue with it to follow the author's course of argumentation with a critical eye, if only to come independently – and not seduced by the book's rhetorical persuasiveness – to agreement with it. For this reason, the discussion of Habermas's book at present is in the somewhat uncomfortable situation of being split between global appreciations of a defensive or critical nature, on the one hand, and the correction of errors of detail, on the other. But what is the significance of amending Habermas's reconstructions of the classical theories of philosophy and sociology, if it has no important consequences for the line of argument of the work as a whole? On the other hand, of what use are global generalizations about the work if they fail to capture the wealth of the book's various discussions? A typical expression of this dilemma, it seems to me, is the fact that many critics are inclined to see, very speculatively and arbitrarily, the cause of the defects of Habermas's vision in his fundamental theoretical positions, although the logical relationship between the components of the theory which are cited is by no means clear. Such an arbitrary, and therefore often erroneous, localization of theoretical weak points in his theory is indeed fostered by Habermas himself when he asserts, 'in good Hegelian terms' (*The Theory of Communicative Action*, (*TCA*), vol. I, p. xxxix), that there is an indissoluble connection between the formation of basic concepts and the treatment of substantive issues. The existence of such a connection will not be denied here. However, a certain measure of doubt as to its inextricability does seem appropriate. Critical interpretations of sociological texts need not, by any means, assume a rigorous connection between the decisions regarding fundamental theoretical questions and the diagnosis of an historical period, which is always based on empirical information. Indeed, even between the solutions of different fundamental theoretical problems, tensions and ruptures can occur.

The following critical examination of Habermas's work takes as its starting point the conjecture that in this work, which claims to be completely coherent, we might find simply a 'personal union' of theoretical positions. More concretely I would like to advance the thesis that Habermas's book treats three sets of questions, all of which are distinct from one another to such an extent that answering one set does not completely predetermine the solution to the others. These three sets comprise the two fundamental problems of sociology, namely the question of human action and that of the conditions of social order, and the question of the central problematics of society in contemporary capitalist democracies. Between the two metatheoretical problems and the empirical dimension there can exist no relationship of logical consequence. Admittedly, a certain conception of contemporary social problems has a motivating function for the posing and answering of metatheoretical questions, but the positing of a determinative relationship between the metatheoretical and substantive levels would make communication between different political-ideological positions inconceivable from the outset. But even between the two metatheoretical questions, a meaningful distinction can be made.

If one takes Habermas's theory as an example, this assertion means that between his theory's contribution to the theory of action, i.e., its taking account of communicative action, and its solution to the problem of social order by means of the duality of system and lifeworld, there lie conceptual and empirical steps which make it clear that other solutions as well to the problem of social order can certainly spring from the soil of communicative action.[1] The following exposition will therefore concentrate on examining Habermas's contribution to the theory of action independently from the contribution he makes to the theory of social order. With respect to the theory of action, it will be shown to what extent the introduction of the concept of communicative action in fact constitutes an advance for mainstream sociological theories of action; on the other hand, however, it will be shown to what extent that concept, like mainstream sociology, continues to ignore a plethora of pressing questions pertaining to the theory of action. As for the theory of social order, the examination of the concepts of lifeworld and system will undertake to demonstrate the indefensibility of Habermas's use of them and to explain how Habermas is led into his unfortunate joining together of hermeneutics and functionalism through the insufficient radicalness of his critique of functionalism and his concomitant failure to recognize the metatheoretical character of the theory of action. I will entirely pass over the more philosophical questions concerning his use of the notion of rationality, and thus questions about the normative implications of a critical theory of society. Concerning the issue of Habermas's diagnosis of the present era, I return to it briefly and only in so far as its plausibility is thrown into doubt when Habermas's broader theoretical grounds are thrown in doubt.

Habermas's most important insight with regard to the theory of action is that the specific structure of human communication is irreducible. As opposed to any reduction of human action which maintains that it is merely technical, instrumental, teleological or oriented solely to success – whatever the counter-concepts might be, and no matter whether they are precise or imprecise – Habermas advanced the view that human beings can have dealings with one another without making each other into means for achieving individually predetermined ends, without closing themselves to the implicit or explicit demands of their fellow human beings for true knowledge, correct conduct and authentic self-presentation. Since Habermas formulated the distinction between 'labour' and 'interaction' in the form of a radical dichotomy, and used this distinction in his critique of Marx's concept of labour, this idea has been hotly debated.[2] This discussion has made unequivocally clear that the distinction proposed by Habermas is defensible only as an analytical one. In every social activity, aspects of both types of action can be found; even for the acquisition of the abilities required for human commerce with things, elementary communicative abilities appear to be a prerequisite.[3] The heart of the distinction does not seem to me to be affected by such criticisms. At bottom, Habermas is directing attention to a fundamental difference in attitude among actors in social action-situations and those in non-social action-situations, although it is certainly true that even my counterpart in a social situation can in many ways be made into a mere object of my influence and of my will. The typology of action put forward in *TCA* (vol. I, p. 384) consists in nothing else than a system of these three types of action: the instrumental, the strategic and the communicative.

Just how meagre this typology is can be shown by even a brief glance at Habermas's own theoretical development. If my own impression and Thomas McCarthy's reconstruction of that development do not deceive me,[4] then opposition to a reduction of action to the 'instrumental' was already a motive of Habermas's thought long before the concept of communicative action had assumed the role of a comprehensive counter-concept. At first, Habermas proposed a concept of praxis informed by the ancient Greek philosophy of praxis and by the early modern resistance to a theory of society influenced by the natural sciences. Even if there are good reasons for introducing the concept of communication or for making a triadic distinction between labour, work and action, as Hannah Arendt does,[5] nevertheless one may ask whether the concept of communication is capable of assuming all the meanings previously carried by the notion of praxis in its fullest sense. For it could indeed be the case that there are more reasons for rejecting the limitation of the practical to the technical than can be derived from the concepts of communication and interaction.

This question becomes even more acute when it is raised not just with respect to the individual theoretical development of Jürgen Habermas, but with respect to the entire history of theory concerned with this matter. Even in classical antiquity, the ideas about praxis were developed, according to Rüdiger Bubner,[6] through the critique of the Sophists' attempt to apply the *techne* model of action to political action. In the eighteenth century, according to Isaiah Berlin and Charles Taylor,[7] an 'expressionistic' counter-model of action as the expression of the actor was developed in opposition to utilitarian tendencies of Enlightenment. This model, which may not be confined to linguistic expression or to stylizing self-presentation, exercised widely ramified influences in post-Kantian German Idealism, in German Romanticism, and in the thought of Karl Marx, whose concept of labour is quite unsuited to serve as an example of the technicist-instrumentalist limitation of the concept of action. An important current of Marxist discussion in this century has concerned itself with the expressive moments of the concept of labour in Marx's early writings and with the constitutive significance of this concept for the critique of political economy. Pragmatism, with its emphasis on creative problem-solving, opposed to the instrumentalist reduction of action an alternative model of action, and was thereby led to reassess playful and artistic commerce with objects. Previously in intellectual history, play and art had, in the most diverse contexts, been presented as counter-notions to instrumentalist reductionism. Durkheim, Parsons, and Gehlen, either within the framework of the theory of action or via a critique of utilitarian views on the social order, each elaborate a conception of 'ritual' as a norm-constituting action as a counter-concept to the instrumentalist restriction of the concept of action. Habermas knows all this. The immediate purpose of the preceding enumeration is to call attention to the fact that a present-day theory of action must be capable of typologically reconstructing all the domains of these phenomena.

How little Habermas succeeds in this regard can also be illustrated by the typology of concepts of action which are widely used in the social sciences, and which Habermas himself presents in the context of his discussion of action's relations to the world and of its aspects of rationality (*TCA*, vol. I, pp. 126ff.). Here he distinguishes the teleological or strategic models of action from norm-regulated, dramaturgical and communicative action. Even a brief comparison of this typology with the concepts of action actually used in the social sciences and in philosophy suffices to show its serious defects. In the case of teleological action, Habermas makes no distinction between an action that accomplishes a previously set end and the type of action stressed by pragmatism and phenomenology, which finds its end within situations. Playful commerce with objects and situations as a type of action is also entirely absent from the typology. The description of norm-regulated action is oriented to the model of norm-observance, while symbolic interactionism and ethnomethodology by contrast emphasize the vague demarcation of behaviour, the meaningfulness of which is situation-specific.[8] Consequently, interaction that is not normatively regulated, or is so only slightly, is lacking in Habermas' typology.

The notion of dramaturgical action refers to the strategic presentation of oneself to a public. As a result, the truly expressionistic model of self-expression in actions performed without strategic intent is also lacking in the typology. The notion of communicative action appears at first (ibid., p. 128) to refer to the type of interaction that is normatively unregulated, or that regulates itself only in the immediate process of negotiations; later (ibid., p. 148) however, it is defined as that kind of action in which all 'relations to the world' become reflexive. This inspection of Habermas's typology makes it impossible to deny that what we have here is neither a suitable précis of concepts of action currently employed nor even a comprehensive typology of a general theory of action, but rather a classification that aims from the start at Habermas's distinction – admittedly a convincing one – of various kinds of possible relations to the world. Thus, we can conclude that Habermas has not really attempted, from the standpoint of the theory of action, to do justice to the diversity of kinds of action, and accordingly has delivered only communication as such as the jam-packed residual category of non-instrumental action.

But the real point of this argument is something else: this relatively schematic construction of the theory of action allows Habermas to avoid making two distinctions, both of which would have significantly widened the field of problems at the level of the theory of social order, and would have placed theoretical obstacles in the way of the solution to those problems within the duality of system and lifeworld. Habermas, on the one hand, insufficiently separates the question of overcoming the philosophy of consciousness from the reduction of the paradigm of purposive activity and the turn to communicative action; on the other hand, he incorrectly identifies a typology of action with a typology of the different kinds of *coordination* of action.

I consider both the supplanting of the philosophy of consciousness and the integration of the concept of communicative action into the sociological theory of action to be of great importance, but I dispute the identity of these two feats. Historically, there has been a pragmatist critique of the philosophy of consciousness without a theoretical model of intersubjectivity, namely that of William James, as well as theoretical models of intersubjectivity based on the philosophy of consciousness, which were put forward by phenomenology and partly by Charles Cooley. Both strands are unquestionably joined together in the work of George Herbert Mead, but they nevertheless remain analytically distinct. A brief characterization of the fundamental premiss of pragmatism's theory of action will make this point clear. This theory does not conceive of action as the pursuit of ends that the contemplative subject establishes a priori and then resolves to accomplish; the world is not held to be mere material at the disposal of human intentionality. Quite to the contrary, pragmatism maintains that we find our ends in the world, and that prior to any setting of ends we are already, through our praxis, embedded in various situations. There is an interplay between the manifold impulses of the actor and the possibilities of a given situation, which can be interpreted in various ways. Between impulses and possibilities of action, the actor experimentally establishes connections, of which, in any given instance, only one is realized; that one, however, is influenced in its particular manner of realization by the other possibilities that have been mentally played through. The course followed by an action then is not one that has been established once and for all time; rather, it must be produced over and over again by construction and is open to continual revision. A model of action that is in this sense non-teleological, that does not confine the situatedness of action to its conditions and means, raises the question of the conditions of the apparently self-evident schematization of natural totalities of action according to means and ends. John Dewey's view of the matter, for example, is that when the imprecise directedness with which customary actions are performed proves insufficient to overcome the resistance encountered in a particular situation, only then is the hitherto implicit intentionality of the action brought into the full light of consciousness and compelled to focus on the situation so as to make itself more precise.[9] Playful self-development and creative solution of problems, as used by the pragmatists, repudiate the primacy of an instrumentalist concept of labour for action just as radically as does the adducing of interaction and communication as kinds of action not accounted for by a model based upon labour.

What then would be the consequences if Habermas had clearly distinguished the two trains of reasoning which lead to the supersession of the philosophy of consciousness and to the emergence of the concept of communicative action? First, it would have been necessary to take into account, within the theory of action, non-teleological forms of dealing with objects in non-social situations. Second, and this is more important, the very way in which end- or success-oriented human action is viewed would change. It would become clear that the setting of ends is a self-reflective and therefore secondary presentation of an action in situations. On the level of the theory of action, a domain would thereby be brought into view, in which all action 'has always been' embedded.[10] Focusing upon this 'domain' permits a more radical refutation of the notion that individual actors enter into action-situations with preconceived intentions than is made possible by the thesis that meanings are linguistically constituted. It is in this domain that the actors' corporeality and prelinguistic sociality must be located. This domain has been examined from very different theoretical vantage points, and Habermas's theory of communicative action provides effective means for rejecting structuralism's claim on this 'domain'. But does his theory succeed in conceptualizing this domain as the lifeworld? If the lifeworld is supposed to be a correlate of communicative action, then there arises the problem that the 'domain' under discussion here is the basis of all action, thus also of teleological action, no matter how it is defined.

Further consequences arise for the positions which Habermas allocates the classics within the history of theory; this, in turn, has indirect consequences for a substantive problem. I believe that Habermas rightly criticizes Weber, Lukács and Horkheimer/Adorno for the defects in their implicit or explicit theories of action, which arise from their deploying a philosophy of consciousness. However, because he does not make a clearcut distinction between a non-teleological and a non-monological interpretation of action, he has unnecessarily to expand a completely justified critique of Weber's concept of meaning, which is neo-Kantian and rooted in a philosophy of consciousness, by imputing a monological orientation in Weber's concept of action (*TCA*, vol. I, pp. 280ff.). As for Parsons's work, Habermas finds it also to have foundations in the philosophy of consciousness (ibid., p. 239), yet does not see that these exist from the outset in a field of tension with other influences, initially brought to bear by Whitehead.[11] The most important consequence, however, concerns Emile Durkheim. At various points Habermas mentions Mead and Durkheim in the same breath as being the originators of the paradigm shift from purposive to communicative action. This classification unquestionably applies in the case of Mead's intersubjectivist pragmatism. However, with regard to Durkheim, it must be qualified to a great extent. Although it can indeed be concluded from his late sociology of religion[12] that he shifted to a theory of extra-ordinary, emotional, direct interaction, there is no basis whatsoever for claiming that Durkheim was at the same time or by virtue of that shift attempting to supersede the philosophy of consciousness. On the contrary: the lectures on pragmatism which he gave after the publication of *Elementary Forms of the Religious Life*[13] clearly show that Durkheim takes the offensive by positing central positions of the philosophy of consciousness against pragmatism. What links Durkheim to an intersubjectivistically oriented pragmatism is the attempt to forge a theory of the social constitution of categories of human knowledge. His first attempt – to be found in the famous essay, coauthored with Marcel Mauss, on primitive classification systems[14] – consists of a theory of the reproduction of social morphology in cultural systems of classification. He then refines this further in the mature sociology of religion. There, Durkheim is concerned with the emergence of social morphology itself out of the religious group experience in collective ritual praxis. He argues that the forces of the collective experienced in 'collective effervescence' and the effects this has on the individual can be interpreted only by the participating subjects as forces which are at work behind the observable things themselves and prevail throughout the cosmos. In the religious group experience, the reciprocal effect of the individual psyches is intensified to such an extent that the connection to collective ideations ensues here, and these then exert their organizing power on the individual perceptions in the everyday world of the individuals. Whereas pragmatism, in other words, emphasizes the constitution of knowledge in practical problematic situations, Durkheim marks the religious experience sharply off from this. He distinguishes brusquely between all cognition directed towards enabling action and a desire to understand which is basic for all religious cosmologies. In his theory of religion, however, he designates the collective praxis of ritual to be the origin of categories. It can be shown that Durkheim's thesis on social constitution is directed against a constitution in everyday *practice* as well as a constitution in the praxis of *everyday* life. Precisely what Durkheim elaborates with regard to the extra-ordinary sociality of the ritual he then disputes with respect to the everyday reality of social life. If Habermas also wishes to include the everyday forms of action that are shot through with religion in his Durkheim interpretation, then he has good reasons for doing so, but he is violating the spirit of Durkheim's work. For the latter feared that such a theory could have irrationalistic consequences and instead defended a traditionally Cartesian concept of consciousness – before and after the shift in the theory of religion. Correcting Habermas's approach in this manner[15] is not only of interest in terms of the history of theory, because Habermas then sets out in a further step (*TCA*, vol. II, p. 133) to fuse Durkheim's notion of a structural change in the collective conscience with a phenomenologically oriented investigation of the lifeworld. In so doing, he proposes that the analysis of the lifeworld be understood 'as an attempt to describe reconstructively, from the internal perspective of members, what Durkheim called the *conscience collective*' (ibid., p. 133). If my reconstruction of Durkheim is accurate, this is an impossible undertaking. For the theory of collective conscience would then have to be regarded as a solution to a problem in the theory of social order that is possible only on the basis of a philosophy of consciousness, a solution that becomes untenable as soon as the switch is made to a non-teleological and non-monological theory of action. On this terrain, the issue in the theory of social order and the question as to the non-conscious lifeworld background of all action would then have to be strictly separated from one another. I will return to this in detail.

As stated above, Habermas identifies in a misleading fashion a typology of action with the distinction among types of coordination of action. A number of Habermas's critics (Berger, Bader, Honneth)[16] have pointed out that in many formulations he connects too closely different types of action and different societal spheres of action, in so far as he speaks of sub-systems of purposively rational or of communicative action. This is a valid criticism, since we must assume that every societal sphere of action exhibits a wealth of different types of action. In *The Theory of Communicative Action*, Habermas appears to want to avoid this problem by talking about types of coordination of action and by introducing on this level of his theory the distinction between success-oriented versus communicatively oriented action. However, since there is no typology adequate to the rich variety of the different kinds of action that correspond to the distinction among different forms of the coordination of action, and since to each of the societal domains and spheres of action only one principle of the coordination of action is ascribed, a linear relationship of correspondence among types of action, types of coordination of action, and societal domains is once again established. Once this relationship has been theoretically established in this manner, then of course no phenomena can block the progress of Habermas's argumentation, and he can shift back and forth between the different levels at will. When considered from the standpoint of the theory of action, this state of affairs is clearly problematic. However, the topic of the coordination of action leads to the second central metatheoretical problem of sociology, namely the question of social order.

Habermas's contribution to the solution of the problems posed by the theory of social order consists in his defence of two opposed conceptions of the theory of social order and in his attempt to join them by using empirical arguments. On the one hand, it is a matter of a type of social order that is supposed to correspond to communicatively oriented action and is represented as being intuitionally comprehensible and rooted in the actors' intentions. To refer to this type of social order, Habermas uses the concept of 'lifeworld'. The precise manner in which this concept is introduced into Habermas's argumentation will have to be treated later. However, according to Habermas, this concept alone is insufficient to solve the problems raised by a theory of social order, as it is constrained by the essential limits of any theory of action. An adequate theory of society must reach out beyond forms of sociality based on primary groups and beyond the intended results of action, and to do this it must critically draw upon functionalist systems theory. Habermas then elucidates the relationship between two models of social order, the 'lifeworld' and 'systems', in a quasi-empirical fashion, that is, first by means of an historical theory about the gradual uncoupling of the system from the lifeworld. Second, he analyses the present relationship among the societal spheres that supposedly correspond to these types of social order, and finally, he introduces a theoretical model, based on the media theory of functionalist theorists, concerning the interactions among these spheres and of the 'mediatization', 'instrumentalization', and 'colonization' of the lifeworld through the imperatives of the system. In order to make perceptible the problems in Habermas's theory, which is sometimes developed at levels of abstraction so high that they make the reader's head spin, it is necessary to scrutinize in order: (1) Habermas's understanding of the status of the theory of action; (2) his interpretation and employment of functionalist systems theory; and (3) his introduction of the concept of the lifeworld into the argument. The problems that appear as we proceed along this path will give the reader an idea of just how infelicitous is the joining together of 'lifeworld' and 'system', of hermeneutic and functionalist conceptions of social order.

1   In many passages of his book, Habermas speaks of essential limits on what the theory of action can accomplish, and of the competition between approaches based on the theory of action and on systems theory as a competition between two different paradigms. This assertion seems to me to require critique, at least as a way of stating the matter; but the unsatisfactory formulation also reveals a questionable understanding of the problem. It is my thesis that, with this formulation, Habermas confounds the distinction between the theory of action and the theory of social order with, on the one hand, the solution to the problem of social order provided by functionalist systems theory and, on the other hand, with the substantive question of the extent to which societal processes occur independently of the intentions of individual actors.

The theory of action does not *per se* compete with the theory of social order. It does not at all contain the empirical assumption that all results of action are covered by the intentions of the actors, or lie within the control and intuitive knowledge of the actors.[17] In fact, the theory of action directly compels us to pose the problem of social order. Every theory of action entails theoretical assumptions about the nature of social order that implicitly or explicitly correspond to it. This is true even of the poorest but very influential theory of action, namely utilitarianism, for which the corresponding model of social order is the market,[18] as well as of theories of action originating in ethnomethodology, which refer to the model of social order based on the fragile interaction among individual human subjects. It is not the case that the theory of action stands in a competitive relation to functionalist systems theory; rather, an anthropologically grounded theory of human action *and* of the basic structures of human sociality resists the unconsidered apprehension of the domain studied by the social sciences in so far as these use the categories of a systems theory that *per se* is not yet tailored to the specific characteristics of this domain. Functionalist systems theory is a proposal about how to solve the problems posed by the theory of social order that is, in relation to the social, still only metaphorical, but might prove to be fruitful after it has been made more specific. If functionalist systems theory should in fact turn out to be fruitful, then this will not be due to the essential limitations of what the theory of action can accomplish, but to its own possible superiority over other models of social order.

Like both Merton and Parsons,[19] Habermas adduces the problem of unintended results of action as an important reason for changing over to functionalist models of social order. This cannot be a compelling reason, since unintended results of action are made the focal point of attention in a large number of theoretical approaches, without leading these theories into functionalism. An example is the political theory of John Dewey,[20] for which the perception and the control of unintended results of group action constitute an important starting point. Some authors, for instance, Blau, Boudon and others,[21] adduce the possibility of unintended results of action as evidence against functionalism, since from no perspective can all unintended results of action be interpreted as functional. This indicates that there is at least a problem in Habermas's distinction between two types of coordination of action. For he presents these types as the two members of a dichotomy in which coordination of action with reference to the intentions directing the action is opposed to coordination of action with reference to the results of action. Now all coordination of action with reference to intentions is extremely unstable, if retro-actions of unintended or unanticipated results of action continuously occur that cannot be consensually interpreted within the framework of the actor's systems of meanings. Conversely, social integration effected by means of the results of action can mean not the interconnecting of the actors through all the results of action, but merely the definition of certain kinds of results that are recorded as legitimate.

The misleading restriction of the theory of action to 'lifeworld' processes leaves its mark at many points in the reconstructions of the history of social theory. To my mind it is wrong, for example, to classify Weber simply as a theorist of action, while failing to consider the ideas which stem from a theory of social order contained in his work – 'Some Categories of a verstehende Sociology'[22] being but one obvious example. The charges against Weber's model of bureaucracy,[23] which Luhmann has assembled from developments in research on the sociology of organization, charges which Habermas repeatedly cites, do not in my opinion show limits of *the* theory of action *as such*, but rather flaws in the Weberian model of bureaucracies, and indicate the need to differentiate between the level of individual action and its rationalization and the rationalization of collective and organized action. Equally, I do not see the point of interpreting Marx's theory of value as an attempt to mediate conceptually between the level of systems processes ('accumulation of capital') and the dynamics of class conflict, since Marx devised the analysis of the value form as an attempt to develop systematically the central economic categories of a social theory meant to address capitalism from the perspective of collectively reversing the fact that social relations had gradually become independent; here Habermas is projecting on to Marx a distinction of his own which does not exist in this form in Marx's work.

However, I also have grave doubts as to whether the history of social theory in the late nineteenth century (*TCA*, vol. II, p. 202) can be described in terms of the division between a German tradition of action theory and a tradition of an economic theory of social order.[24] However, I wanted to refer only briefly to this point; more detailed remarks will focus on the implications Habermas's view of the theory of action has for his interpretation of Mead and Parsons. The relativization of Mead's importance for social theory and the critique of the supposed 'idealism' of his social theory at the end of the section devoted to Mead and Durkheim is as drastic in tone as Mead is central to Habermas's conception because of the 'paradigm shift' from purposive action to communicative action. In his reconstruction of Mead, which on the whole is helpful and influenced by an analytical philosophy of language, Habermas limits Mead's conception of symbolically mediated interaction to the level of communication in signal language. This is a misunderstanding which can arise if one takes Mead's interest in the *origin* of human communication to be his sole interest. However, his works cover the entire spectrum ranging from the dialogue of significant gestures to complex scientific or public political discussions. The simpler forms are viewed not only as preliminary evolutionary stages, but rather also as forms of communication that are always given. The criticism that Mead does not elaborate the difference between the various forms or stages sufficiently is surely justified. As Mead sees it, a fundamental rupture occurs during the period of transition from animal to human in the structure of sociality, a rupture which from the very beginning results in the anthropological conditions for the possibility of an ideal social order, namely, that order which comes about via the institutionalization of discourses. This misunderstanding has to do with the general underestimation of Mead's achievements not only for action theory, but also for a theory of social order – one need only think of his emphatic concept of democracy. To this extent, it provides the basis for Habermas's polemic against Mead, namely that Mead was supposedly not aware of the one-sidedness of his communications-theoretic approach; Habermas claims this is already to be seen from the fact that only those social functions come into view in Mead's work that 'devolve upon communicative action and in which communicative action also cannot be replaced by other mechanisms' (*TCA*, vol. II, p. 110). Mead is accordingly judged to neglect the material reproduction of society and the securing of its physical maintenance and to occlude economics, warfare and the struggle for political power from the theory. In general, Habermas says, Mead ignores the external restrictions (ibid., p. 108) on the development of communicative rationalization.

In my opinion, two distinctions have to be made if we are to assess this criticism of Mead.[25] We should distinguish, on the one hand, between a thematic and a systematic neglect of domains such as the economy, war and politics. Thematically, it is true that in his essential contributions – but one also has to take into consideration his politico-philosophical reviews[26] – Mead concerns himself with problems other than the sociological analysis of the above-mentioned domains. Systematically, however, there is no basis for contending that his concepts of action and social order are too narrow in terms of communications theory. He does not place a naive trust in the development of communication. Rather, the problem as he sees it is how the economically advancing universalization of human social relations could be 'compensated for' culturally and politically. The world market, for example, is in his view a case of advanced sociation to which as yet no forms of social integration correspond. It is precisely not the unleashed dynamics of communicative rationality, but rather complexes now independent and a reduction in their independence that form the level at which he addresses the problem. The second distinction I would like to call for concerns the meaning of the concept of a communicative theory of society. I think one should relate this exclusively to theories which at the level of action theory provide only models of communication and interaction, but should not link it to those which contain or normatively distinguish models of integration via unleashed communication at the level of the theory of social order. Habermas imputes to the concept of social integration a meaning of 'lifeworldly', interpersonal immediacy not to be found in Mead's work. He does not, therefore, take seriously enough the claim made by a conception in the context of a radical American democratism (or a Marxism given a normative twist) to render all structures of social action dependent on the result of collective will-formation. This is expressed crassly when Habermas (*TCA*, vol. II, pp. 117f.) draws a parallel between the semanticization of 'objective' meanings in the functional circuit of animal behaviour and the understanding or the control of social processes by the members of society. Whereas in the one case it is indeed a question of the transition from animal to human behaviour, in the other case it is a question of the collective mastery of the effects produced at any event by action. I see no point in embracing both the natural preconditions for human action and the gradual independence of social relations in the one concept of systemic interconnections; that would indeed be to render uncontrolled social developments natural in origin. Habermas is correct in declaring that the extent to which control is had over these developments is an empirical matter (ibid., p. 118); but, in accordance with his abbreviated understanding of action theory, he bundles this together with the meta-theoretical decision for or against action theory.

Habermas's interpretation of the development of Talcott Parsons's work is impressive owing to its ability to locate ruptures in the considerable continuity of this process – or so the self-stylizations and presentations of the Parsons orthodoxy would have it – and to uncover systematic problems generated by the dynamics of this development. The attempt to deploy in the theory an intrinsic meaning of cultural formations, without succumbing to some transcendentalization of culture (*TCA*, vol. II, p. 231) and the magnificent interpretation of the anthropologizing esoteric late work of Parsons (ibid., pp. 375–84) are, to my mind, among the outstanding accomplishments of this part of Habermas's work. The Parsons interpretation as a whole, however, suffers from the conception of the status of the theory of action criticized above. In Habermas's view, the framework of Parsons's action theory proved 'too narrow for (him) to develop a concept of society from that perspective; thus he felt it necessary to represent complexes of action directly as systems and to convert social theory from the conceptual primacy of action theory over to that of systems theory' (ibid., p. 203). This proposition cannot be adhered to in this form if, as suggested here, one distinguishes the *problematics* of the theory of social order from systems theory's *proposal for a solution* and defines the status of the theory of action accordingly. For then it will be shown that in his *Structure of Social Action* Parsons quite clearly did already advocate not only a voluntaristic theory of action, but also a normativistic theory of social order. Moreover, the chapter in his early work on Pareto,[27] usually neglected in most interpretations of Parsons, contains an interesting attempt to present a concept of the system of action which does justice precisely also to the concatenation of utilitarian actions. Now, Habermas is not attacking the simple existence of attempts by the early Parsons to devise a theory of social order, but rather he is criticizing the supposed isolation of the concepts of action and of social order (ibid., pp. 208–9). In so doing, he proceeds from the notion that it would have been logical to 'connect the concept of action with that of order so that they complemented one another at the same analytical level and thus yielded a concept of social interaction. The concept of *normative agreement* could have served as a bridge between the concepts of value-oriented purposive activity and an order integrating values with interests' (*TCA*, vol. II, p. 213). Parsons, he claims, remains bound to his point of departure, namely the singular action of a single actor. Irrespective of whether this is true of Parsons's work,[28] Habermas's underlying assumption here does not seem tenable to me. It is admittedly correct to design from the very outset the concept of action with a view to the social embeddedness of action, as Mead attempted to do in his conception of the 'social act' as a complex group activity. Yet, Habermas himself does not do this: although he takes the orientation towards interaction into account in introducing communicative action as a type, he nevertheless also develops this type in the context of the individual action of the individual actor. Even if group action or social interaction is made the point of departure at the level of the theory of action, I still do not see how this would solve the problem of the theory of social order itself. The problem of what unintended action sequences should be attributed to and how they are processed is, for example, just as much a problem as it ever was. I cannot see to what extent Parsons's later transition to a functionalist systems theory was *forced* upon him in any way by his original action-theoretic approach. The field of tension in which this theory of action becomes embroiled owing to Parsons's shift is, however, superbly analysed by Habermas. Nevertheless, it would again seem to me that Habermas overdramatizes the results of his analysis by proposing that the harmonistic image of the present era outlined by Parsons can be traced directly back to the initial design of the theory. By contrast, it bears pointing out that Parsons arrives at appraisals that differ substantially from Habermas's (and mine), but not because his theory of modernization did not allow for a dissynchronous intensification in the four dimensions of adaptive capacity, inclusion, value generalization and differentiation of media-controlled sub-systems. Richard Münch's neo-Parsonian critique of Habermas on this point seems justified to me.[29] The potential for an analysis of the present era inherent in a trend towards 'associationism' which Parsons asserts exists is equally not to be trivialized by pointing to individual harmonistic interpretations by Parsons.[30]

Now that we have elaborated Habermas's interpretation of the sociological classics, and this is indispensable if interpretation is as important for the development of systematic argumentation as it is in this thinker's case, let us once again call to mind what was first at issue here.

The foregoing reflection on the status of the theory of action was intended both to stress the inevitable existence of questions pertaining to the theory of social order in the fundamental problems of sociology and to refute the necessity of seeking answers to the theoretical questions of social order by way of functionalist systems theory. For the moment, all that is clear is that the theory of action entails the development of a typology of forms of communal and societal integration, and that the introduction of a theory of communicative action on the level of the theory of action compels the inclusion in such a typology of a type of social order that could be called a social order founded on discursively reached agreement. However, on this level it is still impossible to make any assertion about the normative precedence of this type over other types of social order, or about the empirical relationship among existing types of social order.[31]

2   Habermas gives the impression that the limitations of the theory of action make it necessary to have recourse to functionalist theories of systems. If we are not content to stop at phenomena that occur within the horizon of actors' intentions, or erroneously to explain macrosocial complexes of interrelations with reference to this model, then there seems to be no other choice than to analyse these nexuses according to the example given by systems theory. The only matter of dispute, then, is the claim of functionalist analysis to be exhaustive of the social totality. Habermas

firmly rejects this claim, insisting on the constitution of systemic complexes of interrelations in lifeworldly nexuses of action. Let us examine more closely the procedure, the problems, and the motives of this critical examination and appropriation of functionalism, which is, however, no more than that.

To Habermas, the phenomenon of the interconnection of unintended results of action in the form of self-regulating societal mechanisms seems to be undeniable. He wants to free such mechanisms from the odium of being in their essence evidence of alienation. To this end he frequently emphasizes the problem-solving role of such mechanisms or media, which eases the burden on communication. In the sphere of rational economic activity, which is in conformity with the medium of money, and in the sphere of rational administration, which is in conformity with the medium of power, he sees successful forms for fulfilling societal tasks. In relation to these tasks, the demand for communicative regulation would be out of place, because it would never be capable of competing, from the standpoint of effectivity, with the other kinds of regulation proper to these spheres. The market, in particular, is presented as the prototype of a sociality that, while it is normatively constituted, is itself free of norms. Imperceptibly, Habermas glides from the existence of a type of social order that can be described only by using the means provided by functionalist systems theory to arguing for the indispensability of this kind of social order for the fulfilment of a particular societal task, namely that of material reproduction. 'To be sure', states Habermas,

> the material reproduction of the lifeworld does not, even in limiting cases, shrink down to surveyable discussions such that it might be represented as the intended outcome of collective cooperation. Normally it takes place as the fulfillment of latent functions *going beyond the action orientations* of those involved. Insofar as the aggregate effects of cooperative actions fulfill imperatives of maintaining the material substratum, these complexes of action can be stabilized functionally, that is, through feedback from functional side effects." (*TCA*, vol. II, p. 232)

Not only does Habermas functionalistically conceive of the unintended effects of action a priori as 'latent functions' in this passage; in addition, he also gives a substantializing turn to the formalism of the systems model in the direction of material reproduction of a society.

Neither the one nor the other is self-evidently true. That the problem of unintended results of action does not compel one to have recourse to functionalism has already been stressed numerous times. It is also astonishing, in view of the pervasiveness in the social sciences of a normatively oriented functionalism that concentrates precisely on phenomena of 'symbolic reproduction', that Habermas assigns to functionalism the task of explaining specifically material reproduction. This position contains at least a tendency toward reification of a principle of social order. This tendency is also revealed in Habermas's use of the concepts of system integration and social integration. This pair of concepts has become widely recognized and used following David Lockwood's critique of Parsons from a leftist perspective[32] and has become one of the focal points of the discussion of macrosociological theory. The distinction made by these two concepts in fact expresses the experience of the West European left that smoothly running economic reproduction by no means guarantees the socio-cultural integration of a society, and that economic crises do not necessarily trigger political or socio-cultural crises. With these concepts, Lockwood sought to go beyond the superficial critique of Parsons from the standpoint of the theory of social conflict, and to set against the notion of a system of values common to all the members of a society as a fundamental prerequisite of social order a completely different theoretical plane: that of the real inter-dependence of parts and domains of society. No matter how inexact this attempt to formulate an interesting idea might have been, it was clear that system integration and social integration referred to two dimensions of integration that are always present simultaneously and which did not belong to two distinct societal spheres. Habermas, in contrast, believes that a differentiation between system and lifeworld took place in the course of history; thus he arrives at the proposition that 'societies are *systemically stablized* complexes of action of *socially integrated* groups' (*TCA*, vol. II, p. 152). The scope of societal integration is thus regarded, at least in modern societies, as fundamentally smaller than that of society in general which embraces both system *and* lifeworld.

There is, however, a host of problems specific to Habermas's use of functionalist notions. I would like to call attention here especially to two difficulties. The first concerns the uncoupling from the lifeworld of subsystems of purposive rational action. Within the framework of a Weberian typology of action, this manner of formulation could still be considered to make a certain sense. But Habermas, in order to demonstrate the necessity of 'going over' from the theory of action to systems theory, relies strongly on Niklas Luhmann's critique of Weber and the use of the concept of purpose at the level of system-rationality. Luhmann's critique, however, maintains that there is a rupture between the individual actor's end-oriented rationality of action and the functional rationality of social systems. Therefore, system-rationality does not at all require a rationality of action that is structurally analogous to it. The thesis that there are subsystems of purposively rational action is consequently untenable not only because it allows a societal domain to be based on a single type of action, but also because it assumes that a subsystem can be characterized by reference to the type of action dominant in it.[33] The second immanent difficulty reveals itself when one recalls the argument that Habermas himself used in some of his earlier writings to critique functionalism.[34] There he demonstrated that functionalist analyses in the social sciences encounter what he calls a problematic of the value that should be realized by a social system; this means, such analyses run into the fact that no self-evident, taken-for-granted guiding value is given beforehand to social systems – such as that of sheer self-preservation or of biological survival – but that this value can only be defined by the investigator. This insight ought to lead us to a distrust of any assumption of actually effective teleological tendencies in social systems. Of course, this line of reasoning can be extended beyond the decisionist positing of such guiding values by an investigator, to the question of the guiding values institutionalized in social systems. Then, however, with regard to functional interconnections it is again a matter of tendencies that, from the standpoint of such dominant 'guiding values,' are intended or at least acceptable. From this perspective, real processes that are functional in themselves are theoretically precluded. This is also true of material reproduction, implicit in which is, certainly, the task of self-preservation, but in a modified form. If this is so, then talk of system processes that are uncoupled from the lifeworld but which are nevertheless functional, becomes meaningless.

In recent years, it has been above all Anthony Giddens who has championed – in contrast to Habermas – radical critique of functionalism which does not fall back into methodological individualism and which does not deny phenomena such as homeostatic processes, to the existence of which the programmatic adherents of functionalism like to call attention.[35] Such a radical critique of functionalism is aimed in the direction of a theory of collective action, the focus of which is the intended and unintended results of collective and individual action, and the collective constitution of normative regulations and collective procedures for dealing with normative conflicts. Classic expressions of this way of thinking point to social order resulting from negotiation processes and to the constitution of a collective will.[36] Habermas is unwilling to follow this route. He is forced to adopt a truncated version of the theory of action and to take recourse to functionalist lines of reasoning because he does not see the theory of action in relation to the task of describing collective actions, of describing the constitution of collective actors and identities. In my opinion, he has expressed his motives for not doing this most clearly in the speech he made in Stuttgart when accepting the Hegel Prize.[37] In his discussion of the question of whether complex societies are capable of developing a reasonable identity, he speaks of the two great, influential forms of collective identity in modern history: the nation-state and the political party. In order to judge the claim of these collective identities to rationality, he measures both of them by the standard of whether they embody goals that can be universalized. He adjudges that historically both have played such a role. In the current context, however, a nationalist consciousness means for him the danger of a particularist regression. He also regards the hopes set in the proletarian party as outmoded, after the historical experiences we have had with bureaucratized state parties and reformist parties integrated into the competitive political system of capitalist democracies. We shall not judge the factual basis of these assessments. What is clear, though, is that this judgement sends Habermas on a search for a structure of collective identity that is not very closely associated with the empirically available forms of partial collective identity. The explanation for Habermas's orientation, under Luhmann's influence, towards a functionalism that has been given a critical turn is to be found, in my view, in the above-mentioned assessments and in Habermas's suspicion that any theory centred on the constitution of collective actors (a) promotes the reification of organizations into collective subjects and (b) the assumption made by the philosophy of history that the history of humanity has a single persisting subject. This seems to be the crucial point from which Habermas is led into the dilemma arising out of the union of hermeneutics and functionalism.[38]

3   In Habermas's theory, the concept of the lifeworld fulfils simultaneously two tasks. It characterizes a type of social order and an epistemological position. Using concepts from the tradition of pragmatism and of sociology influenced by pragmatism, the type of social order in question is that called 'democracy' or 'negotiated order'; the epistemological theory is that theory according to which cognition is constituted in a 'world that is there'. I mention these concepts in order to point out that a theory can and must contain both kinds of concepts; they should, though, be clearly distinct from each other. In introducing the concept of the lifeworld into his argument, Habermas does not begin with theories of the constitution of cognition in contexts of everyday certainties of action and of social intercourse, theories that are not fundamentally transcendentalist from the outset like the one Mead develops in his later writings, or the theory of everyday life presented in the works of Lukács during his last period and in the writings of Agnes Heller.[39] He begins, rather, with the contributions made by phenomenology, which have been more influential in the social sciences. He criticizes their use of a model of individual perceptions taken from the philosophy of consciousness and attempts to transform that model in accordance with the theory of communication. This effort is influenced by the findings of analytical philosophy. If this transformation is successful, then we can 'think of the lifeworld as represented by a culturally transmitted and linguistically organized stock of interpretive patterns' (*TCA*, vol. II, p. 124). What the content of this lifeworld is, is of course unknown to the actors; it is merely background, which can become relevant or problematical, depending on the situation.

> From a perspective turned toward the situation, the lifeworld appears as a reservoir of taken-for-granteds, of unshaken convictions that participants in communication draw upon in cooperative processes of interaction. Single elements, specific taken-for-granteds, are, however, mobilized in the form of consensual and yet problematicizable knowledge only when they become relevant to a situation. (*TCA*, vol. II, p. 124)

Up to this point I see no difficulty in principle in Habermas's procedure. This changes, though, with the next step. Habermas is unsatisfied with what he has achieved, inasmuch as the lifeworld concept of the theory of communication 'still (lies) on the same analytical level as the transcendental lifeworld concept of phenomenology' (ibid., p. 135). This plane must be surpassed, however, says Habermas, if the goal is not to remain within the framework of epistemology, but to achieve a demarcation of the domain of investigation of the social sciences. Then, he continues, the lifeworld, which is conceived from the perspective of participants in action-situations, must be 'objectivated'. Habermas sees a first model for how this might happen in ordinary, everyday narrations, which can refer to the totality of socio-cultural facts without necessarily originating from the point of view of a participant in the narrated action. The crucial step, however, is the one that follows:

> This intuitively accessible *concept of the sociocultural lifeworld* can be rendered theoretically fruitful if we can develop from it a reference system for descriptions and explanations relevant to the lifeworld as a whole and not merely to occurrences within it. Whereas narrative presentation refers to what is innerworldly, theoretical presentation is intended to explain the reproduction of the lifeworld itself. (*TCA*, vol. II, pp. 136–7)

The result of this attempt at objectivation is Habermas's contention that the lifeworld fulfils the functions of cultural reproduction, social integration, and socialization. In accordance with these functions that have been identified, Habermas distinguishes three structural components of the lifeworld: culture, society, and personality. By following Habermas in his train of reasoning, we have come to the very same result as Parsons, who at the beginning of the fifties presented his distinction among three levels of systems of action.[40] Still, we have arrived at it along a wholly different path.

Should this coincidence cause us to be sceptical? I think so. After the concept of the lifeworld has been appropriated for the theory of communication and reinterpreted accordingly, Habermas's daring construction presents us with two completely different ideas under the rubric of the objectivation of the participant perspective. The first idea has to do with an objectivation such as an ordinary story-teller or an historian undertakes. The story-teller tells of the knowledge and the action of other actors and objectivates this knowledge and action in so far as he places it within a context resulting from his understanding of the frames of reference within which he interprets the actions of others. He does not become an uncomprehending observer, but an interpretative reconstructor of the subjectively intended and 'objective' meaning of the actions of others. Just as the totality of their lifeworldly background remains essentially non-cognizable for the actors who are the object of the narration, so too does the lifeworldly background of the narrator remain essentially non-cognizable in its totality for him. Our narrator could become the object of narration for a second narrator, and so on, *ad infinitum*. This process would produce ever new 'stories'; and these new stories would perhaps be ever more 'objective', relative to the limited perspective of the original actors. However, in this process no plane would be reached that is essentially different from that of the reconstruction of the meaning of others' actions against the background of a lifeworld.

The other idea that Habermas links to the concept of objectivation does not have to do with the perspective of the story-teller or of the historian, but with the perspective of the epistemologist. The latter can make the mode of constitution of cognition itself, as it is performed by actors or narrators or historians, the object of his reflexion. This is true, of course, even of the phenomenological theorist of the lifeworld. If phenomenology abandons its claim that the objects of cognition are transcendentally constituted, the result is an epistemological theory that attempts self-reflectively to bring into sight the preconditions of cognition. This effort yields corporeality, intersubjectivity, and the structuredness of knowledge as preconditions of all cognition. With regard to this objectivation, it is a matter of a self-reflective confirmation of the preconditions of cognition and action. This confirmation can only assume the character of a formal definition of such preconditions. For as soon as it tries to go beyond a formal definition of them, it becomes a particular theory, which necessarily arises upon a determinate lifeworldly foundation that as such is essentially noncognizable. It is, therefore, no accident that Habermas discovers as the structural components of the lifeworld precisely those dimensions which Parsons identified as the levels at which the concept of system is to be applied in the social sciences. However, no theory about changes of cultural reproduction, of social integration and of socialization can claim to have originated from an objectivation in principle of *the* lifeworld. It holds good also for the human being Jürgen Habermas that the lifeworld environing him, which forms the horizon of his cognition, cannot, in principle, be fully thematized or completely and clearly grasped. The discernment of structural components of the lifeworld therefore cannot smoothly pass over into propositions about the differentiation and structural rationalization of the lifeworld. The epistemologist's self-reflective certainty does not vouch for the empirical plausibility of his further conclusions. That does not mean that these conclusions are wrong; I am only stressing their complete theoretical independence, which, so it appears to me, Habermas conceals. If my reasoning is correct, then neither the objectivation of the lifeworld by the historian, nor its objectivation by the epistemologist, leads us to abandon the participant's point of view for that of the kind of observer who is posited by a functionalist systems theory. We remain, then, participant observers with respect to all socio-cultural processes, even at the highest levels of macrosocial complexes of relations. We are compelled neither by the alleged limitations of the theory of action, nor by the inevitability of functionalist analyses, nor by the theoretical sterility of the participant's perspective, to grasp societal processes conceptually in any way other than in categories of action and of social order grounded in action. Action and social order can be normatively judged according to the degree of which the results of action and the effects of social order can be legitimated from the perspective of the individuals concerned and of course ourselves, that is, the degree to which those results and effects are rational when judged from that perspective.[41]

This critical examination of Jürgen Habermas's *Theory of Communicative Action* sought to call attention to difficulties in the fundamental theoretical argumentations presented in that work, and so to place in doubt the automatism with which a theory of communicative action yields the dualism of lifeworld and system, and the historical diagnosis that the present period is marked by a painless uncoupling of system and lifeworld, as well as by dangers of a 'colonization' of the lifeworld. It would, of course, be inconsistent, after repeated declarations that argumentations on these different levels can be separated, now to draw substantive conclusions about the characteristics of the present era. The programme that has been suggested, namely that of a more broadly based theory of action, the drawing of a clearer distinction between the superseding of the philosophy of consciousness and the intersubjective turn, of a theory of social order centred on the constitution of collective actors – this programme, too, yields no substantive conclusions. Such conclusions likewise could be no more than the speculative transferral of metatheoretical decisions into empirical assertions. On the other hand, it goes without saying that the way this programme is structured is motivated by substantive empirical and normative premises. What this leads to has already been fomulated by several authors:[42] they doubt the alleged ease with which the 'monetary-bureaucratic' complex is uncoupled from the lifeworld; they criticize the lack of a dimension of 'intra-systemic' problems and contradictions; they lament the defensiveness of an argumentation that no longer poses the question of democratic control of economy and state; they point out the hypostatization of 'system' and 'lifeworld' into the societal domains, of state and economy, on the one hand, and the public sphere and the private sphere (family, neighbourhood, voluntary associations), on the other hand (vol. II, p. 309); they find fault with the abstractness of a position that, while it correctly interprets capitalist modernization as one-sided rationalization, supplies no criteria with which meaningful degrees of differentiation could be established.[43] I find all these criticisms convincing, but I do not want to treat them here. The only question which a metatheoretically oriented critique should not, on principle, avoid answering, is whether phenomena that are convincingly analysed by the criticized theory could at all be understood also within an alternative theoretical framework. If we identify the autonomous rationalization of the lifeworld, the painless uncoupling of the monetary-bureaucratic complex from the lifeworld, and the 'painful' colonization of the lifeworld as the three principal notions guiding Habermas's analyses of the problems of the present within the framework of the concepts 'system' and 'lifeworld', then, after the validity of a theory of society proceeding on these two levels has been placed in doubt, we can examine these notions separately with respect to whether they can be transferred into an alternative theoretical framework. I consider Habermas's explanations of an autonomous rationalization of the lifeworld in the dimensions of value-generalization, universalization of law and morality, and progressive individuation, to be an important accomplishment. However, the stress Habermas places on the autonomy of these rationalization processes springs precisely from the pressure exerted against this direction by functionalist models. If one rejects these, however, then it is not the deductive definition of microsocial phenomena on the basis of macrosocial functions that guides us, but a reconstruction of the manner in which societal conditions that have become autonomous can as such issue from the complex of normative traditions and everyday actions, of concrete historical situations and actions, and do so in the face of possibilities of resistance to them that are produced, ever anew. The upside-down world of apparently autonomous social structures is then left behind, at least theoretically. The uncoupling of economic development and the governmental decision-making process from the results of the communication of society's members by means of the privatization of structurally crucial economic decisions and/or undemocratic political structures, as well as the repercussions of 'thoroughgoing capitalization' and bureaucratization in all domains of society, do not require for their explanation the dualism of a theory based on 'system' and 'lifeworld'. There remain, then, the thesis of the 'painless uncoupling' of the processes of material reproduction. This uncoupling is presented by Habermas not as a matter of empirical fact, but as a theoretical inference drawn from the nature of the media of communication, money and power. However, this uncoupling cannot be reconstructed in this fashion in a theoretical framework that refers all phenomena of social order to an actual or virtual collective will of society's members. In such a theoretical framework, 'money' and 'power' would remain at the same analytical level as the other media of communication of systems theory; that is, they would serve to ease the burden borne by communication among society's members, but they could not serve as a substitute for that communication without significant consequences. Surely, the thesis of the painless uncoupling of system and lifeworld cannot have been the cause of Jürgen Habermas's enormous theoretical effort.

7 Complexity and Democracy: or the Seducements of Systems Theory

Thomas McCarthy

There is a spectre haunting Habermas's *The Theory of Communicative Action*, a close relation to the totally reified world that haunted Western Marxism's original reception of Max Weber. In the 1940s Horkheimer and Adorno had in effect abandoned Marx for Weber on the question of the emancipatory potential of modern rationality. The spread of instrumental reason represented for them the core of a domination generalized to all spheres of life. Habermas agrees that the sociopathologies of modern life can be traced to processes of rationalization; however, he stands with Marx in regarding them as due not to rationalization as such but to the peculiar nature of capitalist modernization – and thus in regarding them as treatable through transforming capitalist relations of production. In this respect his position is closest to that of Lukàcs, who attempted to integrate Weber's analysis of rationalization into a Marxian framework. Reconceptualizing rationalization in terms of reification, and tracing this back to the universalization of the commodity form in capitalist society, Lukàcs too could regard the deformations of modern life as specifically capitalist in origin and thus as reversible. It is in fact one of the principal aims of *The Theory of Communicative Action* to develop a more adequate version of the theory of reification. This 'second attempt to appropriate Weber in the spirit of Western Marxism' has three major ambitions: (a) to break with the philosophy of consciousness in favour of a theory of *communicative rationality* which is no longer tied to and limited by the subjectivistic and individualistic premises of modern philosophy and social theory; (b) to go beyond the primarily *action-theoretic* conceptualization of *rationalization* in Weber and his Marxist heirs, back to Marx, in order to recapture the *systems-theoretic* dimension of his analysis of capitalist society – in less historical terms, to reconnect action theory with systems theory by constructing a 'two-level concept of society' that integrates the lifeworld and system paradigms; and (c) to construct, on this basis, a critical theory of modern society which reconceptualizes *reification* as a 'colonization of the lifeworld' by forces emanating from the economic and political subsystems, that is, which traces the sociopathologies of modern life back to the growing subordination of the lifeworld to systemic imperatives of material reproduction.

In this paper I would like to consider several of the ideas basic to the second and third endeavours, with the aim of identifying some potentially troublesome weak spots. I shall be particularly concerned with problems stemming from the appropriation of systems theory. In his early essays Habermas was already concerned to dispel the spectre of a cybernetically self-regulated organization of society, a 'negative utopia of technical control over history' in which humans no longer occupied the position of *homo faber* but that of *homo fabricatus*, totally integrated into their technical machine.[1] This same concern came to the fore in his debate with Luhmann,[2] in the last part of *Legitimation Crisis*,[3] and in his Hegel Prize lecture of 1974;[4] and it has been at least a subtext of most major publications since. It is this spectre that he seeks to come to terms with in *The Theory of Communicative Action*.[5] His strategy is to enter into a pact of sorts with social systems theory: certain areas are marked out within which it may move about quite freely, on condition that it keeps entirely away from others. I want to argue that the terms of this pact are sometimes unclear, that it cedes too much territory to systems theory, and that as a result critical theory is left in an unnecessarily defensive position.

The main lines of Haberma's proposal for connecting the lifeworld and system paradigms are first sketched out with reference to Durkheim's account of how the forms of social solidarity change with the division of labour.

> Durkheim's question, if not his answer, is instructive. It directs our attention to the empirical connections between stages of system differentiation and forms of social integration. We can analyse these connections only if we distinguish mechanisms for coordinating action that bring the *orientations* of participants into harmony from mechanisms that stabilize the non-intended interdependencies of action by way of functionally interconnecting action *consequences*. The integration of an action system is established in the one case through a normatively secured or communicatively achieved consensus and in the other through a non-normative regulation of individual decisions that goes beyond the actors' consciousness. This distinction between *social integration* and *system integration* ... makes it necessary to differentiate the concept of society itself ... [On the one hand] society is conceived from the participant's perspective of the acting subject as the *lifeworld of a social group*. On the other hand, from the observer's perspective of the non-participant, society can be conceived as a *system of actions* in which a functional significance accrues to a given action according to its contribution to system maintenance. (117)

Generally speaking, the problem of 'integration' concerns the mutual adjustment of diverse parts to form a unified, harmonious whole. It moved to the centre of sociological theory with Durkheim's discussions of organic and mechanical solidarity. The latter was rooted in collective consciousness, in shared values and norms, beliefs and sentiments, in individuals' agreement with and acceptance of the group's basic goals, ideals, practices. The former was based on the interdependence of specialized roles, such that the diverse activities of different individuals complemented one another and fit together into a harmonious whole. It was clear to Durkheim that the degree of socio-cultural homogeneity required for mechanical solidarity was increasingly improbable in modern society. And yet he was not willing to view organic solidarity as a full functional equivalent demanded by the division of labour. Thus he rejected Spencer's idea of wholly spontaneous integration of individual interests brought about entirely through mechanisms like the market, that is, not through the conscious harmonizing of value orientations, but through the functional coordination of the aggregate effects of action. For Durkheim, organic solidarity also needed to be anchored in a basic normative consensus. It seemed evident, however, that capitalist modernization destroyed traditional normative foundations without generating suitable modern replacements. The inevitable result was anomie, against which he could in the end only campaign.

Like Durkheim, Habermas rejects the idea of a society integrated solely via the unintended functional interdependence of consequences of action – beyond the consciousness of actors, so to speak, rather than in and through it. He wants to argue instead that every society needs to be integrated in both ways, socially and systemically, and thus is confronted with the fundamental problem of how to combine them. It is this problem that dominates volume II of *The Theory of Communicative Action*. The role of Spencer is played for Habermas by Niklas Luhmann, who has argued at length that modern societies have to develop alternatives to normative integration, which is hopelessly inadequate for dealing with high levels of complexity. The 'world society developing today', Luhmann insists, faces problems that can be solved only at the level of system integration.

The basic reality of society can no longer be said to lie in its capacity to generate and sustain interaction systems. As a consequence modern society cannot be grasped as the sum of personal encounters. This is expressed, for example, in the gulf separating the ethics of face-to-face interaction from objective social requirements in (say) economics, politics or science. In view of this discrepancy, moralistic demands for more 'personal participation' in social processes are hopelessly out of touch with social reality.[6]

If this is so, Habermas noted in his Hegel Prize lecture, then 'individuals henceforth belong only to the environment of their social systems. In relation to them society takes on an objectivity that can no longer be brought into the intersubjective context of life, for it is no longer related to subjectivity.'[7] This 'dehumanization of society' is the systems-theoretic version of that totally reified society Western Marxists had projected in terms of the philosophy of consciousness. To counter it, Habermas undertakes to demonstrate that society cannot be represented exclusively, or even fundamentally, as a boundary-maintaining system. It must be grasped also, and primordially, as the lifeworld of a social group. The central problem of social theory thus becomes how to combine the two conceptual strategies, that is, how to conceive of society as simultaneously socially and systemically integrated.

In earlier writings Habermas made clear the problems that the system paradigm poses for empirical social analysis, which depends importantly on our ability to identify boundaries, goal states and structures essential for continued existence. In *Legitimation Crisis*, for example, he wrote:

> The difficulty of clearly determining the boundaries and persistence of social systems in the language of systems theory raises fundamental doubts about the usefulness of a systems-theoretic concept of social crisis. For organisms have clear spatial and temporal boundaries; their continued existence is characterized by goal values that vary only within empirically specifiable tolerances ... But when systems maintain themselves through altering both boundaries and structural continuity, their identity becomes blurred. The same system modification can be conceived of equally well as a learning process and change or as a dissolution process and collapse of the system.[8]

Any adaptive system has to be able to mediate the relations among parts, whole and environment via 'information flows' so as to 'select' and 'code' stimuli from the environment and to direct its responses to them. What distinguishes societies from organisms is the peculiarly symbolic form of the linkages between the system, its parts and the environment. It is with this in mind that Luhmann introduced *meaning* as a fundamental category of *social* systems theory – with a functionalist twist to be sure: meaning is a mode of reducing complexity peculiar to social systems. Habermas criticized this bit of conceptual legerdemain at some length.[9] He argued, in fact, that it is precisely the dimension of meaning that sets the limits to the application of systems theory to society. For one thing, the whole notion of self-maintenance becomes fuzzy, even metaphorical at the socio-cultural level, where self-preservation is not merely a physical matter. 'The "clearly defined" problem of death and a corresponding criterion of survival are lacking because societies never reproduce "naked" life, but always a culturally defined life.'[10] That is to say, the definition of life 'is no longer pregiven with the specific equipment of the species. Instead, continual attempts to define cultural life are a necessary component of the very life process of socially related individuals.'[11] And yet functionalist analysis requires a reliable determination of essential structures and goal states if there is to be an 'objective' problem to serve as its point of reference. It is for this reason, among others, that the empirical usefulness of the system paradigm at the socio-cultural level has been quite limited and can, according to Habermas, be enhanced only by combining the system and the lifeworld paradigms (that is, by *deriving* the former from the latter). It is only by doing so that we can get at the historically variable interpretative schemes in which societies understand themselves, secure their identities and determine what counts for them as human life.

'Meaning' causes problems not only for the identification of goal states, but for the identification of the boundaries of systems as well. The boundaries of socio-cultural systems are blurry 'because the determination of symbolically constituted limits of meaning brings with it fundamental hermeneutic difficulties' – and this obviously causes problems for empirical systems analysis. In this respect, too, if it is not connected with action theory, systems theory becomes empirically questionable, a play of cybernetic words that only serves to produce reformulations of problems that it does not really help to resolve.[12] The same holds true for the structural features of social systems. Social structures are, after all, patterns of interaction that are relatively stable at a given time. But these patterns may be altered or dismantled as well as sustained by the ongoing interactions of members. This has motivated theorists of various stripes to focus attention on the micro-processes underlying not only the structuring, but the restructuring and destructuring of social systems. 'Process' here points to 'the actions and interactions of the components of an ongoing system in which varying degrees of structuring arise, persist, dissolve or change'.[13] Seen in this light, 'society becomes a continuous morphogenic process'. The implications for the study of social order are not difficult to see: 'Social order is not simply normatively specified and automatically maintained, but is something that must be 'worked at', continually reconstructed.'[14] This holds for formal organizations as well. For example, Walter Buckley summarizes the results of a study of 'The Hospital and Its Negotiated Order' as follows:

> The hospital, like any organization, can be visualized as a hierarchy of status and power, of rules, roles and organizational goals. But it is also a locale for an ongoing complex of transactions among differentiated types of actors ... The rules supposed to govern the actions of the professionals were found to be far from extensive, clearly stated or binding; hardly anyone knew all the extant rules or the applicable situations and sanctions. Some rules previously administered would fall into disuse, receive administrative reiteration, or be created anew in a crisis situation. As in any organization, rules were selectively evoked, broken and/or ignored to suit the defined needs of the personnel. Upper administrative levels especially avoided periodic attempts to have rules codified and formalized, for fear of restricting the innovation and improvisation believed necessary to the care of patients ... In sum, the area of action covered by clearly defined rules was very small ... the rules ordering actions to this end [patient care] were the subject of continual negotiations – being argued, stretched, ignored or lowered as the occasion seemed to demand. As elsewhere, rules failed to act as universal prescriptions, but required judgment as to their applicability to the specific case.[15]

This is indicative of a general line of attack on mainstream organization research taken by action-theorists in the phenomenological, ethnomethodological and symbolic interactionist traditions, among others. Their studies have shown formally organized domains of action to be 'transactional milieux where numerous agreements are constantly being established, renewed, reviewed, revoked and revised.' The formal framework of rules and roles does serve as a point of reference for actual transactions; it is a central element in the 'daily negotiations' through which it is *at the same time maintained and modified.* Far from adequately depicting actual patterns of interaction in the organizations to which they refer, formal organizational schemes are used by participants as

> generalized formulae to which all sorts of problems can be brought for solution ... [They] are schemes of interpretation that competent and entitled users can invoke in yet unknown ways whenever it suits their purposes ... When we consider the set of highly schematic rules subsumed under the concept of rational organization, we can readily see an open realm of free play for relating an infinite variety of performances to rules as responses to these rules. In this field of games of representation and interpretation ... extending to the rule the respect of compliance, while finding in the rule the means for doing whatever need be done, is the gambit that characterizes organizational acumen.[16]

Habermas grants, to be sure, that the question of actual behaviour in organizational settings is a matter for empirical investigation, and he acknowledges that existing studies have shown the classical model of bureaucracy to be strongly idealized. But he seems to suppose that the systems-theoretic model will escape this fate; at least he does not draw the same conclusions with regard to it, as it seems to me he might. Are the membership rules (boundaries) and legal regulations defining formal organizations any different in these respects from other rules and laws? There is no obvious reason for thinking they should be. Habermas insists that however fluid, fleeting flexible action within organizational settings may be, it always transpires 'under the premisses' of formal regulations, which can be appealed to by members. While this *is* certainly a ground for distinguishing behaviour within organizational settings from behaviour outside them, it does not of itself warrant interpreting this distinction as one between a system and its environment. The action-theoretic accounts to which we have referred suggest that the 'buffer zone' of organizational 'indifference' to personality and individual life history, to culture and tradition, to morality and convention is frequently no more effective than the military barrier erected by the American Armed Forces between North and South Vietnam – much of what is to be kept out is already within, and much of the rest can enter as the need arises. If organizations are systems, they are, unlike organisms, systems with porous and shifting boundaries; and if they are constituted by positive law, the legal regulations in question are not merely ideal presuppositions, but elements – very important elements, to be sure – in the representations and interpretations that members deploy, at times with strategic intent, at times in the search for consensus. My point, then, is *not* that there are no important differences to be marked here, but that these systems-theoretic concepts may not be the best way to mark them.

There may be some plausibility to characterizing the market as 'norm-free,' as an ethically neutralized system of action in which individuals interrelate on the basis of egocentric calculations of utlity, in which subjectively uncoordinated individual decisions are integrated functionally. The question I wish to raise in this section is whether anything like this description fits *political* life in modern society. Whereas capitalist economic relations were institutionalized as 'a sphere of legally domesticated, permanent competition between strategically acting private persons' (178), political relations were grounded on the rule of law, basic human rights, popular sovereignty, and other 'moral-practical' consensual foundations. What is it about contemporary capitalism that could make the theoretical assimilation of economics and politics at all plausible?

It is remarkable that Habermas has little to say in *The Theory of Communicative Action* about the political system as such, given that its inclusion in the 'basic' functional domain of material reproduction is central to his reconceptualization of Marx. But what he does say seems consistent with what he has said before – e.g. in *Legitimation Crisis* – and it is thus possible to reconstruct his position, at least in broad outline. The first thing we note is that he usually refers to the 'political system' only when he is discussing problems of legitimation in social-welfare state mass democracies (e.g. 344ff.). Outside of that context he typically talks of the 'administrative system', the 'state apparatus', the 'state administration', or the like. And, in fact, the colonization diagnosis is consistently rendered in terms of the subordination of the lifeworld to the economic and *administrative* subsystems. What is at play here, it appears, is a version of the distinction, familiar among system theorists, between administration and politics in the narrow sense. Thus Parsons specifies the function of the political system in terms of effective attainment of collective goals. The medium of interchange specific to this system is power, 'the generalized capacity to secure the performance of binding obligations by units in a system of collective organization when the obligations are legitimized with reference to their bearing on collective goals and where in case of recalcitrance there is a presumption of enforcement by negative situational sanctions.'[17] The political function is centred in the specific role of office, elective and appointive, with the power to make and implement collectively binding decisions. The political (elective) and bureaucratic (appointive) components of the political system are differentiated out as complementary subsystems, the elected component supplying the 'non-bureaucratic top' of the bureaucratic organization. Thus we have a political system composed of an administrative bureaucracy responsible to elected officers. It stands in relation to other parts of society via the interchange of inputs and outputs over its boundaries. In particular, it requires from the public generalized support and the advocacy of general policies, while it supplies to it effective leadership and binding decisions.[18]

Similarly, if somewhat more cynically, we find in Luhmann a basic differentiation of the political system into politics and administration. The enormous complexity of modern society has to be reduced through authoritative decision-making. Power, a reduction of complexity binding on

others, is a medium of communication that enables decisions to be transmitted – the powerholder's decision is accepted by subordinates as a
premiss for their own decision-making.[19] In modern political systems there
is a fundamental differentiation of roles for bureaucratic administration, on
the one hand, and electoral politics with its specifically political organizations such as parties and interest groups, on the other. The former is
specialized in 'elaborating and issuing binding decisions according to politically predetermined criteria,' the latter in 'building political support
for programs and decisions'.[20] Luhmann regards the public, in certain
of its complementary roles (e.g. 'taxpayer, proponent of resolutions,
complainant, voter, writer of letters to the editor, supporter of interest
groups'), as part of the political system.[21] In complex societies politics and
administration must be kept structurally and functionally separated. Political parties specialize in securing a diffuse mass support for elected leaders,
the state apparatus in carrying out their programmes and decisions.

In *Legitimation Crisis* Habermas explicitly takes issue with Luhmann's
insistence on a strict separation of administration from politics;[22] but his
own descriptive model of advanced capitalist societies seems to concede
that some such separation does in fact obtain.[23] Thus he distinguishes the
administrative system, which is primarily responsible for regulating, complementing, substituting for the economic system, and the 'legitimation
system,' which ensures mass support for this while shielding the administrative system from effective democratic participation. 'Formally democratic' institutions and procedures secure both a diffuse mass loyalty and the
requisite independence of administrative decision-making processes from
the specific interests of the public. They are democratic in form, but not in
substance. The public realm, whose functions have been reduced largely to
periodic plebiscites, is 'structurally depoliticized.'

We find a similar picture in *The Theory of Communicative Action*. The
state apparatus is said to be functionally specialized in the realization of
collective goals via the medium of binding decisions or power (171).
Central to its tasks *in advanced capitalist societies* is that of complementing
the market and, when necessary, filling the functional gaps therein. This it
must do while preserving the primacy of private investment and the dynamic of capital accumulation. Under these circumstances state intervention
in the economy takes the *indirect* form of manipulating the boundary
conditions of private enterprise and the *reactive* form of crisis avoidance
strategies or of compensating for dysfunctional side effects (343–4). At the
same time, the modern capitalist state requires legitimation through democratic electoral processes involving competition among political parties.
There is, writes Habermas, an 'irresolvable tension' between these two
principles of societal integration: capitalism and democracy. For the
normative sense of democracy entails that 'the fulfillment of functional
necessities in systemically integrated domains of action will find its limit
in the integrity of the lifeworld', whereas specifically capitalist growth
dynamics can be preserved only if 'the drive mechanism of the economic
system is kept as free as possible from lifeworld restrictions, that is, from
demands for legitimation directed at the administrative action system'

(345). These opposing principles or imperatives clash head-on in the public sphere, where, according to Habermas, 'public opinion' and 'the will of the people' are a result of *both* communication processes in which values and norms take shape *and* the production of mass loyalty by the political system (346). But he clearly continues to regard the latter as predominant: 'As the private sphere is undermined and eroded by the economic system, so is the public sphere by the administrative system. The bureaucratic disempowering and desiccation of spontaneous processes of opinion- and will-formation expands the scope for mobilizing mass loyalty and makes it easier to uncouple political decisions from concrete, identity-forming contexts of life' (325). The possibilities of participation legally contained in the role of citizen are neutralized. The political content of mass democracy shrinks to social-welfare programmes necessitated by the disparities, burdens and insecurities caused by the economic system. These are compensated for in the coin of economically produced value. As long as capital continues to expand under political protection, as long as there is an adequate supply of compensatory use values to distribute, political alienation does not develop explosive force. Thus the dual task of the state is to 'head off the directly negative effects on the lifeworld of a capitalistically organized occupational system and the dysfunctional side-effects of economic growth steered by capital accumulation, and to do so without damaging the organizational form, the structure, or the drive mechanism of economic production' (347–8).

The correspondences between this assessment of the functions and limits of politics in modern society and those put forward by many system theorists are evident. On the other hand, Habermas's diagnosis is also broadly consistent with leading Marxist theories of the state. The reduction of politics in the narrow sense to the generation of non-specific mass support and the competition for top administrative positions, of the manifest content of politics to the social-welfare state agenda, and of the basic tasks of the state to securing the conditions of capital accumulation while compensating for its dysfunctional side effects have been discussed in both traditions.[24] Of course, in the one case this is meant to be only a description, in the other it is also a denunciation. In Habermas too it is both a description of basic *tendencies* within advanced capitalism and a critique of the consequent disempowering of democratic institutions and processes. His normative point of reference for the latter is not a complete absorption of the system into the lifeworld; in his view, every complex modern society will have to give over certain economic and administrative functions to functionally specified and media-steered domains of action.

There are, broadly, two sorts of questions we might raise in connection with the views on politics expressed in *The Theory of Communicative Action*: questions regarding their adequacy as an account of actually existing political systems, and questions regarding their implications for the utopian content of our political tradition. I am not in a position to deliver any final verdict on the theoretical and empirical adequacy of Habermas's account of the state and politics in capitalist society, but I would like to register some doubts. Recall that for the social systems theorist the differentiation of the political system into bureaucratic administration, party politics and the public is a differentiation among functionally specialized *subsystems* – that is to say, the conceptual tools of systems theory are used for analysing all domains and their interconnections. For Habermas, by contrast, the public sphere belongs to the *lifeworld*, which is indeed uncoupled from the administrative system, but not as a subsystem within the political system – that is to say, we require different categories and principles for analysing the different domains. In one domain interaction is systemically integrated, formally organized, and media-steered, in the other it is oriented to mutual understanding, whether traditionally secured or communicatively achieved. Thus one clue that might be followed in checking the adequacy of Habermas's characterization of the political system is the part which one or the other type of action coordination plays in that domain.

Is interaction in the political sphere systemically rather than socially integrated? Even if we grant for the moment the very reduced – systems-theoretic and Marxist – conception of politics in advanced capitalism to which Habermas more or less subscribes, and further confine our attention to its administrative side, the matter seems ambiguous at best. For one might still ask: Is interaction within large administrative bureaucracies coordinated via functional interconnection of its effects *rather than* via the orientations of actors? Is it integrated like the market, via non-normative steering of subjectively uncoordinated individual decisions *rather than* via normative consensus? The question only has to be posed in this way, it seems to me, to raise doubts about any either/or answer. Obviously much of the activity of such bureaucracies typically involves conscious planning to achieve organization goals. These goals are at least sometimes known to and accepted by organization members – in fact Habermas, following Parsons, designates the 'real value' in terms of which power is to be redeemed as 'the realization of collective goals'; 'effectiveness of goal-attainment' is the corresponding 'generalized value'. It is difficult to see why interaction within these organizations is not socially integrated to the degree that the collective goals really are collective (or at least are thought to be) and the interest in attaining them is broadly shared by members. Habermas is at pains to show that 'power needs to be legitimized and therefore requires a more demanding normative anchoring than does money' (271). Whereas the exchange relation does not obviously disadvantage either of the participants and is apparently in each's interest, subordinates are structurally disadvantaged in relation to powerholders – one gives orders, the other obeys. If the authority of office is not to rely solely on the threat of sanctions (which is, according to Habermas, an inadequate basis for stability) a sense of 'obligation' to follow orders is required. 'Subordinates can examine the goals themselves from normative points of view' and determine whether they 'lie in the general interest', whether they are legitimate. The differences from the money medium are evident. 'Whereas in the case of exchange, judgements of interest do not require mutual understanding among the partners to the exchange, the question of what lies in the general interest requires consensus among the members of a collective ... Evidently power as a medium still retains something of the power to command ... connected with normed rather than simple imperatives' (271– 2). In volume I, the contrast between normatively authorized and simple imperatives is presented as a paradigm for the difference between communicative and strategic action, and in volume II, in the discussion of steering media, the issuing and acceptance of orders is again used as an example of communicative interaction (262). If this is so, it is difficult to understand why interaction mediated by legitimized power is systemically and not socially integrated.

There is another respect in which Habermas grants the premises, but resists drawing the conclusion: the relation of formal and informal organization. It is now a generally accepted fact that the formal aspects of social organizations – the rationally ordered systems of norms and roles, rules and regulations, programmes and positions – are only one side of the coin. The other side is the informal aspects – the concrete norms and values, rituals and traditions, sentiments and practices that inform interpersonal relations within the organization. Habermas notes this fact, but does not permit it to affect his judgement that 'Organizations detach themselves not only from cultural obligations and personality-specific attitudes and obligations, they also make themselves independent of lifeworld contexts by neutralizing informally habitual, ethically regulated action orientations' (309). They are 'domains of action neutralized against lifeworlds' (ibid.). He maintains this while at the same time conceding that 'even within formally organized domains of action, interactions are still interconnected by mechanisms of reaching understanding', without which 'the formally regulated social relations could not be maintained nor the organizational goals attained' (310). He grants that the question of the extent to which formal organization actually structures action and interaction within organizations is an empirical question that can by no means be answered deductively; and he even cites approvingly an empirical study which showed that in government organizations the discrepancies between the idealized model and actual behaviour were considerable (429, n. 6). Yet he insists that social-integrative mechanisms are put out of play in formal organizations; because 'action stands under the premises of a formally regulated domain,' it 'loses its validity basis' (310). That is, members act communicatively only 'with reservation'. They know that 'they *can* have recourse to formal regulations', that 'they are not *obliged* to achieve consensus with communicative means' (ibid.). And yet it seems obvious that there are also situations in which organizational superiors can act authoritatively only 'with reservation', that is, in which they know they cannot achieve their goals without collegiality, cooperation, mutual understanding. The ratio of power to agreement in the actual operation of administrations seems, in short, to be a thoroughly empirical question which allows of no general answer – neither in regard to what is the case nor with regard to some single idea of what ought to be the case. But even if we restrict ourselves to the most bureaucratically hierarchized forms of organization it is not clear that the system integration vs. social integration contrast captures what is specific to them. Recall that system integration was said to stabilize non-intended interdependencies by way of functionally interconnecting the results of action. Correspondingly, systems analysis is supposed to get at these counterintuitive interdependencies by way of discovering the latent functions of action. None of this, it seems to me, fits 'just taking orders' within organizations any better than it does interaction in everyday contexts. We need a stronger theoretical link between 'formally organized' and 'systemically integrated' – stronger, that is, than the fact that the systems-theoretic paradigm has established itself in organization theory. To say that interaction within organizations is not coordinated primarily by traditionally pre-established consensus or by communicatively achieved consensus (in Habermas's strong sense) is not to say that it is not coordinated via actors' orientations at all – e.g. via the giving and taking of order, the threat and fear of sanctions.[25] Of course, the orientations are different in important respects from those which prevail outside hierarchical organizations. But getting at that difference is essential to understanding the type of action coordination within them. The integration of action orientations via everybody following orders seems no less an alternative to normative consensus than integration via latent functions. It is also clear that they need not coincide. I am not trying here to resurrect a pure Weberian model of bureaucratic administration against the now dominant functionalist models, but only to suggest that something of both is needed, neither is by itself adequate – and thus we cannot talk of formal organizations as being systemically *rather than* socially integrated.

Consider, finally, an even more extreme case, a strongly hierarchical, formally organized setting in which the actors have no clear idea of why they are ordered to do what they do. Are their actions then integrated via the stabilization of latent functions? This is not the most immediate answer. Supposing that the top generals, managers, bureaucrats or whatever have worked out and implemented a plan of action, successful coordination of the actions of diverse members might in part be attributed to their astuteness and the efficiency of their organization. This is at least as plausible as attributing it to the working of anonymous control mechanisms. Habermas often equates the fact that the objective sense of an action is not intuitively present to the actor with its being a matter of latent functionality. It could as well be present to other actors who have the authority or power to direct his/her actions.[26] All of this is meant merely to say that system integration and social integration, as they are defined by Habermas, seem to be extremes rather than alternatives that exhaust the field of possibilities: the denial of one does not entail the other. Moreover, if softened to correspond to the inside/outside differences in methodological perspectives, it seems clear that most, if not all, domains of social action can be looked at in both ways. Certainly, organizations, whether government bureaucracies or industrial corporations, can be viewed in action-theoretic terms as well as in systems-theoretic terms[27] – or rather, certainly in action-theoretic terms, very likely in functionalist terms, possibly in systems-theoretic terms as well. It goes without saying that all of this would apply *a fortiori* to the politics wing of the 'political system'.

There are also normative reasons why Habermas should be wary of conceptualizing administrative organization in systems-theoretic terms. He maintains that any complex society will require a high degree of system differentiation. Given what he says about the asymmetry between symbolic and material reproduction in this regard, it is presumably in regard to the latter that we shall have, in part, to rely on mechanisms of coordination other than building consensus in language – which, as he says, can be very time-consuming and is, in many situations, a 'luxury' that can ill be afforded. Surely he does not mean by this that we should aim to construct institutions whose functions are kept latent and in which members just take orders without regard to the legitimacy of goals and the like. In fact, Habermas strongly criticized Luhmann's Gehlenesque dictum: 'The latency of basic problems has the function of protecting structural decisions against insight and variation.'[28] He critically contrasted this 'counterenlightenment' view with the enlightenment goal of maximizing our self-understanding and our ability to 'make history with will and consciousness'.[29] It represents, he said, the most refined form of the technocratic consciousness that today serves to insulate practical questions from public discussion.[30]

Habermas has, it is true, retreated from the almost Fichtean notion of self-transparency that seemed to inform many passages of *Knowledge and Human Interests*. He has found a systematic place in his thought for the inevitably incomplete transparency of lifeworld backgrounds and the substrata of psychic life. The theory of communicative action does something similar, it seems to me, for formal organization and sytemic integration. We shall require economic and administrative mechanisms whose operation does not depend on directly reaching consensus about each decision. In particular, we should not think of direct or council democracy and workers' self-management as the only legitimate possibilities here. We may well need some forms of representative democracy and some forms of public administration. If one accepts this, the decisive question becomes: 'What forms?' And here I want to argue that Habermas has taken over so much of the conceptual arsenal of systems theory that he runs the risk of not being able to formulate in these terms an answer to this question that is compatible with his professed political ideals. I shall come back to this below; for now I want only to look at the question of latent vs. manifest functions. Habermas distances himself from Luhmann's arguments for the necessity of keeping basic problems latent. This is counter-enlightenment. He proposes instead that all problems of general societal significance be submitted to open, unrestricted discussion in a democratic public sphere. Presumably, collective goals would be agreed upon in such discussion and implemented through existing organs of administration. There is no room in this model for keeping functions that are manifest at one level latent at lower levels. So systems-theoretical analysis, which, in Habermas's view, is necessary only to get at latent functions, would exist only to transcend itself continually, that is, to make such interconnections manifest and thus open to discussion and reasoned acceptance or rejection. Perhaps Habermas wants to maintain that latent functions, like background assumptions, are unavoidable and can never be made manifest all at once. Then systems analysis, like presupposition analysis, would be an ongoing, unending task of self-clarification. Of course, this way of looking at things does nothing directly to answer the question we raised above concerning the type of administration that would be desirable in a genuinely democratic society. As I have tried to make clear, whatever answer to this question Habermas might want to advance, it should not be 'systemically rather than socially integrated'.

The normative inadequacy of system concepts for characterizing the institutions of a genuinely democratic society becomes even clearer when they are viewed in the light of Habermas's oft-declared option for some form of participatory democracy. In *Legitimation Crisis* he criticized elite theorists (from Pareto and Michels through Schumpeter and Weber to Lipset and Truman) in these words:

> Democracy in this view is no longer determined by the content of a form of life that takes into account the generalizable interests of all individuals. It counts now only as a method for selecting leaders and the accoutrements of leadership. By democracy is no longer understood the conditions under which all legitimate interests can be fulfilled by realizing the fundamental interest in self-determination and participation ... It is no longer tied to political equality in the sense of an equal distribution of political power, that is, of the chances to exercise power ... Democracy no longer has the goal of rationalizing authority through the participation of citizens in discursive processes of will-formation. It is intended instead to make compromises possible between ruling elites. Thus, the substance of classical democratic theory is finally surrendered. No longer all politically consequential decisions, but only those decisions of the government still defined as political are to be subject to democratic will-formation. In this way, a pluralism of elites replaces the self-determination of the people ...[31]

If self-determination, political equality, and the participation of citizens in decision-making processes are the hallmarks of true democracy, then a democratic government could not be a political *system* in Habermas's sense – that is, a domain of action differentiated off from other parts of society and preserving its autonomy in relation to them, while regulating its interchanges with them via delinguistified steering media like money and power. The idea of democratic participation in government decision-making can be spelled out in a number of different ways, from pyramidal council systems to competitive, participatory party systems in which leaders are effectively made responsible to the rank-and-file.[32] But each of them entails a loss of 'autonomy', 'dedifferentiation' for the political system. Why then does Habermas insist on the continued need for system differentiation in this domain?

One consideration seems to be practicality: how could a participatory democracy operate in a pluralistic society with millions of members sharing no common world view, with a highly differentiated modern culture etc.? There would, it seems, have to be *some* form of representative democracy, *some* type of party system, *some* way of selecting leaders with *some* measure of latitude for decision-making, *some* administrative apparatus for carrying out decisions etc. This is the point, I take it, of characterizing schemes in which all of this is simply thought away as 'utopian' in a negative sense. Even if this is granted, however, the size and shape of the 'some' in each case cannot be determined in an a priori manner. As Habermas has himself stated, this is an open question that can be decided only through learning processes that test the limits of the realizability of the utopian elements of our tradition. Against Luhmann, he argued that even on grounds of effectiveness there is no conclusive argument for shielding the administrative system from participation.[33] Numerous studies have shown that there are very real and rather narrow limits to centralized administrative planning. They may well be inherent in it. This raises the question of whether participation might not actually enhance planning capacity in some situations. As Habermas noted, the rationalizing effect

is difficult to determine, for democratization would, on the one hand, dismantle the avoidable complexity ... produced by the uncontrolled inner dynamic of the economic process. But at the same time it would bring the unavoidable (i.e. not specific to a system) complexity of generalized discursive processes of will-formation into play. Of course the balance does not have to be negative if the limits to complexity ... built into administration are reached very soon. In this case, one complexity that follows unavoidably from the logic of unrestrained communication would be overtaken, as it were, by another complexity that follows as unavoidably from the logic of comprehensive planning.[34]

In short, there is no general answer to the question of where and when and how participatory planning may be more effective than non-participatory planning. It can only be answered by testing and learning in different and changing circumstances.

Furthermore, even where it is less effective in an instrumental sense, we may favour it on other grounds. System complexity is merely one point of view from which to judge 'progress'.[35] Even in the realm of natural evolution, the degree of complexity is not a sufficient criterion for level of development, since 'increasing complexity in physical organization or mode of life often proves to be an evolutionary dead-end'.[36] In the case of social evolution, growth of system complexity must, on Habermas's own principles, be subordinate to the communicative rationalization of life as a measure of progress. Realistically there will have to be compromises and trade-offs. The 'selection pressure on complex systems of action in a world that is contingent',[37] that is, the problem of survival, cannot be wished away. But for critical social theory, the 'utopian' idea of self-conscious self-determination must remain a regulative idea, in light of which we might at least recognize when we are compromising and why.

Social systems theory represents today, no less than it did in 1971, 'the *Hochform* of a technocratic consciousness' that enters the lists against any tendencies toward democratization and promotes a depoliticization of the public sphere by defining practical questions from the start as technical questions.[38] Why then does Habermas now regard it as desirable, or perhaps even necessary, to integrate it into Critical Theory?

The reason clearly cannot be the proved fruitfulness of this approach as a framework for empirical social research. Nothing has happened since 1967 to absolve Parsons from the suspicion of a 'fetishism of concepts' about which Habermas remarked in *On the Logic of the Social Sciences*: 'If one takes seriously his intention, there is in fact a ridiculous imbalance between the towering mass of empty categorial boxes and the slim empirical content they accommodate.'[39] Nor has Luhmann's conceptual expansionism – which, as Habermas remarks, verges on conceptual imperialism – helped matters in this regard. Even in the home territory of social systems analysis, the theory of formal organizations, the question of its empirical-theoretical fruitfulness is, at best, an open one. The disproportion between the complex conceptual arsenal and our ability to 'operationalize' and actually use the notions of 'input' and 'output', 'feedback loops' and 'control mechanisms', 'environments' and 'adaptive capacity' is generally recognized even by its proponents.[40] The abstractness, vagueness, and empirical indeterminacy of such concepts have rendered the predictive power of system models questionable, to say the least.[41] One of the problems, it is widely agreed, is the neglect of internal factors – structures, processes, problems – by organizational systems theorists. In their reaction to classical theory's overemphasis on such factors and its neglect of the impact of an organization's environment on how it is structured and operated and on what goals it pursues, they have too often gone to the opposite extreme: 'Rational planning and decision-making appear almost not to exist . . . and little if any attention is given to interpersonal relations among members.'[42] In short, social systems theory does not recommend itself on grounds of empirical-analytical fruitfulness and predictive power, even in the favoured setting of formal organizations.

On what grounds then does it recommend itself? Why has systems theory proved to be so popular in the theory of complex organizations? Part of the answer might be its appropriateness to 'the type of problems that management encounters in the newer, more technologically complex industries. Here the issue has shifted from efficient task fulfilment to the consideration of structures with the necessary flexibility to ensure system "survival" in the face of rapid change.'[43] Be that as it may, the use of systems theory in the study of formal organizations has in fact been largely 'normative-analytic' rather than 'empirical-analytic'. Though boundaries and goal states cannot be empirically *ascertained*, they can be stipulated or *set*. Systems analysis can then be used as an aid in planning: it provides what Habermas once called 'second-order technical knowledge'. This cannot be what recommends it to him.

Its seductiveness for him derives, I think, from its perceived theoretical virtues. He justified the role that Parsons's work plays in volume II of *The Theory of Communicative Action* by praising it as 'unrivalled in respect to level of abstraction and differentiatedness, social-theoretical range and systematic quality, while at the same time connecting up with the literature in particular areas of research' (199). Likewise, it seems to be Luhmann's conceptual and theoretical virtuosity that Habermas admires above all else. There is of course always the possibility that these virtues are just the other face of the vices mentioned above, that is, one side of that 'ridiculous imbalance' that he noted in 1967. In what follows, however, I shall try to arouse some suspicion concerning system theory's theoretical virtue itself. My strategy will be to refurbish some of the familiar objections to functionalism that Habermas himself once raised, for it seems to me that they have lost nothing of their power.

In the first part of this paper I discussed the lower degree of structural fixity in social as contrasted with biological systems. Change of structure can as well be regarded as a regeneration of the original system as its transformation into a new system. There seems to be no objective way of deciding which description is correct. In *Legitimation Crisis* Habermas suggested that this problem might be overcome if we combined systems analysis with lifeworld analysis in the framework of a theory of social evolution which took account of both the expansion of steering capacity and the development of worldviews. The idea seemed to be that we could then get at the historically variable interpretations of social life in a systematic way and thus ascertain the goal states of social systems in a non-arbitrary manner. Without going into great detail, I would like simply to register my doubt that the problem can be solved in this way. A developmental logic of worldviews and normative structures is not going to help fix the goal states of social systems in a precise empirical manner since at any given formal state of development countless different material conceptions of the good (social) life are possible. Nor will concrete lifeworld analysis do the trick if members' conceptions of social life and its essential structures are multifarious, fluid, flexible, tailored to varied situations, and so forth – as they typically are in modern life. It seems obvious that members of social organizations which are undergoing change may themselves strongly disagree as to whether or not they are also 'in crisis'.

Systems theory is thought (by Habermas, too, apparently) to have overcome at least one central problem of classical functional analysis, which one of its practiners, Emile Durkheim, expressed as follows:

> To show how a fact is useful is not to explain how it originated or why it is what it is. The uses which it serves presuppose the specific properties characterizing it, but do not create them. The need we have of things cannot give them existence, nor can it confer their specific nature upon them. It is to causes of another sort that they owe their existence.[44]

What Habermas refers to as the contributions made by the consequences of patterns of action to the maintenance of the social system cannot of themselves explain why these patterns exist. If the functional consequences are manifest (intended), the explanation presents no particular problems; but if they are latent (unintended, unrecognized), we still have to wonder why such a useful pattern of activity ever arose and why it continues to exist. The systems theorist has an answer ready: Like any cybernetic process, social processes have their 'feedback loops', through which the results of each stage of a cycle are the causes of the next. As Hempel and Nagel pointed out some time ago, however, there are very demanding logical requirements on this type of explanation, and they are not met in social systems research. One might point, in particular, to the unsatisfied requirement of specifying empirically and with some degree of precision the feedback and control mechanisms which are supposedly at work to keep the system directed toward its supposed goals. Without this, social systems theory can 'achieve little more than a translation of old ideas into a new jargon'.[45]

It has generally made sense to approach biological systems as unified, integrated, adapted systems which have been naturally selected, and thus to treat their structures and processes as contributing somehow to system maintenance (though doubts have arisen about the usefulness of systems theory here as well). Does the same approach make sense with respect to social systems? Is biocybernetics going to be any more fruitful a model of society than classical mechanics was? It has some of the same drawbacks, for instance the traditional ideological twist of treating what is social, and thus potentially the object of human will, as natural, and thus purely a matter of objectified relations, objects and events. Habermas hopes to dissolve this solidity in the waters of action theory. But it may just prove to be insoluble. As I have tried to argue, traces of systems-theoretic objectification can be detected in Habermas' treatment of 'the political system'. And they are still present in his extrapolation to political processes in postcapitalist society, which are dealt with solely in terms of the relations between a government administration conceived as *system* and a public sphere conceived as *lifeworld*. The categories remain the same; only the direction of control changes. This approach was suggested in the Hegel Prize lecture of 1974[46] and in *The Theory of Communicative Action* of 1981[47] and is made explicit in a recent essay:

If the inner dynamic of public administration is also to be checked and indirectly controlled, the requisite reflective and steering potentials have to be found elsewhere [than in state planning], that is to say, in a completely changed relation between autonomous, self-organized publics, on the one hand, and the domains of action steered by money and administrative power, on the other. This presents the difficult task of making possible a democratic generalization of interest positions and a universal justification of norms below the threshold of party apparatuses that have become autonomous as large-scale organizations and have migrated, as it were, into the political system ... The social-integrative power of solidarity would have to be in a position to assert itself against the 'power' of the other two steering resources, money and administrative power ... [It] would have to nourish a formation of political will that would influence the boundaries and the interchanges between communicatively structured domains of life, on the one hand, and the economy and the state, on the other ... Forms of *self*-organization strengthen collective capacity for action below the threshold where organizational goals become detached from the orientations and attitudes of members and where goals become dependent on the survival interests of autonomous organizations ... Autonomous publics would have to achieve a combination of power and intelligent self-limitation that could make the self-steering mechanisms of the state and economy sufficiently sensitive to the goal-oriented results of radically democratic will-formation.[48]

This is one view of future possibilities for effectively institutionalizing democratic decision-making processes. I am not interested here in taking issue with it, but only in ensuring that the possibility of democratization as dedifferentiation of economy and state not be metatheoretically ruled out of court by systems-theoretic borrowing.[49] Here, again, the question arises of whether it should be superseded by some non-regressive form of dedifferentiation.

Habermas is certainly correct in arguing that *some* type of functional analysis is essential to the reconstruction of the Marxian project. The idea that history has not been made with will and consciousness, that unplanned consequences, unrecognized interdependencies, uncomprehended systemic dynamics hold sway over our lives like a 'second nature', is quite naturally spelled out by this means. The question is, what type of functional analysis?

We do not need the paraphernalia of social systems theory to identify unintended consequences. Nor do we need them to study the 'functions' that an established social practice fulfils for the other parts of the social network, for these are simply the recurrent consequences of this recurrent pattern of social action for those other parts. If the consequences for a given institution are such as to support its continued existence – the status quo, more or less – they are usually said to be 'functional' for that institution; if the consequences are destabilizing for a given institution – if they necessitate change, more or less – they are usually said to be 'dysfunctional' for that institution. Whether stabilizing or destabilizing, functional or dysfunctional, causal interconnections of this sort can be investigated with comparatively meagre theoretical means. Perhaps the need for systems theory arises in the attempt to comprehend the inner dynamics of expansive subsystems like the economy and the state? I do not know whether or not this is the case 'in the final analysis'; but it does not serve this function in Habermas's argument, for he more or less takes the expansive dynamics of the system for granted in his analysis of colonization. There is no attempt to provide the type of analysis of inner dynamics that Marx was concerned with in *Capital*. And in fact there is some question as to whether this is even on the systems-theoretic agenda. Marx was concerned with internal workings and endogenously generated problems of the economic system. Systems theory directs our attention to problems generated by the environments of systems. One of its virtues, according to Habermas, is that it gets us beyond the strongly idealized models that resulted from focusing on the inner dynamics of a system in isolation. It is, I think, fair to say that the question of whether and how systems theory could be used to reconstruct the expansive inner dynamics of the economic and administrative systems is still open. Until this is resolved, we do not know whether the processes of colonization that Habermas singles out will need to be understood in specifically systems-theoretic terms. (There are of course alternative

frameworks for dealing with phenomena of monetarization and bureaucratization – from Marxist theories of commodification to neo-Weberian
accounts of the bureaucratic state.) And much of what he has to say about
mediatization could be rendered in action-theoretic terms. In short, it is
not clear just where the need for systems theory arises.

If we look to Habermas's favoured formulations, they usually stress the
ideas of 'objective purposiveness', the 'system rationality' of unplanned
adaptive responses, objective (unintended) responses to objective challenges
to system survival. But these holistic ways of talking bring us right back to
the simple fact that the 'needs' of social systems cannot be empirically
established because 'survival' is not a matter of objectively specifiable
parameters. (Did France survive the French Revolution? Did the United
States survive its Civil War? Did Germany survive the First World War?)

To deal with this global level of analysis, in the 1960s Habermas developed the idea of a 'theoretically' or 'systematically generalized history
with practical intent.'[50] He argued that the inadequacies of functionalist
social theory are insuperable so long as it is understood as a form of
empirical-analytic inquiry: goal states are not simply 'given'. On the other
hand, if we do not wish to rest content with using it as a form of
normative-analytic inquiry, we cannot simply stipulate goal states. What
alternative is there? They can, argued Habermas, be hypothetically projected as the outcome of a general and unrestricted, rational discussion
among members, based on adequate knowledge of limiting conditions and
functional imperatives:

> In relation to such criteria, a state of equilibrium would be determined according
> to whether the system of domination in a society realized the utopian elements
> and dissolved the ideological content to the extent that the level of productive
> forces and of technical progress made possible. Of course, society can then no
> longer be conceived exclusively as a system of self-preservation ... Rather, the
> meaning in relation to which the functionality of social processes is measured is
> now linked to the idea of a communication free from domination.[51]

A functionalism of this global sort would no longer be understood on the
model of biology. It would rely, rather, on a 'general interpretative
framework' analogous in important respects to the systematically generalized history used as a narrative foil in psychoanalysis.

> In place of the goal state of a self-regulated system, we would have the antici-
> pated end state of a formative process. A hermeneutically enlightened and
> historically oriented functionalism would not aim at a general theory in the
> sense of the strict empirical sciences, but at a general interpretation of the same
> kind as psychoanalysis ... For historically oriented functionalism does not aim
> at technically useful information; it is guided by an emancipatory cognitive
> interest that aims at reflection and demands enlightenment about one's formative
> process ... The species, too, constitutes itself in formative processes, which are
> precipitated in the structural change of social systems and which can be
> reflected, i.e. systematically narrated from an anticipated point of view ... Thus

the general interpretive framework, however saturated with previous hermeneutic experiences and however corroborated in particular interpretations, retains an hypothetical element – the truth of an historically oriented functionalism is confirmed not technically, but only practically, in the successful continuation and completion of a self-formative process.[52]

This notion of a theoretically generalized narrative, drawing upon both hermeneutical and functional modes of analysis, was the developed form of Habermas's long-standing idea of an historically oriented theory of society with a practical intent.[53] It retained an intrinsic relation to practice: guided by an emancipatory interest, social analysis was undertaken from the standpoint of realizing, to the extent possible at a given stage of development, a form of organization based on unrestricted and undistorted communication. The truth of such analysis could be finally confirmed only through the successful continuation of our *Bildungsprozesse*.

Since the 1970s, Habermas's thought has moved in a more strongly theoretical direction. It is because he wants a *theory* of contemporary society that the systems approach seems so appealing. Habermas once criticized Marx for succumbing to the illusion of rigorous science, and he traced a number of Marxism's historical problems with political analysis and political practice to this source. The question I have wanted to pose here is whether in flirting with systems theory he does not run the danger of being seduced by the same illusion in more modern dress.

8 Communicative Action or the Mode of Communication for Society as a Whole

Hans-Peter Krüger

Habermas pursues an interdisciplinary research strategy in order to provide the foundations for a critical theory of society. There are two sides to Habermas's understanding of the theory and these can be distinguished from one another, even though they overlap in *The Theory of Communicative Action*. On the one hand, a theory of social action that asserts itself *vis-à-vis* systems theory leads to a 'theory of communicative action' which, in the face of systems theory, lays claim to an all-embracing validity with respect to evolutionary theory.[1] On the other, Habermas today considers it necessary also to reconstruct historical materialism, to which the dualism of systems and action theory is alien, in terms of evolutionary theory and presupposing this dualism. The 'theory of communicative action' lays claim to paradigmatic validity with regard to the answer it gives to the question arising in this reconstruction as to the specifics of socio-cultural evolution.[2]

The following problematization of the 'theory of communicative action' refers to both aspects of this self-understanding on Habermas's part.

On the one hand, the mentioned dualism in social theory characteristic of discussions in the social sciences in the United States and the Federal Republic of Germany could surely be resolved by rendering historical-materialistic explanations specific in terms of communications theory. However, the idiosyncrasy of Habermas's approach in *The Theory of Communicative Action* lies in the construction of a typology for kinds of language usage oriented to reaching understanding that can be described in formal-pragmatic terms and thus complements the transcendental-phenomenological model of the lifeworld. This idiosyncrasy does not convince us that he has resolved the presumed dualism in terms of either social theory or communications theory. Instead of a solution formulated in terms of evolutionary theory, Habermas manages to bridge the gap in structuralist terms, and instead of devising a solution in terms of communications theory, he merely doubles up this dualism within communications theory. I shall attempt to justify these assertions immanently in the first part of my article.

If, on the other hand, one abstracts from the reconstructions of the history of social theory from the vantage point of this dualism – and the 'theory of communicative action' stands or falls with these – we have to do with the systematic question as to the importance of a theory of social communication for the theory of social development, i.e. for historical materialism. In specific contexts and forms, social communication functions as the potential for social development. This occurs when, as in the present, it becomes necessary to develop a mode (the manner) of social development. In such a case social communication no longer functions only in the reproduction of the given form of development (namely, social development based on class conflict), but instead also as the potential for changing the social mode of development itself. The question as to the genesis of the manner of development which has traditionally concerned dialectical philosophy has been overtaken in the more recent literature on evolutionary theory by the question of the degree to which evolutionary mechanisms are linked and of the evolution of evolutionary criteria. I shall go into the historical-materialist approach to the problem of a new mode of communication for society as a whole in the second part. This will include a critique of the false interpretation of Marx's approach as presented by Habermas in *The Theory of Communicative Action*.

The 'Theory of Communicative Action' as the Communications-Theoretic Doubling and Structuralist Bridging of a Dualism in Social Theory

The Main Steps in the Formulation of the Paradox of Communicative Rationalization in Habermas's Work

Habermas explicates the approach to communicative action (a) as a theory of communicative rationality which, over and above cognitive-instrumental rationality, also covers moral and aesthetic forms of rationality.[3] The universal concept of rationality is, however, shaped by formal-pragmatic means, i.e. by investigating the formal properties of the ways in which knowledge is used on the part of subjects capable of speaking and acting. In his elaboration of theories of argumentation and learning, Habermas attempts to pinpoint the potential for evolutionary logic inherent in a rationality of action which can still be ascribed to individuals in the form of condensed discourse.

The contextual content of the formal-pragmatic concept of rationality is (b) to be superseded by linking it to the phenomenological concept of the lifeworld.[4] Habermas assumes that communicative action and lifeworld can complement one another. He differentiates between the structural and functional aspects of the lifeworld's reproduction through communicative action. Forms of language usage oriented toward reaching understanding described in formal-pragmatic terms serve as the normative standard here. Habermas founds a communications-theoretic opposition between delinguistified media of communication and generalized forms of communication, an opposition which, as he sees it, transpires to be the opposition in social theory between different principles of socialization. He accepts that the systems-theoretical model of society can be read with regard to material reproduction and limits the validity of his communicative action approach to the symbolic reproduction of the lifeworld.

He intends then (c) to resolve this dualism in terms of evolutionary theory.[5] He claims that in terms of evolutionary theory the communicative action approach (as the complementary gestalt of the concept of lifeworld) must be granted an overriding validity vis-à-vis the systems-theoretic model of society. The communicative action approach supposedly itemizes the specifically socio-cultural criteria of identity for a social system's existence, and in the socio-evolutionary model of learning it shows the formation of innovative evolutionary variants as well as their testing with respect to social integration. The evolutionary interconnection of lifeworld and system, Habermas claims, embraces their uncoupling, the differentiation of both and the paradoxical effect the now independent systems dynamics have back on the modern lifeworld.

The theoretical elaboration of this socio-evolutionary complex, he maintains, required (d) an interdisciplinary theory of modernity which has not been forthcoming to date.[6] The critique of capitalism itself has to proceed from the standpoint of the evolutionary trends of communicative rationalization and social modernization, instead of merging with an evolutionarily backward critique of rationalization and modernization as a whole based on premodern or social-pathological standards. Habermas recognizes that the delinguistified media of communication and/or the systemic steering mechanisms, money and power, are adequate for modern material reproduction in the first place. Only the systems-functional replacement also of communicative action, the medium adequate to modern symbolic reproduction, could be subjected to a realistic criticism.

Finally, Habermas focusses on (e) an analysis of a specifically cultural modernity.[7] On the one hand, he claims, modern culture eludes being given an ideological function by virtue of the fact that its specific validity claims differentiate out at specific levels of action and discourse, and it thus gains relative autonomy and an internal history. On the other hand, as a consequence of the same process mass-based everyday consciousness loses its synthesizing force and energetic motivation. According to Habermas, a new, internally differentiated unity of the expert cultures among themselves and together with communicative everyday practice should emerge from communicative rationalization without relapses into traditional ideologies, into religion and myth.

As Habermas sees it, at present 'the symbolic structures of the lifeworld *as a whole* are being placed in question' (*TCA*, vol. II, p. 403).[8] At first glance, the whole symbolic means of society's reproduction appears to be at stake only because the inexorable autodynamicism of the systems of material reproduction are causing this 'colonization of the lifeworld'. In

The Theory of Communicative Action, however, the formulation of the paradox inherent in the communicative rationalization of the lifeworld plays a decisive role (*TCA*, vol. II, pp. 328, 186, 318; vol. I, pp. 342f.). The differentiation in expert cultures of the validity claims specific to each communicative action leads, for its part, to cultural impoverishment and the fragmentation of everyday communication, as a result of which the modern lifeworld has difficulty resisting its 'colonization'. Both the danger of self-disintegration and the perspective of a unity that is henceforth only procedural in formal terms are, it would seem, inherent in communicative rationalization.

Communications-Theoretic Doubling and the Structuralist Bridging of the Dualism of Social Theory

The idiosyncrasy of Habermas's theory of action

The reasons why Habermas assumes that he can justify the communicative view of rationality only in terms of action theory are compelling in terms of the history of social theory, but not for systematic reasons. He refers to the paradigm shift from purposive rationality to communicative rationality and to the relation of action and systems theory as the 'two basic problems ... which the aporetic explication of the critique of instrumental reason has left behind for us' (*TCA*, vol. II, p. 113). The paradox peculiar to Habermas's overall model arises from his belief that it is possible to approach the paradigm shift to communicative rationality only '*within* the theory of action' in opposition to systems theory (*TCA*, vol. II, p. 113). Nevertheless, however, he wants to provide justifications for the overriding validity for a theory of evolution of the tradition of research into action theory as opposed to that into systems theory (cf. ibid., pp. 143f., 148, 154, 173f.). Given that Habermas is aware of the limits of the action-theoretic procedure of explication as opposed to the systems-theoretical variant (ibid., pp. 113–18, 150–2), then the action-theoretic procedure of explication – the overriding validity of which is to be justified in terms of evolutionary theory – cannot be identical with that explicative action-theoretic procedure which is tied to the limits laid down by its opposition to systems theory. Habermas doubles up the determination of the difference between the two; and it is only in this double distantiation from conventional theories of action that the idiosyncrasy of his 'theory of action' comes to light.

Firstly, the linguistic-communicative specifics of his approach to action expand the bounds of the theory of action, compared with analytical action theory and theories of symbolic interaction. His approach to action bears fruit in terms of the explicative advantages offered by the standpoint of linguistic communication. At the same time, however, the high potential for the socialization and rationality inherent in linguistic communication results from evolutionary processes in society as a whole which cannot be adequately grasped in terms of action theory. Habermas benefits from the evolutionary advantage linguistic communication has in terms of action theory before he has actually explained it in terms of evolutionary theory as a 'pre-adaptation' resulting from earlier processes of evolution.[9]

Secondly, Habermas attempts to liberate himself from the bounds of action-theoretic forms of explication by assuming that communicative action and transcendental lifeworld complement one another. This gives rise to a model of symbolic reproduction of society which is already internally so differentiated in structural and functional terms that one wonders what is actually still supposed to be action-theoretic about this model in the sense of the link to group-specific participant perspectives. However, the transcendental lifeworld allows him to harvest what are in the broadest sense the cultural 'pre-adaptations' of human society, which result from prior evolutionary processes and effectively appear as a transcendental a priori. Habermas makes linguistic-communicative and cultural 'pre-adaptations' of human society accessible to action theory, without having explained their origin in terms of evolutionary theory.

The paradoxical positioning in evolutionary theory of the communicative view of rationality in Habermas's overall conception

The advantages of Habermas's broad view of communicative rationality should not fall prey to a critique of those constructional flaws in which Habermas becomes ensnared owing to the presupposed dualism of action and systems theory.

On the one hand, Habermas attempts in a rational manner to gain uniform theoretical access to the whole breadth and slanting of communicative rationalization. This could serve to ground the possibility of grasping through learning the alternative unity of expert cultures among themselves and together with everyday communication. In this connection, Habermas develops important chains of argumentation on the linguistic unity of the differentiated validity claims, on the intensification of communicative rationalization by means of its being condensed in discourse at higher levels of learning and on the potential of linguistic communication for creativity. The elaboration of all three lines of argumentation contributes to the refutation of systems-functionalist criticisms, according to which linguistic communication is inadequate as a medium and inefficient in temporal terms when it comes to coordination in the development of complex societies. In his refutation, Habermas draws on, among others, Toulmin's theory of argumentation, in which traditionally philosophical problems of a dialectical-logical view of rationality become easier to grasp in analytical terms, mediated historically among other things through the question–answer logic of Collingwood, a neo-Hegelian. In his approach, Habermas also makes rational use of Piaget's work, in so far as the latter strives to provide a genetic explanation of the interconnection of cognitive and moral intelligence based on the coordination problems of cooperative action. This allows specific explanatory steps traditionally taken in philosophical dialectics to be followed in an investigation that is both conceptual and empirical in nature.[10] For that matter, the rationality-theoretic dimension of Habermas's work would offer an opportunity to make an instructive comparison with a dialectical research programme: for example in such an instance as when Habermas after all refers to the procedural concept of argumentation as 'dialectics' and wishes to make the procedural concept of communicative rationality the basis of his critique of society (*TCA*, vol. I, pp. 28, 74). Evidently, even Habermas is left, albeit reluctantly, with a residual problem of the materialist dialectic that forms the path for the philosophical justification of historical materialism.[11] On the other hand, however, Habermas links the theory of communicative rationality to the 'lifeworld' of transcendental-phenomenological intersubjectivity in a problematic manner, namely by means of his formal-pragmatic approach and his assumption that the two complement one another. Habermas's specifically formal and action-theoretical strategy of justification anchors the theory of communicative rationality in the dualism of social theory. The action-theoretic approach inserts at least two actors at the microstructural level of groups and leaves the macrostructural level to be modelled in terms of systems theory. The formal procedure abstracts from the historical contexts and forms of social communication, such as the relations of the 'socium'[12] to its environments, and also leaves them to be modelled by systems theory as far as material reproduction is concerned.

Habermas's idiosyncratic formal-pragmatic view of communicative rationality thus becomes tangled up in a paradoxical situation in terms of evolutionary theory, for it has to prove that its contents are both realistic and yet at the same time critical *vis-à-vis* systems theory (*TCA*, vol. II, pp. 153–6, 173f., 178f., 185, 196f.). This paradoxical situation doubly manifests itself, both in the attempt to explain the genesis and development of modern society and in today's understanding of the problem of the project of Enlightenment in modernity.

The overriding evolution-theoretic validity of the 'theory of communicative action' is defined more closely as the evolutionary priority of communicative learning processes which first make the systems dynamicism structurally possible (*TCA*, vol. II, pp. 283f., 303–4, 312–18). In order to be able to prove this evolutionary priority realistically, Habermas is forced to construe precisely those variants in the structural forms of the possibility for social action as emerging in communicative rationalization which correspond as a presupposition to the systems-theoretic description of modernization. The more realistically Habermas seeks to demonstrate the evolution-theoretic claim of the formal-pragmatic justification of communicative rationality, the more he is forced to pre-empt within communicative rationalization those structural forms and functional divisions that will according to the systems-theoretic model take on functional tasks.

This leads to the paradoxical conception of communicative rationalization as making a system dynamics possible by means of which it itself is retroactively 'colonized', and as following a formally reflexive developmental logic (*TCA*, vol. II, pp. 144–5), according to which communicative rationalization is fragmented and to this extent is unable to resist colonization. Communicative rationalization, Habermas claims, unleashes what then, and this eludes the action-rational perspective, causes its reification and thus ruins it, an intrinsically paradoxical rationalization. What appeared to be a normatively critical standard which could be justified in communicative rationality corresponds as a functionally-divided structural form of action paradoxically to that which is to be criticized. The formal-pragmatic counterpart to the system's mode of functioning has to be pre-empted in the standards of critique in the guise of the possibility for functionally-divided structural forms of social action.

The reification and fragmentation of linguistic-communicative relations are defined at different levels, namely, on the one hand, as the one-dimensional subsumption under system-imperatives and, on the other, communicative rationalization endangering itself in terms of the logic of its development. Nevertheless, the effect of reification cannot merely be of causal origin, but rather also has to be made structurally possible by communicative rationalization itself, if the latter is to be granted evolutionary primacy (*TCA*, vol. II, pp. 325–31, 341, 352–6, 390–403). This standard of critique is assigned general evolution-theoretic validity at the price of its own downfall. Habermas reluctantly prepares the way for the systems-functional replacement of his critical standard, both in his formal-*pragmatic* anticipation of the system's mode of functioning and thus also in the *formal*-pragmatic logic of the self-deterioration of communicative rationalization, its fragmentation and 'decontexualisation'.[13]

The paradoxical positioning of the theory of communicative rationality in terms of evolutionary theory becomes clear for the present in the following consideration. A socio-evolutionary analogy to the emergence of modern society would suggest that communicative rationalization reaches a stage of development in which it overcomes the paradox inherent in it. Wary as he is of myth, religion and ideology owing to the problems they harbour, Habermas is careful when countenancing combinations of expert cultures and their combination with everyday communication. Yet he does so without questioning his formal-pragmatic conception of communicative rationality, which complements phenomenological intersubjectivity. According to this latter view, inherited from transcendental philosophy, communicative rationalization remains trapped in the symbolic reproduction of the lifeworld, and indeed, for all this jettisoning of material reproduction (or precisely because of it) is pathologically endangered. As a communicative approach to *action*, this view of rationality does not match the coordinating function of the economic and administrative *system*. In *formal*-pragmatic terms, all this view of rationality can do is adhere to the assumption of an immanent developmental logic according to which the already reflexive forms of action are again reflected on with regard to the principles of their formal procedures. This meta-reflexion on the reflexive forms of action – which is embedded in a lifeworld reduced to symbols – decontextualizes, i.e. abstracts from the historical and material contexts of the reflexive forms of action.

Even if one were to assume that this decontextualized meta-reflexion could solve its problems of application, this stage of development of the communicative rationalization of the lifeworld nevertheless no longer has a new counterpart in terms of systems evolution (in the 'developmental dynamics', *TCA*, vol. II, p. 144). The new socio-evolutionary learning process can no longer be regarded as such at all, since it contains no meaning comparable to that of the learning process entailed in the emergence of modern societies: structurally, it would not make possible any other mode of systems dynamicism; rather, at best what is (to cite Adorno) *only the negative* determination has to enable a kind of 'decolonization' of the lifeworld to occur instead of its 'colonization'. Equally, there is no stage that follows on the heels of the decontextualized meta-reflexion within the 'developmental logic' (*TCA*, vol. II, p. 144) of communicative rationalization itself. The complete decontextualization of social communication would not only end the development of social communication, but would also render the concept of 'communication' itself superfluous if 'context' is constitutive for it. The *evolution-theoretic* positioning of the view of communicative rationality *ends* in a paradoxical manner since it results from a presupposed *dualism*. Habermas logically seeks a haven in *anthropological* assurances of the material and symbolic reproduction of society as such (*TCA*, vol. II, pp. 138f., 322ff.)

The communication – theoretic doubling of the dualism of social theory

In the foregoing section I addressed as problematic Habermas's attempt to ground his (albeit) meritorious view of communicative rationality in specifically formal-pragmatic terms and as a complement to the transcendental-phenomenological concept of intersubjectivity. This makeshift model in terms of formal pragmatism and transcendental phenomenology does not, however, solve the actual problem, namely how Piaget's psycho*genetic* forms of explanation can be transposed into social theory. Since this makeshift grounding of the conception of communicative rationality does not solve the problem of *socio-theoretical genetic* explanation, the result is a communication-theoretic doubling up of the dualism in social theory presupposed by Habermas.

As the critical use made by research on Piaget following in L. S. Vygotsky's path shows, a linguistic-communicative approach to action is meaningful when it comes to laying the foundations for a social and cultural psychology. The linguistically differentiated unity of 'spiritual actions' (Galperin) and 'communicative actions' (A. A. Leontyev) can be explained genetically as resulting from the coordination problems of cooperative action. The Marxian concept of cooperation is not misinterpreted economistically, but rather expounded as the phase-by-phase developmental interconnection of subject–subject and subject–object relations in play, work, and other 'activities' (A. N. Leontyev), as is necessary for a psychological strategy of explanation. In this explicative approach, it is not necessary to proceed formalistically or intersubjectivistically, since the genetic differentiation of higher planes of action as well as the manner in which they feed back into cooperative contexts of action can be explained.

This concept of cooperation could, if developed as a linguistic-communicative approach to action, surely be made to 'cohere' (*TCA*, vol. II,

p. 399) with K. Bühler's organon model and Habermas's three relations to the world exhibited by communicative acts (*TCA*, vol. II, p. 126). This also applies to Habermas's attempt to reveal the social potential for coordination particular to linguistic communication, the 'coordinating effect of the warranty' (*TCA*, vol. I, pp. 296f., 302, 307ff.) in the problem-conscious front-line position he adopts *vis-à-vis* reflexion philosophies of consciousness as well as vulgar materialist analogies of money and power.

Habermas is conscious of the group-specific limits to validity of the action-theoretical procedure. This is what prompts the question as to how Piaget's genetic form of explanation, including the version expanded to contain the linguistic-communicative approach to action, can be transposed from psychology into social theory. The greatest difficulty in answering this question consists in determining the analogous approach to be taken for the explanation of communication in society as a whole – something termed 'cooperative action' in the communication-psychological explanation, but which cannot be grasped in terms of action theory at the level of society as a whole. However, Habermas cannot eliminate this difficulty, since he has reserved the determination of the structural contexts of society as a whole, and especially that of material reproduction, for a systems functionalist approach. If this difficulty is not mastered, however, then it is not possible to explain genetically either which developmental complex of contextual contents and media-based forms of social communication give rise to a sequence of differentiation among higher forms of communication ranging to discursive argumentation, or through which forms of contextual feedback discourses become relevant for the development of society as a whole. If it does not prove possible to specify an approach to social communication as a whole analogous to that used to explain cooperative action, then firstly the explanation of communication in society as a whole will inevitably be decontextualized and formalized, and secondly, an abstraction occurs in a move away from the objectively and symbolically mediated subject–object relationship contained in the concept of cooperation towards the subject–subject relation, without this yielding an explanation of the developmental connection between the two relations. Habermas does not draw on Piaget's genetic form of explanation, but rather the formal result of this explanation, namely the stage of formal-operational and conventional intelligence. Habermas then subjects this result to a decontextualised self-reflexion aimed at discourse and a meta-discourse that is not linked back to its point of origin.

Habermas avoids the difficulty involved in determining a socio-theoretical counterpart to the psychogenetic explanatory function of the cooperative approach to action by resorting to a makeshift philosophical construction. He evades the group-specific limits to validity inherent in the action-theoretic procedure – something he accepts – by taking up transcendental phenomenology. In this case, however, the difference must be emphasized between the transcendental-phenomenological concept of life-world and a grasp of concrete lifeforms which can be utilized in action theory, as must the difference between the formal-pragmatic model taken and the empiricist-pragmatic investigation (*TCA*, vol. I, pp. 284f., 332). By taking up transcendental phenomenology, Habermas allows the orientation to phenomenological intersubjectivity and formal self-reflexion in the transcendental sense to gain the upper hand in his work. The social genesis of linguistic communication remains engrossed in the horizon of symbols of the lifeworld, which is presupposed and no longer cast into question. The assumption that the formal-pragmatic view of rationality and the transcendental-phenomenological concept of lifeworld can complement one another reactivates the old dichotomies with respect to a typology of action. Thus, Habermas once again ends up juxtaposing the symbolic interactions to an 'instrumental action' deemed *asocial* in advance (*TCA*, vol. I, pp. 277f., 315–18), i.e. a fiction that applies neither to phylogeny nor to ontogeny, neither to social production, social practice, group-specific forms of life nor to child development. If the linguistic form of communication is uncoupled from its context, i.e. from a form of cooperation that calls for social coordination, then all questions as to the objectivation of rationality, especially the question of objective truth, ultimately have to be dissolved into a reference-less realm of intersubjective probability. The transcendental abstraction from the contexts of social genesis and from the manner in which linguistic communication feeds back to whence it originated serves to strip linguistic action which, in its ideal speech situation, coordinates nothing other than itself, of its communicative quality. Habermas transforms the *generalization* of contexts peculiar to linguistic communication into a *de*contextualisation – and this causes his *linguistic* approach to become irrelevant in terms of *communications* theory.

In Habermas's work, a substitute model based on a formal-pragmatic typology and transcendental phenomenology takes the place of an explanation as to how linguistic communication emerges and develops in contexts of society as a whole. He has to limit the applicability of his formal-pragmatic communications-theoretic approach to the symbolic reproduction of the lifeworld. A communications-theoretic approach based in systems theory would be necessary in order to provide a positive explanation for the delinguistified media of communication in terms of the dynamics of the economic and administrative systems. Finally, a third communications-theoretic approach would first have to be developed to account for phenomena of interference caused by delinguistified media of communication and generalized forms of linguistic communication, i.e. according to Habermas, for 'forms of understanding' (*TCA*, vol. II, p. 187). In the meantime, the presupposed dualism of social theory has only been doubled up in terms of a theory of communication with the notion of 'media dualism' (ibid., p. 281).

Dualism's structuralist bridging attempt

Habermas reacts to this simple communications-theoretic doubling up of the dualism of social theory by bridging it via a comparison of the possible structural forms of social action. The attempt at a structuralist bridging of systems-functional and action-theoretic argumentation is intended to enable the evolution-theoretic combination of both kinds of explanation in the socio-evolutionary learning model (*TCA*, vol. II, pp. 313f.).

Habermas has to make use of the structuralist components in this proposed form of explanation in order to bridge individual and social development by means of collective structures. The path which leads from a variant of the rational level of action that is learned individually and group-specifically, all the way to a generally higher level of social rationalization, consists of the formal comparison of structures. The structuralist bridging of individual and societal development coincides with the structuralist bridging of the contents, forms and substantive contents (the contents of the forms themselves)[14] of social communication.

The bridging of these three structural levels becomes clear when Habermas draws up a model of socio-evolutionary learning in terms of its offering a hypothetical causal explanation (*TCA*, vol. II, pp. 314ff.). Habermas compares three structural levels with one another, namely the structures of the institutional complexes functionally necessary for the evolutionary solution of system problems, the structures of rationality embodied in these institutions and those structures of world views which comprise the cognitive potential for the institutional embodiment of these structures of rationality. This comparison bridges the contextual contents (of systemic problems which can now only be solved via evolution), the media forms (media of communication or generalized forms of communication) and the ideational contents (structures of world views) of communication in society as a whole. The dualism in Habermas's social theory – which he extends to include the 'media dualism' – excludes any uniform communications-theoretic explanation being forthcoming for the developmental interconnection of the contextual contents, media forms and ideational contents of social communication. Be that as it may, however, the above-mentioned formal structural comparisons bridge the presupposed dualism, and one could regard them as heuristically meaningful steps on the path to a uniform theory of social communication. Yet, this is contradicted by the fact that Habermas on the one hand has to formulate his hypothetical explanation defensively *vis-à-vis* systems functionalism and in a countermove preinterprets it very much in terms of action theory, without having conducted his own historically concrete investigations. His explanation remains defensive in nature to the extent that the formal comparisons of structure presuppose a systems-functionalist determination of the yardstick taken to measure structure. Habermas can invariably only translate that yardstick, which plays a functional role in the dynamics of the system, back via formal structural comparisons after the event, i.e. 'reconstructively', until he has uncovered the corresponding structure of speakers and world perspectives in the rationalization of the lifeworld which itself comes about through linguistic-communicative action. Even if the formal counterparts to the various structural levels were correct, all Habermas has initially achieved is to have determined the formal-pragmatic *counter*-parts to the systems dynamics in the communicative rationalization of the lifeworld, with the above-mentioned 'paradoxical' consequences. This does not define in an offensive move a developmental course of communicative rationalization that *contradicts* the systems dynamics and its selections. On the other hand, it is not possible by means of a formal structural comparison alone to prove that evolutionary priority should be accorded to one of the above structural levels, something Habermas claims holds for the rationalization by means of linguistic-communicative action of the structures of world views. In the instances where Habermas cites historical investigations to support his assertions, they are structural reconstructions of *pre*modern societal phenomena, such as that of myth by Lévi-Strauss or the kinship system by Maurice Godelier, i.e. of societies in which the lifeworld and the system were, according to Habermas himself, not yet uncoupled.

If one bears in mind that previously in Habermas's writings labour and interaction were treated as separate, unmediated areas, then his reception of genetic structuralism is a step forward: at the level of the group, the cooperative action approach is expanded into one of linguistic communication, and at the level of society as a whole, a structuralistic bridging model is provided – and the heuristic means are given with which a way can be found back to a uniform concept of social development. Habermas now comes up against the conceptual problem of structuralism for social theory, namely the question as to the transformation of structure and the structure of transformation.[15]

Habermas calls it the principal remaining task of his explanatory sketch to situate the socio-evolutionary learning model in the history of social movements (*TCA*, vol. II, p. 316). The media-structural compromise of 'forms of understanding' (ibid., pp. 187f.) in Habermas's model takes the place of the social concept of practice[16] used in historical materialism and its possible interpretation in terms of communications theory as communicative practices which differentiate into discursive practices. Forms of social praxis would appear at first sight as quasi-macrostructural forms of action which transcend the group-specific limits of direct cooperation. However, this in itself could give rise to euphoria from the vantage point of praxis philosophy,[17] whereby the action-theoretic description of direct complexes of cooperation is only extrapolated on to the level of society as a whole. However, an awareness of this problem – which Habermas shares – leads, and here we part company with his work, to the question of what *communications-theoretic differentiation of forms of social praxis* is capable of achieving as *true forms of resolving media dualism*. Surely we have all encountered the constitutional need of modern social practice in Peter Weiss's *Aesthetics of Resistance*.[18]

The forfeited potential of linguistics

Since Habermas ends with the above-mentioned formal structural comparisons at the point where he would have been better advised to begin with the historical genesis of discursive practices from communicative practices, his discursive approach remains embedded in the communication-theoretic doubling up of the dualism of social theory. This doubling up also comes to light from the outset in his view of language. Compared with dialectical logic, systemic and structural linguistics as well as semantics, Habermas proceeds one-sidedly from linguistic pragmatics.

In order to avoid misunderstandings, let me refer to critical tributes to the pragmatic turn to linguistics.[19] I also do not question Habermas's having accomplished a meaningful universalization of formal linguistic pragmatics in terms of three validity claims. Habermas, in my view, provides convincing grounds for believing that illocution does not separate the pragmatic from the propositional contents of meaning, but rather specifies the mode of the validity claim raised with a linguistic utterance in action-related (pragmatic) terms (*TCA*, vol. I, p. 278). This understanding of illocution expands what was referred to as 'intension' in the tradition of formal logic dating from Frege, i.e. as the (action-related) rule for identifying extension.[20] Once the competence to act linguistically has arisen, then it is 'the internal model' and no longer the object of empirical perception which is 'the domain of extension of linguistic utterances.'[21]

It is not the universalization of the turn to linguistic pragmatics in all of the traditional subject areas of linguistics which is problematic. What is problematic is the reduction of the potential for linguistic justification to linguistic pragmatics and the identification of the linguistic-pragmatic turn with the speech act theories of Austin and Searle. The objective meaning of linguistic utterances cannot be clarified independently of the redemption of the respective validity claim. Therein lies the rational content of the pragmatic turn, a turn which counteracts any relapse into philosophically substantialist presuppositions. However, the standpoint of actual language use adopted in speech-act theoretic terms assumes that where intentionality and symbolic interactivity are concerned, they always exist in relation to action anyway. The idea that meaning and validity cannot be clarified independently of the use of corresponding linguistic expressions does not mean that the meaning and validity of linguistic expressions can be sufficiently explained from the standpoint of actual language use grasped in terms of action theory (*TCA*, vol. I, pp. 315–18). The genesis of the general contextual, formal and ideational structural conditions for the possibility of acting linguistically cannot be embraced in terms of *action* theory. An approach that is informed by speech-act theory curtails the objectivity of the meaning and validity of linguistic expressions – this can be grounded only in the context of societal production as a whole – pinning it down to the intersubjective recognition of this objectivity in actual action sequences.

Investigations informed by speech-act theory invariably rely implicitly on the qualities of language discerned by structural linguistics. Maintaining methodological constancy in the characteristics attributed to the speaker and situation can lead to the recognition of the social quality peculiar to language. This social quality peculiar to universal language structures or patterns is inherent in group-specific language use as a universal structural condition of its potential, without it having to be intended. It is only from the structures of potential socialization peculiar to language that justification can be forthcoming for the contradiction of linguistic and social structures, which is of concern to Habermas in socially critical terms as well.[22]

However, Habermas does not make full use either of the extrapragmatic possibilities for justification in linguistics, or of the internal linguistic-pragmatic possibilities for justification that go beyond speech-act theories. He avoids the action-theoretic limit to speech-act theories by drawing transcendental conclusions. His concept gets bogged down in confronting empirical linguistic pragmatics transcendentally and philosophical transcendental pragmatics in terms of speech-act theory. The mutual complementation of linguistic communicative acts with the lifeworld which Habermas assumes is possible and its dualistic opposition to systems logically leads to a false communications-theoretical outlook, namely the belief that discourses cannot arise from the communicative practices of material and social (not only symbolic) reproduction, and that the ideational contents of discourses have no reference outside the symbolic reproduction of lifeworld. Whereas the latter orientation does not allow for the reconstruction of the history of the natural sciences, it is sufficient with regard to the former to point to the possibility of controlling the medium of money – a possibility already structurally evolved, although it has to date been realized for the most part destructively. If it is politically possible to steer a destructive overaccumulation internationally, why should it then be *structurally* impossible to steer the formation of a use value-oriented economy rich in scientific and technical innovations intended to solve global problems through the medium of money? In which case, however, it would not be the medium which steers, but rather the public would steer by means of it.

Social-ontological hypertrophy of methods

As was shown in the preceding sections, the problematic aspect in Habermas's overall model lies in the dualism in social theory which repeatedly comes to light. It is not only a matter of a methodological abstraction or a model-theoretical grounding for a double strategy of conceptualizing the social dimension, but rather of a dualism that coagulates substantively throughout the theory. Habermas extends the original methodological question as to the access to phenomena of the social dimension from the perspective of the participant or observer into a dualism of theories (*TCA*, vol. II, p. 117); and in the final instance a quasi-anthropological reference is ascribed to this, the opposite of the symbolic and material reproduction of society as such. 'System' and 'lifeworld' function not only as methodological and theoretical constructs to permit the investigation of social phenomena *as* system *and as* lifeworld, but rather are also transformed into entities of modernity distinctive in social ontology to which social domains of action are clearly respectively allocated.[23] This foundationalist relapse into a two-substance dualism, obsolescent in terms of the history of philosophy, contrasts conspicuously with Habermas's self-understanding of the theory, namely that it liberates us from foundationalism (*TCA*, vol. I, pp. xii, 397f.; vol. II, pp. 399ff.). Yet it corresponds to the anthropological scepticism, also prevalent in the background of Kant's thought, *vis-à-vis* the dualistically crooked wood from which human beings are carved. In terms of the history of philosophy, it was Hegel's conceptual logic, circumvented by Habermas, that liberated us from the correspondence in the logic of reflexion between the transcendental understanding of self and the semblance that the determinants of reflexion were ontologically appropriate.

At no point in his work does Habermas provide justifications as to how either a material but symbol-free behaviour, or a symbolic but immaterial behaviour, is supposed to be possible as social behaviour at all. Habermas has as a philosopher attached in socio-ontological terms the participant or observer perspective exclusively to either symbolic or material reproduction. This now stands in the way of the explanation he offers as a communications theorist for how the reflexive unity of participant and observer perspective clearly results first from learning to achieve the linguistic unity of communication and thought. Habermas's philosophical preconceptions, and these thwart his communicative approach to rationality developing into a theory of social communication, are probably not understandable unless one considers his philosophical biography. The systematic absence of a theory of his own of the development of modes of production through their socialization has led Habermas from very early on to a highly faltering oscillation in the recognition he accords other theories of this subject domain. He obviously believes himself capable of continuing at least a half-hearted Enlightenment under the protection of this dualistic shield.

The Problem of the Development of a New Mode of Communication for Society as a Whole

Criticism of Habermas's Self-understanding regarding the Marxist Research Tradition

Before I can outline the above issue in a constructive manner, my criticisms will have to be aimed at the self-understanding with which Habermas makes his case for the necessity of a communications-theoretic orientation in interdisciplinary Marxist research.

1   Habermas spares himself the path of providing philosophical justifications for historical materialism by means of materialist dialectics and thus circumvents also the whole history of the problems dealt with by modern dialectics since Hegel. If, as Michael Theunissen has shown, the philosophical draft of a 'theory of communicative freedom' can be found at all in Hegel's 'Science of Logic',[24] and if solid research contributions to the Marxist and Leninist treatment of dialectics are available,[25] and if dialectical logic has proved itself as a means of inquiry into structural logic in Umberto Eco's semiotics,[26] then one could have expected Habermas to take a solid stand on the potential for orientation which dialectical philosophy offers for establishing communications theory. Instead, he would appear to identify the history of the problems dealt with by modern

dialectics with the 'philosophical ballast' (*TCA*, vol. II, p. 383) which led the founding generation of the Frankfurt School to go on the theoretical defensive.

2   Uncoupling historical materialism from materialist dialectics, as occurs in *The Theory of Communicative Action*, is only the first step towards a totally reductionistic interpretation of the 'Marxian approach' (*TCA*, vol. II, pp. 332–42). The section on Marx here is not even of the standard reached in Habermas's *On the Reconstruction of Historical Materialism*. Judging from its positioning, this section would appear only to have the function of helping to establish the self-made image of the Frankfurt tradition, modest by anyone's standards, as that of 'Western Marxism' (*TCA*, vol. I, p. 345; vol. II, p. 302).

   Instead of tackling Marx's overall oeuvre, the Marxian approach is interpreted as being the theory of labour value, although it was something which was not invented by Marx himself, but rather by classical Political Economy from William Petty and Adam Smith all the way to David Ricardo.[27] Even if one disregards Marx's philosophically universal research programme[28] and in turn ignores the writings in the philosophy of history and in social theory he completed in those parts of the programme realized by him; and even if one ultimately takes only the 'Critique of Political Economy', that section of the programme which was for the most part realized,[29] and here, in turn, again examines only the first three volumes of *Capital* – then one sees that the specific characteristics of Marx's contribution apply to a level other than that of the theory of labour value. Marx's genetic presentation of the value-form all the way to the trinitarian formula proves, via an immanent 'Critique of the Political Economy', that the theory of labour value as grounded by classical Political Economy can lay claim to universal validity only under conditions specific to industrial capitalism, which is to say, those of objective production as well as of modern bourgeois society.[30] However, even as a theory of labour value, it cannot lay claim to this already historicized validity, but only if it is grounded – and this was the original step taken by Marx – as the theory of surplus value and of value modifications.[31] Indeed, Marx understands that the intrinsic limits set to the capitalist modes of production are precisely that which at present empirically finds large-scale confirmation in the industrialized countries: namely, the fact that *work* (as such) ceases to be *the* pillar of material production and *the* social measure of wealth.[32] Marxian philosophy, which made possible the critique of the theory of labour value, cannot itself then be attributed to foundations provided by the theory of labour value.

   If questions of social theory are directed to Marx's work, then Marx's explanation of the developmental connection between modes of production,[33] social formations,[34] and ways of life[35] has to be taken up, instead of holding these questions up to the theory of labour value, which was not designed to deal with them in the first place. Indeed this explanation cannot be press-ganged into the dichotomy of system and lifeworld characteristic of Habermas's theory. In what Habermas himself terms a heavily stylized interpretation of Marx, assertions are made which again bypass the specifics of the Marxian consciousness of the problem.

According to Habermas, Marx was convinced a priori that capital was nothing other than the mystified focus of a relation between classes. Habermas believes that Marx uses the model of the unity of a fragmented moral totality, which prevented Marx from adequately accounting for the high structural degree of differentiation of modern societies, leading him instead to proclaim a kind of triumph of the lifeworld over the system of the desecularized labour force (*TCA*, vol. II, pp. 332–41). Habermas's portrayal is ultimately aimed at showing that the unsuccessful explanation of reification in terms of labour theory found a counterpart in Marx's work in a kind of romantic revolutionary stance.

I may not be able to make out Marx's strategic orientation in this complementation, but certainly can discern in it the background history constitutive for the image of Marx in the Frankfurt School. The economistic revision of the Marxian approach by leading German-speaking representatives of the Second International was followed by an historico-philosophical subjectivism which surrounded[36] the proletarian class subject in the aura of it being declared to constitute an historical-teleological guarantee. The continued development of the Marxian research programme which, without doubt, was necessary on the threshold of the epoch that began with our century lay and lies beyond this complementary position.

As Marx's developmental-theoretic classification of primary, secondary and tertiary formations shows,[37] his approach was not one of reducing the explanation of formative development to labour and class theory. Also, the discovery of class structures and the attempt to explain social phenomena in terms of class theory had been provided long before Marx, among others, by the historians of the French Revolution during the Restoration.[38] By contrast, Marx inquires how the mode of social development based on class conflict came about, was reproduced and can be replaced, without the achievements of civilization in the capitalistic formation of society being destroyed by some lapse back into a pre-class level of social development or reinstating master–servant relations. The classification of the capitalistic formation of society in terms of developmental theory resulted as a part of the inquiry into how, in the as yet still capitalist means of reproducing class conflict, the material conditions and structural possibilities already arise which would allow class conflicts, being the decisive form of development in civilized societies, to be overcome.[39]

Marx's attempts to classify social formations in terms of developmental theory remained incomplete. In his late works Engels in particular emphasized, as opposed to the ongoing economistic revision of the Marxian approach, that, for historical reasons understandable given the battle lines adopted *vis-à-vis* German idealism, he and Marx did not deal very systematically with questions of the mode of social formation as opposed to problems of material production.[40] It is characteristic of the strategy championed by both that the traditional manner of pure philosophy should be sublated, practically and theoretically, by systematically linking their historico-philosophical orientations to an investigation of the way in which social formation ensued with interdisciplinary research. In this sense, it becomes possible to thematize historico-philosophical modal determinants in terms of communications theory, as, for example, when A. A. Leontyev examines the Marxian concept of 'forms of intercourse' in terms of social communication.[41]

3 The 'theory of communicative action', which is rich in reconstructions of the history of social theory, excludes, of all things, precisely that research tradition which would have merited priority in the light of the subject-matter concerned. This could give rise to the impression that Marxist research is only now beginning to discover the key significance of problems of linguistic communication. L. S. Vygotsky[42] made a great contribution by showing as early as the late 1920s how Marx's philosophically universal programme of research can be given a specific form in the historical-materialist grounding of a complex social and cultural psychology, namely, through the interdisciplinary investigation of the linguistic unity of communication and thought. The turn he inaugurated in Marxist research towards implementing Marx's philosophical research programme in terms of communications theory has been confirmed in the writings of A. N. Leontyev, P. Ja. Galperin, A. R. Luria and D. Elkonin, as well as being given thorough foundations expanded interdisciplinarily, and empirically substantiated by their own investigations by A. A. Leontyev and V. P. Lomov in particular.[43] Long before Habermas, this research tradition was characterized by a critical reception of Piaget, and one which Piaget himself appreciated.

On the Presupposition of Natural History and the Context of Human History in the way Marx Approaches the Problem

Biocommunication: a natural-historical presupposition of social communication

Since Habermas delegates social modes of production as the context of social communication to systems theory and, equally in his conception of the lifeworld symbolistically abstracts from individuals as natural creatures, he also excludes nature-determined genetic dimensions of the context of social communication. By contrast, however, the shift to a communications-theoretic perspective in the conceptualizations of evolution in the natural sciences,[44] especially the biocommunications-theoretic view of evolutionary theory, which had already been redefined in terms of behaviour theory anyway,[45] permits a link to be established with communications theory from the side of social theory.

Biocommunication represents a significant selective advantage which changes the whole natural structure of selection, since by means of it 'individually acquired experience achieves a new status; once it does, the threshold to the human being has been crossed.'[46] Biocommunicative learning processes permit the individual acquisition of the experiential patterns of the population, the individual-historical cumulation of experience and its transmission, which leads to ontogeny feeding back positively into phylogeny. By means of biocommunicative learning processes, a population-specific measure of coupling among evolutionary mechanisms is achieved,[47] and consequently, the genesis of evolutionary criteria no longer has to be explained teleologically.

Communications research renders superfluous the senseless dispute on the question – put wrongly in the first place – as to which preliminary form of analytically distinct and natural-historically pre-projected properties of the human being were supposedly predominant during the transition to social evolution. The human being is not the product of any subsumptive recombination of factors, such as tool manufacturing, society-like interactions or precultural traditions, but rather the product of the evolution of the mode of social development itself. This evolution takes place initially in the context of the 'prehistory of human society'.[48]

On the context of human history in the problem as raised by Marx

In view of the failure of the 'theory of communicative action' to indicate the macrostructural context for the transition in the history of humankind to a new mode of communication in society as a whole, and in view of Habermas's disorienting interpretation of Marx, it would seem worthwhile to reconstruct Marx's own description of this problem.

Marx already distinguished the modes of production of social formations according to whether the 'natural relation' is still dominant in them or has already ceded dominance to the 'social, historically evolved elements'.[49] The societal *production* process took shape by becoming the societal *labour* process through the social division of labour in general, in particular and individually. Given this presupposition, the cooperative organization of immediate production 'constitutes the starting-point of capitalist production. This is true both historically and conceptually.'[50] Capital thus rests substantively on abstract labour. It does not reproduce itself in general until after the production and reproduction process has been industrialized in a manner adequate to it.

With the intensive expansion of the reproduction of capital, its universal developmental tendency stands in contradiction to the stuff of abstract labour on which it rests – culled from the history of humankind. The specifically capitalist unity of production and consumption through a now autonomous exchange of commodities is not an undifferentiated unity, but rather a process that contradicts itself in crises; nor is it a self-contained process, but rather a process which is linked to 'conditions extraneous' to it ranging from nature all the way to culture.[51] The production and realization of relative surplus value is tied to an intensive expansion of the productive and consumptive 'cycle' of capitalist reproduction. This expansion can, if mediated by the agency of the state as a monopoly, take the shape of a destructive impact on the natural environment and the existential foundations of social life. However, it can also take place in a progressive manner to the extent that the 'culture of all characteristics of social man ... equally (becomes) a condition of production based in capital.[52] Marx investigates the progressive developmental tendencies of capital first with a view to the scientific-technical emancipation of the form of socialization embodied by the immediate production process away from the limitations of the labour process. In the reproduction of what was still the industrial means of production, it was necessary to go through further, new divisions of labour, as well as new forms of combination and technical objectifications of these divisions. In the scientific-technical revolution, science and social communication – the two differentiated conditions and results of social reproduction – are fed back into the production process.[53] The specificity of both does not rest substantively on labour, but rather stems from the cultural mode of socialization of social reproduction, something Marx frequently refers to in the classical German tradition as directly social activity.[54]

Marx examines the progressive developmental tendencies of capital secondly with a view to the transition from commodity exchange, which has an independent status under capitalism, to the planned proportioning of the overall process of reproduction. Capital presupposes that the exchange of activities is independent *vis-à-vis* the production and consumption process. This is the case with commodity exchange, since labour, from the standpoint of society as a whole, cannot be exchanged as an act, i.e. not primarily as an activity, but rather has to be exchanged in a 'form of being', that is, in the material form of the product.[55] Now the mechanism of capital leads, however, to a drastic curtailment not only of the socially necessary working hours, but also of circulation unproductive for the realization of surplus value. Marx calls this the revolution of the means of communication and transportation. Although, historically speaking, he could have had only the railways and telegraph in mind, he is nevertheless already comparing the significance of this revolution with the significance of the industrial revolution.[56] By means of today's combination of innovative production and communications technologies, a tendential synchronization of the whole process of reproduction could be achieved which would render the *independent* exchange of commodities presupposed for the reproduction of capital superfluous, and thus also the proportioning of the whole process by *crises* after the fact. This extends to include retaining money as a sign of steering the proportions of the national economy.[57]

Thirdly and finally, Marx discusses the progressive developmental tendencies of capital with a view to new production by producers and consumers. The switch from the natural and traditional reproduction of individuals as labourers and individual members of a class over to the 'social individuals' produced by modern culture bursts the productive and consumptive cycle of the reproduction of capital in a progressive manner.[58] As opposed to the production of commodities, in the cultural form of production 'production ... cannot be separated from the act of production', or an 'interval between production and consumption' arises only for the material agent of what is, nevertheless, a cultural usage.[59] As opposed to the exchange of commodities, the exchange of cultural capabilities results in actuality, i.e. the exchange of material symbolic agents functions *culturally* only if it corresponds to the *actual* exchange of *activities*. Historically, Marx was thinking of culture as ranging from general education all the way to a possible generalization of the acquisition of knowledge in sciences and the arts. He studied 'services' the purchase of which 'by no means entails the specific relation of labour and capital' in terms of these being forms of transition from commodity exchange to the exchange of activities.[60]

The tendency towards the dissolution of the substance of capital is recognizable from these three aspects. The different forms of the division of labour in society as a whole are revolutionized in general, in particular and individually.[61] The previous developmental interconnection of the modes of production and social formations, however, rested on these divisions of labour and their reproduction in class society.[62] The progressive sublation of the conditioning of capital means more than a change in formation within class society. It calls for the unleashing of developmental tendencies already inherent in capitalist society which, nevertheless, can only be realized in this society through conflict. Marx summarizes these in terms of the 'conscious reconstruction of human society' which succeeded the 'prehistory of human society'.[63] The universal tendency of capital is that the 'process of development [is] itself posited and known as a prerequisite of the same.'[64] Marx and Engels no longer have a substantialized concept of 'consciousness'. They view 'consciousness' in its immediate reality as linguistic praxis and in its thus socially mediated reality as 'conscious being'.[65] Language is understood in genetic terms as the need for dealings between individuals, i.e. for social communication.[66] Social communication and cognitive reflexion are fused in language. As distinct from purely sensuous mirroring, language functions in rational knowledge as that 'mirror' through which reflexion on reflexion (discursive thought) becomes possible. 'Objectification' by definition presupposes a communicating commonality.[67] Language is, genetically speaking, not only a product of social reproduction, but rather becomes the 'self-evident existence' of the common body.[68] Marx explicitly refutes the economistic transfer of the effect of the reification of the money form (as a value form) on to the concept of language.[69] W. Hartung has shown that instrumentalist concepts of language fail to grasp the social character of language and cannot draw on Marx's thought.[70]

According to this, the 'conscious reconstitution of human society' contains the change in the history of humankind from a mode of social development based in class conflict to one based in culture. However, the developmental interconnection of the modes of production, social formations and ways of life is always cultural in nature, in that it is mediated through sets of signs[71] which are determined objectively and subjectively. Objectively, cultures are sets of signs that are ordered in such a way that, unlike the material substitution of elements of social production, the social structures of natural acquisition can be passed on by them and actualized through them. Subjectively, sets of signs function as culture to the extent that they make 'activity' possible, i.e. the formation in history of the individual of personality structures, according to which objectively meaningful behaviour can be produced as subjectively meaningful action.[72] 'Conscious reconstitution' does not simply call for the cultural mode of producing, but rather for such at the already modern level of development of the linguistic unity of societal-practical communication and discursive thought.

It is a matter of putting these philosophical orientations on principle on Marx's part into interdisciplinary practice. In consequence, only the strategy for grounding such a theory of the social mode of communication with links to interdisciplinary research will be of interest.

On the Development of a New Mode of Communication Geared to Society as a Whole

In the development of class society to date, forms of the linguistically differentiated unity of social communication and discursive thought have become only partial facts of reason. Investigating whether these forms can be developed into a functionally efficient mode of communication for society as a whole necessitates our first distinguishing between at least three aspects. I shall reformulate both the explanatory advantages and the possible resolution of the shortcomings in the explanation provided by the 'theory of communicative action' in terms of these three aspects: the formation of a new *mode of communication for society as a whole* can be thematized as the contradictory developmental interconnection of *communicative activities* (in Habermas's work the communicative approach to action), *communicative practices* (the structuralist bridging, in one sense) and *communicative relations* (in Habermas's terms, tasks delegated to systems theory).

1   Communicative *activities* are personality structures in keeping with which the reproduction of *immediate* forms of cooperation are coordinated. They are created in the process of the 'individual's socialization',[73] which takes place in the context of group-specific *ways of life*. Individual life becomes directly social in nature in personal relations with other individuals. The concept of 'way of life' emphasizes the socio-cultural structure of the natural-social expressions of life by individuals in groups. The reproduction of group-specific ways of life depends objectively on the relations and material living conditions in society as a whole,[74] and subjectively on the development of individuals into personalities. 'Personality' can be examined as the developmental interconnection of activities, actions and operations.[75] Attributing objective and subjective determinants alternately to the way of life could be effected by specifying 'forms of individuality'.[76] The underlying thesis of a social psychology that follows in the footsteps of Vygotsky and A. N. Leontyev consists of the following with regard to communication (A. A. Leontyev) and thought (Galperin). Communication and cognition develop from communicative and intellectual actions embedded in as yet still *pre*linguistically motivated activities of life into the specific *activities* of linguistic communication and of discursive thought. This linguistic-communicative or intellectual activity then develops, for its part, further via its own levels of action and operation. This restructures and generalizes the point of departure of an as yet still prelin-

guistically motivated, but in A. Luria's sense already 'sympractical' activity of life. Perception, will formation, and cognition can become subject to rationalization through their linguistic organization.[77] The psychogenesis of the linguistic unity of communication and cognition makes possible a rational potential for creativity which is new in terms of evolutionary development. This emerges in the linguistic-communicative use of discursive-cognitive structures and in the discursive-cognitive use of linguistic-communicative structrues.[78] The genesis of the metalinguistic form of resolving contradictions between the two forms of usage presupposes that linguistic communication and discursive thought are already produced and received in terms of a 'textual language.'[79]

Contextually speaking, certain *ways of life* and the emergence of discursive *practices* from communicative practices both already interfere in the text-linguistically differentiated units of communication and cognition. Textual units and their metalinguistic units not only develop within the resolution of contradictions (structurally, from heterogeneities) between 'meaning' and 'sense' (A. N. Leontyev, J. M. Lotman) in contexts determined by the way of life, but rather also in the resolution of the contradictions between the texts and those contexts as are not determined by ways of life. The question whether group-specific ways of life can be reproduced socially itself leads to an expansion of the context to include the prerequisites, conditions and consequences of this reproduction in society as a whole.

2   The question as to the capacity for objective reproduction of group-specific ways of life distinguishes with respect to the life utterances of the individuals between *acting* and *behaving*. Individuals initially act in direct cooperation according to subjective structures of activity. In acting, however, the individuals are behaving objectively, i.e. they fulfil functions of reproduction in society as a whole which go beyond the group-specific context of reproducing their way of life. Communicative *practices* initially represent socio-cultural forms of dealing with one another that have evolved strata-specifically, and that serve to coordinate the social reproduction of cooperations that are spatio-temporally *indirect*. Problems of the social intermediacy (communicability) of cooperation arise in the process of object-bound and productive natural acquisition as well as in the socio-practical reproduction of both the modes of production and social formations, as well as in the intercollective reproduction of group-specific ways of life. The reproduction of socially mediate cooperation includes an at least symbolic emancipation from the experiential knowledge acquired in direct cooperation. The historical consequence of the genesis of communicative practices from symbolic via ideological to discursive practices cannot be dealt with in depth here. In my opinion, it would be possible to show in terms of the history of sciences, for example, that if the reproduction of indirect forms of cooperation (in the appropriate contexts of the modes of production, social formations and ways of life) is necessarily and intensively subject to consistent expansion, then the discursive

practices required differentiate out into natural, social and human sciences[80] which feed back steadily into their original contexts.

3   The integration of discursive practices in a *mode of communication for society as a whole* in which the developmental complex of the modes of production, social formation and ways of life are coordinated cannot emerge from the simple addition of the specific contents and forms of these practices. This integration requires that the principal solutions for contextual and textual contradictions be grounded discursively in the first place and institutionalized in an ensemble of communications media that are public.

An integration of this type, however, could not function as a mode of communication for society as a whole unless the communication *relations* were changed. I understand the latter to mean those general prerequisites of social communication which optimize linguistic communication without having to be actualized linguistically. This involves, in negative terms, the exclusion of any monopolization of the means of communication, and in positive terms, specific communications technologies.[81] The prime criterion determining such *communications technologies* would be that they enable general participation in public communication and simultaneously relieve the output of linguistic communication by operationalizing linguistic levels of action.

The developmental interconnection of levels of activity, action and operation already pinpointed in the above-mentioned Soviet research to date allows us to anticipate the following: the communications-technological operationalization of previous levels of discursive action will lead to a restructuring of linguistic activity at a higher discursive level of argumentation. If the development and dissemination of such communications technologies is successful, a type of communications media will be available for the first time in human history which does not have a reifying effect, as is still the case with industrial communications media – if only from a technical standpoint, since the new type would itself be the product of the operationalization of discursive argumentation. The linguistically differentiated unity of communication and cognition could not in any case be stabilized as a means of communication for society as a whole without the existence of such technologies. The use of such communications technologies, which is generally taken as a matter of course, returns us to the original question as to the psychogenesis of communicative activities which might then be differently structured.

Habermas, Foucault and Luhmann would seem respectively to declare the action side to communicative activities, the structural side to communicative practices and the functional side to communicative relations to be the reference point for their respective models. Providing the still absent justifications for a theory of modes of communication for society as a whole will involve an arduous process of elaborating the fundamentals of the theory. Anyone who, like Habermas, gives in to Popper's ideological verdict on dialectics cannot go down the path to a synthesis. In today's discussion on the principles of theory we have yet to rediscover what

Hegel understood as 'the idea', the portrayal of which Lenin recognized was surely the 'best description of dialectics', and to rediscover what Hegel examined as *the nature of the copula in judgement* in his critique of Kant's formalism, and in which, as Lenin saw it, the 'materialist roots' of the dialectics of the concept lay.[82]

9 The Linguistification of the Sacred and the Delinguistification of the Economy

Johannes Berger

Any survey of sociological writings over the last two decades invariably evokes the impression that social theory formation remains under the firm control of functionalism. Although there have been significant projects put forward on the part, for example, of French structuralism, these were never quite accepted by mainstream sociology. Critical Theory has restricted itself for some time now merely to nurturing its tradition in the form of new editions, and 'genuine' Marxism, which during the protest movements caused some disturbance with its critique of 'bourgeois thought', can no longer ignore the crisis it has been caught in for some time. Are all serious attempts at a theory of the social totality bound for better or for worse to functionalist criteria? Those who have fought their way through Habermas's *The Theory of Communicative Action* (*TCA*) may have noticed this bond, with either resignation or satisfaction. 'No theory of society', writes Habermas programatically (*TCA*, vol. II, p. 199) 'can be taken seriously today if it does not at least situate itself with respect to Parsons.' In fact, if we prophylactically equate those writings which are taken seriously with those that should be (though this need not be the case), then, at least in West Germany – compared with the positivism dispute of twenty years ago – the ongoing standardization of intellectual methods is striking. Theories that lay claim to describing society as a whole tend to take the concept of functional differentiation as their guiding light; (four) functional areas of society are distinguished from one another, levels of the order of socialization (interaction, organization, society) marked off from one another, and types of coordination developed (social and systemic integration; economists will perhaps talk of a 'Luhmann-Schluchter-Habermas theorem') – as if this were a matter of course. The German contributions are characterized by their being variations of Weberianism (left Weberians vs. right Weberians). Habermas's 'theory of communicative action' is an impressive testament to this state of affairs. For Habermas, Weber's theory of rationalization 'still holds out the best prospect of explaining the social pathologies that appeared in the wake of capitalist modernization' (*TCA*, vol. II, p. 303). For long stretches the book reads like an attempt to reformulate Weber's 'diagnosis of contemporary society' (loss of meaning and freedom through the secularization of religion, the monetarization of labour and the bureaucratization of task performance) within the interpretative framework of the interaction of 'system' and 'lifeworld'. We must concede, however, that quite unlike functionalism, the author all the same tries adamantly to maintain links to Marx's oeuvre. Thus, the concluding remarks are entitled: 'From Parsons via Weber to Marx'.

Habermas's study is admittedly less concerned with Marx than with Western Marxism (*TCA*, vol. II, p. 332). But the theory of communicative action is Marxist through its reference, however modified, to the theme of 'crisis and critique' excised in functionalism. Habermas's book claims to provide a critical theory of society (cf., in particular, *TCA*, vol. II, pp. 374ff.). This is brought into being by liberating the project from the constraints of the older Critical Theory promulgated by Horkheimer and Adorno. In what follows, I shall concentrate on discussing the question as to what potential avenues for critique are open to a Critical Theory freed from the claims of a philosophy of consciousness and reformulated in light of the tradition stretching from Weber to Parsons. I shall start by sketching out Habermas's main intentions, for these hold together what are otherwise the highly tangled and twisted threads of his thought. I shall completely ignore questions of interpretative accuracy, although the sections on Marx and Weber especially prompt critical discussion. I neither wish to join in the widespread lament that the book is so long and so unreadily digestible, nor tarry with praising its richness of thought; instead, I shall press ahead directly to the core of the theory. What does the theory of communicative action wish to achieve and what does it accomplish with respect to explaining the process of capitalist modernization?

Habermas intends his study as the development of a 'theory of communicative action that clarifies the normative foundations of a critical theory of society' (*TCA*, vol. II, pp. 396f., and vol. I, p. xl). The core of this theory (*TCA*, vol. I, p. 275) involves the elaboration of the idea that understanding through language or communicative rationality is the proper – and not only a derivative – mechanism for coordinating action. However, the extended passages on 'the foundations of theory' are not an end in themselves, but serve to provide the basis for a theory of society. Social theory needs normative foundations which can be obtained through a theory of action that functions reconstructively. The assumption that a theory of action should form the basis for social theory is the point of departure; this is by no means obvious and certainly requires further justification. Another standpoint is possible, e.g. if we merely detach the concept of modernization from that of rationality (*TCA*, vol. I, p. 6). For Habermas, it is the problem of rationalization which connects the theory of action with the theory of society. He derives the interlocking of the two from Weber's sociology where, according to Habermas, action was interpreted in terms of the guiding idea of purposive rationality. The *constraints* of a theory of action founded on the concept of purposive rationality then prejudice the direction of Weber's social theory. The narrow basis of Weber's action theory then gives the latter's social theory a one-sided weighting (*TCA*, vol. I, pp. 273, 339f.). Habermas adheres firmly to the notion that a theory of society must proceed from action and its rationality, but he seeks a more comprehensive concept of the rationality of action than merely purposive rationality. This concept is communicative rationality as prefigured in the tradition stemming from Mead and Durkheim. It is expressed in all modes of behaviour for which reasons can be given. It is embodied in the central experience of the 'unconstrained, unifying, consensus-bringing force of argumentative speech, in which different participants overcome their merely subjective views and, owing to the mutuality of rationally motivated conviction, assure themselves of both the unity of the objective world and the intersubjectivity of their lifeworld' (*TCA*, vol. I, p. 10).

The idea of communicative rationality as the normative foundation for a theory of society is suitable for a theory that proceeds *reconstructively* only to the extent that such rationality is already inherent in the basis for validity being granted to a discourse, i.e. – and this is the Hegelian element in Habermas's work – it has already become 'true in practice'. But Habermas does not rest content to search for the presence of reason in the irreducible presuppositions of (rational) speech, but rather postulates – in a sense different from Horkheimer and Adorno's *Dialectic of Enlightenment* – an *increase* in communicative rationality in the course of modernization. The mechanism of linguistic communication based on validity claims develops in the course of the process of the linguistification of the sacred, reaching an ever more unadulterated form (*TCA*, vol. I, p. 342). 'In modern societies', the book concludes, 'there is such an expansion of the scope of contingency for interaction loosed from normative contexts that the inner logic of communicative action "becomes practically true" in the deinstitutionalized forms of intercourse of the familial private sphere as well as in the public sphere stamped by the mass media' (*TCA*, vol. II, p. 403).

The linguistification of the sacred in the domain of symbolic reproduction (the family and the public sphere) is, however, only one side of a rationalization process; the other is delinguistification among forms of material reproduction – and this includes the economy and state administration (!). The latter becomes the domain of a purposive rational action that no longer relies on language as a mechanism of consensus. The fact that Habermas does not merely swap the concept of purposive rationality for that of communicative rationality (or strategic action; I shall return to this terminology below), but splits the process of rationalization into these two diametrically opposed concepts, is, to my mind, the book's fascinating key argument. In the course of modernization, what happens is not simply that purposive rational orientations spread, as Weber suggests (in Habermas's interpretation); nor does organic solidarity simply acquire a progressive preponderance over mechanical solidarity, as in Durkheim; similarly, history does not end hopelessly in the context of total blindingness engendered by instrumental reason, as in Horkheimer and Adorno. Rather, like two sinusoids that cross one another, increasing communicative rationality in the 'lifeworld' entails greater purposive rationality in the 'system'. The basic problem of the continuation of the modernization process consists then in the difficulty that a *further* extension of purposive rationality forces the reverse to occur in communicative rationality. However, unlike in the case of the sinusoids, it is not a matter of a cyclical development; the threat to communicative rationality by the further expansion of purposive rationality does not produce a lower threshold where purposive rationality diminishes and communicative rationality increases again. The opportunities for consensus provided by reaching understanding in language are, rather, *secularly* threatened, without the increase of purposive rationality itself generating a countertrend.

Distinguishing between two diametrically opposed types of rationality with irreducible criteria of rationality avoids the shortcoming of the phenomenological tradition, namely the simple disolution of societies into processes of communication (*TCA*, vol. II, p. 2). 'Precisely insofar as social integration has more and more to be secured via communicatively achieved consensus, there is a pressing question as to the limits of the integrative capacity of action oriented to reaching understanding, the limits of the empirical efficacy of rational motives' (*TCA*, vol. II, p. 111).

In keeping with this line of argument, Habermas develops a two-stage concept of society: society must be conceived of as lifeworld and as systém at the same time (*TCA*, vol. II, p. 254). Society is accessible from the participatory perspective of acting subjects as a normatively integrated lifeworld; as a functionally tuned system it is accessible from the observational perspective of (system-theory schooled) sociologists. Accordingly, there are two types of action coordination: either via the consensus of the participants, be it secured by world-images or produced linguistically; or via 'functional connections' (a somewhat vague idea). Habermas introduces Lockwood's far-reaching distinction of system integration and social integration, which was expanded into a critique of Parsons, but surprisingly, without explicitly referring to him. The systematic development of Lockwood's idea is what takes Habermas beyond Parsons. The 'rationalization of contexts of communicative action and the emergence of subsystems of purposive-rational economic and administrative action' are, as Habermas does not tire of stressing, 'processes that have to be sharply distinguished' (*TCA*, vol. II, p. 303). Because Parsonian functionalism – according to Habermas – treats both processes as equals at the level of basic concepts, it cannot describe the pathologies of modernization.

Partially following Weber, Habermas depicts the process of societal rationalization as the expansion of subsystem-specific types of purposive rational action (*TCA*, vol. I, p. 284), and in part presents it functionalistically as increased complexity or an expanded steering or (adaptation) capacity. Cultural rationalization or the rationalization of the lifeworld (and here I am bundling together things Habermas wished to keep separate) is a multi-faceted process whose components[1] Habermas analyses in a series of different approaches. These analyses and the fusion of these components in the process of rationalization of the lifeworld are one of the book's exceptional achievements, one that has, to my mind, no equal among contemporary studies.

To fail to recognize the importance Habermas ascribes to the distinction between rationalization of the lifeworld and rationalization of the system would be to miss the book's central intention completely. With his theory of communicative action Habermas explicitly claims to be able to identify and explain the 'pathologies of modernity' which other research strategies ignore for methodological reasons (*TCA*, vol. II, p. 378). At the level of critique the theory of communicative action claims superiority over all comparable undertakings, be it Marxist orthodoxy – which is not specified more closely – and which adheres to, so it is claimed, a point of departure that is over-economistic in focus. (On pp. 342ff. in vol. II, the old objections raised against Marxism, namely its economistic approach and its monism, are reproduced without the justifications for these claims being improved in any way.) A critical advantage is also claimed over the older Critical Theory, which failed because of the exhaustion of the paradigm of a philosophy of consciousness (*TCA*, vol. I, p. 386). An even greater superiority in critical power is claimed over approaches in the social sciences which obstruct any path along which they might identify or explain pathologies which can be reliably diagnosed only through a theory of communicative action, either owing to their methodological foundations or their cognitive interest. These pathologies, which can be discovered only using the basic conceptual framework of a communicative theory, all converge in the idea that (at least under 'advanced capitalism') a communicatively structured lifeworld becomes crushed, or, so Habermas says, by formally organized subsystems of purposive rational action. The 'unleashed functionalist reason of system maintenance', according to a dramatic and ambiguous formulation in the first volume, 'disregards and overrides the claim to reason ingrained in communicative sociation' (*TCA*, vol. I, p. 399). That *all* 'social pathologies ... are today becoming increasingly visible' is to be explained by the fact that 'communicatively structured domains of life are being subordinated to the imperatives of autonomous, formally organized systems of action' (TCA, vol. I, p. xl). But neither the secularization of world views ('cultural rationalization', according to conservatives) nor the structural differentiation of society as such (as some in the ecology movements maintain) is pathological in the sense of a faulty development. What is pathological is the 'cultural impoverishment that threatens a lifeworld whose traditional substance has been devalued' as a result of the separation of elitist 'expert-cultures' from the culture of everyday life (*TCA*, vol. II, pp. 326, 330) – Weber's thesis of the 'loss of meaning' (*Sinnverlust*). Equally pathological is the intrusion of forms of economic and administrative rationality into domains which reproduce themselves via processes of reaching understanding in language – Weber's thesis of the 'loss of freedom' (*Freiheitsverlust*). It is no coincidence that Habermas speaks of 'pathologies' in the Durkheimian tradition and not of 'crises' in the Marxist tradition: crises lead either to a resolution or to destruction; resolution is 'self-purgation' and destruction is 'self-destruction'. Pathologies continue or are stopped from the outside. As faulty developments, pathologies can be *corrected*. The division of labour itself is not, according to Durkheim, such a faulty development, but becomes one only if it is pressed ahead with too rapidly and to too great an extent (thus Luhmann's claim that societies can falsely differentiate themselves). It is not inequality as such that disrupts a society, but only coerced inequality; thus it can be avoided by guaranteeing legal, political and social equality of opportunity. Then class conflict cannot come about, for this has its roots in economic crises. In that case a situation in which the proletariat has 'nothing to lose but its chains' does not occur at the outset. In this manner, sociology as a whole has followed Durkheim and not Marx.

Now the inherent threat to the possibilities of reaching understanding in language and the chances for achieving a consensus which stem from the constantly expanding 'monetary-administrative-bureaucratic complex' (the term occasionally used to describe the modern 'Leviathan') results from a paradoxical development – paradoxical in so far as the overburdening of the lifeworld by increasing 'system complexity' (*TCA*, vol. II, pp. 343, 375) first becomes possible through the prior rationalization of the lifeworld itself (ibid., p. 317). 'The rationalization of the lifeworld makes possible the emergence and growth of subsystems whose independent imperatives turn back destructively on the lifeworld itself' (*TCA*, vol. II, p. 186). The degree of causality intended varies in the different instances in Habermas's book between necessary condition, causation, an opening up of the options etc.; at times, Habermas claims merely to describe and interpret. 'In a differentiated social system', one important passage reads,

> the lifeworld seems to shrink to a subsystem. This should not be read causally, as if the structures of the lifeworld changed in dependence on increases in systemic complexity. The opposite is true: increases in complexity are dependent on the structural differentiation of the lifeworld. However, we may explain the dynamics of this structural transformation ... it follows the inner logic of communicative rationalization. (TCA, vol. II, p. 173)

Implicit here is a pronounced, quite idiosyncratic theory of evolution which seeks to explain the origin of modern societies by expanding the basic ideas of Piaget's cognitive psychology into a cognitivist theory of social evolution. This states that the rise of modern societies must be conceived as the translation of a prior cultural rationalization into a social counterpart. The threshold of modern societies is crossed precisely at the point when (and because!) progress in rationality already exists on a cultural level and, as it were, it steps out of the monasteries and into social reality (*TCA*, vol. I, p. 216).

In what follows I wish to forgo a critical discussion of the strand of evolution theory Habermas' book contains. I shall instead concentrate on a second main strand, namely the diagnosis of contemporary society, in the context of which Habermas exploits the conceptual framework of a theory of communicative action.

The diagnosis of contemporary society is, as stated, developed in the framework of a theory of communication. The intention of this approach is to abandon the 'paradigm of the philosophy of consciousness – namely, a subject that represents objects and toils with them – in favor of the paradigm of linguistic philosophy – namely, that of intersubjective understanding or communication' (*TCA*, vol. I, p. 390) A parallel formulation relates to actors rather than cognizant subjects and is expressed as abandonment of a means-end scheme in favour of a schematization in terms of the symbolically mediated interaction of at least two subjects capable of language and action. For the whole book seeks to initiate or accomplish the change of paradigm from teleological to communicative action (*TCA*, vol. I, p. 339). According to Habermas, the tradition of sociology, at least from Marx, via Weber, to Parsons, rests on overnarrow action-theoretic foundations. Here action is understood as 'poiesis' and not as 'praxis'. The model taken for interpreting action was the individual craftsman purposively working on an object. The means–ends scheme derived from this is indeed not designed to fit Ego-Alter situations.[2] The 'teleological model' does not provide an accurate account of the process of reaching intersubjective understanding in language. It is therefore only logical to replace the teleological model of action by a (more encompassing) communicative model which encompasses all aspects of the rationality of action.

In Habermas's eyes, the overnarrow base of the traditional theory of action is thus the ultimate reason for the deficiencies of the diagnosis of contemporary society. And, conversely, only on the basis of a theory of communicative action can an exhaustive diagnosis of contemporary society be made. There is no denying the theoretical progress made by substituting the communicative model of action for its teleological counterpart. My objections are as a consequence directed not against the replacement of the means–end scheme by that of communicative rationality, but against the idea that a reorientation on the level of the theory of action *itself* already guarantees a better social analysis. It is my contention that the close links between the diagnosis of contemporary society and a specific version of the theory of communictive action are the cause of the specific weakness of Habermas's own diagnosis. In order to explain this objection, I shall first outline my critique of Habermas's particular version of the theory of communicative action and then turn to the arguments which are at the roots of Habermas's diagnosis of contemporary society.

Let me initially touch on three points briefly: (1) the confining of phenomena of power and dissent to an obscured background; (2) the polarization of two forms of action (instead of their multifarious interlocking) as well as the inconsistencies in that polarization; and (3) the allocation of action types to domains of action.

1 The point of reference for the analysis of factual interactions becomes the 'potential for rationality' already inherent in the 'validity basis of speech' (*TCA*, vol. I, p. 339). Microsociologically speaking, aspects of dissent and of the power relations embedded in speech-situations (cf. Foucault's microphysics of power) are background *vis-à-vis* the primary

interest in 'achieving, sustaining and renewing consensus' (*TCA*, vol. I, p. 17). And from a macrosociological perspective, the course of history is stylized as a process in the course of which communicative rationality, already present in communicative action, gains increasing recognition at least in the sphere of the lifeworld. Does not Habermas's argument against Mead – that he neglects 'economics, warfare, and the struggle for political power' (*TCA*, vol. II, p. 110) – also apply to him? The author could matter-of-factly insist that each book must first be measured against its own intentions and that the primary question here is therefore whether he has succeeded in adequately reconstructing the rationality potential inherent in language. Nonetheless, the bias towards consensus generates a rationalistic weakness of the theory which, e.g., excludes or at least casts insufficient light on obstacles to communicative reason rooted in instinctual drive structure or the hierarchical nature of social relations.

2   What is decisive for the shortcomings of the diagnosis of contemporary society is not the paradigm shift of action-theory as such, but rather Habermas's characteristic contrasting of two types of action. Moreover, specific obscurities and inconsistencies slip into this crucial contrast that have consequences for the overall analysis of society.

Habermas safeguards himself against an assessment of his work that misunderstands him as equating communicative action with linguistic communication: interaction must not be assimilated to speech (*TCA*, vol. I, p. 96). However, types of social action can be distinguished according to the *kind* of coordination of action involved. This is the case with communicative action involving processes of reaching linguistic understanding. Communicative action ensues when reaching linguistic understanding is the mechanism for coordinating action. Yet is there any form of action that is not linguistically mediated? Thus, in the table on p. 329, vol. I, success-oriented action ranks among the types of linguistically mediated interaction. Moreover, just as communicative action contains teleological components, so, too, teleological action contains communicative elements. One can reach a linguistic understanding successfully and succeed communicatively. The two figures of action cannot be disentangled as easily as Habermas imagines. Communication is possible for communication's sake and in order to achieve a specific purpose; just think of the wily travelling salesman using personal conversation as part of his sales strategy. Similarly, one can be interested in goal-oriented activity in order to increase the chances for communication.[3]

But perhaps the two types of action cannot be distinguished suitably from one another in terms of whether they are mediated linguistically or not, but instead according to their inner telos. Along this line of demarcation Habermas distinguishes between success – and communication-oriented action. The two forms are not just analytical types: concrete actions can supposedly be classified from this viewpoint (*TCA*, vol. I, p. 285). Success-oriented action is defined more closely as stragtegic action. Strategic action is governed by egocentric calculations of utility (ibid., p. 94); communicative action, by contrast, exists when the actions of the agents involved are coordinated not through egocentric calculations of success, but through acts of reaching understanding' (ibid., pp. 285f.). This delimitation recalls both Durkheim's identification of morality with altruistic attitudes and the exclusion of all egoistic action from the moral sphere. Either the Ego seeks its own success or the achievement of consensus with Alter. Communicative action is essentially behaviour-oriented toward consensus; and agreement lies at its core. Whoever, on the contrary, acts strategically only wishes to have an impact on others; whoever acts communicatively seeks to achieve linguistic understanding. On this basis, a critique of social conditions that reduce the other person to a means can then be developed (see the key passage, *TCA*, vol. II, p. 196). This form of differentiating between two types of action is problematic, not only because it creates an inflexible dichotomy of concrete actions such that an action can fall under only one of the two specified types and cannot involve a mixture of the two, but also because the boundary between the two types of action shifts. For example, the non-communicative type of action is labelled alternately with terms such as teleological action, instrumental command, strategic action, purposive-rational action etc. (see, for example, *TCA*, vol. I, pp. 232f.). Sometimes purposiveness is contrasted with communication, then strategic action with communicative action, purposive rationality with communicative rationality. Are all these contrasts equivalent? Habermas admits (ibid., p. 101) that all action has a teleological structure. Even communicative behaviour follows plans (*TCA*, vol. II, p. 127). If this is the case, then a sharper distinction must be made between aims and purposes, and purposes must be defined more closely as intended success. Either instrumental command or communicative understanding is the telos of rationality, says Habermas (*TCA*, vol. I, p. 11). This is the old, hotly disputed distinction between labour and interaction, although criticism would appear to have led to nothing but a reformulation of this distinction in concepts of strategic and communicative action. The original critique of Habermas's version of the relation between work and interaction implied that the two moments did not constitute sharply separated functional orders of instrumental and communicative action, but rather, precisely as Habermas himself says in the quotation from Piaget (*TCA*, vol. I, pp. 14 (note) and 409), that 'two types of reciprocal action ... combined in social cooperation: the "reciprocal action between the subjects and objects", which is mediated through teleological action, and the "reciprocal action between the subject and other subjects", which is mediated through communicative action.' Furthermore, it is by no means evident that, for instance, purposive rational action is of the same breadth as the strategic action of *homo oeconomicus*; and the latter need not be the same as action that instrumentalizes the other person only as means for egoistic ends. As Weber says,[4] a person acts in a purposive rational sense if he orients his action toward ends, means, and side-effects, and he rationally weighs both the means against the ends, and the ends against the side-effects, as well as finally also the various possible ends against one another.' The institutionalization of purposive rationality is not *ipso facto* identical with an increase in the *inversion* of ends and means, if only for the reason that the latter are based on structures other than that of goal-oriented action. When Weber, for example, represents state administration as being superior to all other forms of administration with respect to efficiency, this precisely does not mean that in it the inversion of ends and means reaches its zenith. The institutionalization of purposive rational economic and administrative action is precisely not meant as the institutionalization of conditions in which others are perceived solely as a means. It is at least questionable with regard to *administrative* rationality whether this must be conceived of as a domain of selfish calculation or even of the inversion of ends and means. In short, if it is a matter of distinguishing between purposive rationality, namely the realization of a plan, and communication, then the two types are interwoven; if it is a matter of the inversion of ends and means, then this inversion cannot simply be universalized. Rather, the task of theory consists in uncovering the origins of such an inversion. Marx's proposal was to identify the transition from an orientation toward use-values to one toward exchange-values as the core of this inversion and to trace the history of its morphology from this point of departure.

3   The most far-reaching consequence of the theory of action is, however, the firm allocation of types of strategic and communicative action to specific functional areas of the social system. Not only are, for instance, all residues of practical rationality thereby elided from strategic action; in a further step, this type of action is then allocated to an area in which it becomes the dominant type of action. In the diagnosis of contemporary society, the domains of the family and the public sphere are allocated to communicative action, those of the economy and state to purposive rational action (where, e.g., does the traffic system belong?). The latter are *systemically* integrated via the media of money and power, the former *socially* integrated via the medium of language. In my opinion, the intentions of Lockwood's distinction are missed if the effectiveness of various mechanisms of integration is allocated to specific functional areas of society. These mechanisms of integration are perceived more clearly if all social subsystems are thought of as integrated both systemically and socially. Bowles and Gintis,[5] for example, construe the connection between structures and actions along these lines.

It follows from this, for instance, that labour is not just an expenditure of labour power in the manner of machine performance; it shatters the framework of instrumental action understood as the technically applied appropriation of natural objects. It is rather an ensemble of economic, political and cultural practices, structured by the capitalist relations of production. By means of such a concept, processes of business management can, for example, be analysed; this is, by contrast, not the case if we use only a concept of instrumental action.

This brings me to the diagnosis of contemporary society as engendered by a theory of action and which amounts to the assertion that communicative rationality is threatened by a steady increase in the domain of purposive rationality (cf. *TCA*, vol. I, p. 342).

The prevalent theme of the critique of society is this threat to or restriction of the possibility of consensus-formation in the familial and public spheres as a result of the expansion of the 'monetary-administrative complex' beyond the boundaries of the subsystems of economy and state. Instead of confining itself to the domains of economy and state administration, where it suffices, instrumental rationality intrudes into communicatively structured areas of life and thereby causes disturbances in the symbolic lifeworld (*TCA*, vol. II, p. 307). What is worthy of criticism, if we follow Habermas, is not that the economy and the state are organized according to purposive rational criteria, nor that areas of formerly communicative action are transformed into subsystems of purposive rational action, but rather that this process does not stop at the boundaries of the economy and the state. 'It is characteristic of the pattern of rationalization in capitalist societies that the complex of cognitive-instrumental rationality establishes itself at the cost of practical rationality; communicative relations are reified' (*TCA*, vol. I, p. 363). Habermas reformulates the theme of reification to be found in Critical Theory, regarding it as a process of the deformation of the lifeworld by processes of bureaucratization and monetarization. The *site* of reification is *not* the factory, and its source is not a particular form of organization of alienated labour; it is located, rather, at the border between 'lifeworld' and 'system', and consists in the deformation of lifeworld structures by forms alien to everyday practice. Actions, Habermas maintains, can be coordinated either systemically by the media of money and power, or socially by processes of reaching linguistic understanding. Material reproduction is the domain of system integration, symbolic reproduction is the domain of social integration. Material production can be handed over 'painlessly' (!) to the steering mechanisms of non-linguistic media. The switch from symbolic reproduction (socialization, cultural reproduction and social integration) over to system-integration, however, is pathological. With regard to aspects of rationalization, the switch of the economic – which has separated out from comprehensive life-contexts and has been normatively neutralized (Polanyi) – over to non-linguistic steering mechanisms (for this realm can be handed over to system-integration just as 'painlessly' as can state adminstration) is not in itself problematic. Pathologies result only at the *battle front* between 'system' and 'lifeworld', and even there only in *one* direction, namely the switch of the 'system' over into the 'lifeworld'.

If one follows Habermas, one must distinguish between a domain of progressive linguistification and one of progressive (legitimate) delinguistification. In the course of development, a linguistification of the 'sacred' has ensued in the lifeworld or a switch from normative social integration over to discursive will-formation. Evidence for this is to be found in numerous examples that can be taken from the everyday practice of family life and child-raising. (Mothers today tend to ask their children when crossing the street whether they are sufficiently motivated to do so.) This process of linguistification is understood by Habermas as progress in the dimension of rationality. Of course, this linguistification of norms leads to an enormous overburdening of action coordination. After all, norms are supposed to reduce the contingencies of action. This is the idea behind the sociological concept of institutionalization. Institutions limit contingencies of action by designating only certain ideas as acceptable. If this normative basis of action has to be justified linguistically, uncertainties in action and an overburdening of the coordination of action are the result. Such a linguistification cannot occur in all domains of society, for this would lead to the collapse of social cohesion. A solution to the problem of linguistification emerges when this process is matched by delinguistification in other areas of action, which Habermas pinpoints as the economy and state subsystems. The overburdening of coordination via linguistification, on the one hand, corresponds, on the other, to an unburdening of coordination by a switch to the steering mechanisms of power and money (cf. *TCA*, vol. II, p. 378). A critical phase of development arises only when those domains of action which cannot forfeit a reliance on language (social integration, cultural tradition and socialization) are also switched over to delinguistified action coordination. In the economic sphere, language can and must be forfeited; it would only have a disruptive effect there. But the 'lifeworld' cannot give up that which would impair the 'system'. And conversely, the same process that represents a progress in systemic rationalization (its switching over to steering mechanisms) constitutes a step backward in rationalization in the 'lifeworld'.

Habermas's key idea can be understood both as an attempt to mark his work off from the revolutionary idea of wanting to shape all social relations according to principles of communicative rationality (socialism based on Soviets) and as the recognition of the evolutionary advantage of the development of purposive-rational subsystems – an advantage that we cannot abolish or go back behind without relapsing behind the stage of modernization already attained. Just as in functionalism, there can be no further stage of social evolution following the stage of functional differentiation, but only regression behind an attained level of differentiation, so, too, the process of the uncoupling of 'system' and 'lifeworld' can only be continued, but not reversed or overcome.

A critical discussion of this analysis could, in principle, also be carried out by contesting that deformations of genuinely communicative internal structures of the lifeworld by the encroachment of forms of economic and administrative rationality, or by classifying this as the ineluctable social costs of social rationalization. Habermas would probably ascribe objections of this type to functionalist reason (the critique of which is the prime object of the second volume). According to Habermas, only the conceptual framework of communicative action avails the perspective from which the process of social rationalization can be understood as a contradiction between linguistically engendered lifeworld structures and the growing complexity of subsystems of purposive rational action. The theory of communicative action, however, seems able to grasp *only* this contradiction, and either completely ignores or pays slight attention to the internal contradictions of the 'system' itself and to such contradictions as arise from the intrusion of lifeworld by orientation into the subsystems of purposive rational action. An analysis that focuses on the threat to communication rationally posed by the expansion of the 'monetary-bureaucratic complex' fails firstly to grasp contradictions in the area of system-integration and, secondly, does not embrace specific problematic situations that result from the intrusion of 'lifeworld' principles into the subsystems of purposive rational action.

Let us take the first objection first, namely that Habermas on the whole paints an inadequate picture of intra-systemic problems and contradictions. This objection can be best described in terms of three separate points.

1 The subsystem analysis can be summed up in three statements. *Firstly*, economic system and state administration are formally organized domains of action; *secondly*, they are differentiated via the media of money and power; and *thirdly*, they constitute the domain of purposive rationality.
(a) Compared with the family and the public sphere, the economic system certainly exhibits a high degree of formal organization. Nonetheless, I would prefer to analyse the economic system not just from the perspective of formation of formal organizations, but also from the vantage point of the dualism of money-steered markets and organizations based on rulership, which are each organized according to different principles of rationality. This line of analysis has been taken up in the 'institutionalism school' ranging from Marx to Williamson.[6]
(b) The media of money and power are not distributed, as Habermas's analysis suggests, between the economic system and the state apparatus. On the one hand, action *in* organizations is not mediated by money alone; sociological analyses of industry discuss, for example, commands by persons, hierarchization, formal procedures, and technologization as mechanisms of action coordination.[7] On the other hand, although the rational orientation of profit has been based on a calculation of all costs and income in monetary terms, it is still pertinent to distinguish between monetary steering and profit orientation. All discussions of the possibility of limiting the profit-principle while retaining market allocation would otherwise become obsolete.
(c) Since it is bound to the view that purposive rationality expands successfully, the analysis suggests that apparatuses function efficiently and thus disregards the internal problems with which formal organizations must contend. That such organizations do not just fulfil functions, but also serve the perpetuation of domination is a viewpoint just as neglected as is the whole analysis of the barriers to rationality-limits in formal organization-formation, which is inspired by a critical reading of Weber in the sociology of organization.

2 The diagnosis of contemporary society developed within the referential framework of the theory of communicative action ignores such analyses of the instabililities of the economic system as have been developed from Marx to post-Keynesianist variants, for example Harrod. Stable subsystems expand more or less as though 'self-propelled'; their growth destablizes only the lifeworld, but not themselves. In the analysis of contemporary society there is little room for such a thing as that which Marx terms the 'immanent contradictions in the production of relative surplus value'.

When Habermas addresses crises of the economic system, this tends to occur in the form of the argument of the 'blanket that turned out to be too short': it is still just large enough to cover the industrial conflict between labour and capital, but too small for 'disparity problems' that show up at the edges. Nor does Habermas deal systematically with the effects which the implementation of restrictive forms of labour in factory and administration has on the area of symbolic reproduction. This point has to do with the fact that in Habermas's work reification precisely does not arise *ipso facto* from the replacement of language by money and power, but only in instances when this replacement happens in an area in which language cannot be dispensed with, namely in the formation of communities, in cultural reproduction and in socialization.

3 As regards interferences between economy and state: the diagnosis of contemporary society is permeated by a bloc-like notion of the monetary-administrative complex. By their equidirectional growth, the two subsystems cause fewer problems for one another than for the lifeworld. This line of analysis has questionable consequences for attempts to grasp self-blocking mechanisms of welfare-state capitalism. Such self-blockages result from the interferences of economy and state; crisis-retarding state interventions could, for example, have a crisis-producing effect precisely because they block the mechanism by which the industrial reserve army is the central precondition for the growth of capitalist systems.[8] I naturally do not wish to claim that Habermas is not familiar with such ideas; he has provided much inspiration for analyses of the welfare state. But such a critique lies on the margins of the road taken by the analysis of contemporary society presented by the theory of communicative action.

A *second* line of criticism against the slanting of Habermas's diagnosis of contemporary society can be developed if we conceive of the fact that Critical Theory analyses lifeworld–system interferences only in *one* direction and does not take note of the equally significant expansion of lifeworld principles into subsystems of purposive rational action. The latter tendency has been addressed by conservative critiques of society. The subsystems no longer function owing to interference from lifeworld principles. For example, trends toward the humanization of labour or democratization of the economy could be interpreted as the interference of communicative rationality into formally organized subsystems. In fact, neither the stage of development characterized by welfare-state capitalism nor the social conflicts thereof are adequately described by the statement that some 'functionalist reason gone wild' threatens the communicative infrastructure of the lifeworld. Broader problematic situations would be uncovered by the more abstract proposal that the jurisdiction of 'principles' for particular areas of action has substantively become questionable. The uncertainty as to which principles should be used to decide which problems has become universal – a result of the interpenetration of system and lifeworld. By means of explanation, let me draw on Bowles and Gintis's attempt to describe current conflicts in terms of the polarity between *rights in persons* and *property rights*.[9] Principles such as 'communicative rationality', 'purposive rationality', or 'property rights' and 'rights in persons' can hardly be kept in quarantine. For example, the disputes in the mid-1970s over the restructuring of the economic system after the 'end of the postwar period' could be described as the attempt to decide whether property rights or economic civil rights would determine the accumulation process. And it is directly relevant to chances for reform whether the demarcation line between conflicting principles runs between 'system' and 'lifeworld' or between economy and state.

In the theory of communicative action, in other words, only the assimilation of the realm of genuine processes of reaching linguistic understanding to media-directed sybsystems is declared pathological, whereas the delinguistification of the economy is regarded as a quite normal development. By contrast, the act of generalizing the idea of 'boundary-crossing' principles – i.e. the attempts of social groups to transfer practices which follow different rationality patterns on to social situations in which they no longer apply – would not just complete the portrait of welfare-state capitalism; it would also shed a different light on the question of the possibility of social change. Habermas, in good Marxist fashion, links protests to conflicts. However, he considers the 'old' conflicts to be settled and thus the old protest-potential (of the workers' movement) to be tamed, for it purportedly no longer substantially disturbs the 'system'. The new conflicts arise along the seams between 'systems' and 'lifeworld' (*TCA*, vol. II, p. 395). As long as system/lifeworld conflicts were limited to the sphere of material reproduction (as is the case, for instance, when the social state takes members of a lifeworld only in their role as consumers and clients), the process of modernization could successfully ignore the protest of those affected: 'Along the front between system and lifeworld, the lifeworld evidently offers stubborn and possibly successful resistance only when functions of symbolic reproduction are in question' (*TCA*, vol. II, p. 351). Now, the Marxian theory of social change is indeed in need of revision on two substantial counts: the assumption that the working class is the subject of historical change, and the idea of an emancipation of the working class at a 'higher stage' of society that follows capitalism. With the abolition of a distinct bringer of social change, the clear direction this change was supposed to take is also lost. But must we consequently abandon the idea of instrinsic system limitations? Just as functionalism since Durkheim can speak only of differentiation, so, too, Habermas can submit only that objectively the process of switching over to linguistic steering mechanisms has gone too far. If the process of capitalist modernization has been able to disregard the protests of those affected successfully for such a time as areas of material reproduction were affected, why should the resistance then become 'possibly successful' when 'systemic imperatives' pervade the 'lifeworld'? The book comes no closer to giving a satisfactory answer to this question than it does to outlining the causes for the 'irresistible [!] inner dynamics' of the subsystems (*TCA*, vol. II, p. 331). Only communicative rationality, according to Habermas (ibid., p. 339) 'gives an inner logic . . . to resistance against the colonization of the lifeworld by the inner dynamics of autonomous systems'. For success, however, not just consistency, but also resources are necessary.

Such resources might be found in the fact that a process of development can exhaust its own preconditions and thus precipitate a 'turning point' or a 'structural break' in development: there is some evidence that such a 'structural break' took place in the mid-1970s. If this is correct, then the plausible conclusion would be that one should again take up the analysis of the developmental potential of welfare-state capitalism, whose internal and external limits are beginning to be visible today – an enterprise which certainly does not lie beyond the boundaries of Critical Theory.

10 Modernity as Project and as Field of Tensions

Johann P. Arnason

The 'Concluding Reflections', in which Habermas summarizes his theory of communicative action and defends it against misunderstandings, contain among other things a passage which at first reads like a far-reaching relativization of the preceding theoretical construction:

> The test case for a theory of rationality with which the modern understanding of the world is to ascertain its own universality would certainly include throwing light on the opaque figures of mythical thought, clarifying the bizarre expressions of alien cultures, and indeed in such a way that we not only comprehend the learning processes that separate 'us' from 'them', but also become aware of what we have *unlearned* in the course of this learning. A theory of society that does not close itself off a priori to this possibility of unlearning has to be critical also in relation to the pre-understanding that accrues to it from its own social setting, that is, it has to be open to self-criticism. Processes of unlearning can be gotten at through a critique of deformations that are rooted in the selective exploitation of a potential for rationality and mutual understanding that was once available, but is now buried over.[1]

If a model of action rationality based on the 'magnificently one-sided developments' of modernity can and must first prove itself in dialogue with premodern modes of thought and non-European traditions, then the claim to unconditional validity – which remains essential to the concept of reason even when it has been reformulated in terms of a theory of communication – is tempered by the openness of a culture which subjects itself to questioning. The project of a reconstructive theory, grounded in a rationalized lifeworld, can no longer be seen as a methodological alternative to hermeneutics; it must, rather, encounter hermeneutics on its own ground by expanding and concretizing the idea of 'fusion of horizons' in such a way that it involves different cultural universes as well as different traditions within a shared cultural field. The confrontation with other interpretations of the world is made more acute by universalistic approaches, and this will – according to Habermas – lead to a more adequate self-understanding of modernity as well as to a clearer distinction between universal and particular structures of the lifeworld.

This line of thought is obviously more than a tactical concession to critics. The renunciation of foundationalist claims – and this renunciation applies both to the self-understanding of modernity and to the social theory anchored in it – is rooted in the philosophy of science and history to which Habermas has always adhered; his critics did not first have to tell him that every exercise in theory-building is problematical and every historical achievement double-edged. If the 'reconstructions of universal and necessary presuppositions of communicative action, of argumentative speech, of experience and of objectivating thought, of moral judgments and of aesthetic critique'[2] are undertaken with such reservations, they are protected against any relapse into either a transcendental quest for ultimate foundation or a historicist absolutization of progress.

Despite these clear and well justified pointers, the approach outlined above is not pursued in a more concrete form. A self-critique of modernity, enriched and put to the test by comparative cultural analysis, is envisaged as a long-term goal. But the substantive and the methodological implications of this stance for a positive theory of modernity are left largely unexplored. This failure to realize a clearly formulated programme is indicative of more fundamental difficulties; more precisely, it reflects built-in conceptual obstacles that have to do with Habermas's version of the distinction between modern and premodern forms of thought. His basic concepts sharpen this dichotomy in such a way that there is no scope for a mutual – or mutually instructive – understanding; all that can be achieved is a one-sided and pre-programmed comparison. If the specific characteristics of mythical and traditional world views are reduced to symptoms of an inability to grasp the differences between object domains (particularly those of the natural, the social, and the subjective world) as well as between the ways of relating to them, there is no scope for an authentic fusion of horizons. From this perspective the latent meaning of the 'opaque figures' and 'bizarre expressions' can represent only a negative counter-example or an embryonic anticipation of the modern structures of consciousness. One might want to understand the observation cited at the beginning as the first step towards an unprejudiced dialogue; the resultant theory of rationality could then go beyond the superficial opposition of differentiated and undifferentiated world views and try to compare traditional patterns of relativizing the contrasts between nature and culture or subject and object with the modern tendency to radicalize such distinctions.[3] Even so, it will have to be admitted that Habermas imposes a priori constraints on the critical and comparative analysis of world views. As we have seen, he speaks of rationality and processes of reaching understanding, but neither of interpretation nor of experience. In the final instance, his programme is aimed at retrieving a universal but hitherto partially repressed potential, of which alien cultures have presumably retained something, and is not oriented towards the understanding of alternative forms of interpretation and life; this one-sided slanting rests on a more general conceptual strategy which devalues the role of creativity and openness to the world as constitutive aspects of culture and lays the main emphasis on a closed and universal paradigm of rationality.

The perspective I have just recapitulated forms the background to the observations below. They will make no positive contribution to the intercultural dialogue which Habermas both recognizes as the final standard of justification and yet tries to disarm in advance by means of restrictive assumptions. Rather, the remarks are preparatory steps towards a more direct examination of the 'text case', in the sense that their main aim is to clarify the nature of the above-mentioned conceptual barriers. But I shall be able to address only one aspect of this within the bounds of the present essay. The discussion will focus on what is simultaneously a restrictive and an emphatic concept of modernity – that is, of the interrelations between its cultural, political and economic determinants as well as of the variations possible within this framework. This concept imposes narrow limits on the self-critical confrontation with earlier developmental stages and alternative lines of development. It can, however, be relativized in two ways: with reference to the programmatic propositions quoted above and on the basis of its hermeneutical presuppositions. From the latter point of view, the theory in question is – as we shall see – a partial elaboration of a pre-understanding of the problem of modernity. The claim to superiority and universality which Habermas reads into the self-understanding of modernity is derived above all from a specific interpretation of its cultural foundations; the obverse of this foundationalist privileging of modern culture is a reductionist conception of economic and political structures which supposedly can therefore develop, achieve a certain degree of independence and give rise to alternative systems only within the scope prescribed by the cultural pattern. My critique will take this side to Habermas's model as its starting-point. If it can be shown that the economic and political aspects of modernity cannot be encapsulated in the categories provided by the twofold paradigm shift – from purposive to communicative action and from instrumental to systemic rationality – then the overall interpretation and thus also the role it attributes to culture becomes questionable. I shall, in conclusion, suggest some more concrete guidelines for a continuation of the critique at this level; we must forgo pursuing them *in extenso* in the present text.

The problematic of modernity has, in its function as both testing ground and legitimizing frame of reference, become the focus for a research programme which Habermas hopes will vindicate his 'conceptually strategic decisions'. The theory of socio-cultural evolution, in which the construction of the new paradigm is supposed to culminate, must above all be able to explain the formation and implementation of distinctively modern structures. On the other hand, the categorial framework which Habermas devises is explicitly linked to a 'basic philosophical intention' which can be 'related to an implicitly invoked *self-understanding* of modernity'.[4] A concept of modernity adequate to this dual task begins to emerge at an early date in Habermas's work, although it is not until a later stage – above all in connection with the redefinition and clarification of his relationship to the Marxist tradition – that it begins to take on a more concrete shape. This line of argument can be compared to other neo-Marxist approaches to the extent that, by thematizing a more comprehensive context, it is meant to correct the traditional Marxist equation of modernity with a supposedly self-transcending dynamic of capitalist development.[5] But Habermas's revision of Marxism also has some distinctive characteristics; among other things, he wants to render the theory of modernity more receptive to arguments developed by some critics of modern culture and theorists of modern art.

Habermas's reconstruction of modernity in terms of social theory begins with the differentiations and tensions which are at the core of the capitalist system. As he sees it, Marx limited the analytical and critical potential of his image of society by overgeneralizing specifically economic mechanisms; this tendency manifests itself even at the most elementary level, i.e. in the labour theory of value. By contrast, Habermas wants to interpret the problematic of 'real abstraction', which Marx associated with the value-form, in such a way that the analogous and increasingly important subsumption of social life under mechanisms of state control can also be included. It should be noted that this does not presuppose a radical autonomy of the political sphere. Habermas takes for granted that the modern state was from the outset subordinated to 'the functional imperatives of the new mode of production';[6] he therefore insists on the bourgeois nature of the absolutist state and accepts Hobbes's *Leviathan* as an adequate account of this. The political sphere thus appears only as an extension of the social space structured and controlled by capital. It is only when the legitimizing foundations of the modern state are taken into account that we can speak of more autonomous developmental tendencies or even of a potential counterbalance. The modernization of economic and political structures can take place only within the framework of a more comprehensive process of rationalization, and the latter also involves the adaptation of legitimate power to democratic principles and procedures. This means – as Habermas sees it – that modern societies have to understand themselves in terms of a 'primacy of the lifeworld in relation to the subsystems separated out of its institutional orders'.[7] We shall later consider some implications of the concept of the lifeworld for action theory and communication theory; at this stage the crucial point is that the 'insoluble tension' between capitalism and democracy cannot be reduced to an inter-systemic conflict. Rather, Habermas proposes to ground the autonomous and potentially emancipatory logic of the political sphere, which limits the preponderance of capitalism and to a certain extent co-determines the development of the modern state, in specific patterns of interaction and interpretation, and it would then be the generalization of these which marks the final breakthrough to modernity. The complex arguments that lead to a reconstruction of 'modern forms of reaching understanding' take as their starting point the fundamental insight that the dissolution of traditional structures leads both to a 'linguistification of the sacred', i.e. to basic religious norms being replaced by more or less rationalized processes of consensus formation, and to the categorial separation of object and action domains which had previously been fused in religious world views. The problematization of the contents of the cultural spheres is inextricably bound up with this formal differentiation: to the extent that the critical potential of language is freed of ritual and dogmatic barriers, the world views which had once generated an undisputed order now dissolve into disputable and competing interpretations, the rules of social life disband into criticizable conventions in need of legitimation and the socio-cultural patterns of individuality disintegrate into selective elaborations of an anthropological substratum which cannot be reduced to them. The dominant trait is, in other words, a specifically modern under-determination of cultural foundations.

We can now define the pre-understanding mentioned at the outset somewhat more closely. It refers, as we have seen, not only to normative structures, but also to the 'societal environment' as a whole. A particular constellation of economic, political and cultural structures appears as the distinguishing characteristic of modernity. The model which Habermas uses can, to begin with, be understood as a far-reaching correction of the traditional Marxist diagnosis of the present. For Habermas, the emancipatory perspective which is supposed to guide the resistance to the systemic logic of capitalism can neither be grounded in a self-destructing dynamic of the process of accumulation nor in a metasocial residue that would be immune to subsumption and reification (the most influential variants of Marxism combine both postulates in the vague notion of the development of the productive forces). Rather, Habermas wishes to show that the interrelations between the dominant structure and its tendential counterweight – in other words, capitalism and democracy – are constitutive for both sides and become increasingly complex in the course of capitalist development. On this view, the economic class relation between capital and wage labour still constitutes the core of the capitalist order, but the systemic logic that corresponds to it has to be mediated through the agency of political and cultural institutions. The obverse of the subsumption of various domains of life under the logic of capital is the transposition of processes of reproduction and symptoms of crisis into extra-economic and non-class specific spheres. The alternative to capitalism that is built into the socio-cultural context, i.e. the radicalization of democracy, can – as Habermas sees it – meet the intrinsic standards of modernity only if it is adapted to the differentiation of economic and political structures which initially takes place under the conditions of capitalist development, but is also compatible with other forms of society. This alternative does not go beyond the horizons of capitalism by fixating on some irreducibly anticapitalist contents or aims (such strategies cannot cope with the increasingly abstract and elastic mechanisms of subsumption), but rather through a relativizing potential that can be mobilized against imperatives and determinations imposed by the system.

The underlying structure of modernity, if defined in this manner, is perhaps best described as a field of tensions that can neither be absorbed by a system nor by a strategy of transformation. It is by reformulating this pre-understanding in terms of action and systems theory that Habermas, drawing on various traditions, is first able to turn this field of tensions into a unified if incomplete 'project of modernity'. The analytical distinctions formulated in *The Theory of Communicative Action* are based on the real differentiation of spheres of action and culture in the modern world; the integrative ideal of a unity of reason is redefined in terms of latent aspects of the rationality of action and linked to the practical task of rendering them more explicit, but it can only be justified at the more general level of a theory of language. It is modernity's experience of itself which makes the 'universal conditions of possible understanding' accessible to reflection, but they in turn lend to the modern world an ultimate coherence that is not exhibited by its manifest structures. The notion of a 'project of modernity' thus presupposes a rationalizing and harmonizing transfiguration of modernity. By contrast, the following discussion will explore the overhastily abandoned model of a field of tensions and defend it against harmonizing interpretations. This, however, first of all requires a broader frame of reference; some of the thematic complexes which Habermas confines to the wings owing to their peripheral or derivative nature will serve as the point of departure for my criticism of his central theses.

If criticizing the open or implicit absolutization of capitalist relations and thematizing other determinants within a more comprehensive framework is one of the main tasks facing a theory of modernity, then the latter must concern itself with the questions posed by the genesis and expansion of a non-capitalist variant of modern society.[8] It is certainly not because of any illusions about the results of such developments that Habermas has not developed a detailed critique of them; he regards Soviet-type societies as 'a worse variant of that ... which one wanted to combat'.[9] The meagre role played by the problematic of 'Eastern-bloc socialism' in his analysis of modern society is thus all the more surprising. The sparse remarks on this topic that can be found in his more recent writings do not add up to a consistent model, but they will at least allow us to pinpoint the conceptual obstacles that stand in the way of further progress.

Habermas suggests in his discussion with Andrew Arato that the particularities of the 'bureaucratic-socialist' line of development should be explained in terms of a variant of the basic structure of modernity. The most important precondition of modernization would accordingly be 'a by and large rationalized lifeworld', in which money and power are anchored as media, i.e. are given a positive legally institutionalized form.[10] The primacy of money – and consequently of the self-propelling economic process of accumulation – is characteristic of the capitalist path of development, whereas the primacy of administrative power is expressed in the *étatisation* (*Verstaatlichung*) of economy and culture; the latter process takes a particularly radical turn when a party-state is involved. This thesis contains a highly condensed 'theory of the contemporary age', which needs to be examined from various angles. First of all, the notion of a common constellation from which the two lines depart is questionable. The Soviet variant of modern society emerged in a historical context which was starkly different from Western conditions, and a theory which abstracts from this background – that is, from the specific interrelations of its economic, political and cultural aspects – can explain neither the revolutionary transformation nor its results. In *The Theory of Communicative Action* Habermas skirts round this difficulty by limiting the comparison to 'post-liberal societies'; he thus contrasts the Soviet model with organized capitalism. But the term 'post-liberal' is misleading, since the modernizing process which took place in pre-revolutionary Russia cannot be regarded as a simple – even if ultimately unsuccessful – imitation of liberal capitalism. Rather, a quite unique formation emerged that is not to be confused with either the central or the peripheral variants of capitalism, and which despite its short lifespan set the scene for later developments.

We might disregard this historical context if it could be shown that the consolidation and further development of the Soviet model has led to the functional primacy of administrative planning, for this would allow a systems-theoretical comparison with the role of the market economy in capitalist societies. Such an approach would focus less on common preconditions than on a retrospective neutralization of differences; in this way, the question of the 'evolutionary significance of bureaucratic socialism' could be separated from the analysis of its historical origins. In order to buttress this line of argument, Habermas refers to crisis tendencies and socio-pathological symptoms which originate, in one case, from the 'over-stretching of the medium of legal-administrative power' and, in the other, from an absolutization of economic imperatives.

But on closer examination, there are some reasons to doubt that this comparison – conceived as it is in media-theoretic terms – does justice to the Soviet model. To speak of an over-stretching of legal-administrative power is misleading inasmuch as not only the crisis of Stalinism, but also the difficulties in overcoming the crises of the post-Stalin era were closely related to the unavoidable but impossible task of placing the power structure on legal foundations. A limited but real modification of legal patterns lies behind the officially proclaimed 're-establishment of a socialist legality'; the patterns in question were not just ignored in an earlier phase, but were systematically designed to guarantee a broad space for direct ideological legitimation as well as for the arbitrary exercise of power. Since both were taken to the point of excess, thus threatening the very existence of the system, measures of rationalization became necessary, which, however, had to avoid impairing the institutional nucleus of a form of domination based on the fusion of economic, political and cultural-ideological control mechanisms and objectives. The 'constitutionalization of the relations of force' (Habermas) is permissible only to the extent that it is compatible with their prior totalization. This form of modernity is therefore to be distinguished from the capitalist version with respect to the overall constellation of economic, political and cultural determinants, not just in regard to the more prominent role of a subsystem-specific medium within what is then regarded as an unchanging and common framework. But, at the same time, the structural core of this form gives rise to tensions and disjunctions which are hard to explain on the basis of the Habermasian crisis theory. On the one hand, sphere-specific – i.e. economic, political and ideological – principles of organization and orientation are defined in the monolithic and comprehensive terms needed to facilitate the subsumption of social life under a unified power apparatus; in a 'mono-organizational' society, dissonances between these separate perspectives of totalization do not result in open social conflict, but this does not mean that they are automatically neutralized by the coordinating centre. At the level of the economy, a model of industrialization and accumulation – or, to use Gyorgy Markus's term, a system-specific 'principle of maximization' – is implemented and backed up by a claim to superior substantive rationality which may gradually lose its mobilizing force, but cannot be officially discarded. The distinctive characteristic of the political order is a systematic *étatisation* of society, intensified and transfigured by the party's monopoly of power. The ideological framework takes the form of a closed world view which presents itself as a 'superscience' and has maintained its claim to universal applicability despite the various adjustments that proved necessary during the post-Stalin era. While the complex relationships and interferences between these structural principles cannot be discussed here, it is clear that the crisis potential of the overall pattern cannot be reduced to the 'paradoxes of plan rationality'.

This becomes even more obvious if we take into account the other side of subsumption. The autonomous dynamics and tendencies of each sphere reassert themselves in such a way that they may, up to a point and in certain respects, contribute to the reproduction of the system, but the more far-reaching consequences threaten both its functional coherence and its official image. The well-known role of the 'parallel economy' and the periodically recurring, but never consistently implemented attempts at economic reform are representative of this. At the political level, the principle of the sovereignty of the Party is never explicitly called into question; but as experience has shown this does not exclude either a far-reaching independence of individual sectors of the apparatus, or the counter-tendency towards a growing personalization of the centre of power, which in extreme cases can go as far as to engender a new form of charismatic rule that superimposes itself on the Party's sovereignty. Finally, the official ideology has, to an increasing extent, to be supplemented by other value-orientations and traditions that are neither randomly malleable nor clearly subversive.[11] This subliminal syncretism does not correspond to the interpretative patterns which Habermas regards as characteristic of advanced modernity; as he sees it, the differentiation of value spheres and validity claims should result in a tendential immunization of culture against ideological reinterpretations, whilst the enlightening effect inherent in this trend is factually thwarted by the fragmentation of everyday consciousness. But in the 'state socialist' constellation, both the relative weight of the components and the overall effect differ from this model. Here, a perverted universalism claims to base itself on objective interests and the 'scientific world view' which sanctions them, rather than on a collective will-formation and criticizable norms; at the same time, the dialectical form of thought, originally linked to the self-reflexion of modernity, is transformed into a diffuse pseudo-ontology which serves to justify the de-differentiation of social and cultural spheres. And as suggested above, this kind of universalism is dependent on the complementary contributions of more or less openly particularistic ideologies which, at the same time, derive their strength largely from reactions to the dysfunctional and regressive consequences of the official dogma.

The Habermasian image of modernity centres – as we have seen – on a constant and universal pattern; all that can vary are the forms of integration, i.e. the relative weighting of the subsystem-specific mechanisms of coordination. Their culturally and normatively grounded differentiation from each other and from the lifeworld must, by contrast, be regarded as invariable. Objections to circumscribing the changing relations between economic, political and cultural structures in such a manner soon arose from our brief overview of the Soviet model. Here, we encountered a constellation which seems to be characterized by simultaneous and interconnected trends towards the amalgamation, absolutization and fragmentation of all three spheres. A more detailed analysis could partly link up with the ideas of East European dissidents and partly draw on some versions of the theory of totalitarianism, such as those of Hannah Arendt, Cornelius Castoriadis and Claude Lefort. Habermas seriously considered neither course.[12]

But it is not only the a priori minimization of contrasts between different lines of development that is open to criticism. The very idea of parallel trajectories set against a shared background is questionable; it obscures the fact that the non-capitalist variant of modernity arose in the concrete historical context of a world increasingly unified but not homogenized by capitalist development. The revolutionary transformations from which Soviet-type societies emerged were primarily due to a particularly explosive collision between an expanding capitalism and a non-capitalist environment, and the latter continued to exert a strong influence on the shape of post-revolutionary conditions. If we approach the problematic of 'Eastern-bloc socialism' from this angle, it points to a more general path of inquiry, one that Habermas has concerned himself even less with. Although he specified in his studies on the reconstruction of historical materialism that the 'dynamics of an antagonistic world society' should be one of the central themes of a theory of social evolution, his theory of modernity disregards the international interconnections and processes which have elsewhere been subsumed under the concept of the capitalist world system – as in the Marxist tradition – or that of a world society, for example in the sense of Luhmann's 'real unity of a shared world horizon'. In his positive definition of modernity, Hebermas consistently elides the worldwide expansion which Marx still saw as a 'civilizing mission of capitalism'. Similarly, in his critique of unbalanced and pathological patterns of modernization, Habermas collapses the specific problematic of the developmental divide between centre and periphery into a general theory of accumulation and crisis. His theoretical disinterest in this dimension of the modern world is all the more striking given that it was from it that he first culled the metaphor which best summarized his diagnosis of contemporary society, namely 'the colonization of the lifeworld'.

A brief comparison with another – and very different – theory of modernity will show the relevance of this topic to the question of constants and variables in the modernizing process. Immanuel Wallerstein has developed a theory of 'historical capitalism' which, despite all partial revisions and unresolved issues, retains at least one central proposition throughout: the *differentia specifica* of modernity is the formation of an economic world system, i.e. an international division of labour without an overarching political organization. The primacy of the economic sphere can thus be demonstrated only if the functions of cultural traditions and political institutions are viewed from the perspective of a self-reproducing world system.[13] One need not approve of the economic-deterministic thrust of this approach in order to accept the relevance of the first step for a correction of Habermas's theory. Neither the emergence of the capitalist world economy in the course of European expansion nor its subsequent structural changes can be explained in terms of a subsystem embedded – in the final instance – in normative structures. Rather, it signals the breakthrough to a new level of system formation in the economic sphere and at the same time a shift in the balance between economic, political and cultural structures; the latter change cannot be reduced to the 'overstretching' of a specific mechanism of coordination. Habermas's overhasty equation of monetarization and capitalization, based on a combination of the Parsonian theory of media with traditional Marxist notions, can also be relativized in another way by means of the concept of the world system. As Wallerstein has shown, the monetary form of the surplus product does not *ipso facto* imply the universalization of wage labour; it can, and must, rather be linked to a whole spectrum of other forms of both the regulation of labour and the reproduction of labour power. The various institutional bases for capitalist relations are at the same time ways of incorporating and restructuring other forms of society upon which capitalism relies in its capacity as a world system; the fact that the non-capitalist environment plays a constitutive role in capitalist development and supplements its mechanisms in all spheres of social life is the obverse of the unique expansionary and developmental capacity manifested by the capitalist economy.

On the whole, earlier Marxist theories ignored this dialectic of capitalism and its Other. The incorporation of the non-capitalist periphery into the reproduction of capitalism was regarded, above all, as a result of the latter's internal contradictions; the only controversial issue was at best the question whether this was a permanent but derivative phenomenon or merely a symptom of crisis specific to one particular phase. With the concept of the world system, the approach undergoes a decisive change: the system now contains its Other as a co-determining component from the outset and down to the very core of its structures. But as long as world system theory accepts the primacy of the economy, this co-determination may seem to be secondary. Its scope is broader and its importance more obvious at the political level. According to Wallerstein, the modern state is 'a crucial mechanism for the maximal accumulation of capital'.[14] But if its role cannot be reduced to this, that is not only because of the 'global bursts of juridification' which Habermas interprets as successive partial victories of democracy over the systemic logic of capitalism. A theory of modernity which thematizes the state only as a bone of contention between system and lifeworld – or put differently, between capitalism and democracy – cannot do justice to the complex modern process of state formation; in particular, its roots in non-capitalist configurations of social power and its significance as a further development of their potential are obscured. This process involves not only the growing autonomy and gradual rationalization of the state, but also the trend – alternately blocked and intensified – towards the subsumption of various spheres of social life under the logic of the state. This aspect of modernization is one of the necessary – but, owing to their intrinsic dynamics, also transfunctional and potentially dysfunctional – conditions for the emergence and existence of the capitalist economic system. As Fernand Braudel has shown, it was not just the universalization of commodity production which led to the breakthrough of capitalism; rather this was brought about by the intersection of a tendentially worldwide market economy with increasingly centralized structures of domination.[15] It would consequently seem advisable to replace the conventional periodicization of capitalism in terms of a liberal and an organized variant with a three-phase model. The formative phase is characterized by the symbiosis of pre-industrial capitalism and the absolutist state; the latter influences the economic sphere both via direct participation in it and by supporting monopolistic strategies.[16] The next phase, often called competitive or liberal capitalism, can in retrospect be reduced to the regional, partial and temporary separation of state and capital, and it is followed by a phase of their renewed interpenetration.

The economistic misinterpretation of this context still prevails in the contemporary Marxist theories which see the modern state only as a functional – and, according to some of them, readaptable – appendage to capital. It can most easily be corrected by pointing to the wider-reaching structural and genetic interconnections. Capitalist development is not co-determined by the modern state *in abstracto*; rather, it takes place in constant interaction with the concrete structures and processes of the modern state system. In the latter context, the accumulation of abstract wealth – which appears at the economic level as the system-specific goal of production -constitutes a power resource that co-determines the dynamics of competition and monopolization to a great degree, but not *ipso facto* in a decisive way. Furthermore, the mutually complementary modernization of state organization and the capitalist economy can – as Norbert Elias's pioneering studies have shown – be regarded as the continuation of a two-track process of structural change that was well under way in the High Middle Ages; the result was, already in the premodern phase, the development of a money economy and the rise of the bourgeoisie on the one hand, and a gradual centralization of feudal structures of domination on the other. This thesis is plausible not least with regard to the concluding phase of European expansion – i.e. the 'era of imperialism' – and the subsequent crisis in the world system triggered off by the First World War. Various critics of orthodox theories of imperialism have justifiably emphasized the central role which in this context was played by both the precapitalist power elites of the eastern European empires and by the corresponding cultural patterns.[17] We have to do here not – as has sometimes been erroneously claimed – with the simple perseverance of traditional forms, but with an independent and explosive – albeit ultimately secondary – further development of non-capitalist structures, closely linked to the dynamics of capitalism.

It could also be shown that Habermas underestimates the autonomous developmental patterns of the modern state in another respect: with regard to the normative meaning of democracy and its progressive implementation. If the main thrust of political modernization is reconstructed – as he does – in terms of the process of juridification which sets in with the early bourgeois state and reaches its zenith in the social and democratic constitutional state, some distinctive counter-tendencies go unnoticed; they can be reduced neither to interruptions nor to relapses, nor indeed to inherent ambivalences in the medium of law. Their common denominator is rather the ongoing attempt to hold the logic of democracy in check by means of procedures for restricting it and taking the sting out of it. The contrasting tendencies – the radicalization and the containment of democracy – have a common point of departure. The absolutist state, which Habermas places at the beginning of the process of juridification, appears in retrospect to be a complex mixture of heterogeneous elements that can be distinguished clearly from one another only in the light of later divergences and alternatives. For our present purposes, it is enough to note that the absolutist state set in motion three historical innovations which, via successive changes and in varying combinations, all co-determined the results of the democratic revolution. The cultural model of absolutism involves, firstly, a personalization of power which, while linking up with traditional forms of legitimation, opens up new perspectives through a shift towards the direct sacralization of unlimited power. The theoretical understanding of the forms of domination which constitute further steps on this path still leaves much to be desired. Although the concept of charismatic domination, which dates back to Weber, and the concept of Bonapartism, frequently used by Marxist theorists, have diametrically opposed starting points, both are too unspecific to do justice to the phenomena concerned (the former approach leads to the premature construction of a supra-historical model, the latter to the over-generalization of one particular constellation). Secondly, it is not only the intrinsic dynamism of bureaucratization analyzed by Weber that can be traced back to absolutist times, but also the closely related attempts to elaborate the fundamentals of a norm-free *raison d'état* subject to no democratic principles. To borrow Ernst Fraenkel's terminology, which Arato uses in his analysis of the Soviet model of society, one could also speak of a growing independence of a decree-based state (*Massnahmenstaat*) vis-à-vis a state regulated by norms. This trend is the common ground of political projects which at first sight are poles apart, such as, on the one hand, the idea of sovereignty beyond law which manifests itself most adequately in the state of emergency, and on the other hand, that of a dictatorship freed from moral and legal conventions, but supposedly guided by insight into the objective laws of progress. Finally, the above two trends should be distinguished from the role played by the state in forming and consolidating collective identities. Further developments at this level depend above all on the degree to which and the manner in which nationalist orientations and ideologies, on the one hand, and social transformations by revolutions from above or below, on the other, can be coordinated with or incorporated into the process of state formation. The most extreme phenomena that appear in this context have been addressed by theories of totalitarianism, whereas the search for a more comprehensive conceptual framework has sometimes led to more or less critical recourses to Hegel's theory of the state.[18]

Unit now there has been no theory of the modern state which could do justice to these different aspects and the varying relationships between them; the tasks that face such a theory can, however, be specified clearly enough to bring to light the obverse of Habermas's over-rationalized model of the modern state. In this sense as well it would be more appropriate to speak of a field of tensions rather than a unified project of modernity. If we take the international context into consideration, it becomes even clearer that the specifically modern possibilities of development, inherent in the separation of state and society, cannot be reduced to the process of democratization. In the societies which are caught up in the global process of modernization at a later date and become directly or indirectly dependent on its pacemakers, the intervention of the state in social life – most easily legitimated in terms of developmental strategy – can take on new forms which, on the one hand, imitate the models first invented in the centres of the world system and, on the other hand, outdo such models by drawing on statist or imperial traditions. A theory of the modern state must take into account the possibilities exemplified by such combinations. It should be noted that their development depends on the additional influence of other factors; as the experiences of this century have shown, the state's political instrumentalization and ideological expropriation of social movements is of particular importance.

Habermas's theory of modernity is, as the misgivings outlined above suggest, too restrictive in design and therefore not able to embrace the variety and variability of the relations between economic, political and cultural determinants of the modern world. In relation to the bourgeois-capitalist line of development, its historical background and the alternative competing against it today, we have seen that a wider and more flexible conceptual framework is necessary. But it would also seem appropriate to distinguish between a primary, but not self-contained dynamic of modernization, and a secondary but not epiphenomenal offshoot. In other words, the core structure of modernity develops in a historical context which also includes traditional, i.e. non-capitalist and non-democratic, structures as constituents which persist and can be developed further.[19]

Habermas's simplifying reconstruction of modernity is based on a specific combination of concepts from action and systems theory; the question thus arises as to which underlying assumptions and prior decisions have been encoded in these. As we have seen, Habermas regards the normative anchoring of the media of money and power in a 'by-and-large rationalized lifeworld' as the most general precondition for modernization. We shall return below to the cultural-theoretic premises of the connection Habermas makes between the concept of the lifeworld and a theory of rationality; for the time being we are concerned with the interpretation of the polity and the economy in terms of a theory of media.

Talcott Parsons's theory of media of communication, i.e. of generalized steering mechanisms which regulate the differentiation of function-specific subsystems and the exchange relations between them, is taken as the point of departure. Habermas concurs with Parsons that money and power can – at least up to a point – be thematized in this way. But as he sees it, the most serious weakness of a theory of media is its inability to grasp the difference between communication and steering. Parsons therefore neglects to consider the question under what conditions and to what degree the diverse media can be detached from the context of everyday linguistic communication and thus from their basis in the lifeworld. Habermas accordingly relativizes the structural analogy between money and power: since power relies on legitimation, it requires 'a more demanding form of institutionalization'. On the other hand, he doubts that the concept of media can be generalized beyond the context of the economy and the state administration – on the grounds that, in other domains of social life, the action-coordinating mechanisms are much more closely bound to linguistic processes of reaching consensus. The critique of Parsons thus remains within an overall conceptual framework which is largely indebted to him.

By contrast, the changes Niklas Luhmann has made to the theory of media of communication are not taken into account. They would be relevant to the issues addressed here to the extent that a less deductivistically structured model would permit much more flexible relations between the media and the systemic context. In Luhmann's opinion, the function of the media consists not only in structuring the exchange processes between subsystems; in their capacity as 'additional mechanisms' (*Zusatzeinrichtungen*), which serve to transmit reduced complexity, they also structure the relations of the overarching system to its environment. They regulate both action and experience and can therfore be integrated into the systems-theoretical perspective only by means of a corresponding redefinition of the concept of meaning. The greater emphasis on intepretative and communicative aspects is intended to enable the concept of media to provide the hitherto – to Luhmann's mind – missing link between the respective strategies of systems theory and the sociology of knowledge.[20]

If taken as a point of departure for an analysis of the relations between economic, political and cultural structures, Luhmann's theory of media would clearly emphasize other features than that of Parsons. The fact that Habermas prefers the latter's approach can be explained only in terms of the logic of his own project. His use of systems theory presupposes the primacy of action theory and is further conditioned by the concept of the lifeworld. Once he has, in a first step, constructed the complex concept of communicative action, he introduces the complementary concept of the lifeworld and then goes on to demonstrate that the latter itself needs to be supplemented by the system-theoretic concept of society. The mechanisms of action coordination burst the framework of the lifeworld to the extent that they must also embrace 'the counter-intuitive aspects of the context of societal reproduction'. The theory of media is meant to give a more detailed acount of the systemically stabilized contexts of action. In other words, the degree to which action coordination has become independent of action orientation can be judged on the basis of the autonomy and range of the respective media.

The approach to systems theory thus depends on the conceptualization of the relationship between these two dimensions of action. Habermas criticizes the competing paradigms in social theory partly for a restrictive definition of action orientations (this is true above all of the teleological and strategic models of action which thematize action only as purposive activity) and partly for their lack of an adequate grasp of the problem of action coordination (this leads, on the one hand, to relapses into utilitarian conceptions of order and, on the other hand, to premature concessions being made to systems theory). The nucleus of Habermas's own strategy for reconceptualization, the concept of communicative action, is intended to throw new light on both issues. It highlights precisely the point of intersection between action orientation, including the references to the world that are constitutive for the formation of action goals, and action coordination, i.e. the interlinking of individual acts into a pattern of in-teraction. This dual meaning becomes particularly clear when Habermas uses the term *verständigungsorientiertes Handeln*. This can be understood both as action oriented towards mutual understanding and as action oriented – or coordinated – *by* mutual understanding; Habermas wants to combine both meanings without obfuscating the difference between them. The model of communicative action 'presupposes language as a medium of uncurtailed communication whereby speakers and hearers, out of the con-text of their preinterpreted lifeworld, refer simultaneously to things in the objective, social, and subjective worlds in order to negotiate common definitions of the situation'.[21] The 'uncurtailed communication' thematizes and problematizes the whole complex of references to the world that are partially and implicitly taken into account in less complex models of action. The telos of understanding, rooted in language, thus appears as a second-degree action orientation, more demanding and comprehensive than those of the first degree. But in this process, speech and understanding are not related to one another 'as means to end';[22] the interrelation be-tween them does not, as a consequence, form a closed structure of action. One can speak of communicative action only when the linguistic processes of consensus formation have become linked, on the one hand, to the fully developed teleology of 'active interventions in the world', and, on the other, to interactive structures which, while they cannot take shape or function without speech acts, cannot be reduced to these. Action-orienting perspectives and action-coordinating mechanisms thus converge at the level of linguistic communication; neither as a purposive activity nor as a form of interaction can the latter be said to constitute an action type of its own, and it is precisely for this reason that it can alternately function in a stabilizing and in a transforming capacity as an agency of mediation between the two dimensions of action.

Our main concern here is with the consequences this has for social theory. The central positioning of communicative action leads to the structural and evolutionary primacy of the form of understanding, i.e. ultimately, of the intrinsic structures of the world view it contains. It is at this level that the degree to which one-sided action orientations can become independent and be rationalized in terms of their intrinsic criteria is established. And the sphere of the influence of specialized and neutralized steering media depends on the more or less extensive release of purposive action from communicative contexts. This conceptual scheme excludes specific action orientations at the level of economic and political structures. Given that they are subsystems of purposive-rational or strategic action, both spheres are entrusted to the theory of media. The special characteristics of economic and political activity are thus subsumed under an undifferentiated and derivative pattern of action, the institutional preconditions of which point – in the final instance – to the context of uncurtailed communication. The cultural sphere, i.e. the lifeworld, is thereby given a privileged position: it guarantees the ultimate unity of action orientation and action coordination as well as determining the degree to which they can be separated. At first sight, one could object that Habermas developed his concept of the lifeworld in explicit contrast to culturalistic reductionism. If, however, the specific social components of the lifeworld are conceived of as the sum total of 'the legitimate orders through which participants regulate their memberships in social groups and thereby secure solidarity',[23] then the analysis still remains within the bounds of a culturalist framework in the wider sense which occludes economic and political aspects. Admittedly, according to Habermas, the material reproduction of the lifeworld takes place in the medium of purposive activity, but this latter aspect is considered only in terms of its constituting the transition to systemic contexts and does not lead to further differentiation at the level of the lifeworld itself. The 'appropriation of nature by the individual within and through the agency of a determinate form of society', to use Marx's words, is as absent from the intrinsic structures of the lifeworld as are the autonomous processes of the political sphere and their fluctuations between the opposite poles of collective self-determination and de-socialized power.

But if we want to reconstruct the less rigidly fixed pre-understanding behind this conceptual delimitation, the already mentioned critical position *vis-à-vis* the Marxist diagnosis of the times can be taken as a guideline. The reformulation of the Marxian approach which Habermas strives for can, in this context, be compared with other objections and suggested corrections to Marxism. Some of them are rooted in the theories of culture, whereas others are more directly related to the problematic of power. The first group includes both the diverse forms of criticism that have attempted to explain Marxism's failures in terms of its ties to the cultural horizon of bourgeois society, and conceptions, which differ just as much among themselves, of a cultural revolution; the latter hope to overcome subaltern notions of emancipation either through a more emphatic autonomy or through a more complete sublation (*Aufhebung*) of culture. By contrast, the power-theoretic perspective has in some cases been in closer contact with political practice, but lacked the appropriate conceptual tools; when it takes a more explicit turn, it is often associated with a sharply anti-Marxist stance. For Georges Sorel, the most fatal weakness of orthodox Marxism was its blindness to the difference 'between power, which is geared towards becoming authority and attempts to achieve automatic obedience, and *violence* which seeks to break this authority'.[24] Without a clear commitment to the latter, the revolutionary movement would – as he saw it – lose sight of its real aim: 'the creation of free people'. At approximately the same time, Lenin encountered the same problem from a very different angle. Despite his self-deceiving orthodoxy, he never came as close to the original intentions of Marxism as did Sorel; in making the issue of power more central to Marxist thought, he also immunized it against a more critical analysis by couching it in a dogmatically simplified theory of class. A more balanced view of the problematic, going far beyond Sorel's one-sided intuitions and Lenin's systematic self-misunderstandings, was developed by some later critics of classical Marxism. They tried to account for the misfortunes of the revolution on the basis of an intrinsic logic of the struggle for or the accumulation of power – be it in the sense of a 'bureaucratization of the world', the rise of a new power elite, or the impotence of social movements *vis-à-vis* the structural constraints of competition between states. To complete the picture, we must mention Hannah Arendt's comprehensive attempt to develop a new theory of power, not least in the light of misjudged or repressed revolutionary experiences.

In this context, Habermas's theoretical programme would appear to be heavily loaded in favour of the culturalist approach. The decisive significance attributed, firstly, to linguistic communication with regard to social action, secondly, to the form of understanding with regard to the lifeworld, and, thirdly, to the lifeworld with respect to the logic of democracy admittedly does not guarantee an inviolable autonomy of culture, but it does secure a primacy of the latter over the polity and the economy in the logic of development. Seen thus, Habermas's critique of the older version of critical theory, and above all of its classic formulation in the *Dialectic of Enlightenment*, is aimed against a synthesis of the culture-theoretic and power-theoretic lines of argument which foreshortens both of them and sees the logic of domination as a common denominator. But if we want to put his own synthesis to the test, the first question to be asked is whether the restrictive conception of the economic and political domains of action is defensible, and whether the conceptual scheme summarized above does not neglect the specific action-orientations characteristic of these dimensions of social practice.

Taking up the questions left open by Marxian theory, it is possible to show that not only action-coordinating but also action-orienting structures, i.e.

those which are constitutive for goal setting and references to the world, are part of the economic sphere. The most suitable point of entry into this discussion is the labour theory of value, which, according to Habermas, anticipates in pioneering fashion the tasks today facing a critical theory of society. From a methodological point of view this theory had, or so he contends, 'a status similar to that which the action-theoretical introduction of steering mechanisms had for Parsons', and yet also 'from the start a critical sense that is absent in Parsons'.[25] The difference between concrete and abstract labour, which Marx himself termed the 'salient point' of his critique of political economy, should accordingly be equated with that between action tied to a lifeworld context and the functional pattern of the capitalist process of accumulation. If the critical intention behind this distinction is to be developed according to the standards of contemporary critical theory, it must draw on the more precise and abstract concepts of Parsonian systems theory. But on closer examination, the interpretation of exchange value from the viewpoint of a theory of media, which is meant to establish a link between Marx and Parsons, reveals so many gaps that it cannot serve as a balanced reconceptualization of the theory of value. It begins by avoiding the most acute problem of interpretation: we have to do not simply with a discrepancy between trailblazing insights and inadequate concepts, but with a paradigm conflict at the very core of the theory. The 'physiological' concept of abstract labour as the non-specific, infrasocial expenditure of labour power, which Marx defined unequivocally when introducing this concepts, is incompatible with the interpretation of the value-form as a specific mechanism of sociation (*Vergesellschaftung*) which affects both labour and its products. It is the second perspective which predominates in Marx's more concrete analyses, but it is never spelled out in explicit contrast to the other one. A more systematic reconstruction would show that the value-form cannot be treated as an objectification of the most elementary and general content of productive activity; rather, it is a complex structure, characteristic and constitutive of a societal form under which the totality of the process of production is subsumed. This line of argument would not only lead to the upgrading of underdeveloped aspects of Marx's theory, but also help to pinpoint the conceptual limitations and short-circuits which lead to reductionistic regressions on the level of historical materialism in general and the theory of value in particular.[26] For our present purposes, the most important aspect is the specific goal which results from a global transformation of the production process: the accumulation of abstract wealth. This development is inseparable from a wider context which is as irreducible to exchange value as a medium as it is to labour as a physiological process. On the one hand, as Marx occasionally intimated but never argued in systematic fashion, the abstract category of use value and the corresponding view of the world as a 'system of general utility' both belong to the overall structure of real abstraction. On the other, the institution of money, which Marx termed the 'general form of wealth' and at the same time the 'material representation of the totality of wealth', and with it all the cultural and political preconditions for it, must be regarded as constitutive for this overall structure. Money must not, therefore, primarily be conceived of as a steering mechanism differentiated out for special purposes. Some seminal and hitherto neglected ideas on this topic are to be found in Simmel's *Philosophy of Money*.

In the light of these interconnections, obvious in retrospect, but touched on only superficially by Marx, we can now specify somewhat more closely the significance of the physiological concept of labour. Within the theory of value, this concept attests to the same trend towards naturalizing the labour process as is expressed at the level of a theory of history in the absolutization of the productive forces. The 'process between man and nature' is in both cases separated from its social context. But this has less to do with definitive limits of the paradigm of production than with a defensive closure, intended to stave off the self-relativization of the paradigm which would otherwise suggest itself. A more thorough and unprejudiced thematization of the social context as a whole and the value relation in particular would ineluctably cause us to focus on those political and cultural determinants which play a part in structuring and finalizing the pattern of production. Ignoring this problematic has, in particular, an impact on the goal of production, which constitutes an indispensable but notably neglected component of the Marxian model. As we have seen, the concept refers – within the analysis of capital – to the accumulation of abstract wealth, and this is in turn linked to a permanent revolution of the productive forces and to an inherently limitless expansion of mastery over nature. To describe, by contrast, precapitalist modes of production as globally oriented towards use value would be a misleading oversimplification; the abstraction inherent in the concept of use value – which refers in the final instance to capitalist relations – obscures the respective specific goal-values which arise from the interplay of highly different structures of needs, domination and integration.

The following analysis will take its bearings from this under-thematized context of the paradigm of production and draw some lessons for the theory of power. This should not be mistaken for a reduction of the political sphere to configurations of power. Given, however, that any incursion into this area must inevitably make use of the notoriously contentious concept of power, a discussion of the latter is a necessary preliminary to any further development of action theory.

Hannah Arendt's work provides us with an analysis of the specifically modern structures of power and their inherent action orientations that draws on Marxian concepts and at the same time goes beyond them. She considers the in principle limitless accumulation of power – which first asserts itself in the form of imperialist expansion and later strikes back with intensified destructiveness at the internal structures of the nation–state – to be the political counterpart to the limitless accumulation of capital and at the same time to be the most general precondition for totalitarian rule.[27] What remains unclear is whether one should derive this structural change in the political sphere either from the absolutization of an action pattern initially valid only in the economy or from the functional imperatives of the capitalist economic system. The former course leads to the highly unorthodox thesis that it was not the democratic revolution but rather imperialism which achieved the political emancipation of the bourgeoisie and the assimilation of political praxis to the latter's class habitus; the latter approach would, by contrast, be exposed in part to the very objections that can be raised against the Marxist diagnosis of the times.

We can take as the guideline for our further discussion the concept of abstract power, i.e. power separated from the contexts of action and communication within a political community and programmed for its unlimited expansion and intensification. The reference to the Marxian problematic of real abstraction is, however, too vague for a more detailed comparison. On the other hand, Arendt formulated the anthropological presuppositions of her theory of power in such a one-sided contrast to Marx that she can no longer draw on the ideas which go beyond the narrow version of the paradigm of production. Some other theorists of power have entered into a more constructive dialogue with historical materialism and made more systematic use of Marx's work. In such cases, a Marxian theory which focuses primarily on production and appropriation is either supplemented by an analysis of power structures that has a similar conceptual frame (this is the course Leszek Nowak takes in his outline for a 'non-Marxian historical materialism')[28] or retrospectively annexed as a component of a power theory that was initially generated without reference to it. The latter approach is, in more or less pronounced forms, characteristic for the projects which today compete with one another in this field. They tend to reproduce the mostly latent dual meaning of Marx's concept of production, which associates the expansion of control with structure-building activity – in other words, the technical domination of the world with the practical constitution of that world – in a sharper and more generalized form. The inclusion of these themes in a theory of power also serves to explain the reservations shown towards the well-known Weberian definitions (not to be confused with Weber's more concrete insights), which overemphasize intersubjective relations at the cost of other aspects of power structures. The scope and substantive meaning of the ability to impose one's own will on others depend, on the one hand, on the range of resources mobilized for this purpose and, on the other, on the ability to determine and transform the horizons and goals of behaviour.

The common background does not exclude radical differences on other points. Anthony Giddens relates the concept of power to the 'transformative capacity' of human action in general and regards productive activity as a particular case of the exercise of power and the accumulation of resources; it is only in specific historical circumstances that it takes priority over other forms. Michel Foucault, by contrast, wishes to overcome the subject-centred preconceptions of traditional theories of power, in particular the conflation of power and sovereignty, and to replace them with relational and processual concepts which would do justice to the above-mentioned dual character of power. Norbert Elias rejects the attempts to conceptualize power on the basis of an individualistic theory of action and advocates instead a model which points not to systemic contexts but to the interdependencies and reciprocal controls of 'humans in the plural', to action-theoretic conceptions that are bound up with individualistic premisses. Pierre Bourdieu's theory of power is perhaps best understood as a combination of the above three perspectives which, however, at the same time boils them all down to a simplifying model. The metaphor of a force field, which is at the centre of his image of society, refers to polycentric contexts of interaction and thus strictly limits the independence of power structures and processes *vis-à-vis* the actors, while on the other hand subsuming the actors within the field under the universal pattern of strategic action.

In view of these differences it would appear all the more important that the theories of power described converge in two points: they take the maximization of power, i.e. the accumulation of power resources, to be an action-orienting component of the social domain or at least a basis for more manifest action-orientations, and they stress, to use Luhmann's words, the 'intrinsic value (*Eigenwert*) of unsociability', that is, the productive and structure-forming role of antagonistic forms of sociality. The two viewpoints are clearly interconnected: conflict can be recognized as an autonomous principle of structuration to the extent that it impresses specific purposes on social action.

We cannot pursue these issues further here. But it should be clear that the media-theoretic conception of power cannot avoid a critical debate with these alternative positions.[29] I have already briefly pointed to the historical experiences which *prima facie* speak in favour of the latter approaches – or, more precisely, in favour of their shared presuppositions. The role played by political determinants in the historical development of capitalism and the even greater part they took in the genesis and consolidation of a non-capitalist model of society are too autonomous and complex to be understandable in terms of a theory of media. With respect to the capitalist epoch, one cannot deny the existence of a context-bound and ambivalent primacy of the economy; a mode of production aimed at maximizing abstract wealth and internationalizing exchange relations can impose its imperatives on the other domains of social life much more effectively than can precapitalist economic systems, but the dynamics of expansion and accumulation which it simultaneously engenders increase the space within which extra-economic processes can unfold according to their own laws. For our present purposes, it is enough to mention the processes of state formation, state intervention and interstate competition. For all their dependence on the development of the economic world system, a quick glance is enough to show that they cannot be confined to a secondary or derivative role. At an early stage, they contributed decisively to the formation of the system, and later on, they not only gave a particularly explosive twist to the latter's internal conflicts, but also greatly facilitated the destruction or absorption of antisystemic movements. Their role becomes even more central in post-revolutionary societies; these are, as we have seen, characterized by the fact that economic and cultural mechanisms of control are fused with political ones. If we bear this theoretical and historical background in mind, it will be easier to show which additions and modifications must be made to the concept of abstract power as both an object and a driving force of accumulation. The parallel to Marx's conception of value and capital as abstract wealth, clearly stated but not developed further by Hannah Arendt, must now be reconsidered in the light of the essential but controversial connection between labour and the value-form. As I tried to show, the analysis of the commodity form, its components and its derivatives – which in Marx's thought is vitiated by a naturalistic reductionism – can make a relevant contribution to social theory only if it does not focus on the substance of value as the product of abstract labour, but rather on the subsumption of the labour process as a whole under the value relation. The latter must, furthermore, be connected to a more comprehensive context, i.e. one that includes political and cultural determinants. A similar perspective suggests itself for a theory of power: in line with the model of subsumption, the concept of abstract power could refer to the structures and processes which transform the different components of the social world into more or less mobilizable power resources or objects of the exercise of power. Reactions and countertrends are, of course, as inseparable from this homogenizing and levelling process as they are from the subsumption under capital. Hannah Arendt's notion of abstract power is defined in primarily negative terms – its main characteristic is the separation from and undermining of communicative contexts – and therefore too undifferentiated to be of much use for an analysis along these lines. On the other hand, its positively defined counterpart, i.e. the authentic power which coincides with a communicative community and stands in sharp contrast to violence, is too narrowly demarcated for the transformation into abstract power to be explained otherwise than in terms of an abrupt collapse or of the loss of the political dimension.

Further exploration of these issues is beyond the limits of the present paper. But to conclude the discussion of the concept of power and its relationship to action theory, let us return briefly to the problematic which Habermas thematized only from the point of view of action orientation and coordination. As we have seen, the concept of strategic action serves to neutralize at the level of action orientation the differences between the economic and political spheres and to justify their subordination to a common pattern anchored in the cultural sphere. The above objections suggest that a less hierarchical and homogenizing model would be in order, and that we should include among the economic and political determinants of action some domain-specific action orientations that can neither be reduced to a common denominator nor limited to a derivative role. This does not mean that they are unrelated to the cultural context. To clarify this point, it may be useful to confront the present line of argument with other interpretations of modernity which – unlike that proposed by Habermas – do not ground their culturalist diagnoses on the highly abstract presuppositions of communicative action and communicative rationality, but rather relate them to concrete and dominant semantic contents.

In the present context, two variants of this line of argument are particularly noteworthy. According to a plausible but not uncontroversial interpretation of Weber's theory of modernity, the project of rational world domination is a specifically modern action orientation which tendentially has an impact on all areas of life. This involves a form of rationality that has emerged in specific historical circumstances and in which principles of order and efficiency – in other words, the imperatives of organization and performance – are linked.[30] Capitalism and bureaucracy, the two formative powers which Weber believed were decisive for the modern world, clearly combine both elements in different ways; the same can be said about the two different models of economic and social organization which today dominate the scene. Castoriadis has radicalized and problematized this Weberian perspective in a way that also seems relevant to the questions raised by Habermas's approach.[31] If we assume that the project in question does not simply manifest itself in a gradual progress towards greater practical control over the environment, but also and more importantly – as Weber saw – in the belief that calculating reason can expand its realm *ad infinitum*, a further conclusion suggests itself: the underlying meaningful orientation which Weber describes as 'belief' is not reducible to its rationalized and rationalizing superstructures; it should rather be located at the level of the 'imaginary significations' which we cannot grasp directly, but only through an analysis of their alternative or complementary interpretations. From the imaginary vision of a rationally organized and inherently limitless accumulation of power, Castoriadis derives the partly overlapping and partly divergent projects of an infinitely expanding domination of nature, a metasocial and universally valid economic rationality, an unlimited economic growth and an all-embracing planning of social life.

As this example shows, the recourse to an underlying imaginary layer of culture opens the way to a more differentiated analysis of modern action orientations. Because of their openness and indeterminacy, the imaginary significations can acquire additional and more specific contents in the context of economic and political structures. As the above considerations suggest, the imaginary core – the phantasm of unlimited rational mastery – could be linked to the dynamics of abstract wealth in one sphere and abstract power in the other. In both cases, the dominant economic or political category is co-constituted by a cultural interpretation (i.e. through the specification and contextualization of an imaginary signification), but in such a way that the scope for autonomous economic and political processes and a relative primacy of economic or political structures is greatly enlarged. But although Castoriadis notes that the imaginary core of capitalist development is open to alternative practical and ideological interpretations, he has so far paid too little attention to the specific contrasts between its economic and political offshoots, and this also leads him to minimize the corresponding differences between Western and Soviet patterns. It would, however, be equally misleading to postulate a direct link between intrasystemic differentiation and intersystemic polarization. The primacy of the economy in one case cannot simply be counterposed to the primacy of the polity in the other; rather, the different overall structures function in such a way that a central but not unconditionally dominant role is in one instance assigned to the autonomous dynamic of capital and in the other to the unified power apparatus of the party-state. The ideological derivatives of both 'paths of modernization' oscillate accordingly between absolutizing market rationality or state control on the one hand and more complex constructions, which supplement both principles with further claims to legitimacy, on the other.

The action orientations that are built into modern economic and political structures and projected on to the level of global societal alternatives cannot be defined without taking the cultural sphere into consideration. We therefore need a concept of culture that would allow us to interpret the relationship between the spheres not in terms of the one-sided and unambiguous programming of action orientations by a world view and a form of understanding, but rather as a specification and extension of the cultural components through their incorporation into economic and political contexts. As mentioned above, the concept of imaginary significations provides a promising point of departure for such an approach. With this in mind, we have still to engage critically with Habermas's theory of culture.

Before doing so, however, let us return briefly to some conceptual distinctions in his theory of action. As we have seen, the concept of action orientation reduces references to the world and the purposes of action to a common denominator. Purposeful intervention in the world, which is emphasized in the teleological concept of action and at least presupposed in the other concepts mentioned by Habermas (those of normative, dramaturgical and communicative action), relies on a testable and transmissible knowledge of the objective world. Conversely, the intrinsic relation of this knowledge to action determines its categorial framework – if not in the narrow sense of a nomological knowledge tied to the functional radius of instrumental action, then at least in the sense of an interpretation of the world in terms of things and events that is from the outset tailored to match purposive action. More complex models of action add further determinations to this underlying pattern and thus open up new domains of meaning. Intervention and interpretation, accomplishing an action and gaining access to the world, determine each other reciprocally at all levels. We shall later return to the presuppositions of this construction with regard to a theory of world views; on the level of action theory, Habermas relies on the above-mentioned line of argument which reduces the relations between cultural, political and economic determinants of action to the asymmetrical interdependence of communicative and strategic action. Our critique of this reduction has some implications for the very concept of action orientation. If the economic and political goal-values of action – which culminate on the one hand in the accumulation of abstract wealth and on the other in the accumulation of abstract power – presuppose a shared meaningful context that is also elastic enough to permit divergent interpretations, then it is evident that we should distinguish between *horizons of action* and *goals of action*. The emphasis on a substantive differentiation of the goals, in opposition to the levelling concept of strategic action, serves to underline not only the far-reaching autonomy of the practical level *vis-à-vis* the interpretative one, but also the surplus meaning constitutive of the latter and the irreducibility of each level to the other.

This new perspective has, among other things, a direct bearing on the issue of a specifically modern understanding of the world. To be more precise, it leads to the question whether one should speak of a specifically modern world view or a specifically modern field of tensions between divergent interpretations. It will prove easier to analyse further implications if we take into account the analogous problems which result from the concept of action coordination. The power-theoretic arguments, which we used to counter the levelling of concrete action orientations in the concept of strategic action, also speak against equating – at the level of basic concepts – the sociation of the actors with their consensus-based or functional harmonization. *Action coordination* must rather be viewed as a special case of the *interweaving of actions*. Only given this presupposition can one adequately thematize the 'intrinsic value of unsociability' (Luhmann) and the many shapes of its combination with more positive forms of sociality. Elias emphasizes, to mention but one important example, the indissoluble linking of processes of functional differentiation and integration to processes of competition and monopolization; the power-theoretic perspective from which he analyses the latter involve also the insight that 'there are types of interdependency which drive Ego and Alter to wage war against and kill each other'.[32] In other words: if it is true that 'the human species maintains itself through the socially coordinated activities of its members',[33] we should also bear in mind not only the fact that the human species has repeatedly damaged itself in irreparable ways and might possibly destroy itself through the socially interwoven activities of its members, but also something Marx had already stressed, namely that sometimes 'war developed earlier than peace'.[34] The most destructive forms of interaction can have an impact that leads to major changes in the patterns of self-conservation.

Conflictual interdependence is not only characteristic of power structures; the primacy of action geared toward consensus must also be relativized with regard to cultural preconditions. The Weberian diagnosis of the times is a convenient starting point for a discussion of these issues. Although Habermas rightly stresses its relevance as a challenge to Critical Theory, his reading of it is open to objections: the twin theses of a loss of meaning and a loss of freedom, which he attributes to Weber, add up to an oversimplification of the latter's argument. For all its incompleteness, Weber's image of advanced modernity is more complex and nuanced than Habermas's version of it would suggest. Rather than a global loss of meaning, Weber diagnoses a simultaneous levelling and fragmentation of semantic contents (the question of freedom can, for the time being, be left aside). Although the traditional interpretative patterns are – as he sees it – invalidated by the absolutization of a calculating reason and the transformation of the cosmos into a causal mechanism, the interpretative functions of culture are nevertheless shifted on to heterogeneous value-principles which compete with one another through their respective totalizing claims and cannot – because of their incommensurability – merge in a synthesis. In the final instance, both aspects, levelling and fragmentation, must be viewed in light of the comparative analyses of civilizations. In the latter context Weber is not only interested in tracing the gradations and ramifications of rationality, but also in distinguishing mutually exclusive stances toward the world, each of which has specific interpretative contents of its own. The ability to engage critically with the constitutive stance towards the world of another culture is clearly inseparable from the relativization of one's own self-understanding and understanding of the world, which is brought about by the dissolution of traditional all-embracing interpretations and the radicalization of latent oppositions. This specifically modern openness towards the Other is the polar opposite of an equally modern homogenization of the world by means of instrumental reason.

Habermas cannot be accused of completely disregarding this problematic. The concept of communicative action is not aimed against the pluralism of life forms and value orientations; it is intended to embrace 'only formal determinations of the communicative infrastructure of possible life forms and life histories'.[35] And it would be even less justifiable to criticize him for neglecting the structural and dynamic aspects of social conflict. Action conflicts and mechanisms of conflict regulation play an important role in his outline of a theory of socio-cultural evolution. In this way, he wants to preserve some basic insights of historical materialism while tuning them to greater precision (it is not, however, altogether clear how much of this is then incorporated into the theory of communicative action).[36] To begin with, he distinguishes 'normal action situations' from the more difficult tasks involved in consensual regulation of conflicts; the institutions responsible for the latter area on the whole develop more slowly, and they can therefore coexist with more advanced elementary structures of action for the duration of a whole evolutionary phase. But they nevertheless play a particularly important role in evolutionary breakthroughs. On the other hand, the dialectic of progress consists not least in the fact that central and permanent conflicts – which arise from the 'differential exercise of social violence' and can neither be overcome by genuinely consensual solutions nor contained by procedures that have lagged behind evolutionary change – speed up the development of the world views which legitimate domination and in so doing generate intellectual resources that can promote further development of the ability to regulate conflicts.

From the viewpoint of the forms of understanding, Habermas thus thematizes social conflicts partly as external barriers and partly as productive challenges. But it is doubtful whether this approach does justice to the complex interrelations of the two sides of social life. In particular, we need to consider to what extent social conflicts do not only disturb or stimulate processes of reaching understanding, but can also co-determine their shape and direction by influencing the interpretative patterns which underlie them. In this respect, Habermas's work follows the model of ideology critique: universalist norms and ideas which serve to legitimate particular interests can also be invoked by a critique geared toward emancipatory aims and deployed against the existing social order. An example of a different approach would be Alain Touraine's analysis of the relations between antagonistic social movements, especially the workers' movement and the bourgeoisie. As he sees it, alternative versions of a shared but underdetermined cultural model (in the above-mentioned case, the idea of progress) enter into conflict, and on both sides the cultural component is as essential to the constitution of the movement as the power component is with respect to determining and implementing the concretized cultural patterns. On the one hand – and in contrast to the formal and procedural presuppositions on which, or so Habermas claims, the interplay of ideology and ideology critique is ultimately based – epoch-specific contents are constitutive of the common basis, and yet they are, on the other, sufficiently flexible to be appropriated by antagonistic collective actors and translated into rival projects.

The theoretical implications of such comparisons should, of course, not be overestimated; they can at best serve to illustrate the contrasts between overall perspectives. In the above context, we have to do with links between divergent theories of the development of world views and different conceptions of social conflict. Habermas's emphasis on autonomy, universality and clearcut directions with regard to the former leads *ipso facto* to a limitation of the role conflict can play in relation to forms of understanding. The underlying cultural structure of modernity, in which the rationalization of world views supposedly culminates, should also be examined from this point of view. Here we must confine ourselves to a few preparatory remarks.

The uniformity of a culturally encoded interpretation of the world and an institutionalized form of understanding must clearly not be confused with conflict-free harmony. As Habermas stresses, one of the characteristics of the modern world is that it reserves a space for conflicting interpretations which also co-determine the development of social movements. He counts 'anarchism, communism, and socialism' as well as 'syndicalist, radical-democratic and conservative-revolutionary orientations to fascism and National Socialism'[37] among the specifically modern reactions which, for all their differences in terms of motivation and direction, nevertheless have a common point of departure. These ideological constructions, which are more or less closely connected with social movements, still have 'the form of totalizing conceptions of order addressed to the political consciousness of comrades and partners in struggle'[38] in common with early modern ideologies and traditionalist reactions. On the other hand, they adhere to the logic of modernization in that they oppose moral-practical or expressive criteria to an absolutized or systemically reified purposive rationality. This explains their affinity to 'counter-movements' of another kind which do not operate on the level of collective action, but rather within the differentiated spheres of culture, and aim at a balanced coordination of the separate validity claims. According to Habermas, non-objectivistic approaches in the humanities are representative of this trend, as are attempts to supplement universalistic ethics with references to the calculation of consequences and the interpretation of needs, or the return of realist or *engagé* trends within post-avant-garde art.[39] The common underlying intention of these initially spontaneous and fragmentary attempts at mediation is first articulated systematically at a higher level of abstraction. This task is fulfilled by the 'philosophical discourse of modernity', i.e. by the repeatedly blocked or disoriented search for a concept of reason that would do justice to the modern structures of rationality, those embedded in the lifeworld as well as those embodied in differentiated institutions. The search begins with a critique of the subject-centred and monological model of rationality, geared towards the determination of facts and the adjustment of means to ends. But beyond this point, several options are available. On the one hand, cultural traditions are conjured up as a counterweight to a self-absolutizing cognitive-instrumental reason; on the other, a form of purposive rationality enriched with normative and expressive elements and dedicated to the telos of self-realization is expected to secure the substantive unity of reason and emancipation. Habermas attributes the latter strategy to praxis philosophy in the widest sense. Both suggested solutions are, however, rejected by the 'counter-discourse of modernity' which, beginning with Nietzsche, uses the inadequacies and aporias of an absolutized purposive rationality as a pretext for putting reason itself on trial. A sufficiently complex model of rationality that would neither offer irrationalism a point for attack nor grant it some exterritorial domain is, according to Habermas, to be gained only by recourse to the communicative reason that has – together with its perspectives on the world – 'always already been embodied' in everyday communicative practice. However, this involves appealing to a pregiven understanding of the world which is not open to question within the framework of modern structures of consciousness. This is evident, among other things, from the assumption that the discourse and counter-discourse of modernity are, despite the controversy surrounding the concept of reason, articulated within a common and overarching argumentational framework.[40]

This model has some obvious advantages. It integrates three different levels, namely politically effective ideologies (i.e. those represented by social movements), culturally critical innovations and philosophical discourse into a common frame of reference without blurring the distinctions between them. At the level of social movements, it takes a very wide spectrum into account, the heterogeneity of which attests to the internal tensions within modernity. And it makes the self-thematization of the modern world appear less the result of a process of maturation and more the focus of a permanent conflict. Yet it also immunizes against interpretative conflicts the supposedly ultimate foundations of modern culture and the developmental logic inherent in them. The modern interpretation of the world, based as it is on a clear differentiation between objective, social and subjective reality, can accordingly be as little relativized or problematized as can 'the modern form of understanding which has been crystallizing in the West since the eighteenth century',[41] which integrates the universal perspective of the Enlightenment into a more concrete structure of the lifeworld. There is, in other words, no radical conflict of interpretations at the heart of modernity, but only the fundamental pattern of the Enlightenment, the uneven development of which provoked on the one hand the artificial resuscitation of outdated forms of thought and, on the other, global and undifferentiated negations that could be given concrete form only by borrowing from traditions or reinterpreting emancipatory perspectives.

Habermas has to postulate the existence of a coherent, unambiguous and closed core structure of modern culture, in order to be able to create categorical barriers against the intrinsic dynamics of the polity and the economy, and to counterbalance them with a potential corrective: the 'unfinished project' of a rationalized, reunified and sovereign lifeworld. The latter construct is given clearer historical contours by virtue of its being equated with the telos of the Enlightenment. But this also raises the question of a specifically modern response to the Enlightenment that should be taken into account as such, i.e. not only in its secondary and subliminal manifestations. Such an extension of the frame of reference would decisively undermine the idea of a unified modern world view.

As both recent and older studies have convincingly shown, the complex of Romantic structures of consciousness constitutes such a response.[42] For a theory of modernity which wants to retain a link to Marx while going beyond the bounds of his work, the most convenient starting-point is a brief reference in the *Grundrisse:* 'The bourgeois viewpoint has never advanced beyond this antithesis between itself and this romantic viewpoint [i.e. the longing for the "original richness" of premodern forms of life], and therefore the latter will accompany it as legitimate antithesis up to its blessed end.'[43] Since the transformation of Marxism into an institutionalized ideology was – to say the least – not a step beyond the 'bourgeois viewpoint', as far as the overcoming of the legitimate antithesis was concerned, it would seem advisable to generalize the Marxian diagnosis. In that case, we would have to do with an internal polarization of modern forms of consciousness and/or with an internal structural split in the self-thematization of modernity. If, however, we wish to interpret the opposition between Enlightenment and Romanticism in this manner, both sides call for a clearer and more complex definition.

Adorno and Horkheimer developed a critical concept of the Enlightenment which they applied not only to the whole trajectory of bourgeois society, but also to a pattern of civilization which antedates it and continues to influence the forces that strive to transcend it. But since this line of argument collapses the structures of particular epochs and cultures into a universal logic of domination, it offers no alternative to classical Marxism when it comes to a more concrete analysis of the modern world. Other theorists have been more concerned with the Enlightenment as a specifically modern project, bound up with particular cultural contents and driving forces, and subjected it to a critical examination. As we have seen, Castoriadis takes the imaginary absolutization of rational mastery to be of crucial importance, whereas Foucault perceives the real infrastructure of processes of Enlightenment to reside in a new organization of power. The two otherwise very different approaches converge in one crucial assumption: on this view, the Enlightenment model of rationality is structured in terms of disposition, control and the increase of power in such a manner that it cannot be explained by reference to the one-sided development of cognitive-instrumental reason, but rather presupposes a specific world project. Seen from this vantage point, the idea of a communicative rationality does not constitute a definitive break with earlier conceptions. A theory which not only thematizes the intersubjective context of objective knowledge and the internal relations between interpretation and communication, but also attempts – above and beyond this – to determine universal and necessary rules for the communicative use of language, is open to the suspicion that, for all its efforts to broaden and diversify the idea of reason, it remains bound to the imperatives of control.

Following Hans Blumenberg, who in turn draws on the work of Rothacker, we can use the concept of meaningfulness (*Bedeutsamkeit*) to characterize the Romantic countertrend.[44] Put briefly, the concept refers to the ability and the need to establish meaningful relations between the human world and the world as a global context. If we relate this notion to Schleiermacher's proposition that in reality Enlightenment, or clearing something up, means clearing out in the sense of a clean sweep, we arrive at a preliminary definition of Romanticism, in the widest sense of the term. It is essentially the defence of meaningfulness against subsumption under the meaning – destroying mechanisms of an Enlightenment geared towards the expansion and rationalization of power and embodied in the reified economic and political structures of the modern world. The stages and variants of the Romantic consciousness can, among other things, be categorized in terms of whether the perspective which provides meaning is primarily anchored at a cosmological, a social or a subjective level. The traditionalist utopia, to which the above quotation from Marx refers, is thus only one of many variants of Romantic thought. At the other end of the spectrum we encounter its self-reflexive form: an attempt to place the ability to 'take a deliberate attitude towards the world and to lend it significance'[45] at the centre of a theoretically articulate and research-oriented image of man and society.

The point is not to oppose Romanticism to Enlightenment as an alternative project, but rather to underline a constitutive polarity of modern structures of consciousness that can express itself in highly different constellations. Given this presupposition, a theoretical elaboration of the self-understanding of modernity must proceed in a manner unlike that pursued by Habermas. The critical but neither aporetic nor methodologically pre-programmed self-reflexion of the Enlightenment would not exhaust itself in the correction of hitherto existing imbalances, but would expand to include on the one hand a distantiation from the imperatives of control, regardless of the sublimated form these may take, and on the other an open-ended dialogue with a legitimate and articulate opponent. A more concrete analysis of modern interpretations of the world and their ideological derivatives would, in addition, have to take into account the polarizations, partial convergences and hybrid forms of the two fundamental tendencies. The action-orienting ideologies of the social movements mentioned above also contain, to a varying degree, a Romantic streak. The picture becomes even more complex if we also consider the role of nationalism. The latter is linked to the Romantic consciousness above all through the phenomenon of the 'imagined community';[46] as to the social movements, they have in part been directly influenced and in part externally conditioned or retroactively absorbed by nationalism.

In light of the interrelations between Enlightenment and Romanticism, we must relativize the categories and demarcations which constitute – as Habermas sees it – the ultimate premisses of the modern world view. A critical examination along these lines would lead to the reconstruction of a 'discourse of modernity' in which the central categories – nature, society and subject – were not implicitly accepted, but problematized and opened up to conflicting interpretations. A positive reception of Romantic motifs can, for example, be seen in the diverse endeavours to thematize the moment of creativity and to point it up in opposition to the monological concept of nature, to a normativist concept of society and to the idea of an inner nature tending towards expression. On the other hand, a critical line of argument, which relies directly or indirectly on Romanticism, leads to the exposure of the imperatives and structures of power which lie behind identitarian modes of thought, normative patterns of sociality and images of the self-positing subject. A perspective expanded in this manner would first allow us justifiably to speak of a radically decentred understanding of the world; it would also provide a new focus for the comparison with other world views and traditions.

Postscript (October 1989)

This paper was written in 1984. Extensive additions and afterthoughts would obviously be in order, but in the present context they must be limited to one aspect of the argument: the attempt to use the problematic of Soviet-type societies as a starting point for an alternative to Habermas's theory of modernity. Recent events – not only the 'Gorbachev phenomenon', but also other developments more or less directly linked to it – have thrown new light on some of the questions discussed above. More specifically, a general crisis of the Soviet system now seems to be developing more rapidly and at the same time provoking a broader range of responses than most observers would have expected five years ago.

The overall pattern of the crisis can, in my opinion, still be analysed in terms of the model sketched on pp. 186–9. But on the other hand, an additional factor has been thrown into much sharper relief than before, both as an organizational principle and as a source of crisis tendencies: the imperial dimension of the Soviet system. If the party-state with its peculiar fusion of economic, political and cultural patterns of power can be regarded as an alternative 'path of modernization', it must also be analysed in relation to the processes of imperial regeneration, consolidation and expansion (their global background was briefly discussed on pp. 191–3). The diffusion of the Soviet model beyond its original context was partly a direct consequence of its imperial dynamics (as in Eastern Europe), partly associated with a comparable revolutionary detour to imperial restoration (as in China). Most importantly for our present purposes, it seems clear that the general crisis of the Soviet model was above all sparked by a growing discrepancy between imperial constraints and aspirations on the one hand and systemic patterns and resources on the other.[47] This general diagnosis can be specified in terms of the three structural trends mentioned above: the fusion of the three spheres; the subsumption of each of them under a specific self-absolutizing principle; and the gradual strengthening of centrifugal and fragmenting tendencies within each sphere.

The command economy, which developed as a result of the Stalinist revolution from above, was subordinated to a more comprehensive accumulation of power; it was, in other words, a technique of state formation on an imperial scale, rather than a strategy of economic development. But at the same time, it was legitimated as a superior and definitive form of economic rationality, and it gave rise to highly resilient power structures with their own logic of expansion and maximization. This hypertrophy of the economic factor within the totalitarian pattern affected both the centre and the periphery of the empire; the persistence of dysfunctional and unreformable structures within the Soviet Union was reflected in the counterproductive imposition of the Soviet model on more developed economies. As a result of the overextension of the imperial project during the Brezhnev era, these weaknesses became increasingly acute, but the short-term response to them generated new crisis symptoms. The military economy developed in contrast to – and at the expense of – the civil one; this discrepancy in terms of both organization and performance led some analysts to forecast a progressive militarization of the regime and the society as a whole, but in retrospect it seems to have had a rather different effect.[48] The backwardness of the civil sector undermined the military strength of the Soviet Union, weakened its international position and made the need for structural reforms more obvious. The growing gap between the two economies was, in other words, a symptom of systemically induced fragmentation, rather than the first step towards a redistribution of social power in favour of the military apparatus.

The universalistic self-interpretation of the party-state has served to legitimize imperial aspirations, but imperial achievements have also helped the state to mobilize nationalistic undercurrents. If the combination of these two aspects made the political centre more resistant to change and contestation, it was by the same token bound to aggravate the fractures built into the very reproduction of the regime. The consolidation of the party-state apparatus during the Brezhnev era did not benefit all sectors to the same degree (the army was clearly a privileged case), but to the extent that it resulted in a certain differentiation of positions and interests, the role of the party leadership shifted from despotic rule towards a balancing and coordinating function. At first this constellation seemed more compatible with imperial aims than the original Stalinist pattern had been; when the leadership was transformed into a gerontocracy, and supreme power was transferred to a nonentity in 1984, the degeneration of the centre – facilitated by its more conservative role – had obviously gone beyond acceptable limits and made it vulnerable to the innovative strategy of an outsider. The pendulum swung back to the *other* built-in deviation from the principle of party sovereignty: the emergence of a charismatic leader who has tried to outflank the apparatus by building other bases of power.

Finally a few words should be said about the ideological component and its contribution to the crisis. Although there is no reason to believe that the official pronouncements about the terminal crisis of capitalism were ever taken at face value, there is no reason to doubt that ideological blockages prevented the Soviet leadership from grasping the significance of the transformations that were taking place in the capitalist world; this applies to recent technological breakthroughs as well as to the emergence of a more multipolar state system. At first, the growing dependence of a fossilized Marxism-Leninism on a more vigorous but less presentable nationalist imagery made matters worse: this combination was particularly conducive to delusions about the ability of the Soviet state to meet new challenges and adjust to international realignments. But at a certain point, the progressive ideological decomposition seems – in combination with other factors – to have taken a new turn. The nationalistic priorities of a new leadership, concerned with the survival of the Soviet Union as a great power, led it to take a more openly critical view of the ideological and institutional patterns which it had inherited.

It would thus seem that an analysis of the problematic and changing relationships between economic, political and cultural structures, as well as of the repercussions within each sphere, is the most rewarding approach to the present crisis. More specifically, it serves to show how the latter differs from the crisis model which Habermas includes in his theory of the two paths of modernization. It can also help to understand the responses to the crisis. If there is such a thing as a 'Gorbachev project', it can – as the learning processes and readjustments of the last few years have shown – be defined only in very general and flexible terms: as an attempt to restructure the unity of economic, political and cultural patterns of power in such a way that the autonomy of each sphere would be much more openly recognized and effectively guaranteed. There is, however, no functional frame of reference and no stable relationship of forces on which a more precise and durable version of this strategy could be based. Both inside the Soviet Union and within its sphere of influence, the first serious innovations set in motion a complex interplay of social forces, and the theoretical model suggested above does not permit any predictions about its results.

11 A Reply

Jürgen Habermas

In philosophy and the sciences, just as in literature, an author is indebted to his readers, and the more he is able to learn from their criticism the more he has to thank them for. I would like above all to thank the editors of this volume for having helped to promote a discussion that has had more difficulty getting off the ground in West Germany than in an English-speaking context, where it has developed rather more easily.[1] I am aware that I have not put forward a mature theory but have, at best, marked out a theoretical approach which serves to link a philosophy committed to understanding itself as a postmetaphysical enterprise with certain areas of the social sciences. It was my concern in writing *The Theory of Communicative Action* to provide the foundation for a project sufficiently fertile to be pursued, as it were, radially, in different directions. Since then, I have published the Christian Gauss lectures. These gave me the opportunity to fill in some of the gaps in my theory by providing philosophical foundations for the necessary paradigm shift from a theory of consciousness to a theory of communication.[2] I have further elaborated my approach to discourse ethics and examined it in the context of developmental psychology.[3] And finally I have deployed the concept of modernity – developed until now only in terms of social theory – in the context of the radical critique of reason, which has always been of central importance to Critical Theory, in order to counter objections raised by neo-Structuralism.[4] I am currently engaged in clarifying the complex relationship between law, morals and ethical life (*Sittlichkeit*) as well as reviewing my (perhaps over-presumptuous) theses on juridification.[5] I feel that what is called for is an elaboration of argumentation theory and the theory of truth as well as a clarification of specific questions in the domain of a formal-pragmatic theory of meaning. Only three of the essays in this volume touch on philosophical issues in the narrow sense. I shall, in consequence, both in the first, philosophical, section of my reply and in the second, action-theoretical, section, where philosophical and sociological questions touch on each other, devote rather more attention to criticisms that have appeared elsewhere. In the third section, set aside for social-theoretical questions, I shall focus more closely, although not exclusively, on the contributions to this volume. I shall not be able to do justice to the points raised by J. P. Arnason, who took his critique as an opportunity to put forward a counter-project. I shall concentrate rather on clearing up misunderstandings, correcting mistakes and eliminating shortcomings in the logical foundations of my work. Thus I can also not comment on the two excellent monographs by Helga Gripp and Stephen K. White,[6] which both centre more on description than on critique.

On the Concept of Communicative Rationality

Charles Taylor's objections to my theory are to be seen in the context of his own theory of language, which follows in the tradition of Humboldt's work in the same area. In responding to them, I shall be able to open the discussion with some general observations on the conception of language as utilized in a theory of intersubjectivity. Martin Seel aims his remarks at the foundations of the theory, namely the manner in which a procedural concept of reason is explained in terms of the theory of language. He pursues the question of how this form of reason can preserve its unity given the plurality of different aspects of validity. In this context I would like to return to the problem Schnädelbach discusses, namely the purely descriptive use of the concept of rationality and the fallibility of such deliberations on underlying principles. In arguing against Kuhlmann's work, I distance myself from any claim to provide ultimate foundations.

Charles Taylor reconstructs my concept of language accurately from the perspective of Humboldt's philosophy of language. The distinction be-tween the structure of language (the linguistic structure or organism of language) and the practice of language usage (the living process of speech) – in other words Humboldt's distinction between language as *ergon* and as *energeia* – has certainly been taken up by more recent theories of language (*langue* vs. *parole*, linguistic competence vs. linguistic performance). At the same time, however, it has been deprived of a decisive dimension, namely that of the intersubjectivity of possible understanding. Neither Saussure nor Chomsky conceives of conversation as the crux of language, as Hum-boldt did.[7] Taylor correctly perceives that the theory of communicative action can be understood as an attempt to develop a theory of society from precisely this approach to the theory of language. Yet, there is a tension in Humboldt's writings between the basic presuppositions with which he works, which are grounded in a theory of intersubjectivity, and the figures of thought in which these are couched, which are taken from a philosophy of the subject. My theory is drawn more towards the one pole, Taylor's more towards the other. This is the source of the controversy between us.

Before proceeding further, it would therefore be advisable to review the issues involved.

Humboldt specifies the status of the linguistic medium of reaching understanding in a manner similar to that adopted by Hegel to designate objective Spirit. Language acts upon the speaking subject as an incisively moulding, and suprasubjective force without – as is the case with the contingent influence of nature – facing him as something purely external. The structure of language maintains and renews itself solely through the linguistic community's practice of reaching understanding. The language system makes speech acts possible which, in turn, reproduce the language and in so doing, make innovative changes in it, however imperceptible these may be.[8] All else depends on which model Humboldt adopts when conceiving of the mediating unity of linguistic structure and linguistic practice. Is the whole of language a self-referential subject which holds the living process of language together by means of its synthesizing achievements – or is this synthesis accomplished solely within those forms taken by the diffracted intersubjectivity of dialogue? Humboldt did not completely relinquish the model of the self-referentiality of the active, knowing subject. His notion of language as an organism clearly still bears the Romantic traits of language as an expressive whole that externalizes its essential powers and assures itself of its creative subjectivity by contemplating these objectifications. Humbold't concept of language would seem simply to be a variation on Hegel's concept of the concrete universal: language as such relates to the multiplicity of national languages, and these in turn relate to concrete speech acts as the moments of the universal, the particular and the individual in the processual matrix of relations of a particular totality.

On the other hand, these basic concepts of a philosophy of consciousness do *not* in fact enable Humboldt to lend validity to the insight which was of paramount importance to him, both as the liberal philsospher of a bourgeois individualism and for his philosophy of language. He is convinced that

the individuality of a language is only such by comparison, and that its true individuality reposes in the given speaker at any time. This must be considered if the concepts are to be sharply defined. Only in the individual does language attain its final distinctness. Nobody conceives in a given word exactly what his neighbour does, and the ever so slight variation skitters through the entire language like concentric ripples over the water. All understanding is simultaneously a non-comprehension, all agreement in ideas and emotions is at the same time a divergence. In the manner in which language is modified by each individual, there is revealed, in contrast to its previously expounded potency, a power of man over it.[9]

Of course Humboldt is not an empiricist trying to pull the rug out from under the feet of the process of reaching understanding and hold the identity of linguistic meanings to emanate from the randomly iterated intentions – constantly superseding each other – of single, isolated speakers. For him, the intersubjectivity of a common perspective does not dissolve, for example, into a series of isolated I-perspectives which are merely reflected in one another; rather, it arises at the same time; and from the same source as intersubjective validity of semantically identical linguistic expressions and is of equal origin (*gleich-ursprünglich*). But Humboldt is no less adverse to understanding language as a totality; for this would necessarily prejudice the initiatives and yes/no positions of autonomous and at the same time unique subjects by creating a pre-understanding that determines the course of all things to come, as it were. Humboldt wants to give adequate consideration to *both* aspects, i.e. the unavoidable and also counteractual supposition that all participants involved use the same expressions in a semantically identical manner, for, without this idealizing precondition, they would not be able to enter into dialogue in the first place; and also to the fact that the intentions of the speakers invariably deviate from the standard meanings of the expressions used and that this difference casts its shadow over all linguistically-achieved mutual agreement (*Einverständnis*).

It is my impression that Taylor does not pay sufficient attention to this difference. Certainly, I- and We- perspectives are supposed to complement one another; but in Taylor's work the latter then take precedence after all. Taylor speaks of temporary breaches in a processually secured consensus, such that the breaks which have occurred have to be sealed over by processes of reaching understanding. We can detect signs of a Romantic concept of language in this view in which the synthesizing achievements and the unifying productive capacities of a Spirit of Language functioning self-referentially are held up as a first principle. The organic life of the linguistic totality branches out via the structural differences of national languages right into the multiplicity of speech acts, yet asserts itself within all these differentiations as the *superordinated* universal. To counter this totalizing concept of language, Humboldt rightly brings into play the diffracted intersubjectivity of a form of reaching understanding that allows the *divergence*, within the successfully achieved consensual agreement itself, of individually nuanced thoughts and feelings.

Objective agreement about something in the world – i.e. agreement the validity of which is open to question – is dependent in fact on the creation of an *intersubjective* relation between the speaker and at least one listener capable of taking a critical position.[10] The model of dialogue, taken from the ideal of Platonic dialogue,[11] implies a notion of dialogic synthesis which no longer ensures – as the reflexive force of the 'I think' does – the presence of monologic unity within the multiplicity of representations. Rather, consensus achieved through communication depends both on the idealizing supposition that an identity in linguistic meanings already prevails and also on the power of negation and the autonomy of unique, non-substitutable subjects – from whom intersubjective consent to criticizable validity claims has to be obtained anew in each case. All consensus achieved within discourse rests on the power of negation held by independent subjects, who, by entering into an interpersonal relationship, reciprocally acknowledge the accountability (*Zurechnungsfähigkeit*) of the other, whereby such competence is taken to mean that they orient their actions toward validity claims.

Even when applied to linguistic phenomena, self-consciousness – the basic figure of thought used in the philosophy of the subject – does not offer a sound basis for a theory of society. If the subject relates to itself at the same time as it knows its objects, then it encounters itself in the double position of being both a single empirical entity in the world and as the transcendental subject facing the world as a whole. It finds itself in the position of being one amongst many and as one against all (Henrich). Between these two positionings of the subject there is no space left for the symbolically prestructured, linguistically constituted domains of culture, society and socialized individuals.

Things are altogether different with respect to the basic figure in communication theory, namely that of subjects capable of speech and action reaching understaning about something in the world. What is constitutive for it is the relation of an ego to an alter ego, *of simultaneous and equal origin*. Between the two, the space opens up for an intersubjectively shared life world; communicating parties are situated within the horizons of this lifeworld when they refer to objects or states of affairs in the world: 'For such designation use must be made of a sensuous concept that nevertheless abstracts from all qualitative differences, a concept that embraces the I and the You in one sphere, and yet allows for a mutually determining division within this sphere. The notion of space (which refers to the personal pronouns) is such a concept.'[12] A communication-theoretical concept of society hinges on this social space for a lifeworld inhabited in common that emerges in the course of dialogue. Humboldt already understood speech acts to be linkages for interaction; he conceives of reaching understanding as the creative mechanism in socialization – initially as the mechanism of action coordination and social integration, but then also as the medium both of socialization and through which cultural traditions continue to be handed down. Language, world view and form of life are interwoven.

I have referred to these interdependencies because I want to make a point which Wilhelm von Humboldt brought up, pre-empting George Herbert Mead by a hundred years, so to speak. For Humboldt already conceives of reaching understanding as a mechanism which *socializes* and *individuates* in one act. In the structures of diffracted intersubjectivity – which demand of the competent speaker that he or she master the system of personal pronouns[13] – singularization is just as impossible without the inexorable compulsion to universalization as is socialization without concomitant individuation. Language contains 'the possibility of universal understanding within the shell of the most individual expression', it 'connects by virtue of singling out'. On the other hand, the person who communicates with others will at the same time also 'augment his individuality in the course of this effort', in order to step beyond the dividing boundaries of his individuality.[14] And what holds true for individuals is of course doubly true for nations: 'In its capacity for making divisions between different people it (language) unifies the difference of individualities by means of the mutual understanding of foreign speech, without at the same time detracting from them.'[15] Language compels the individuation of peoples and single persons, 'but in such a wonderful manner that precisely by virtue of this division it awakens a feeling of unity; indeed, it appears as a means of at least creating such as an idea.'[16]

The idea to which Humboldt is alluding here lends expression to the rational potential of speech – that is, the telos inherent in the very process of reaching understanding through language. This goal of reaching universal understanding has to make itself felt as a tendency permeating society as a whole, because and in so far as the latter makes use of the mechanism of reaching understanding for its own coordinating purposes.

Although he in no way denies that communicative rationality is potentially contained in rational speech, Taylor objects at this point that my explanation of such a rationality is false, because I explain it in terms of a formalist and cognitivist ethics. Here, Taylor is too quick to introduce philosophical ethics into the debate. In my opinion, communicative rationality precisely does not amount to the sum total of its moral-practical components. Everyday communicative practice covers a wider range of validity; claims to normative correctness constitute merely one of numerous validity aspects. It is only when conflicts of action are to be re-solved with the consensus of the participants in terms of this *one* aspect that moral issues arise. Philosophy can take such questions as its point of departure in order to explain the moral point of view from which they can be answered rationally, i.e. by providing good reason. Such an ethics cannot, however, exhaust the rational content (*Gehalt*) of everyday communicative practice, but can grasp it only in terms of one aspect, and only within the framework of a normative theory. Taylor could agree to these reservations and insist nevertheless that his objections can be raised not only against a procedural ethics but against procedural rationality as a whole. The case Taylor makes against a procedural ethics is also directed against communicative rationality *as a whole* if this is understood solely as a procedural unity. Does not *every* concept of rationality have to remain enmeshed with the substantive contents of a particular form of life, with a particular vision of the good life?

This question leads us back to the paradigm shift, signs of which are already apparent in Humboldt's philosophy of language, at least if it is read strictly from the vantage point of a theory of intersubjectivity. According to such a reading, the moments of the universal, the particular and the individual are no longer tied into the ongoing process of self-relation of a higher-level subjectivity. Rather, they are released from the relation to a totality and are conceived of as equiprimordial reference points of a process of differentiation that moves outward radially in three directions. As a mechanism of socialization, the first act of reaching understanding itself sets a dialectic of universalization, particularization and individualization into motion, a dialectic which leaves *only* the differentiated *particular* in the position of an individual totality. General structures of the lifeworld, collective forms of life, and individual life histories arise within the structures of the diffracted intersubjectivity of possible understanding and are at the same time differentiated. The ego is formed equiprimordially as a subject in general, as a typical member of a social collective, and as a unique individual. The universal, particular and individual constitute themselves radially, as it were – and no longer as moments bound within a totality. Humboldt made this clear with reference to the example of the cultural development of civilized peoples.[17]

Here the individual language, the development of ideas, and the national character are so interlinked that inner correspondences obtain between the linguistic images of the world and the socio-cultural forms of life of the linguistic community. However, the same national languages not only constitute the delineating borders of a form of life, they serve simultaneously as a medium that traverses these borders, a medium where the different totalities – each of which is the spirit of a people (*Volksgeist*) – meet the others and, each from its respective standpoint, come to an agreement on the world of all that is knowable 'lying between them'.[18] In other words, languages, as the form-giving principles guiding the shape taken by the individual totality of each respectively particular view of the world and way of life, only have an effect to the extent that, by virtue of their universalistic core, they enable translations to be made from each language into every other language and determine the point of convergence towards which all cultural developments are aimed. In this respect Humboldt speaks of the 'constant and uniform effort' 'intellectual power'. 'Its purpose is comprehension. Thus, nobody may speak to another person in a manner different from that in which the latter, under identical conditions, would have spoken to him.'[19]

By putting it this way, Humboldt had already given a normative twist to what – in formal-pragmatic terms – can be read as the rational potential of speech in the necessarily idealizing suppositions of communicative action. Of course, the grammatically regulated world views and forms of life appear only in the plural; yet they constitute totalities which are not in turn overshadowed by a supertotality, but rather correspond to one another in terms of their formal and most general structures. Because all lifeworlds have to reproduce themselves through the agency of action oriented towards reaching understanding, so the general character of communicative rationality stands out within the multiplicity of concrete forms of life.

If moral philosophy appeals to this universalistic potential of speech – and Humboldt did indeed derive something like a cosmopolitan ethics of reaching understanding from this basis[20] – then it can in fact develop a formal or procedural ethics only from it. In so doing, moral philosophy has to accept that with the concept of morality only one of various general aspects of the rationality of linguistically structured forms of life can be reconstructed – and this only from the reflexive viewpoint of a participant in the argument who is hypothetically considering whether to advance normative validity claims. It must also be conceded with regard to such an ethics that it can explain only the formal conditions of valid moral judgements, but not the empirical conditions under which moral views can be put into practice. Any universalistic morality is dependent on supplementation by structurally analogous forms of life. The circumstances under which it can count on such supplementation is less a question of moral philosophy than of social theory.[21] One cannot, however, develop an ethics of language on a Humboldtian plane – as Taylor does – and at that same time endeavour to reconnect the universal core of morality to the ethical life inherent in concrete forms of life.[22]

Of course, the reproduction of the lifeworld feeds off the contributions to communicative action, while the latter at the same time feeds off the resources of the lifeworld. But the structures of the diffracted intersubjectivity of possible understanding prohibit this cycle from spreading out into a totality. To the degree that the reproduction of the lifeworld is no longer merely channelled through the medium of action oriented towards reaching understanding, but – with the lifeworld's increasing rationalization – is a burden placed on the interpretative achievements of the actors themselves, so the universal structures of the lifeworld contrast all the more with the particular configurations of forms of life that simple overlap one another. In the face of such totalities thus reduced to a merely empirical status, the approach taken by a theory of intersubjectivity restores to favour what Hegel had discredited, namely the distinction between form and content.[23]

However, Taylor is right in challenging another of my positions on the basis of Humboldt's insights. In *The Theory of Communicative Action* I treated somewhat unfairly the world-disclosing (*welterschliessende*) function of language. In contrast to theories of meaning oriented towards conceptions of denotation or representation, Taylor himself has developed an expressivist theory of language that goes back to the work of Herder, Hamann and Humboldt.[24] He frees the linguistic constitution of a world view from its foreshortening by a semantic ontology interested solely in a grammatically regulated pre-understanding of reality. Using Humboldt's work, Taylor demonstrates how every language opens up a grammatically prestructured space, how it permits what is in-the-world to appear there in a certain manner and, at the same time, enables interpersonal relations to be regulated legitimately as well as making possible the spontaneous self-presentation of creative-expressive subjects. 'World disclosure' means for Taylor, as for Humboldt, that language is the constitutive organ not only of thought, but also of both social practice and experience, of the formation of ego and group identities. And yet Taylor here again tends to totalize this world-disclosing function of language. In so doing, he falls victim to an epistemological perspectivism which in fact Humboldt had avoided.

Humboldt conceives of the different linguistic views of the world as *converging* rays that illuminate that same world as 'the sum of the knowable'. This convergence arises by virtue of inner-worldly processes of learning in which the world-disclosing force of an interpreting language has first to *prove itself* within the world. Of course, in line with changes in a language's system of rules, the conditions under which sentences formulated in a language are valid also undergo change. But whether such conditions of validity are actually fulfilled to such an extent that the sentences can function within their language games depends not only on the world-disclosing force of language, but also on the successes within the world of the practice that it makes possible. Because all other linguistic functions (in other words, the representation of states of affairs, the establishment of interpersonal relations, and the expressive self-presentation of speakers) are intimately connected with criticizable validity claims, everyday communicative practice – including the cultures of experts that arise from it – can develop an obstinate meaning of its own that transcends all local boundaries. Thus, the modes of action constituted by a linguistic view of the world operate in the light of a communicative rationality that imposes an orientation toward validity claims on the participants and in this way triggers off learning processes that may have a retroactive effect on the previous understanding of the world. Taylor is wrong to allow this problem-solving capacity of language to disappear behind its capacity for world disclosure.[25]

Martin Seel endeavours to elaborate a 'plural, non-integral and yet non-separatist' concept of reason – one that is postmetaphysical. In this respect, I am fully in accord with his intentions. Seel also perceives quite accurately the situation in which I had to defend the procedural unity of communicative reason, whose moments of validity have split off from one another, on *three counts*: against two variants of a dialectics of reconciliation, which still conceives of reason as the whole, and against a scepticism of reason, which enters into such totalizing concepts only in order to denounce them from the perspective of 'the Other of reason'. These argumentational strategies, all three of which are directed against the procedural concept of communicative reason, lead up blind alleys: the neo-Aristotelian and neo-Hegelian just as much as the neo-Nietzschean variants. On the one hand, Taylor, in a manner similar to Bubner, reduces practical reason to a faculty of judgement which has always unquestioningly conformed to the horizon of a particular, already accepted form of life and therefore remains positioned *below* the level at which a distinction can be made between theoretical, moral, aesthetic and technical questions (and at which they can be treated hypothetically).[26] On the other hand, Thomas McCarthy also admonishes me for the fact that the concept of communicative reason has to do justice not only to the Kantian differentiations, but also to the Hegelian motif of reconciliation, albeit without revealing how we would then be able to rescue universalism without tacitly adopting Hegel's concept of the concrete universal.[27] And lastly Martin Jay, in his study of the concept of totality in Western Marxism, also discovers traces in my work of what he terms a 'Marxist holism'; I have met this objection, and similar ones raised by Bernhard Waldenfels, at a metacritical level, namely with arguments intended to show why the neo-structuralist attempts to break out of the philosophical discourse of modernity are doomed to failure.[28]

Irrespective of this common battle front, Seel is convinced that my attempt to generate a *postmetaphysical* and yet *non-defeatist* concept of reason by means of an analysis of speech acts must fail. He initially believes it is inconsistent to assert philosophically that communicative reason preserves an at least procedural unity within the plurality of its validity claims and at the same time to maintain sociologically that the discourses on truth, justice and taste – which have differentiated out into expert cultures – cause the moments of reason to diverge to the point of mutual indifference. Only one of the two, he thinks, can be true – either the intergration in the lifeworld of the differentiated aspects of validity, or their separation into specialist areas. I fail to see why this *first objection* should hold water. One must clearly distinguish between the following analytic levels.

1 *Communicative action*. Speech acts can link the action plans of one actor with those of other actors via rationally motivating achievements in reaching understanding – rather than by exerting influence, i.e. empirical intervention. I infer the rationality of such convincing motivations from the (credible) guarantee that a speaker gives that, if necessary, s/he is in a position to honour with good justifications the claim s/he raises for the validity of that speech act. For, in language usage oriented toward reaching understanding, the speaker raises exactly three validity claims with one (grammatically correct, i.e. understandable) utterance, one of which can respectively be emphasized depending on the mode of communication adopted. The yes/no positions of the hearer *vis-à-vis* the offer contained in a speech act are rationally motivated if they rely on a resource for justifications that is internally linked to the meaning and validity conditions of the sentence uttered. Each 'yes' requires that the possible negation of this disputable validity claim can implicitly be denied. Such rationality is *located in* the idealizations built into communicative action. The *concept* of rationality includes the pragmatic roles of criticizable validity claims which are at the same time geared towards intersubjective recognition. The theory of argumentation provides a promising *methodological means* for explicating this concept. The internal interconnection of the meaning, validity and justification of validity claims demonstrates, namely, that naive everyday practice itself refers to the possibility of argumentation. This does not mean, however, that communicative action is located in argumentation. The theory of argumentation merely contributes to clarifying what the conditions for a consensus motivated by justifications are that already play a role in communicative action.

2 *Rationalization of the lifeworld*. The concept of communicative rationality does not just apply to the processes of intentional consensus formation, but also to the structures of a state of pre-understanding already reached within an intersubjectively shared lifeworld. The latter demarcates in the shape of a context-forming horizon the respective speech situation; at the same time, as an unproblematic and prereflexive background it plays a constitutive role in the achievements directed toward reaching understanding. Lifeworld and communicative action thus relate to one another in a complementary fashion. As a consequence, communicative rationality is embodied just as much by the structures of the undiffracted intersubjectivity of a *pre*-understanding guaranteed in the lifeworld as it is by the structures of the diffracted intersubjectivity of possible understanding to be achieved by each respective actor him/herself.

Given that the concrete forms of life reproduce themselves via the agency of validity-oriented action, those substantive a prioris of the linguistically-constituted views of the world inherent in a particular form of life are subjected to an incessant test; they have to prove themselves in inner-worldly practice and they change in the wake of inner-worldly processes of learning. A directional dynamics is built into the communicatively structured lifeworld in the form of the polarity between a state of pre-established pre-understanding and a consensus to be achieved: in the course of time, the reproductive achievements switch from one pole to the other. The structural possibility of such a rationalization of the lifeworld is initially to be gained using a formal-pragmatic analysis. Yet a global description of this process of whatever sort, e.g. as the 'linguistification of the sacred', first becomes possible if we move with a methodologically controlled shift in perspective from a formal-pragmatic to a sociological investigation. The structural components of the lifeworld can be recognized as culture, society and personality only once such a shift in perspective has been accomplished; only then can we also decipher within the long-term morphological changes in these components those historical trends, the vanishing points of which reveal the hypothetical goal states of a *rationalized lifeworld*. In the case of culture, these would be a state of the constant revision of fluidized traditions, i.e. traditions which have become reflexive; in the case of society, a state in which legitimate orders depend on discursive procedures for positing and justifying norms; and in the case of personality, a state of the risk-laden self-steering of a highly abstract ego-identity.[29]

3   *Expert cultures and lifeworld.* Max Weber drew attention to those 'cultural value spheres' which gain a relative autonomy in modern societies, namely science and technology, law and morality, art and criticism. He thus focused our attention on phenomena by means of which we could study the *tendencies toward rationalization in the domain of culture.* Seen from an internal perspective, expert cultures form around such complexes of issues as have been gradually disengaged from the unfiltered stream of tradition in terms of respectively one specific aspect of validity (such as questions of truth, justice or taste). The professional processing of these complexes stresses in an ever more one-sided fashion the intrinsic logic and the mutual indifference of purely theoretical, purely moral and purely aesthetic questions. One of the signs of European modernity is the fact that these mutually distinct elements of a reason which is still held together only by the procedure of argumentation can no longer be compensated for by an *integration of contents* a posteriori. To date, all attempts at rehabilitating world views have failed. Nevertheless the question still arises as to the synthesis of these intrinsically separated elements of reason not only from the point of view of their pre-established procedural unity, but also with regard to their interdependent collaboration. Yet in this context one must be careful not to bundle together the philosophical inquiry into the conditions under which such interdependencies are possible and the empirical question as to the facutal existence thereof. One must above all distinguish between the question how aspects of rationality that were initially eliminated from other value spheres can now be taken into account *within*

one and the same value sphere under the sign of the respectively dominant validity claim, on the one hand, and the completely different question how expert knowledge can be transformed back into the diffuse processes of reaching self-understanding in everyday life, on the other. I have briefly addressed the problems of mediation *within* the spheres of science, morality and art elsewhere.[30] From the same internal perspective the problems of the mediation *between* expert cultures and lifeworld arise in the form of questions to the relation of theory and practice, morality and ethical life, art and life.

I have shown in a different context[31] that in this respect philosophy and art criticism fulfil very similar tasks – namely to bring radically one-sided and professionally processed stocks of knowledge into the culturally barren flow of tradition in the hermeneutics of everyday life. In everyday hermeneutics, the aspects of rationality that diverge from one another within the expert cultures are always originally treated – albeit at different levels of differentiation and in changing combinations – as a syndrome. The logic of such an expansion of everyday hermeneutics has certainly by no means been sufficiently elucidated, but Seel would seem to connect this immanent theoretical question prematurely with the empirical question, namely via which channels and with what differing effects the interchange between expert cultures and forms of life factually occurs in modern societies. This question can itself not be answered independently of a sociological investigation of the exchange between media-steered subsystems and the quite differently structured domains of the lifeworld.

4 *'Reconciled' vs. rationalized forms of life.* However, Seel draws our attention to an important problem in this context. If one separates the *form* of the increasingly general differentiated structures of the lifeworld from the *contents* of increasingly particularized totalities of forms of life (which are nevertheless intermeshed in the form of 'family resemblance'), then the concept of the rationalized lifeworld can no longer embrace what was once meant with the concept of the good life. The conflicts within modern lifeworlds have, after all, not diminished with the advancing rationalization of the lifeworld. Rather, the forms in which social pathologies manifested have multiplied – loss of meaning, anomic conditions, psychopathologies are the most noticeable, but by no means the only symptoms[32] – I still explain these pathologies by referring to the mechanism driving capitalism forward, namely economic growth, but I *assess* them in terms of the systemically induced predominance of economic and bureaucratic, indeed of all cognitive-instrumental forms of rationality within a one-sided or 'alienated' everyday communicative practice. I attribute the *one-sided* rationalization, and the *preponderance* of one complex of rationality, to the uneven exploitation of the resources for rationality made available culturally. The yardstick thus used intuitively to measure the deformation of forms of life consists of the idea of the free interplay of the cognitive-instrumental with both the moral-practical and the aesthetic-expressive, within an everyday practice which must be open to an *uninhibited* and *balanced* interpenetration of cognitive interpretations, moral expectations, expressions

and valuations. Now Seel justifiably asks whether the concept of communicative rationality can itself yield this clinical intuition of a 'counterbalancing interplay' or whether in fact the latter does not precede the former. If the second were the case, he infers, then reason should precisely not be explained in the sense of a *communicative* rationality.[33]

I am of the opinion that social pathologies can be understood as forms of manifestation of systematically distorted communication, in which case it would, however, have to be possible to find justifications for the normal forms of undistorted communication in the framework of a theory of communication. I have at least sketched such in my 'Considerations on a Pathology of Communication'.[34] Forms of social repression can take root unobtrusively in the pores of processes of reaching understanding in such a manner that the forms of diffracted intersubjectivity are damaged and at the same time rigidify. If the external organization of speech relays no longer concealable pressure on to the inner organization of speech, then the latter loses its flexibility and permeability because the internal links between meaning and validity, meaning and intention, and meaning and accomplished action are *interrupted*[35] and block the intermodal transfer of validity, i.e. the coercion-free transformation of the same propositional contents from one mode into another.[36] Precisely that capacity for flexibility is blocked which is of such central importance to Seel, namely, the 'capacity to change rational perspectives' which he terms 'the capacity for interrelational judgment'. This faculty of judgement (which Seel rightly distinguishes from Aristotelian *phronesis* as an ability to apply rules) is indeed bound up with the performative stance of the communicative *actor* and to this extent is anchored in a practice which *pre-dates argumentation*. In the final instance, we must perhaps leave the answer to the clinical question of whether a given form of life allows more or less space for trends towards an undamaged, correctly spent life to this 'faculty of judgement', even if we cannot conceptualize such in terms of a theory of argumentation.

We can deal swiftly with the *second bone of contention* in light of this consideration. Given that each type of argumentation is specialized in only one validity claim, such premises and presuppositions remain ignored within its bounds as would require clarification in terms of other validity claims, i.e. within different forms of argumentation. The conclusions I infer form this are, however, not the same as those reached by Seel. The different forms of argumentation form a system precisely to the extent that they *refer internally to one another* owing to their need for supplementation. Now, the switch from one form of argumentation to another is sometimes motivated internally and sometimes by bottlenecks in the course of argumentation. At times, such a transition needs to be prompted from without, namely by problems which confront us. The *manner* in which the transition is effected is regulated by the logic of argumentation; *whether* and *when* we are supposed to accomplish it depends on the faculty of judgement inherent in communicative action itself. There are no meta-discourses for this. There are in fact no meta-discourses whatsoever; every discourse is, so to speak, equally close to God. This should be no cause for astonishment. In the different types of argumentation, communicative action encounters only reflected forms of itself. For this reason, speech act theory engages at a level lower, so to speak, than does the theory of argumentation, although the latter in turn provides a methodologically sounder approach to explicating the meaning of validity claims.

A *third objection*, which is aimed at the false intellectualization of non-theoretical matters, arises from the fact that Seel first falsely connects argumentation and life practice, then skips over the analysis of speech acts, and resorts immediately to the semantic analysis of forms of utterances. I shall come back to this. If one, by contrast, bears in mind that the practice of reaching understanding is stratified in terms of actions and discourses, then it inevitably appears natural first to identify the validity claims at the level of communicative action in terms of speech acts – in the context of functions of reaching linguistic understanding – and subsequently to explain them in terms of argumentation at the level of discursive forms of justification. I have already recalled that three inner-worldly linguistic functions contrast with the constitutive linguistic function of world disclosure: the presentation of factual matters, the creation of interpersonal relations and the expression of subjective experiences or expressive self-presentation. How these four functions are fulfilled can be measured in terms of the following validity claims: aesthetic harmony (or evaluative cogency),[37] propositional truth, normative rightness and subjective sincerity. The meaning of these validity claims can be gleaned from the manner in which they can be justified when they are problematic. The justification of aesthetic evaluations is, as Seel pertinently remarks, slanted towards emphasizing the validity of the work evaluated in the grammatical role of its being a reason for assuming world-shaping (*weltbildend*) modes of perception. Value standards and the corresponding evaluative utterances can be validated only indirectly, namely by means of authentically world-disclosing productions. Things are different in the case of factual, normative or experiential utterances. Here, their justification aims at proving the existence of factual matters, the acceptability of modes of action or norms, and the transparency of subjective experiences.

The justification of problematic validity claims can, in *all* these cases, occur only given pragmatic presuppositions of argumentation, and this means with an attitude in which we suspend the validity naively imputed to value standards, facts, norms and experiences, and instead deal *hypothetically* with the validity claims which have been *left open*. This distantiation from the lifeworldly pressure to experience and to take decisions characterizes the transition (from communicative action) to all forms of argumentation, and by no means signifies entry only into a theoretical discourse. If this transition provides the foundations for 'a genuinely theoretical relationship' to virtualized innerworldy phenomena, then we address not only matters of fact, which may or may not be the case, 'theoretically', but also treat norms, which can be valid or invalid, or experiences, which the speaker may or precisely may not have meant in such and such a way, in the same manner. We can most certainly not make random use of such a change of attitude, which breaks with the 'natural attitude towards the world'. I can only doubt Cartesian doubt pragmatically if I rely on the experience that real problems *arise*, and are not simply created arbitrarily. Yet we *have to face* such problems as we encounter them – this is not a question of the faculty of judgement. The transition to lines of argumentation is, on occasion, not the 'most rational' answer to a problematic situation. However, this will be revealed only with the passage of time, and is thus again not a matter of a personal faculty of judgement. It is only in the course of hypothetical retrospection that, for example, we gradually come to suspect that following the defeat of the Nazis spontaneous retribution in the form of a purifying revolt would have been a better alternative than decades of smouldering soul-searching.

Herbert Schnädelbach problematizes the concept of communicative rationality from a completely different viewpoint. He draws our attention to the fact that this concept contributes nothing to clarifying the normative foundations of a critical theory of society if it can also be used in a descriptive manner:

> It may indeed be the case that communicative action always involves unconditional claims being made, but this does not qualify it to provide foundations for Critical Theory. To do so, it would itself have to be open to critical assessment. In other words, the theorist would have unconditionally to provide the unconditional standards for critique from the outset and s/he will never be able to derive these from the subject-matter via hypothetical rule reconstruction.[38]

Schnädelbach bases this objection on doubts as to the internal interconnection between description and evaluation of justifications, an interconnection I used in attempting to make the unavoidability of rational interpretations plausible.[39] Let me start with a brief remark on the term 'normative'.

We attribute normative contents to dispositional concepts of rationality which we explicate by means of the ability to adhere to the rules of an intuitively guided praxis. The meaning of normativity changes with the status of these rules. Grammatical or mathematical rules (the renowned examples of Wittgenstein's 'game rules') have a different status and a different form of normative validity than do morally-binding norms of action, cultural value standards or necessary, transcendental conditions. Normativity in a practice that is regulated accordingly (and a practice that is 'rational' in the sense of rule-competence refers in this sequence to the well-formedness or analytical truth of linguistic expressions or mathematical propositions, to the moral rightness of actions, to the preferability of ends, and to the absence of alternatives to non-substitutable modes of action. Communicative rationality has 'normative' content in the sense that those pragmatic rules are normative which generally play a constitutive role in the practice of subjects capable of language and action trying to reach understanding about something in the world. They are similar to transcendental conditions to the extent that we cannot avoid making certain universal presuppositions when using language in order to reach understanding. On the other hand, they are not transcendental in the strict sense for (a) we can also act in a non-communicative manner and (b) the ineluctability of idealizing supppositions does not imply that these will in fact be fulfilled. Irrespective of how we define more closely the normativity of this peculiar form of pragmatic idealization, the element of unconditionality inherent in the neutralization of spatio-temporal contexts by validity claims would already suggest that we have to do here with normativity in a relatively strong sense.

Schnädelbach, however, doubts whether this normativity innate to the rational potential of speech also extends to the theory describing it; he enquires whether it cannot be attributed completely to the object side. Let us assume that our concept of communicative rationality can be used in a purely descriptive manner. In such a case, without making a value judgement or being prejudiced, we would nevertheless still impute to communicative actors that they cannot avoid making certain pragmatic presuppositions, harbouring idealizations and orienting themselves towards validity claims – and above all, that they are unable not to learn. We would maintain that there is an internal linkage between linguistic communication and processes of learning, whereby the fact that better insights cannot be intentionally forgotten but only repressed is part of the logic of such processes. And an analysis that is descriptive in terms of attitude and intention would, if it were to deploy the concept of communicative rationality at all, arrive at statements such as the assertion that persons, to the extent that they only act communicatively, are subject to normatively substantive rationality constraints and in this sense submit to an objective order of preferences. In such a case, however, the further-reaching methodological question – as to the form in which the concept of rationality is used – would be of no consequence for the substantial contents of the theory. We clearly do not need to pursue this consideration any further, because I am of the opinion that we cannot in the first place assume that the precondition of impartiality is given, an assumption on which it rests.

I maintain (a) that the social scientist must use language oriented toward reaching understanding – as the original mode of linguistic usage – if s/he is to have hermeneutic access to his/her object. I also maintain (b) that we cannot understand an utterance without knowing the reasons that can be given for its validity. And I maintain finally (c) that we cannot understand such reasons without at least implicitly judging the soundness thereof; communicative acts (by both laypersons and scholars in a similar manner) demand interpretations that are rational in their approach. I shall return to the first two assertions later. Schnädelbach is correctly interested first and foremost in (c): can we not, assuming that (a) and (b) are true, understand reasons and at the same time desist from evaluating them?

An example that supports my thesis would be that of a proof, say, of the binomial theorem. We understand a mathematical proof only to the extent that we can reconstruct it ourselves; in which case we will accept it to be true or know why it is false. Let me give three other examples in terms of diminishing plausibility: justifications for metamathematical positions in the debate between intuitionists and formalists; reasons for the superiority of Newtonian over Aristotelian physics; and explanations for what appears from the perspective of the speaker to be unmotivated laughter in the audience. Needless to say, the interpreter can in each case desist from taking a position, i.e. from evaluating the reasons. Yet such a reaction amounts to confessing that I have not *yet* correctly understood the problematic assertion or utterance. Even in the last case, which is at first sight least plausible, the interpreter does not know how s/he should understand the audience's reaction until s/he can decide on the basis of available evidence whether some of the listeners have discovered an unintentional joke in his/her utterances or whether they have misunderstood her/him, or indeed have been mocking her/him – and if they did indeed laugh at an unintended joke, whether this really was a joke or why it seemed one only to them. S/he must understand the reasons which could be given for considering this laughter true laughter, i.e. considering it a 'valid' utterance in this sense. Wittgenstein maintains that we can understand an utterance only to the extent that we share the pre-understanding of the language game in question and concur with one another with respect to a mutual form of life. Gadamer is of the opinion that we understand an utterance only to the extent that we reach an understanding on the thing in question. Both are right – one with respect to the lifeworldly background, the other with regard to the contents of what is said. Those linguistic theories which claim that the boundary between lexical and empirical knowledge is permeable, and that the transition from linguistic knowledge to knowledge of the world is fluid, address the same question.

I by no means wish to imply with the above that such a form of hermeneutic understanding (*Sinnverstehen*) as includes evaluating the potential reasons for the validity of the understood utterance is to be equated with a yes/no position – in the manner in which someone participating in topical contexts of action takes a yes or no position on a validity claim that has been raised factually and, in so doing, takes on certain obligations with regard to the further course of interaction. The role of interpreter and of actor are not identical.[40] Understanding does not of course mean agreement.

Schnädelbach closes his critical remarks by observing that Karl-Otto Apel understandably adheres to the transcendental-pragmatic claim to providing final foundations, because critical unconditionality is not possible without a foundationalist approach. Wolfgang Kuhlmann puts forward the same thesis, albeit for reasons different from those just described and rebutted.[41] Were Kuhlmann or Schnädelbach to be right, were some transcendental, ultimate foundation to be the only alternative to the failed historico-philosophical justification of the critical potential of a theory of society, then it would no longer be possible to construct such a theory in the form of an unambiguous postmetaphysical project.[42] Kuhlmann at first provides a quite accurate description of the fallibilist self-understanding of an explication of the concept of communicative rationality carried out with philosophical means – a philosophical project which accommodates itself, in line with the division of labour, to cooperating with other reconstructive disciplines. Such an undertaking is postmetaphysical in that it forgoes any self-certain conceptions of an hierarchy of sciences with a fundamentalist philosophy at its head, and does not claim to possess a privileged knowledge, truth or certainty in its own theory formation *vis-à-vis* theory formation in the individual disciplines. From this standpoint, philosophical theories are, in principle, accorded the same status as theories in the empirical sciences; they are justified in terms of their own criteria and evaluated at a metatheoretical level from the point of view of coherence, in terms of how well they fit together with other theories.[43]

Kuhlmann, however, attempts to show in his trenchant article that if linked to such a fallibilist self-understanding, the theory of communicative action becomes caught up in a dilemma. The principle of fallibilism, he claims, cannot be applied to itself, i.e. cannot in turn be justified in terms of fallible statements. It is by no means my intention to intervene in the long-running argument between Albert and Apel, for I by no means understand 'fallibilism' to be one or the other version of a demanding Popperian theory, but merely a simple grammatical matter. We understand the expression 'justify' when we know what we have to do in order to redeem a universal, i.e. trans-spatio-temporal and in this sense unconditional, validity claim by deploying reasons. This can be the case just as much with regard to the truth validity of an assertoric statement as it can with respect to the validity a normative statement has as being right. We understand the term 'justify' when we know the rules for an argumentational game within which validity claims can be redeemed discursively. Now, we can make these rules the object of a theory of argumentation or truth – or, if we have to do with special discourses, we can make it the object of a moral theory or a philosophy of science. Yet, justifying these theories – as is the case with justifying a theory *per se* – must itself fit into the framework of an argumentational game to the same extent as must the justification of harmless, e.g. practical everyday utterances. Certainly, the claims made of justifications vary according to the argumentational form and context. Yet, which reason counts as a good or indeed as the better reason for what object in what context has to be assessed in terms of standards which under certain conditions become problematical and in turn require justification. Justifications must always be provided in one and the same place – there are no meta-discourses in the sense that a higher discourse is able to prescribe rules for a subordinate discourse. Argumentational games do not form a hierarchy. Discourses regulate themselves. Discourses are in principle open. And it is impossible to predict the outcome of discourses, that is, except from the perspective of an observer who is not a party to the discourse, yet who has to enter into another discourse in order to be able to justify his/her prognosis.

In short, the fact that we cannot once and for all fit reasons, or types of reasons, into an hierarchy – which would be headed by 'final' reasons – is part of the grammatical role played by the term 'justify'. In view of their superiority in the final instance, such reasons would have no clear meaning if we adhere to the grammar of the word 'justify'. We cannot simply freeze the context in which we here and now consider a certain type of reason to be the best and we cannot exclude a priori that other types of reasons would have a greater validity in other contexts. This does not strip the validity claim redeemed with the help of these reasons of one iota of its unconditionality. The fallibilist meaning of an argumentational game takes into account only that universal validity claims have to be raised factually – namely, in our respective context, which does not remain stationary, but rather will change. We cannot predict whether the unavoidable changes in context will have an effect on what is accepted here and now as sufficient justification. We do not, however, need to deny this abstract possibility in order to preserve the performative sense inherent in accepting justifications: with every assertion 'Mp' we ineluctably express that we are convinced of the definitive truth of 'p' as a statement the validity of which is accepted. This final validity to which we thus lay claim is part and parcel of the grammatical role played by the term 'true' just as is the awareness that reasons which are sufficiently convincing today *could* tomorrow be devastated by criticism.

As a consequence, Kuhlmann's premisses are untenable – by which I mean the division of theoretical statements into two groups: those with a hypothetical status and others by means of which we justify the fallibilist nature of that status. Statements have a hypothetical status only for such time as we hold their discursive review to be incomplete. We also speak of scientific hypotheses in this sense – they require *further* review before we can accept them as true. Yet we hold accepted scientific theories to be true; from a performative point of view we must hold them to be definitively true – if this were not itself a pleonasm. To hold something to be true means to hold something to be definitively true. And to know something means that that something can be criticized. *Both* belong together. One without the other would cause the grammar of the language game in which the terms 'true' and 'untrue' have their place to collapse. The presumption of fallibilism refers solely to the fact that we cannot exclude the possibility of falsification even given convincingly justified theories which are accepted as valid. Otherwise we have not understood what 'to be justified' means. We differentiate in philosophy and science between hypotheses and valid theories, between hypothetical assumptions and valid theoretical sentences. It is not, however, the principle of fallibilism which discriminates between the two types of expressions, but solely our decision whether we consider – for the time being – a discussion to be finished or not. I therefore understand fallibilism only in the sense of a grammatical explanation which must itself naturally be justified and is therefore in principle itself open to revision. Again, each is part and parcel of the other in such a way that a dilemma of self-application cannot arise. The fact that our reasons are truly good reasons and suffice to satisfy ourselves about the truth by no means alters the fact that what we – finally – hold to be true can in principle turn out to be error.

Perhaps the disagreement between Apel, Kuhlmann and myself focuses not on fallibilism, but on truth theory. I do not understand the discourse theory of truth to mean that the consensus achieved discursively is a criterion of truth (as was the case in some of my earlier statements); rather, it should explain via the discursive redemption of validity claims the meaning of each element of unconditionality which we intuitively link with the concept of truth. Albrecht Wellmer describes this succinctly as follows:

> Part of the idea of truth is that there will not in the future be sound counter-arguments against what we now view to be true, and this includes our manner of talking about the world and formulating problems not being cast into doubt in the future by lines of argument being raised against it. In this sense, we can readily accept that the imputed 'ideal speech situation' and equally the anticipation of an infinite consensus both have an effect in every (factually) discursively achieved consensus.[44]

It is solely these strong idealizations that render the meaning of the unconditionality of the validity claimed for our knowledge compatible with the principle of fallibility of all knowledge.

The theory of communicative action behaves assuagingly towards over-exaggerated transcendental demands for justifications; on the other hand, it takes on the role of an agitator *vis-à-vis* the slender premises of empiricism.[45]

Problems of Theories of Meaning and Action

The contributions to this volume, being predominantly sociological, on occasion reveal a reception of my theory that is restricted to their particular discipline. This is expressed not by the fact that they completely legitimately confine themselves to certain topics, but rather is revealed by a prejudiced understanding of my underlying assumptions. This is particularly true for a theory which places the concept of communicative action in the centre of the stage and with it the action-coordinating role of processes of reaching understanding. I analyse these with the aid of a theory of speech acts expanded into a formal pragmatics (and not reduced back to a theory of intentionality). (a) I wish to explain to my partners in philosophical discussion (including Seel and Wellmer) why I drop the premises of a semantic theory of meaning developed from Frege to Dummett, and to remind my partners in sociological discussion that one does not understand the theory of communicative action unless one is prepared to acknowledge a formal-pragmatic theory of meaning. (b) Problems which have arisen from the line I draw between illocutionary and perlocutionary speech acts prompt me to return once again to questions of a typology of actions. (c) Finally, I shall treat the wide range of objections raised against the rationalistic and harmonistic illusions with which an 'idealistically' charged concept of communicative action supposedly encumbers a sociological theory of action.

Defenders of formal semantics will certainly be provoked by the proposition that reaching understanding in language terminates in the intersubjective recognition of criticizable validity claims and is therefore a phenomenon which is not grasped by a semantic analysis of the meaning of statements, but rather necessitates a pragmatic analysis of *successful* utterances. Rolf Zimmermann has criticized the theory of communicative action from this viewpoint.[46] He believes that I have been led, by overgeneralizing the specific case of action oriented toward reaching understanding, into carrying the *social* aspect of an orientation to validify into the theory of meaning and falsely making it the central aspect of language itself.[47] Zimmermann does not perceive that formal pragmatics generates solutions to problems which have themselves arisen in the theoretical tradition that dates back to Frege. If my proposals are conceived of as an internally-motivated extension of formal semantics, then certain barriers to their being understood can be overcome.[48] I shall subsequently discuss a difficulty in the analysis of commands which has in the meantime prompted me to amend my theory.

To start with, a few key words concerning the most important stages on the path from formal semantics to formal pragmatics.[49] Frege's theory, which emerges from a double critique of psychologism and reference semantics, is our point of departure. Meanings are to be analysed as something objective and publicly accessible by addressing the formal characteristics of their linguistic expression. It is no longer the designation of an object by a name that is the model for linguistic meaning, but rather the relation between sentences and states of affairs. In this context, the sentence forms the most elementary unit constituting meaning. Now, the decisive step is to link meaning and truth validity. Taking a simple assertoric sentence, Frege develops the thesis underlying truth semantics: one understands the meaning of a sentence if one knows the conditions under which the sentence is true. In this connection, Frege distinguishes the assertoric force which makes a sentence an assertion from the propositional content of what is expressed. *What* is asserted can be completely explicated with reference to the conditions of truth; all the assertoric force adds to this is *that* these conditions are considered to be fulfilled. The statement 'p' expresses both at once.

For this reason, the analysis of linguistic meanings can confine itself to analysing sentences and can abstract from the pragmatic rules concerning the use of the sentence. In addition to this semantic abstraction, Frege also makes a more inconspicuous cognitivist abstraction, deriving all meanings from propositional contents and indirectly from the meaning of assertoric sentences or propositions. A third abstraction relies on the objective concept of truth, which Davidson was later to explain by means of Tarski's theory of truth, stripping it of the Platonistic connotations Frege had given it. Truth conditions construed purely semantically explain what makes a sentence true, and do not, for example, extend epistemically to a knowledge of truth conditions that can be imputed to a speaker or hearer. The sphere of application of formal semantics is, owing to these abstractions, initially quite restricted.[50] Attempts to relax such abstractions later advance the development of the theory of meaning further. Let me remind you (in reverse order) of Dummett's verificationist theory, which renounces the limitation to an objective concept of truth, of the modal theories from Stenius to Searle, of Frege's attempt to expand the analysis of non-assertoric forces, and of Austin's speech act theory, which drops the semantic abstraction once and for all. And, finally, I understand formal pragmatics as a theory that succeeds in overcoming even the barriers of the empiricist ontology within which all the aforementioned three extensions of formal semantics move.

Dummett links truth conditions to the knowledge which the speaker and hearer have of them. Truth conditions would continue to be of no consequence for an understanding of the meaning of sentences if they were not known to be such. Now, this turn away from the objective conditions which render a sentence true in favour of focusing on the epistemic conditions under which the speaker and hearer are able to identify and recognize truth conditions is intended not only to explain the understanding of sentences. It is intended at the same time to extend the sphere of application of formal semantics to include types of sentences which had hitherto eluded analysis. If, namely, the reasons which the speaker can cite for the possible truth of a sentence are constitutive for its meaning, and if in this manner the meaning is linked via potential justifications to the truth validity of a sentence, then counterfactual utterances, modalized utterances, utterances with a temporal index etc. are all open to an investigation based on truth semantics. Dummett does not thereby start to doubt cognitivist or even semantic abstraction. For the verificationist procedure which he puts forward in order to determine truth conditions can be carried out monologically and is tailored solely to the truth conditions of assertoric sentences. Verification cannot at this point already be equated with the intersubjective generation of a discursive redemption of *different* validity claims.

The post-Wittgensteinian modal theories which nevertheless take up Frege's work, such as those devised by Stenius, Kenny, Tugendhat and others, can be understood as attempts to relax the cognitivist abstraction: the intention here is to open up the 'forces' – now understood as illocutionary – to a purely semantic analysis. This approach rests on the simple ontological model of Austin's two 'directions of fit'; the assertoric force represents the agreement between sentences and states of affairs, and the imperativist force represents the adjustment of the latter to fit the former. This model has the advantage of introducing both fundamental modes with reference to 'conditions of satisfaction' which, although differentiated in terms of conditions of truth and success, nevertheless continue to be based on the ontological presuppositions of language as a mirror of the world, and thus remain restricted to the fundamental relation between sentences and states of affairs. Illocutionary forces need not be conceived of as modes of sentence usage, i.e. pragmatically, and the semantic abstraction involved can therefore be ignored. This also explains the limited explanatory potential of this approach. For the whole breadth of illocutionary forces can by no means be derived from the assertoric-imperativist dual mode. Even the most elaborate taxonomy[51] cannot succeed in embracing even the most important modes or classes of speech act: normative obligations, orders and declarations all evade – as do expressive utterances – any attempt at classification which functions using exactly two relations between language and the objective world, and in so doing remains bound to the logocentrism of Frege's semantics.[52]

It is, after all, Austin who, following the later Wittgenstein, takes the decisive step towards an analysis of speech acts and overcomes the semantic abstraction. He resolutely replaces truth semantics with a use theory of meaning and substitutes an analysis of the use of sentences in utterances for the analysis of sentences. This affords him the freedom to uncouple the illocutionary forces from the prototypical case of an assertoric sentence. Austin starts to part company with an ontology which is tailored exclusively to the objective world as a totality of existing states of affairs and which results in special emphasis being placed on assertoric sentences and propositional truth. His concept of an illocutionary act opens up the complete spectrum of speech to linguistic analysis. Wittgenstein's thesis that meaning is to be sought not in the relation of sentences to something in the world but rather in the use of these sentences as regulated by convention turned the attention of philosophers of language to the wealth of such language games which regulate the use of sentences in the context of particular forms of life 'grammatically'. Yet, this liberating turn away from the world of existing states of affairs back to the contexts of the lifeworld not only pushed all the abstractions of semantics à la Frege and Davidson to one side but also renounced, in addition to the reference to the objective world, the *internal* relation between meaning and validity – or rather assimilated a form of validity that had been equated with truth validity to the social validity of cultural practices. Such an adjustment may suffice for an inquiry undertaken solely out of a therapeutic interest. Yet, anyone who maintained an interest in explanation and wished to elaborate a theory of the usage of meaning in the form of a theory of speech acts without at the same time reducing linguistic analysis to the task of a broader ethnolinguistic description of family resemblances in the widest sense was faced with the objection that there are an innumerable number of context-dependent ways of using each sentence. Austin had to search for a systematically motivated classification of speech acts – in other words, for *universal* rules for the typical use of sentences in utterances – precisely because he did not wish to sacrifice the theoretical orientation on the altar of contextualism.

Austin's own analyses of usage types, carried out inductively, admittedly did not lead to theoretical generalizations. By contrast, Roman Jakobson's systematics of language functions, which took up Karl Bühler's work, though motivated by an interest in theory, nevertheless remained entrenched in the framework of an empirical pragmatics which could not come up to the insights provided by formal semantics or linguistic phenomenology. It was then possible to subject language games and the elementary units thereof, namely speech acts, to renewed formal analysis only if one could succeed in guaranteeing speech act theory a point of reference as objective as that attained by formal semantics via the linking of meaning and truth. Searle returned to formal semantics for this reason. We found that an alternative availed itself if we followed Humboldt's transcendental conception of language, for this retains the reference of the different linguistically constituted views of the world to an objective world. In his transcendental pragmatics Apel has always energetically propounded the validity of this universalist core *vis-à-vis* the pluralism of Wittgenstein's language games.

Taking Apel as my point of departure, I then forged a link to Austin (and the early Searle) by means of the idea of (a) providing justifications for Bühler's language functions in terms of a theory of validity; (b) by generalizing the objective concept of truth conditions in terms of validity conditions as a whole (including normative rightness and subjective truthfulness) while renouncing the ontology of *one* world; (c) by taking the epistemic turn inaugurated by Dummett further through connecting these conditions of validity to an intersubjective concept of justification via argumentation; and finally (d) by recognizing the illocutionary component of speech acts to be the linguistic expression of the raising of validity claims which can be redeemed in discourse. I have elaborated this idea in the form of a formal-pragmatic theory of meaning.

It proceeds from the simple notion that we understand a speech act if we know the conditions which make it acceptable. We have to do here with objective conditions of validity from which the semantic content of linguistic expression used can be derived not directly, but only by means of the epistemic claim raised by the speaker for the validity of his utterance while accomplishing his illocutionary act. This validity claim relies on a potential of reasons with which it can, if necessary, be redeemed in discourse. The reasons interpret the validity conditions and to this extent are themselves part of the conditions which render the validity claim worthy of recognition in intersubjective terms and make the respective utterance acceptable. This step first truly effects the turn away from formal semantics to pragmatics heralded by Wittgenstein and Austin, and it achieves this in such a manner that the cognitivist and objectivist abstractions are completely overcome. This, in turn, necessitates a revision of the ontological basic concepts established in philosophy, which I shall not go into here.

The above brief review of the history of the theory of language was intended merely to show that the understanding of linguistic expressions already calls for an orientation toward validity claims and that a rationally motivated force already inheres in processes of reaching linguistic understanding. If understanding a speech act depends on knowing the conditions for its acceptability, then the speaker's illocutionary aim – to be understood – points to the further aim that the hearer should accept the offer made with the speech act. Acceptance or agreement on the part of the hearer is equivalent to recognition of a validity claim raised by the speaker. It is based on the good reasons which the speaker offers in order to redeem the validity claim in discourse (or on a credible guarantee provided by the speaker that, if necessary, such reasons could be stated). And the hearer, with his/her 'Yes' to a validity claim accepted as worthy of recognition, i.e. by accepting the offer made with the speech act, as a rule takes upon him/herself certain obligations relevant for the further sequence of interaction – e.g. to meet a request, to trust a confession, to believe a statement, to rely on a promise or to obey an order. This quite simply has consequences for the further course of interaction, be it with the speaker or with other participants or persons affected; and it explains why acts of reaching linguistic understanding – which consist of a nucleus of an offer made with a speech act and a yes/no position – *are able* to take on functions of action coordination in the first place. What distinguishes the approach taken by formal pragmatics from that of formal semantics is the insight into the internal interconnection of understanding (*'Verstehen'*) and processes of reaching understanding (*'Verständigung'*). I by no means, as Jeffrey Alexander believes, confuse linguistic understanding and agreement.

To understand an expression means, however, to know how one can use it to reach an understanding with someone about something. One can already see from the conditions for *understanding* linguistic expressions that speech acts which can be carried out by means of such expressions are oriented toward *reaching understanding*, i.e. toward achieving a rationally-motivated agreement between parties to communication about something in the world. One would have utterly misconceived what it means to understand the meaning of an expression were one not to know that this is intended to serve reaching understanding about something, i.e. to bring about agreement – and the concept of agreement involves its being 'valid' for the participants. The dimension of validity is innate to language. I believe that Zimmermann's notion of the orientation to validity claims being *carried* from the domain of social action *into* the genuine sphere of speech and understanding language is an empiricist misunderstanding.[53] The orientation toward validity claims is among the pragmatic conditions for a possible understanding being reached, i.e. of understanding language *per se*.

Someone trained in formal semantics is likely to present simple demands as an incisive example disproving my proposal. It appears to be the case that a foreigner who has just arrived in town already understands a child's (begging) request to 'give me some money' if s/he knows the conditions under which the action requested can be successfully carried out.[54] It would appear that a normative validity claim is not even involved here, or rather that it first comes into play if we also take into account the pragmatic context within which the speech act – to be analysed semantically as a request – can be considered pragmatically to be begging.[55] I wish, in opposition to such a contra-intuitive reading, to stick by the analysis carried out in the *Theory of Communicative Action* (vol. I, pp. 298ff.): the knowledge of the conditions for success to be gleaned from the propositional component of a demand does not suffice in order to understand the illocutionary meaning, i.e. the request's specific character as a demand. Rather, the hearer must understand the normative context which authorizes the speaker to make the demand and thus legitimates the expectation that the addressee has reasons to carry out the action demanded of him/her in the first place. Otherwise the hearer has no knowledge of the conditions for his/her agreement: it is this agreement which first justifies his/her entering into obligations which are relevant to the further sequence of the interaction – in this case, handing over 'some money'. A knowledge of (a) the conditions for success must be accompanied by that of (b) those conditions under which the speaker has reasons to consider demanding the contents of (a) valid, i.e. normatively justified – e.g. that children are allowed to beg from foreigners in the streets of Lima.[56]

Now what is decisive here is that we cannot conceive of situations in which a request would be understandable *per se* without it being authorized or backed up by *some* normative background *or other*, however weak this may be, and be it simply that one should *per se* help children or people in distress, whereby being in distress belongs precisely to a request's pragmatic preconditions. Admittedly, there is the borderline case of normatively non-authorized demands, such as the demand by a bankrobber that the cashier s/he threatens hand over money. In such cases, the conditions of normative validity must be *replaced* by conditions for sanctions which complete the conditions for the acceptability of the demand: 'Hands up!', exclaimed while pointing a revolver, shows that a validity claim has been replaced by a power claim and that the demand is to be understood in the sense of the factual expression of someone's will, whereby the one person's will is simply imposed on the other. The potential for sanctions contingently linked with the demand grants the speaker the certainty that the addressee has good reasons to conform.

I was mistaken to treat this borderline case of a pure imperative backed up by power as a class of speech acts in its own right. As Zimmermann, Tugendhat and Skjei point out, because of this I managed to embroil myself in self-contradictions. I have already revised this position in my reply to Skjei:[57] I now consider simple or normatively non-authorized demands to be a parasitical case. As a sociologist, I should have known that a continuum obtains between power that is merely a matter of factual custom and power transformed into normative authority. *All* imperatives to which we attribute an illocutionary force can therefore be analysed in line with the model of normatively authorized demands. What I falsely took to be a difference at a categorial level thus shrinks to the status of a difference in degree. The bankrobber's demand, sanctioned by his 'Hands up!', belongs to those *borderline* cases of a manifestly strategic usage of speech acts, whereby the deficit in illocutionary force is replaced by a reference to potential sanctions. This usage is parasitical to the extent that the understanding of such a speech act takes a form borrowed from the conditions under which normatively authorized demands, i.e. demands not stripped of their illocutionary force, can be used.[58]

In general, the strategic use of illocutionary acts functions under conditions of latently strategic action: the speaker must not 'concede' the existence of perlocutionary effects – the side effects of a consensus seemingly achieved communicatively which s/he may *trigger off* in the hearer in the form of obligations relevant to the further sequence of interaction. The objections raised by Alexander in his essay reveal to me yet again that my usage of Austin's expressions 'perlocutionary' and 'illocutionary', diverging as it does from conventional philosophical usage, leads to misunderstandings. This prompts me to provide some *terminological clarification*.

I shall initially distinguish more clearly between the *immediate* illocutionary aim (or success) of the speaker – namely that the hearer understands her/his utterance – and the *more far-reaching* aim that the hearer accept the validity of the utterance and thus take on obligations which are relevant to the further sequence of interaction. The illocutionary success in the *narrow sense* consists of understanding, whereas the illocutionary success in the *broader sense* consists of a consensus which effects coordination, i.e. *an interactive success*. I had hitherto only termed those effects 'perlocutionary' as were not related internally to the meaning of the sentence uttered, whereas this expression usually applies to *all* those effects the speaker has on the hearer which go beyond *mere understanding*. Given that, as we have seen above, the dimension of validity is inherent in this use of language, it would appear advisable to consider the illocutionary aim to be not just understanding an utterance (with a concomitant knowledge of the conditions for its acceptability), but also to include the agreement reached with the hearer, i.e. the hearer's acceptance of the offer made with the speech act. This, an illocutionary aim in the widest sense, is achieved solely by carrying out the illocutionary act. I wish to stick by this usage of the term. However, in approximation of the usual philosophical usage, I shall label all effects that go beyond this 'perlocutionary'. For example, the conviction that gradually forms in the hearer when he accepts that a statement is true could just as easily be prompted by a lie and then represent precisely the type of effect which the speaker wishes strategically to achieve. This terminological concession compels me to differentiate within the class of perlocutionary effects: between effects which arise from the semantic contents of what is said in the course of obligations relevant to the further sequence of interaction, and such effects as occur contingently independently of grammatically regulated interconnections. I wish thereby to correct the mistake I made of equating this distinction in the theory of meaning with the action-theoretic distinction between strategically and non-strategically intended perlocutionary effects.

I term those effects strategically intended which come about only if they are not declared or if they are caused by deceptive speech acts that merely pretend to be valid. Perlocutionary effects of this type reveal that a use of language oriented toward reaching understanding is deployed for strategic interactions. I have referred to this as the 'use of language with an orientation to consequences' (*TCA*, vol. I, p. 293) – a one-sided and latently achieved subordination of illocutionary acts under conditions of success-oriented action on the part of the speaker. In line with this terminological revision, one can on longer consider *all* perlocutions to be[59] latent-strategic action. In opposition to Jeffrey Alexander, let me emphasize that the distinction between *communicative* and *strategic* action is not influenced by this.

I define communicative action, by stating among other things that action coordination must come up to the conditions for agreement reached without reservation by communicative means. The demand that illocutionary aims be pursued 'without reservation' is intended precisely to exclude cases of latent strategic action. In the case of strategic action, linguistic processes of reaching understanding are (generally) not resorted to as a mechanism of action coordination. Here, we can no longer explain the coordination of different plans for action by referring to conditions for an agreement achieved in communication that culminates in the intersubjective recognition of criticizable validity claims. Instead, we must fall back only on the conditions for the reciprocal influence the players attempt to exert on one another in the course of purposive action oriented towards their own respective success. My critics have on occasion overlooked the fact that *both* models of action impute to the actors a capacity for setting ends and for goal-oriented action as well as an interest in executing their own plans for action.[60] Other critics also support their arguments by referring to the fact that, here as there, a teleological structure of action is presupposed; however, they identify the pursuit of illocutionary aims without reservations (as is envisaged in the model of communicative action) and the pursuit of perlocutionary aims through the agency of illocutionary successes already achieved with the egocentric pursuit of one's own interests and aims permissible in the model of teleological or strategic action, and this leads to one model merging with the other.[61] Such an identification is impermissible, even if the description of both cases is based on the same teleological language game of end-setting actors who pursue goals, achieve results and trigger off effects. For the illocutionary 'ends' of reaching understanding cannot be defined without referring to the linguistic means of reaching understanding: the medium of language and the telos of reaching understanding intrinsic to it reciprocally constitute one another. The relation between these is not one of means and ends. As a consequence, 'aims' which an actor pursues in language and can only realize together with Alter cannot be described as if they resembled conditions which we can bring about by intervening causally in the world. For the actor, the aims of action oriented toward success and reaching understanding are situated on different levels: either in the objective world or, beyond all entities, in the linguistically constituted lifeworld. I do not mean to say that speech is a self-satisfying action that bears its purpose within it and is to be distinguished from such actions as are aimed at purposes external to them. However, we must in both cases distinguish between the ontological presuppositions and the perspectives as well as attitudes of the actors; we must conceive of the aims and the realization of set purposes in a respectively different manner.

In the process in which speaker and hearer reach an understanding about something with one another, for them the illocutionary aims of understanding and consensus lie *beyond* the world *in* which the actor intervenes purposively in order to achieve a goal. Illocutionary aims can, from the perspective of the participants, be achieved only within the dimension of world-disclosing language itself, and in such a manner that the intersubjective recognition of disputable validity claims depends on the autonomous agreement of a subject who is held to be accountable. Illocutionary aims can, in other words, only be achieved cooperatively and are never, as it were, at the disposal of an individual party to interaction. Strategic action also occurs under conditions of the double contingency of actors equipped with a freedom of choice. Yet these purposive actors, who condition one another with a view to their own respective success, can be reached by one another only as entities *within* the world. They have to attribute successes and failures solely to themselves, namely as the result of their own causal intervention in the supposedly regular nexus of *innerworldly* processes. The same is, of course, true of collective actors who are first constituted as such in the cooperation of individual actors.

Furthermore, communicative and strategic action do not differ primarily in terms of the attitude of the actors, but rather with respect to structural characteristics. A formal-pragmatic analysis of successful speech acts is needed precisely because in communicative action the structure of language usage oriented toward reaching understanding is superimposed on the underlying teleological structure of the action, and subjects the actors to precisely such constraints as compel them to adopt a performative attitude that is more laden with presuppositions than the objectivating stance of the strategic actor. Interaction mediated through acts of reaching understanding exhibits a both richer and more strictly limiting structure than does strategic action.

As game theory has shown, strategic action has served to generate a model. If one does not allow oneself to be deluded by a semanticist theory of meaning, i.e. does not draw a line separating the illocutionary binding (bonding) effect from speech acts and thus condemn the former to context-dependent forms of usage, then one will have no difficult in recognizing that the two other models of action known in sociological theory are both borderline cases of communicative action. Just as normative and expressive language usage are both tailored to fulfil one respective function of language, so too norm-guided and dramaturgical action are suited to one specific aspect of validity respectively, namely to the legitimacy of admissible interpersonal relations and the authenticity of self-presentation. The above-mentioned models represent borderline cases (and not, as I had mistakenly believed, 'pure types') of action oriented toward reaching understanding to the extent that in them the dynamics of reciprocally taking positions on criticizable validity claims that is essential to communicative action is suspended: in the one case by means of a presupposed value consensus and, in the other, by an empiricist reinterpretation of self-presentation oriented toward reaching understanding as impression management.[62]

In the light of these philosophical observations a number of the global misgivings that Alexander, Berger, Dux, Joas and others have with respect to my basic action-theoretic assumptions evaporate. I in no manner identify the practice of speech with that of social action; I do not fail to see that social interaction of all types is mediated by language and that strategic interactions also demand discerning achievements in understanding and interpretation. However, because the structure of language usage oriented toward reaching understanding imposes certain attitudes and perspectives – incompatible with an attempt geared directly towards one's own success in influencing one's opponent – on the communicative actor, my distinction between the two controversial types is not *only* analytical. The sociological observer is also in principle able to distinguish between communicative and strategic action by means of those attitudes which, from the perspective of the actor, comprise a complete alternative.[63]

This ideal-typical division, i.e. a division made by using clear criteria from language pragmatics, but by no means merely analytic in nature, does not simply strip the complex concept of social cooperation – what Marx termed 'labour' – of its relevance: something that plays a great role in social reality need not also be fundamental in conceptual terms. Moreover, the degree of rationality of strategic action can vary; seen empirically, it seldom meets the standards of game theory and decision theory.

It should now also be clear that approaching an analysis of action oriented toward reaching understanding from the vantage point of speech act theory by no means implies assimilating this action to the model of discourses that serve to relieve action. Action oriented toward validity is not, as Dux believes, assimilated to the argumentational treatment of validity claims which have become problematical. Nevertheless, let us remember that with the validity claims factually raised and recognized within an action-coordinating role, an element of unconditionality enters into everyday communicative practice. Criticizable validity claims have two faces: as claims, at least from the viewpoint of the participants, they transcend all merely local agreements and base themselves on a subversive, continually flexible potential of disputable reasons. Yet they must be raised *here* and *now* within specific contexts and with coverage provided by an unquestioned cultural background and accepted (or rejected) with a view to non-reversible action sequences. The social reality of the lifeworld consists of such action sequences as are interlinked via criticizable validity claims. Apel uses the vivid image of the interlocking of the ideal communication community and its real counterpart, which sounds almost too Kantian. The 'Doctrine of the Two Realms' has been completely overcome. The structure of a use of language oriented toward reaching understanding demands idealizing suppositions on the part of the communicative actors; yet these notions function as social facts and are, as is language *per se*, constitutive for the form in which socio-cultural life reproduces itself.

Alexander maintains that in the concept of communicative action I conflate 'ideological' questions with metholodogical and empirical issues. I am supposed to have secretly smuggled 'value postulates' into the argument via the definitions of reaching understanding and action oriented toward reaching understanding, instead of declaring them openly. The identification of understanding language with an agreement achieved in communication ostensibly serves to effect this. To leave this misinterpretation aside for the moment, what Alexander overlooks is the intention of the overall project. I would never have tackled a formal-pragmatic reconstruction of the rational potential of speech if I had not harboured the hope that by means of this approach I would be able to generate a concept of communicative rationality from the normative contents of the universal and ineluctable presuppositions of a *non-circumventable* practice of everyday processes of reaching understanding. It is not a matter of this or that preference, 'our' or 'their' notions of rational life; rather we are concerned here with reconstructing a voice of reason, which we cannot avoid using whether we want to or not when speaking in everyday communicative practice. Perhaps I surreptitiously culled from my definitions something I thought I had found by means of reconstruction – it is, at any rate, this concern that criticism should focus on.

Those who reproach me for ignoring materialist components suspect that another type of idealization lurks within my theory. This objection takes various forms. Johannes Berger suspects that my conceptual strategy is underpinned by an intention to divide, as did Durkheim, all social action into moral or immoral action from the viewpoint of altruism and egoism. Johannes Weiss also maintains that communicative action above all owes its integrative capacity to the moral power of normative validity claims.[64] These doubts do not hold for the simple reason that I merely introduce norm-regulated action as a borderline case of communicative action: the rationally-motivated binding (bonding) effect of speech acts extends across the whole spectrum of illocutionary powers which are differentiated according to the respective language involved and appear in respectively different constellations depending on the linguistic view of the world and form of life. It is precisely this internal differentiation of the spectrum of validity and the interplay of cognitive, expressive and aesthetic validity claims with those that are of a conventional, moral and legal nature which grants everyday communicative practice autonomy from (and a state distinct from) normative contexts (which, by the way, comprise only one of three components of the lifeworld (background).

Weiss and others have rendered their objection more specific by claiming that the concept of communicative action would seem to promote the rationalist illusion that language could engender within itself illocutionary binding (bonding) effects, whereas in fact the binding (bonding) effect of communicative acts can arise only 'given certain social and institutional constellations as well as psychological dispositions'; and 'it is these empirical conditions for the development and binding character of rationality which the explanations offered by an empirical theory of society must aim to address'.[65] It is precisely this that I maintain; however, the pragmatic concept of language allows for another, non-empiricist description of the same thing. I have left no doubts as to the fact that the concept of action oriented toward reaching understanding developed in 'Intermediate Reflections: Social Action, Purposive Activity, and Communication' must be supplemented by a complementary concept of lifeworld as elaborated in 'Intermediate Reflections: System and Lifeworld'. We would in no manner be able to explain how everyday processes of consensus formation repeatedly succeed in crossing the threshold posed by the risk of dissent built into the practice of reaching understanding in the form of criticizable validity claims were we not able to take into account the *massive preunderstanding* of participants in communication. This is to be found in the self-evident features of an intuitively present, prereflexively known form of life presupposed to be unproblematical to which they have become culturally accustomed and which has to be imbued in them through socialization. Subjects acting communicatively are dependent in their seemingly superficially autonomous achievements in reaching understanding on the resources of a background knowledge of the lifeworld over which they have no control. Now what is important is the philosophico-sociological double aspect in terms of which the lifeworld can be analysed more accurately. It is not I who push both analytical levels 'into one another in a way which is, for all the convergence of approaches to problems, inadmissible' (Weiss, 'Verständigungsorientierung', p. 113).

An analysis with a *formal-pragmatic* thrust of forms of life constituted in language that views the latter as comprising a lifeworld behind the backs of the communicative actors makes it plausible that, from the perspective of the actors, the processes of socialization are generally accomplished in a matter-of-course, normal and coercion-free manner if these do not cross the threshold into a domain where they manifest conflicts. Only if we change the methodological position taken and make the reproduction of the lifeworld a *sociological* topic do those circular processes come into view which occur in and though the medium of action oriented towards reaching understanding. To put it clumsily, it is only once we have switched from a Humboldtian to a Parsonian perspective that everyday communicative practice reveals itself – both with respect to disturbances in it and its functioning – to be the product of a cooperation of cultural tradition, social integration and the socialization of individuals, whereby cooperation arises under the compulsions of material reproduction. Clearly, these constellations determine the interactions networked in social spaces and historical times in two ways: the actors *encounter* them as determinants of the action situation, because the latter restricts the actors' scope for action; and as resources for action oriented toward reaching understanding they at the same time *make possible* what the actors experience as a formative process and attribute to themselves as spontaneous achievements. This second aspect, from which society appears as the sum of enabling conditions, cannot be subjected to empirical analysis. Indeed, society can be thematized from such a vantage point only if we couple the sociological concept of lifeworld to its formal-pragmatic counterpart. Hans Joas is not the only person to misunderstand this methodologically decisive step,[66] namely linking the basic concepts of the sociologically described components of the lifeworld (culture, society, person) with the formal-pragmatic description of the lifeworld's resources (background knowledge, forms of solidarity and skills). The latter, for their part, ensure that the lifeworld is fed into communicative action via the branches of the propositional, illocutionary and intentional components of speech acts.

If one perceives that sociological statements *presuppose* the above-mentioned change in perspective, then one will realize that even the strongest variant of the charge of idealism is unfounded. Berger makes such a charge with respect to the microsociological level by stating that the fixated focus on consensus formation blocks phenomena of dissent or power from sight. Axel Honneth repeats this objection, claiming that a lifeworld structured in communicative terms is conceived in such a manner that 'all success-oriented attempts at asserting interests' have to be excluded from it.[67] The concept of power, he continues, is no longer introduced in an action-theoretic context, but rather only in systems-theoretic terms.[68] This is not the case: for the simple fact that power as a 'steering medium' first arises in modern societies, from which it would then follow that all premodern societies have to be defined as power-free.[69]

Whereas communicative action requires cooperation with a view to a situation-specific agreement on the basis of which each of the participants can realize his/her own interests and plans, strategic action occurs in any random form of conflict or cooperation; the degree of conflict depends contingently on the degree to which the respective interests diverge or converge. Phenomena of dissent and power cut across this dimension of conflict and cooperation; however, they vary in a complicated manner according to the type of action. Agreement and disagreement are complementary phenomena in the dimension of understanding reached through language. They are to be measured (in the final instance) in terms of the yes/no positions adopted toward validity claims. Strictly speaking, disagreement can arise only under conditions of action oriented toward reaching understanding; it changes into one phenomenon of conflict among others as soon as (at least) one of the participants considers disagreement no longer from a performative perspective as a problem of failed processes of reaching understanding, but rather as an occurrence in the world that can be empirically influenced. Admittedly, communicative action also affords broad space for manoeuvre with respect to the processing of now manifest disagreement; from costly argumentation, through everyday repair work, diverse forms of leaving-things-be and of neutralization, to intentional ambiguities and fictitious agreements which nevertheless no one challenges. Precisely the 'non-agreements that have been made manageable' communicatively to which Weiss draws our attention[70] are possible only thanks to the exceptionally flexible, inscrutably backgrounded instrument of colloquial speech. Moreover, one must bear in mind the fragile nature (elaborated by ethnomethodology) of an explicitly achieved agreement as well as the fact that this applies only with temporal restrictions. At the level of communicative acts, the diffracted intersubjectivity of possible processes of reaching understanding is, after all, opposed by seamless integration effected via unambiguously stable and indisputably sound agreements. The continual risk of misunderstanding, disagreement and a lack of comprehension is held in check only by the counterfactual validity of strong idealizations. Yet, the conflicts which are, as it were, open to use for strategic action, are, with the exception of a few borderline situations, almost always framed in background assumptions or conventions on which there is a consensus; this holds true for conflicts that are legally organized as well as for those which do not have any formal basis.

Just as dissent can be allocated to action oriented toward reaching understanding, so too power can initially be allocated to strategic action. I treated the concept of power in this manner as early as 1971, namely as 'the ability to prevent other individuals or groups from realizing their interests. As a rule, power is asymmetrically distributed; one side can then impede the other in the strategically-effective pursuit of its interests, or the one can impose its own interests on the other.'[71] Power, influence and domination are the different external forms taken by power, whereby power transformed into normative authority as it were changes sides depending on the type of action. As soon as power is linked to legal-normative validity claims, it penetrates the structures of action oriented toward reaching understanding:

> We speak – in cases of the factual use of violence or the permanent threat of open violence – of power being manifestly exercised ... By contrast, the legitimate use of power is based on recognized norms ... I understand domination to be only a special case of the exercise of power. Power is always built into valid norms if the reciprocal behavioural expectations license the satisfaction of needs only under the proviso that one foregoes satisfying *other* needs that have already been interpreted.[72]

Macrosociological power relations are mirrored in that microphysics of power which is built into the structures of distorted communication. This position also need not be raised as an objection to my work.[73]

The misunderstanding that I am forced by the categories I use to exclude phenomena of dissent and power from the lifeworld is, in turn, I suspect, to be attributed to the formal-pragmatic concept of lifeworld being mistaken for its sociological counterpart. From the perspective of the actor it is indeed factually the case that the assumption of a *mutual* lifeworld is suspended in strategic action – the lifeworld ceases to be available as a resource for action coordination. Yet, seen sociologically, strategic interactions also belong to a society conceived of as the lifeworld.

I sense that the same overhasty connection of philosophical and sociological approaches lies behind the objections which Günter Dux raises.[74] I am somewhat dumbfounded by the assertion that I have raised communicative action and its institutional order 'to a level of symbolic self-understanding that is set off from the real pursuit of interests'. Naturally, in legitimate orders complexes of interests are integrated with value orientations. Normative validity claims state that institutions deserve (albeit, usually counterfactually) recognition because they embody generalizable interests. This naturalistic element gains entry into discourse ethics – in the formulation of a principle of universalization which has often aroused the suspicion that Kant was thus being betrayed to utilitarianism. If I understand Dux correctly, then he returns from a sociological viewpoint to the neo-Aristotelian theme of the relation of morality and ethical life. Proceeding from Parsonian premises, Alexander and Münch concern themselves with the same problem. Both believe that I do not differentiate sufficiently between the cultural validity of norms and the institutionalization thereof in the system of societal community; put in Parsonian terms, only within a 'community' can norms first be integrated with the motifs and traditions of a concrete form of life in such a fashion that their (assumed) ideal validity can be transformed into the factual validity of social obligations: 'Rationality is not only an intellectual construct of meaning, but in the form of normative rationality it is coupled with the action of the community.'[75] I do not challenge this assertion, but Münch actually describes the uncontroversial matter at hand in a different way from mine. To my mind, the manner in which Münch and Alexander wish to distinguish *cultural* from *social* validity is not without its problems.

Irrespective of whether we conceive of society in communication-theoretic terms as a lifeworld or follow Parsons in considering it a system of action, in both cases culture, systems of institutions, and personality each form a different level of analysis (whether as 'structural components' or precisely as 'subsystems'). From this sociological perspective, complexes of validity (in the sense of validity claims worthy of recognition) are situated at the level of cultural symbolism, whereas factually functioning, i.e. *de facto* recognized complexes of validity are attributed to the level of society. Now Münch determines the relation between ideal validity and social validity as one of 'objective' vs. 'intersubjective' validity. He draws for the purpose of interpretation *ad hoc* on Popper's Three World Doctrine and the latter's truth theory (with the correlates of 'truth-in-itself' and 'truth-for-us', or 'resemblance to truth' respectively). Entities in the third world are to be accorded objective validity – like thought in Frege's work – whereas the intersubjective validity of 'held-to-be-true' or 'held-to-be-correct' are situated in Popper's second world, i.e. at the level of social interaction. This uncoupling of ideal validity and acceptability (however idealized it may be) is intended to take into account the fact that 'a social consensus is always limited spatio-temporally in terms of a community, i.e. it is a specific consensus'.[76] This conceptual strategy initially has two unfortunate consequences. It has to rely on a Platonic theory of meaning and a realist theory of truth, a position which is surely hard to defend given the state of philosophy today. It has, moreover, to conceive of discourses as the result of diametrically opposed trends towards rationalization and communalization and divide them up into the corresponding types.

Supposedly, 'rational' discourses focus on clarifying questions of validity whereas 'discourses of will-formation' centre on generating consensus. This differentiation between types of discourses devoted specially, on the one hand, to objective validity and, on the other, to intersubjective processes of reaching understanding leads to false conclusions. For argumentation, e.g. theoretical discourses established in the scientific community, do not exclusively serve the purposes of critique, i.e. the 'creation of disturbances in communication' (Münch, p. 112); post-Popperian theories of science have clearly elucidated that the scientific community, which is by no means so undogmatic, evidently wishes to gain acceptance for its theories. Nor can everyday processes of consensus formation be stripped of their reference context to transcend validity claims in such a way that all that remains of rationally motivated consensus is the factual bindingness of a socially predominant opinion.[77] One must, by contrast, conceive of the 'rational discourses' established in expert cultures as the validity-specific differentiation and corresponding institutionalization of a sub-class of the discourses that crop up rather more accidentally in everyday life; subsequently both must be described as reflexive forms of a structurally-similar communicative practice embedded in the lifeworld. All these forms of communication call for an orientation toward validity claims that go beyond spatio–temporal contexts, although not all in the same way.

If one takes this into consideration, then one also avoids the further difficulty of having to describe the lifeworldly contextualization of everyday knowledge as the irrational background of a merely emotionally harboured and ritually secured pre-understanding.[78] According to our intuitive experience, the lifeworld constitutes itself as absolutely certain *knowledge*. Münch has to shift this knowledge on to the level of culture, where he then has to situate religious world views which function to generate meaning. This compels him to anchor not only the lifeworld but also religion at such a deep level in terms of basic concepts that the decline of religious world views which is to be observed in empirical reality is then excluded at the analytical level. Such phenomena as are grouped around the factual recognition of counterfactual validity claims resist any Parsonian description; I pinpoint them initially at the philosophical level of a formal-pragmatic investigation carried out from a first-person perspective. They need not, however, be lost from view following the transition to a sociological approach because the *same* phenomena of a communicative action nourished from the resources of the lifeworld would then return as products of the interaction of structural components of the lifeworld. Clearly, they can now be explained in terms of the functional linkages of cultural tradition, social integration and socialization. This is the advantage of arriving at one's conceptualization of society from philosophical premises and not having to secure it after the event with the aid of philosophical hypotheses.

This leaves Hans Joas's objection that my theory of action does not do justice to the variety of action types. I have the impression that Joas loses sight of my approach with his references to play and art. 'The playful and artistic interaction with objects' is just as little constitutive for *social* action as is purposive action as a whole. I am concerned with an explanation for social action, not with constructing an anthropology of action as a whole. The juxtaposition of communicative and strategic action has the advantage with regard to my socio-theoretic aims of stressing consensus and influence – those two mechanisms of action coordination which, from the rationality-theoretic viewpoint of whether the rational potential of speech has been exhausted or not, form completely alternative options. I am able to embrace the phenomena which are of relevance to social action within these concepts. This is also true for problem-solving and creative/end-generating behaviour. The problem-solving and world-disclosing capacities of speech are, in fact, central to those functions of language which, following Bühler and Jakobson, I distinguish from one another and take into account in a pragmatic meaning theory.[79]

There can also be no talk of the theory of communicative action limiting the analysis to simple interactions between individual actors. The interactive relation between Ego and Alter provides only the paradigm for the formal-pragmatic investigation; the sociological analysis of the lifeworld lends itself equally well to embracing collective actions and actors as well as individual actions and individual actors. However, the intersubjectivity-theoretic description of collective actions protects the speech of collective actors from those hypostatizations to which action theories based on praxis philosophy have repeatedly succumbed. Joas and Honneth wish, if I have understood them correctly, to add a further variant to approaches in praxis philosophy developed from Marx to the younger Marcuse (and up to the late Lukács), based in this case on Mead's work. I have elsewhere stated why I do not feel that such an approach will bear fruit.[80] My assessment relies on a critique of the philosophy of consciousness and on a paradigm shift which stands and falls with the pragmatic concept of language.

The former, the critique of the philosophy of consciousness, leads, if carried out consistently, to the latter, the paradigm of reaching understanding. Admittedly, there have repeatedly been attempts to develop a notion of intersubjectivity from an underlying subjectivity on the basis of a philosophy of consciousness, be it Fichte's *Science of Knowledge* or Husserl's *Cartesian Meditations*. Semantic nominalism, from Grice to Bennett and Schiffer, is but one variant of this. The only interesting thing about these endeavours is the reasons for their failure. On the other hand, critiques of the philosophy of consciousness have also emanated from the behaviourist camp, in Morris's work, from the existentialist-ontological camp, namely Heidegger, and from the formal-semantic corner, in Tugendhat's writings. Yet, only a language pragmatics that reaches back to Humboldt's work and takes up motifs from the thought of Mead, Wittgenstein, Gadamer and Austin can introduce a paradigm into the debate which does not merely undercut the paradigm of self-consciousness that dominated modern thought in a reductionist manner, but also replaces it without a loss of sensitivity towards problems.[81] A critique of the philosophy of consciousness conducted from the vantage of a pragmatics of language sheds light on the scene in which sociological action theories must also operate: the listing ship of praxis philosophy can probably not be righted using spare parts gleaned from the dry dock of symbolic interactionism and social phenomenology.

Problems of the Two-level Concept of Society: System and Lifeworld

The sharpest criticism is levelled not against the concept of communicative action, but rather against a conceptualization of social life which supplements the concept of lifeworld – developed in action-theoretic terms – with borrowings from systems theory, and thus from the outset exposes itself to charges of its being an eclectic fusion of heterogeneous approaches, models and procedures. Unfortunately, readers of my earlier writings transpose conceptions on to the theory of communicative action which it was supposed to amend, and in so doing draw false parallels between types of action and types of order. Nevertheless, as the author of that theory I bear the responsibility for unclear or contradictory formulations, and would thus like to take this opportunity to tidy them up. Thomas McCarthy's instructive essay contains the most detailed criticism of my determination of the relation between system and lifeworld. Drawing on his study I shall group the often overlapping objections and hone them to such a critical point that I am then able, so I hope, (a) to reformulate my basic assumptions in a manner which will shed clear light on them. I shall (b) treat the criticism of the thesis of the uncoupling of system from lifeworld in like manner. To the extent possible in the present context I shall, lastly, (c) go into the objections which are in part normative and in part inspired by Marxism, challenges which I welcome, for they enable us to perceive that the theory of communicative action is not a completely unpolitical project.

In his essay, McCarthy has already enumerated the most important motives for linking the concept of system with that of lifeworld. Seen in terms of the history of social theory and philosophy, two strands of traditional theory branched out following the devaluation of the concept of totality, namely approaches based on action theory and those founded in a macrosociology oriented toward the model of sociation provided by the market. Although I believe that the attempts at remerging the two traditions which this provoked, particularly the endeavours of Durkheim and Parsons, failed, my own proposal moves along the same theoretical lines. I connect the concept of lifeworld developed in an action-theoretic frame with the concept of a boundary-maintaining system, which itself cannot be justified by reference to action theory. I do this because it appears to me to be especially well-suited for outlining certain pathological phenomena of modern society, namely what Marx termed 'real abstractions'. The third motive for the suggested type of paradigm combination results from the methodological difficulties facing systems theory in the social sciences: the definition of the boundaries and goal states of social systems ceases in principle to entail problems only once the descriptions conducted in the system language can be referred to phenomena previously identified in another theoretical language. The fourth motive is provided by problems that have arisen from my own work. Inconsistencies in my 'Technology and Science as Ideology' were, as Honneth has convincingly shown, due to my drawing an overhasty parallel between action systems and action types. As a consequence, I already attempted in *Legitimation Crisis* to combine the concept of lifeworld developed in *On The Logic of the Social Sciences* with a conceptual framework with which I had acquainted myself in the course of the controversy with Luhmann. To my mind, the empirical utility of the systems-theoretic approach for an analysis of crises in economic and administrative systems was proved in the studies conducted at the Max Planck Institute in Starnberg, particularly those carried out by Claus Offe. Yet, the first attempt stopped short at a muddled theoretical adding-together of 'lifeworld' and 'system'. I wished to tackle all these difficulties in the second volume of *The Theory of Communicative Action*. This project has itself now sparked off an opaque controversy which certainly can also be attributed to its not having been elaborated with sufficient precision in that volume. I shall therefore attempt first to clarify the way in which I deploy the concepts of 'system' and 'lifeworld' as analytical concepts of order. I shall then proceed to discuss the uncoupling of system and lifeworld in modern societies as well as the normative implications entailed by the diagnosis of the present age laid out in such a conceptual strategy.

I initially treat social and system integration as two *aspects* of societal integration which must be considered *analytically* distinct. It is in terms of these aspects that concepts of order can then be introduced into the argument, concepts which in the preliminary definition of society as 'the systemically stabilized contexts of actions of socially integrated groups' also pinpoint aspects of the same object that can only be distinguished from one another analytically. The aspects refer to two classes of mechanisms of societal integration: exchange and power mechanisms vs. consensus-forming mechanisms (which bring about agreement on values, norms and linguistic communication). These mechanisms generate social order from interactions; their mode of operation can, however, be specified with reference to the structures of action. Whereas mechanisms of social integration proceed from action orientations, system-integrating mechanisms penetrate through and beyond action orientations and integrate action consequences (irrespective of whether these were intended as results or rather occur as an unintended outcome).

Mechanisms of social integration are related *internally* to structures of action oriented toward reaching understanding, whereas the mechanisms of system integration remain *external to the structures of action*. This is, however, not the case for the *steering media* 'money' and 'power', which differentiate out from the universal medium of ordinary language taking the form of special codes. Yet these steering media have a specific de-worlding effect; even their integrative achievements do not fall within the bounds of the horizon to which the participants in interaction orient themselves.

This explains why the participants remain intuitively aware of orders established by social integration even if this takes the form of a pre-reflexive, by no means readily available or recallable background knowledge. Orders created by system integration are, by contrast, as a rule counterintuitive in nature. Both aspects of the social order are in a respectively different sense 'far from consciousness', i.e. distant from the immediate experience of the participants in interaction. This difference can, for example, be seen in the modes of operation of structural anthropology and political economy: the former searches, to overstress the case, for society as the ethnically subconscious, whereas the latter pursues society as second nature. Now, if one hunts for the dimensions in which the respective degrees of societal integration achieved can be measured, one inevitably comes up against the two underlying conceptual models.

Social integration is to be measured in terms of criteria of internal stabilization and the preservation of ego and group identities that depend on what actors attribute to themselves. System integration can be assessed in terms of criteria of external stabilization and the preservation of the boundaries of a system *vis-à-vis* its environment. That which, in borderline cases, becomes respectively subject to crisis and threatened in its existence (*Bestand*) is in the one instance linked internally to the self-understanding of those concerned and, in the other, accessible only to objective observation. It is always *the same* society which is caught in the grips of such crises of identity or steering,[82] but each of these processes can be grasped only in terms of one of the two aspects of societal integration.

Taking social integration as our guideline – and if we follow the structures of action oriented toward reaching understanding – we come across the concept of lifeworld which this implicitly rests on; if guided by the notion of system integration – and if we follow the functionally connected action consequences – we come across the concept of a boundary-maintaining system which this implicitly rests on. The formal-pragmatic analysis of communicative action affords us access to the complex structure of a lifeworld in which orders of legitimate behaviour created by social integration represent but one of three components. By contrast, compared with the psychological system and in the midst of organic systems, that social system which exists within an overcomplex environment and can augment its existence therein comprises merely the special case of a universal mode. We have to do here, in other words, with the suitable interpretation in the social sciences of the basic concepts and assumptions of general systems theory. Yet it is not the two concepts themselves which are subjected to criticism, but the decision to merge system and lifeworld into aspects from which society can respectively be analysed as a whole. Some initial methodological clarification is in order.

Functional analysis, with its classical conceptual tools, is, as McCarthy shows once again, relevant to an analysis of social phenomena in terms of *both* aspects. It is not this method itself which discriminates between the two forms of viewing society, but rather the fact that the method is linked to a system-environment model There can, in other words, be no talk of my having wished to confine functionalism to the observation of phenomena of material reproduction. And it is equally misleading to suppose that processes of symbolic and material reproduction can only be grasped in terms of one respective aspect. An approximate description can be given of all phenomena using *each* of the two aspects – although there is a difference in depth of field. It is always possible to approach from its own perspective the manner in which a lifeworld reproduces the material conditions for its existence; yet whether these processes have become so opaque and complex as to be inadmissibly foreshortened by being examined from this perspective and can thus be *better* explained under the aspect of system depends on the degree of differentiation within a society.[83] Conversely, systems analysis will also always embrace those contributions which cultural tradition, social integration and socialization make to stabilizing boundaries in an over-complex environment; in doing so, however, it must treat the internal limitations that symbolic structures impose on the steering capacity of a system as contingent data without being able to explain them adequately, for example, with the aid of a developmental logic.

The relation I established between social integration and action orientations, between system integration and action consequences also caused some confusion. The problem of unintended action consequences can, of course, also be treated from the perspective of the lifeworld. In more complex cases, this analytical strategy soon comes up against limitations if it is meant to clarify how aggregated action consequences reciprocally stabilize one another in functional contexts and thus engender integrative effects. Such investigations must be based on a more appropriate model; and of those on offer today, that of system-environment seems to afford the greatest explanatory potential.[84]

Finally, the use I made of the distinction between the participant's perspective and that of the observer when elaborating the two aspects was evidently misleading. We have to do here with the justifications for the methodological primacy of the analysis of the lifeworld. Since we can gain access to the object domain in question, namely social action, only hermeneutically, *all* social phenomena must initially, irrespective of whether this is explicitly stated or not, be described in a language which takes up from the language of the actors to be found in this object domain. Given that the objectivist language of systems theory does not do this, systems analysis must rely on a different portrayal of the object domain – and here I suggest using a primarily communication-theoretic approach. With systems theory, the phenomena which have been made hermeneutically understandable are described in a manner independent of the language and self-understanding of the actors. This objectivating change in stance triggers off an alienating effect, repeated with each individual systems-theoretic description of a phenomenon previously grasped from the participant's perspective. Thus, Luhmann owes his *literary* influence to the baffling effect of an intelligently objectivating translation which permits us to see the sobering obverse of phenomena with which we are well acquainted.

Many critics have allowed themselves to be misled by what they believe to be the allocation of either system integration or social integration to one respective type of action. They then infer that the system and lifeworld aspects are also allocated to particular action types. Since strategic and communicative action are mutually exclusive, analytical aspects would therefore *from the outset* be reified into different action domains. I made this mistake in 'Technology and Science as Ideology'; I have introduced the two-level concept of society in order to correct it.

Needless to say, mechanisms of system integration have an impact over and beyond contexts of communicative action. Of the four mechanisms I treated, three are neutral *vis-à-vis* the two action types, namely segmentary differentiation, stratification and political organization. Only the steering media of money and power demand a strategic stance on the part of the actors (albeit naturally not always at the highest level of purposive rationality). The mechanisms of social integration are, by contrast, defined in such a manner that they rest on the structures of action oriented toward reaching understanding. As the lifeworld, however, by no means offers an innocent image of 'power-free spheres of communication', the presuppositions for orientation toward reaching understanding are met without reservations, i.e. without deception and self-deception, only if the improbable conditions of non-repressive forms of life prevail. Otherwise, social integration proceeds via norms of domination which sublimate violence, on the one hand, and consensus formation in language which fulfils the conditions for latent strategic action, on the other. To this extent, social integration is also not allocated a priori to some specific type of action.[85]

However, this relatively clear picture changes if one takes that evolutionary trend into consideration which I have described as the 'uncoupling of system and lifeworld'. McCarthy has elucidated my proposition that both aspects of society, which are initially introduced merely as different perspectives adopted in observing the same phenomena, also acquire essentialist connotations for modern societies and open up a view of differently structured domains of social reality itself.

With regard to the aspect of system, societies as a whole constitute what Marx termed materialistically society's 'metabolic processes' with nature. This metaphor suggests that we should conceive of society in terms analogous to one large organism which reproduces itself via interchange with its organic and inorganic environments. The system-environment model also first proved its value in biology. In general systems theory it has been connected to cybernetics and research into artificial intelligence in such manner that it is more suited to applications in the social sciences than are the earlier biological equilibrium models which have played a somewhat doubtful role in sociology and in particular in theories of social evolution. Now, the characteristic constitutive for system formation is differentiation between internal and external perspectives, whereby the system is supposed itself to accomplish the maintenance of the system-environment distinction. My thesis of the uncoupling of lifeworld and system only implies that the dynamics – typical for the system character of society as a whole – of demarcation *vis-à-vis* a more complex environment *infiltrates* into *society itself*. The model of an organism suggests a harmonious relation between the parts and the whole. The system model, by contrast, submits that subsystems mark themselves off from one another in the course of processes of differentiation and define themselves reciprocally as environments: they comprise environments for one another, and the whole system also constitutes an environment for them. As long as one makes purely analytical use of the system model – as does Parsons, and as do his pupils Alexander and Münch in even stricter fashion – then random processes of differentiation can be described as the formation of subsystems in this manner. However, the minute one makes essentialist use of this model, as does Luhmann, then one can first talk of subsystems in the strict sense once such system-environment boundaries as society maintains as a whole *vis-à-vis* external and internal nature can be discerned *within* society. Yet, if we do not abandon the methodological primacy of the lifeworld, such subsystems cannot be identified independent of the inner-societal perception of these by that society's members themselves.

Such perceptions as allow one to infer the existence of subsystem-specific boundary-making first appear in modern societies. The philosophical discourse of modernity that I have analysed elsewhere is proof of how, in eighteenth-century Europe, the uncoupling of system and lifeworld within modern lifeworlds was interpreted as 'diremption' – as the splitting-up and objectification of the customary traditional forms of life. Hegel reacted to this by devising his notion of the 'positive' and with his conception of the ruptured totality of ethical life. Marx later proceeded more specifically from alienated industrial labour and class antagonisms and spoke of a 'real abstraction'. The main strand of social theory – from

Marx via Spencer and Durkheim to Simmel, Weber and Lukács – has to be understood as the answer to this entry of system-environment boundaries into society itself, to the genesis of this 'internal foreign country' – an expression Freud coined for the individual subconsciousness, for the person's id – which has been understood as the hallmark of modernity.

Now, a third level of what have since become autonomous functional contexts – media-steered subsystems – marks itself off from the level of simple interactions and that of organizational forms of precapitalist labour and premodern domination still perceptible within the lifeworld. It is not until the emergence of capitalism that an economic system arises which can be described (in an essentialist sense) as a subsystem with its own environments: it regulates internal (commercial) dealings as well as exchanges with the non-economic environments of both private households and the state now placed at a distance from it via its own, i.e. monetary channels. The institutionalization of wage labour and of the individual household of private employees, the institutionalization of the fiscal state and the client relation that obtains between citizen and public bureaucracies are *experienced* as *incursions* into the traditional forms of labour and life. Complementary *environments* arise to the extent that the production process is adjusted to function in terms of wage-earning employment organized along factory lines and the state apparatus is linked back to production via the taxes paid by employees and is thus gradually expanded into an all-embracing administration. We have to do with painful processes of dissolution and 'abstraction' from the point of view of these environments and from the vantage point of those who see themselves as having been placed at a distance from these changes and cut off from the new, objectified, organizationally-structured realities. Numerous controversies were triggered off by my gathering these processes together and concentrating them in the concept of the uncoupling of system and lifeworld.

Again, it is less the proposition of the uncoupling of system and lifeworld itself that is contentious, but rather the consequences the proposition has for the description of modern societies. The differentiation of subsystems which are integrated via the steering media of money and power is initially an observation that is historical in nature. Seen methodologically, the process is at the same time the precondition for a use of systems theory that is no longer solely analytical in thrust; rather, such a theory is now deployed to investigate 'real abstractions'. This usage has a descriptive and a critical side to it. I shall first detail the former with respect to the question as to whether this use actually results in the reification of an aspect which is only properly considered if treated as analytical.

Let us turn first to what is meant by this proposition. It describes the fact that, with the advent of the capitalist economic system and a state apparatus in which power linked to an office or person has been assimilated to the structure of a steering medium, action domains have differentiated out that are primarily systemically integrated. These are now integrated only indirectly through the agency of consensus mechanisms, namely to the extent that the legal institutionalization of steering media must be *coupled* to normative contexts of the lifeworld. In this context, the express-

ion 'norm-free sociality' led to misunderstandings. It is obvious that commercial enterprises and government offices, indeed economic and political
contexts as a whole make use of communicative action that is embedded in
a normative framework. Leaving aside the fact that the functional contexts
of media-steered subsystems cannot simply be marked off topologically
from one another and made to match certain institutional complexes, my
thesis amounts merely to the assertion that the integration of these action
systems is *in the final instance* not based on the potential for social
integration of communicative actions and the lifeworldly background
thereof – and these systems make use of both. It is not binding (bonding)
forces, but rather steering media that hold the economic and the administrative action system together. This is to be seen, among other things, from
the fact that these action domains are *constituted* in law rather than their
internal communicative structure merely being given a legal superstructure.
The case taken as standard here is always subject to the proviso of recourse
to prior formal regulation (whether it is the regulation in civil law of
commercial dealings between commodity owners or the quasiauthority
comprised by the regulation of internal dealings between members of the
organization).

In this respect, action domains which are primarily integrated socially
behave *asymmetrically*. However, the talk of the uncoupling of system and
lifeworld unfortunately also conjures up images of the lifeworld being
stripped of mechanisms of system integration. In this regard I am quilty of
a reifying use of language: the lifeworld is 'uncoupled solely from media-
steered subsystems, and of course not from the mechanisms of system
integration as a whole. Both (1) epistemic and (2) action-theoretic reasons
speak in favour of there being an historical trend toward the uncoupling of
'system' and 'lifeworld' in this asymmetrical sense.

1   Whereas one can study modern societies in general from the viewpoint
of both aspects, economic and political contexts can be adequately grasped
at this stage of system differentiation only as part of the description of
media-steered subsystems. They cannot be sufficiently explained in terms
of aspects of the lifeworld, as can be seen from the history of social theory.
This indisputable experience has, however, been overgeneralized by system functionalism. My critique of Parson's media theory was intended to
demonstrate that the concept of media developed using the case of exchange value can be applied, and then only in part, only to political power,
but not to value-commitments, influence, or even love, truth etc. One can,
therefore, define the lifeworld *negatively* as the totality of action domains
which cannot be bent to conform to a description of media-steered
subsystems.[86]

Nevertheless, system integration also extends throughout contexts of
communicative action; these remain accessible to an analysis conducted
from the viewpoint of system aspects, and require such an analysis.

2   *Action-theoretic* reasons also speak in favour of the real uncoupling
effect of steering media and the subsystems that have differentiated out
through their agency. Although social integration occurs via communica-

tive action, action domains of the lifeworld which are primarily integrated socially are, as I have already stressed, neither free of power nor free of strategic action. On the other hand, the steering medium mechanism of system integration clearly possesses an affinity to purposive-rational action orientations; such is revealed by an analysis of media-steered interaction.[87] In their capacity as special codes, steering media branch off from normal language. They are tailored to meet standard situations and, on the basis of a built-in structure of preferences, condition action decisions without resort having to be made to the resources of the lifeworld. This language, specialized and impoverished at once, disconnects action coordination from those relations to a lifeworldly totality via which communicative action remains bound up with culture, society and the person *as a whole*. Normally, the strategic actor retains his/her lifeworld at least as a fallback even if this has lost its coordinating efficacy; switching over to media-steered interactions, however, is accompanied by a specific 'de-worlding' effect which is experienced in the form of an objectification of social relations. The acting subject is able to retain his/her success-oriented and – in borderline cases – purposive-rational stance, but only under conditions of an *objective inversion of the ends set* and *the means* chosen, for the medium itself is now the transmitter of the respective subsystem's system-maintaining imperatives. This inversion of means and ends is experienced in the form of the reifying character of objectified social processes. I would thus miss the point if I were to continue to speak, as I did in earlier publications, of systems of purposive-rational action.[88] Media-guided interactions no longer embody an instrumental, but rather a functional form of reason.

Despite the action-theoretic characterization of steering media, the media-steered subsystems of other action domains cannot be demarcated in terms of action types. Strategic actions do not only occur here; and it is not only strategic actions that occur here. The steering media can only be grasped by referring to those sequences of interactions which produce and secure systemic integration. It is possible to identify this interwoven layer – of *direct* relevance for integration – within the network of interactions by reference to the characteristics of interaction mentioned above. These, however, are not suited for the task of demarcating media-steered subsystems as a whole. Other empirical indicators are available here – the constitutive legal form given to social relations and a level of organization at which organizational aims are detached from motivations of membership.

What remains are the objections made to the systems-theoretic concept of power. In my opinion, public administration, which must of course be separated from processes of legitimation and the public sphere as a sphere of the lifeworld, can be described in societies of our type as a subsystem operating as if it were a steering medium. Precisely the way political parties operate – 'extracting' mass loyalty from the public sphere – is an indication of the extent to which the administrative system has made will-formation in the political public sphere an objectified part of its evironment. I cannot answer the interesting objections raised by McCarthy in detail, especially as empirical investigation is needed to shed clear light on the matter in hand. I wish, however, to emphasize once again that according to my analysis the political system, owing to the nature of the medium of power and the way in which it is institutionally anchored in the lifeworld, remains far more dependent on its environments than does the economic system.

My attention has also been drawn to the fact that the necessarily schematic form the presentation in *The Theory of Communicative Action* ineluctably created the static impression that I believed the process by which these subsystems become independent had already come to an end. In fact, we have to do here with historical trends that are by no means linear; the model which I had in mind was Marx's analysis of the gradual permeation of life by the capitalist mode of production. The subsumption of living labour under the commodity form is an oversimplifying theoretical expression for infinitely multi-layered and ramified processes that are far removed from the limiting value of completely commodified labour power and, incidentally, also set processes of decommodification in motion, as Claus Offe has shown.

The objections raised by McCarthy and others ultimately made clear to me that the use that I believe I should make of systems-theoretic considerations must be specified more closely. Linking these back methodologically to the primacy of the analysis of lifeworld suffices to shield me from a now independent system functionalism that serves as a world view. And the concept of media is indispensable for the description of modern societies. However, I am by no means sure whether a surplus value will accrue to social theory from the most recent developments which systems theory has undergone and which have been labelled autopoiesis.[89] I react utterly pragmatically to the question McCarthy puts somewhat over-dramatically, namely how much must be 'borrowed' from systems theory if we are to be able to continue at the best possible level what Marx initiated with his critique of political economy.

To this point, mention has been made only of the descriptive thrust of an essentialist use of systems theory. I do not wish *per se* to link the *critical* thrust of such an analysis to the inversion of ends and means. To do so would be to provide a consistent translation of Marx, for he imputed a fetishizing effect to the switching of social action from an orientation toward use values over to one toward exchange values. What I do not see, however, is how a system rationality, be it the market-mediated rationality of the medium of money or the organization-mediated rationality of the power medium, can be criticized from this action-theoretic vantage point and then rejected for being inverted purposive rationality. Structural incompatibilities first arise between media-guided interactions and the conditions under which symbolic structures of the lifeworld have to reproduce. I justified this strong thesis, on the one hand, by arguing that the concept of media cannot be transposed on to the domains of cultural tradition, social integration and socialization, and, on the other, by outlining that these three functions can be fulfilled only via the medium of communicative action and not via the steering media of money and power: meaning can neither be bought nor coerced. To note that the action systems specialized in material reproduction have opened up to being steered by media is initially merely an empirical observation[90] and this immense process was certainly not 'painless'.

The gradual formation of media-steered subsystems can already be seen as an analogy to Marx's real abstractions; this does not in itself, however, give rise to pathological effects, which first result from endogenously generated systemic disparities (crises) being shifted into the lifeworld.[91] I therefore by no means paint a picture of the efficient functioning of 'self-propelling' subsystems, as Berger believes. The objections he raises to a linear diagnosis of our age which one-sidedly addresses the case of replacing the missing potential for reaching understanding with steering achievements of the monetary-administrative complex – i.e. which addresses the colonization of the lifeworld by systemic imperatives – are justified. Such an approach creates an ahistorical picture which blocks from sight the traces of a countervailing restriction of these imperatives by lifeworldly principles. My 'four stages of juridification' leave no doubts as to the success of these countertrends; yet, in view of the topical question how the 'crisis of the welfare state' can be solved productively, the contemporary trends, which Berger cursorily mentions, deserve a more thorough analysis.[92]

This brings me to one of the essential motives behind the disquiet of many of my leftist critics, namely the question whether the critical use of systems analysis does not in truth mean a rejection – dressed up as a criticism of normative conceptions of the socialist or even only radical democratic tradition. If this were the case, then I would of course not have found the energy to write such an intricate book. But this is not the place for confessions.

A theory of society which has renounced all the certainty of a philosophy of history without having renounced its claims to having a critical edge can perceive its *political* role to rest only in heightening, with somewhat sensitive diagnoses of the times, the attention we pay to the substantial ambivalencies displayed by the contemporary historical situation. Only a knowledge of structurally anchored developmental trends that run in opposite directions can help one to become aware of possibilities for practical intervention. My remarks on this at the end of a book on the foundations of critical theory of society could inevitably only be brief; the layout of the theory had to speak for itself. The proposition of the uncoupling of system and lifeworld leads to the description of mutually-contradictory tendencies. The one group of trends ensues from the – still class-specific – anchoring of the steering media in the lifeworld and presses for the implementation of lifeworldly imperatives in the form of restrictions imposed on the capitalist mode of operation in the economic system and the bureaucratic mode in the administrative system. The other group, the countertrends, overlay the lifeworld with forms of structurally-alien economic and administrative rationality. The former signifies a strengthening of 'the institutional framework that subjects system maintenance to the normative restrictions of the lifeworld,' the latter a consolidation of existing class structures and thus of 'a base that subordinates the lifeworld to the systemic constraints of material reproduction and thereby "mediatizes" it.'[93]

The prolongation of these colonizing tendencies points to a barbaric state which Marx had characterized in his day as the complete subsumption of the lifeworld under the imperatives of a production process which had been uncoupled from concrete labour and an orientation toward use values. I by no means opt for such a state when I emphasize the intrinsic evolutionary value exhibited *per se* by steering media such as money and power, i.e. irrespective of the class-specific distributory effects their institutionalization has. However, I believe for empirical reasons that there is no longer much prospect of the democratic reshaping from within of a differentiated economic system solely by means of worker self-management, in other words by switching its steering from money and organizational power *completely* over to participation. This by no means implies a defence of the capitalist labour market, which retains as the norm a linking of income and labour as well as lifelong, full-time occupation. I have dealt with the crisis of the welfare state in 'The New Obscurity'[94] and have attempted to draw conclusions from our experiences to date with the compromise at its heart. We are faced with the problem of how capabilities for self-organization can be developed to such an extent within autonomous public spheres that radical-democratic process of will-formation can come to have a decisive impact on the regulatory mechanisms and marginal conditions of media-steered subsystems in a lifeworld oriented toward use values, toward ends in general. This task involves holding the systemic imperatives of an interventionist state apparatus and those of an economic system in check, and is formulated in defensive terms. Yet, this defensive resteering will not be able to succeed without a radical and broadly effective democratization.

The normative criticism which McCarthy, Honneth and Joas make of what they presume are the conclusions to be drawn from my diagnosis of contemporary society proceed from a counter-model based in praxis philosophy. The latter cannot exist, whether one likes it or not, without adhering to the untenable premise that it must be possible to conceive of the autonomous self-steering of a complex society as self-consciousness on a large scale. This figure of thought does not, however, do justice to the pluralist traits of a decentred society.[95]

Hans-Peter Krüger also seems to orient his outline for a future 'integrative fusion of discursive practices into an overall social mode of communication' towards this idea; he would otherwise not call my attention so energetically back to Hegel at the end of his interesting essay. I am happy to see what is, to my knowledge, the first sign of a discursive reception of my work by colleagues in the GDR, whereas it was until now treated only polemically.

Krüger rightly points to a problem evidenced in every attempt to make fruitful use of genetic developmental psychology for a theory of society since the days of Lucien Goldmann. How can the cognitive structures which Piaget attributes to the individual consciousness simultaneously be construed as structures which are both from the outset transsubjective and built into objective Spirit? For my part, I conceived, without much ado, of the world view structures studied by Weber in his sociology of religion as the cultural embodiment of cognitive structures because this interpretation is, after all, not only already to be found latently in the middle period of Piaget's work, which takes up Durkheimian insights, but also has already been rendered even more plausible by Lévi-Strauss's studies. World views or cultural systems of interpretation belong to that part of the stock of lifeworldly knowledge which has already passed through communicative explication and has sedimented once more in habitualized background knowledge. The individual structures of consciousness acquired and developed in processes of socialization merely reflect these prior structures of the lifeworld. In other words, these do not need to 'bridge' some dualism or other.

The picture painted thus far is clearly still static and does not explain the social character of the corresponding processes of learning, particularly those of a moral nature. Max Miller, following Vygotsky (and taking up Oevermann's conception of an 'objective hermeneutics') has developed a sociological theory of learning that goes beyond Kohlberg's approach, yet refers in turn to ontogeny. The problem of the social institutionalization of new structures of consciousness which Krüger raises can probably be solved only by means of a theory of collective learning processes. Klaus Eder has now taken a notable step in this direction.[96]

Other misunderstandings that also crop up in Krüger's work have no doubt already been cleared up. System and lifeworld by no means behave towards one another as macrolevel to microlevel. The lifeworld continues to be the more comprehensive concept of order given that the media-steered subsystems are differentiated out from the social component of the lifeworld via the specialization of the universal medium of language. To this extent, the material reproduction of the lifeworld is not 'leased out' to systems theory. Production relations and class structures can in no fashion be adequately grasped by means of systems theory, because modes of production and social formations depend on the manner in which mechanisms for system integration are institutionally anchored in the lifeworld.[97]

What I have learned from Krüger's essay is that Marxist thought has returned to the approaches to language theory first taken by Vygotsky and Luria, for example by interpreting the central concept of the form of exchange in terms of communication theory. I take the interesting pointer to the writings of A. N. Leontyev and others as a stimulation to study a scholarly tradition that I have hitherto neglected. Yet Krüger's use of this body of thought, whereby he distinguishes between three analytical levels of communicative activities, practices and relations, does not quite make sense to me. One gains the impression from his deliberations that the concept of 'social mode of communication' confuses two things that must be kept separate: on the one hand, communications technologies which make possible higher-level, condensed forms of public communication, and, on the other, steering media which systemically regulate social information flow. It is perhaps the line of inquiry engendered by a socialist planning theory which suggests an overhasty connection between these qualitatively different forms of communication.[98]

With regard, finally, to my drawing on Marx's work – there can be exquisite disagreements about how to read a text, particularly where Marx's writings are concerned. Nothing was further from my mind than an exegesis of Marx; I was interested solely in comparing the transition from concrete to abstract labour with the switch from communicative action to media-steered interaction in such a manner that my analysis of social pathologies would become understandable as a study of 'real abstraction'. Furio Cerutti has defended Marx against the objections I had raised in a philologically well-founded article.[99] If one adopts his interpretation, then numerous, much more far-reaching points of convergence emerge – all the better.[100]

Johann P. Arnason's substantive essay draws on yet another Marx. He links the Marxian model of subsumption and Adorno's thoughts on an instrumental reason that has opened out into a negative totality with the approaches to a theory of totalitarianism developed by Hannah Arendt, Claude Lefort and Castoriadis. A new version of a theory of violence emerges from this which, seen through the eyes of dissidents, views the development of capitalism and that of bureaucratic socialism as subject to a sweeping 'logic of domination'. This constitutes an alternative to my explanatory approach, one which also places *different* phenomena at the centre of the stage. Competing theories have, of course, to be measured in terms of how well they explain which phenomena. Such a discussion would burst the framework of what has already become an overly extensive reply. It remains for us to await the book which will no doubt soon mature from Arnason's fruitful thoughts.

The motifs which Arnason goes into at the end of his essay under the heading of 'romanticizing countertrends' express themselves in doubts whether the concept of communicative reason is sufficiently developed in self-critical terms to do justice also to the polarity inherent in modern consciousness between the fulfilment of meaning and emancipation, between self-realization and autonomy.[101] These motifs have also been eloquently expressed in the neo-Structuralist critique of reason; they are also the driving force behind Ulf Matthiesen's highly original connection of Husserl's late philosophy and the sociology of the sacred that Bataille developed on the basis of Surrealism.[102] A concept of lifeworld charged, as it were, with heterological magma serves Matthiesen as a foil with which to provide an enjoyably readable critique of what he claims is a communication-theoretic appropriation of basic concepts from social phenomenology that remains bound to rationalism.

I hope that my lectures published meanwhile on the philosophical discourse of modernity provide an answer to such objections as are raised against the purported purism even of a form of reason that is embodied in language. The neo-conservative suspicions which K. H. Ilting, M. Kriele, H. Lübbe, G. Rohrmoser, R. Spaemann and B. Willms have voiced since the mid-1970s cannot be accorded the same status as the objections which stem from a radical critique of reason. My thanks go to Herbert Scheit who, with great patience, has surveyed these neo-conservative objections – treated as the misgivings of the political police – and disarmed them,[103] although the premiss from which they all proceed is not applicable: I have never had the false ambition of wishing to develop something like a normative politicial theory from the principle of discourse.

Bibliographical Note

The following essays have appeared in periodicals:

Jeffrey Alexander, 'Habermas's New Critical Theory: Its Promise and Problems', *American Journal of Sociology*, 91 (1985–6), pp. 400–24.

Johannes Berger, 'Jürgen Habermas, *Theorie des Kommunikativen Handelns*', *Telos*, 57 (1983), pp. 194–205 (an abridged version of the text reproduced here).

Hans Joas, 'The Unhappy Marriage of Hermeneutics and Functionalism', *Praxis International*, 8 (1988), pp. 34–51 (an abridged version of the text reproduced here; Translator: Raymond Meyer).

Thomas McCarthy, 'Complexity and Democracy, or the Seducements of Systems Theory', *New German Critique*, 35 (1985), pp. 353–65.

Herbert Schnädelbach, 'Transformation der Kritischen Theorie', *Philosophische Rundschau*, 29 (1982), pp. 161–78.

All the other essays were written specially for this volume.

Notes

NOTES TO CHAPTER 2

1 Cf. Durkheim's critique of Mead's terminology in Habermas, *The Theory of Communicative Action (TCA)*, vol. II (Boston, 1987), pp. 57–62.

2 For a critique of Parsons see, amongst others, ibid., p. 234. Parsons does not succeed in allocating the lifeworld an appropriate position in his systems theory. Despite his point of departure, which stresses the primacy of action theory, 'Parsons dispensed with introducing the systems concept via the theory of action.'

3 Cf. the discussion of lifeworld in ibid., p. 119.

4 Cf. Marvin Minsky, *Computation* (Englewood Cliffs, N.J., 1967), p. 105.

5 Cf. the process of juridification. Cf. also the discussion in *TCA*, vol. II, ch. 6.2.

6 Cf. the example given by Ernst Tugendhat: a search is made for people on a mountainside who answer 'here' when asked where they are. The answer is nonsensical if we have to do with a radio-link. Cf. E. Tugendhat, *Traditional and Analytical Philosophy: Lectures on the Philosophy of Language* (Cambridge, 1982), Lecture 4.

7 Predominantly in his discussion of Mead in *TCA*, vol. II, ch. 1, in particular pp. 40–2.

8 In this context, Piaget perhaps possesses a theory both better than and unlike Mead's: the fact that I adopt the perspective of the other person to my mind presupposes that I have already identified *my* perspective. Perhaps Piaget is right, and at the beginning the two perspectives are not distinct from one another. According to him, 'egocentricism' means first of all ignoring your perspective and then ignoring my own perspective, precisely because the child does not yet perceive a clear difference.

9 Cf., for example, *TCA*, vol. II, pp. 87–92.

10 Cf. the critique of Weber in ibid., pp. 323–6.

11 Cf. Jürgen Habermas, *Moral Consciousness and Communicative Action*, tr. Shierry Nicholsen Weber and Christian Lenhardt (Cambridge, Mass., 1990), pp. 43–115.

12 Cf. *TCA*, vol. II, p. 183.

13 Cf. ibid., p. 109.

14 Cf. also Charles Taylor, 'Die Motive einer Verfahrensethik', in W. Kuhlmann (ed.), *Moralität und Sittlichkeit* (Frankfurt, 1986), pp. 101–35.

15 Cf. *TCA*, vol. II, pp. 146–8.

16 Cf. also Charles Taylor, 'Neutralität in der politischen Wissenschaft' in *idem*, *Erklärung und Interpretation in der Wissenschaft vom Menschen* (Frankfurt, 1974) [*Explanation of Behaviour* (London, 1964)], pp. 14–64.

17 Cf. Charles Taylor, 'Legitimation crisis?' in *idem*, *Philosophy and the Human Sciences: Philosophical Papers 2* (Cambridge, 1985), pp. 248–88.

NOTES TO CHAPTER 3

1 J. Habermas, *The Theory of Communicative Action (TCA)*, vol. II (Boston, 1987), p. 398.

2 *TCA*, vol. I, p. 318; cf. J. Habermas, 'Erläuterungen zum Begriff des kommunikativen Handelns' in: *Vorstudien und Ergänzungen zur Theorie des kommunikativen Handelns (VE)* (Frankfurt, 1984), pp. 571–606, here pp. 600 and 606.

3 J. Habermas, 'Replik auf Einwände', in *VE*, pp. 475–570, here pp. 521, 539, 559; cf. *TCA*, vol. I, pp. 73 and 363 and Habermas, 'Philosophy as Stand-In and Interpreter', in *Moral Consciousness*, p. 19.

4 *VE*, p. 522.

5 Ibid.

6 E.g. *TCA*, vol. I, pp. 330 and 336f., and vol. II, pp. 148ff.; *VE*, pp. 522, 557, 589f. and 593.

7 *TCA*, vol. I, pp. 18 and 22.

8 At least four meanings of the expression 'validity-related' need to be distinguished more clearly from one another than Habermas has done: the *relation* of *many* speech acts to validity (and also of non-verbal forms of expression); the *orientation* to validity of *some* speech acts with which a claim to validity is made (assertions, imperatives, questions); the role of *statements thematizing* validity which, however, does not necessarily refer to argumentation; and the *explicative* function related to validity as is ascribed solely to statements in argumentation.

9 *TCA*, vol. I, pp. 444f.; cf. explanations in Habermas, 'Wahrheitstheorien' in *VE*, pp. 127–183, here especially pp. 174ff.

10 J. Habermas, 'Questions and Counterquestions' *Praxis International* 4 (1984), pp. 229–49, here pp. 237f.

11 *TCA*, vol. I, p. 41.

12 Moreover, Habermas's in my opinion unfair treatment of the indirect forms of speech stands in the way of sensitive treatment of the question of comprehensibility; its explanation cannot simply be left to a competing (intentionalistic) theory of meaning. Cf. *TCA*, vol. I, ch. 3, and *VE*, pp. 543f. and 549f.

13   *TCA*, vol. I, pp. 24f.
14   With regard to the steps involved in such a differentiation, see M. Seel, *Die Kunst der Entzweiung. Zum Begriff der ästhetischen Rationalität* (Frankfurt, 1985), ch. 2 especially 2.b.
15   My presentation dispenses with consensus-theoretic premises and the equation of practical and moral rationality. In contrast, the orientation to utterance forms is also provided for by Habermas, cf. *TCA*, vol. I, pp. 39ff. and pp. 19ff., and *VE*, pp. 530 and 127ff.
16   Seel, *Kunst*, ch. 3.
17   An obvious example taken from the special theoretical context of philosophy: '. . . the central experience of the unconstrained unifying, consensus-bringing force of argumentative speech' which Habermas cites by way of illustration at the beginning of his book (*TCA*, vol. I, p. 10) cannot be explained theoretically in terms of its being this central experience. This does not constitute a flaw in Habermas's theory: it shows a limit(ation) of philosophical theory (or at least of its argumentative possibilities). The theorist has to translate this – his intuition – into assertions about the constitution in language of the social world (and into arguments that support these assertions). The experience gained in the contemporary lifeworld, if not the experience of a communicative life-form, then at least of that which is communicative (not only) in contemporary life-forms, could be addressed non-reductively only in the interpretation of aesthetic objects. The theory could only switch gears at this level to its disadvantage; the theorist can do so, of course, albeit not 'simply' (because aesthetic media of reflexion, unlike arguments, are not at hand), but rather by adopting the form of the aesthetic essay, but then he would no longer be speaking as a theorist.
18   *TCA*, vol. I, p. 318; cf. the explanatory passage in 'Wahrheitstheorien', *VE* pp. 174ff.
19   Habermas discusses the questions touched on here in his 'Discourse Ethics: Notes on a Program of Philosophical Justification' in *Moral Consciousness*, pp. 43–115, in particular p. 98ff., and in Über Moralität und Sittlichkeit: Was macht eine Lebensform "rational"?' in H. Schnädelbach (ed.), *Rationalität* (Frankfurt, 1984), pp. 218–35; Habermas coined the conspicuous term of 'application discourse' in the lecture (given at the University of Bielefeld on 14 June 1985) on 'Moral und Sittlichkeit – treffen Hegels Einwände gegen Kant auch auf die Diskursethik zu?'
20   *TCA*, vol. I, p. 444, notes; although Habermas speaks at this point only of dependencies in the acceptability of various speech act (with the same propositional content), in the systemics of his theory this model is impermissibly (because only seemingly analogous) transposed to the relationship of the forms of argumentation (with structurally different patterns).
21   *TCA*, vol. I, p. 364.
22   J. Derrida, *Writing and Difference*, tr. A. Bass (London, 1979), pp. 422–42, especially p. 423, and *On Grammatology*, tr. G. C. Spivak (Baltimore, 1977), Part I, especially pp. 17ff. and 87f.; 'Die différance' in Derrida, *Randgänge der Philosophie* (Frankfurt, Berlin and Vienna, 1976), pp. 6–37.
23   On the interpretation of the concept of rules presupposed by these remarks, see A. Wellmer, 'On the Dialectics of Modernity and Postmodernity', in *In*

Defence of Modernism, tr. David Midgley (Cambridge, 1988).

24 On the meaning of the faculty of judgement in the context of a critique of plural reason, cf. H. Schnädelbach, 'Bemerkungen über Rationalität und Sprache' in D. Böhler and W. Kuhlmann (eds), *Kommunikation und Reflexion* (Frankfurt, 1983), pp. 347–368.

25 This section associates concepts from the first version of the introduction with the critique of the faculty of judgement in I. Kant, *Werke*, ed. W. Weischedel (Wiesbaden, 1956), vol. V, pp. 171–232.

26 *TCA*, vol. I, p. 73.

27 Cf. R. Zimmermann, *Utopie-Rationalität-Politik: Zu Kritik, Rekonstruktion und Systematik einer emanzipatorischen Gesellschaftstheorie bei Marx und Habermas* (Freiburg and Munich, 1985), Part II, pp. 19ff., especially p. 21, and A. Wellmer, *Ethik und Dialog: Elemente des moralischen Urteils bei Kant und in der Diskursethik* (Frankfurt, 1986), pp. 140f.

NOTES TO CHAPTER 4

1 It is remarkable, for example, that in the comprehensive collection of critical essays on Habermas collected by J. B. Thompson and D. Held, *Habermas: Critical Debates* (London, 1982), there is only a single reference to the Habermas–Parsons link. It is Giddens ('Labour and Interaction', pp. 149–61 in ibid., p. 160) who notices and regrets the connection; he refers to the link, however, only in connection to Habermas' internalization theory, neglecting the much more important theme of normative evolution.

2 Thompson's fine essay in the collection he edited with Held first drew this statement to my attention.

3 For my own argument with Weber on these points, see 'The Dialectic of Individuation and Domination: Weber's Rationalization Theory and Beyond' in Sam Whister and Scott Lash (eds), *Max Weber, Rationality, and Modernity* (London, 1987), pp. 185–206.

4 Habermas explores here precisely the issue that was at the centre of Parsons' late work, *The American University* (Parsons and Platt, Cambridge, Mass., 1973). In that work Parsons argued that as modernization proceeds, the differentiated subsystems of societies increasingly become coordinated by different versions of the 'rationality' value. In fact, he suggested that this becomes the major mode of intersystem coordination. Parsons argued that cognitive rationality – the theoretical standard of empirical truth – was the cultural medium through which coordination occurred and that the university was the crucial institutional vehicle. The differentiated value and institutional spheres of modern society, then, are coordinated because each depends upon the university's 'outputs' of rationality, e.g. in the training of their personnel, the evaluations of their products and the justification of their performance. Parsons identified four different types of coordinating rationality: economic, political, integrative and value. On the one hand, this discussion indicates an extraordinary convergence on a detailed and profoundly significant empirical point. For example, like Parsons, Habermas pinpoints the crucial role that professionals play as mediators and carriers of modern rationality (*TCA*, vol. I, p. 253), and his emphasis on the

uncoerced equality of the communicative situation can be seen – in the light of this reference to professionals – as parallel to Parsons's later emphasis on the emergence of collegial in contrast to hierarchic and market organization in modern societies. (On this point, see Sciulli's far-reaching analysis of the Parsons/Habermas convergence, 'The Practical Groundwork for Critical Theory: Bringing Parsons to Habermas (and Vice-Versa)' in Alexander (ed.) *Neofunctionalism*, Los Angeles and London, 1985.) On the other hand, Parsons's understanding of rationality remains more cognitivist and limited than the one developed by Habermas.

5 Gadamer (*Truth and Method*, New York, 1975, p. 245) states the problem well, though his work does not go far toward resolving it:

Does the fact that one is set within various traditions mean really and primarily that one is subject to prejudices and limited in one's freedom? Is not, rather, all human existence, even the freest, limited and qualified in various ways? If this is true, then the idea of an absolute reason is impossible for historical humanity. Reason exists for us only in concrete, historical terms, i.e. it is not is own master, but remains constantly dependent on the given circumstances in which it operates.

NOTES TO CHAPTER 5

1 Hereafter cited as *TCA*.

2 Habermas does not go on to thematize how interests and interpretations are related to one another, or how interests are criticized and compensated through interpretations. He obviously assumes that the lifeworld background provides the necessary resources. In any case, consensusses are achieved because they solve the problems of action in the common interest of all parties involved (*TCA*, vol. I, pp. 88f.).

3 Habermas does explain at one point (*TCA*, vol. I, pp. 89f., n. 25) that, when making use of normatively regulated action, one at least has to act *as if* the legitimacy of norms of action were secured; however, his theory of norms unequivocally claims to do more than this.

4 This in particular links Durkheim's theories to Descartes, a connection often mentioned in the literature.

5 Mead's conception of phylogeny is generally retained. Nevertheless, this contains strategic references for a reconstruction which can be redeemed from the vantage of an anthropologically substantiated point of departure. Cf. in particular G. H. Mead, *Mind, Self and Society* (Chicago 1934 [1965]), pp. 227ff.

6 I do not go into Habermas's reference to ritualization in the domain of animals here. Based on a closer examination of the mechanism of ethological ritualization, it would seem fruitless to deploy it for the formation of rites in one way or another.

7 E. Durkheim, *Soziologie und Philosophie* (Frankfurt, 1967), p. 105.

8 The idea that subjectivity takes shape in the sphere of religion – or more precisely, based on the subjectivity of gods – is or was a view widespread in Starnberg in other fields as well. Cf. R. Döbert, *Systemtheorie* (Frankfurt,

1973), pp. 103 and 113. This inverts the relationship and falls behind Feuerbach in terms of a critique of religion, even if Feuerbach was not in a position to do justice to the subject matter in the form of a systematic reconstruction.

9   Mead, *Mind*, p. 265.

10   Cf. also Habermas, *Moral Consciousness and Communicative Action*, p. 25.

11   For more detailed comments on the structure of legitimation, see Dux, *Strukturwandel der Legitimation* (Freiburg, 1976), and on the legitimation of early forms of domination, Dux, 'Egalität als Selbstbehauptung. Zur Genese von Norm und Recht', *Quaderni Fiorentini. Per la Storia del Pensiero Giuridico Moderno*, 13 (1984), pp. 191ff. Intellectuals have always overestimated the legitimacy of a social order and its individual norms. As described above, Habermas believes that the viability of a lifeworld simply requires an awareness that one lives in legitimated relationships – this is decisively devalued by our own lifeworld: I simply cannot think of a single domain of life whose life-forms could be ascribed outright legitimacy – even though an awareness certainly does exist of that at least problematical legitimacy involved in conducting everyday life. At the same time, life is being conducted in them. If one agrees with Habermas in defining the social world as the world of legitimately regulated relationships, then this social world has collapsed in the present day.

12   As we know, Habermas also draws on ontogeny for an understanding of historical development, but only for 'heuristic' reasons. Cf. Habermas, *Zur Rekonstruktion, des historischen Materialismus* (Frankfurt, 1976), p. 177. History, however, necessarily has to be created by drawing on ontogeny. On its systematic justification, cf. Dux, *Die Logik der Weltbilder. Sinnstrukturen im Wandel der Geschichte* (Frankfurt, 1982), pp. 54ff.

13   In his notorious work of 1943, K. Lorenz advanced precisely the opposite theory: namely that it is the innate forms of behaviour which have been dissolved; the triggering characteristics were preserved as patterns of judgement in the social domain ('Die angeborenen Formen möglicher Erfahrung', Zeitschr. f. Tierpsych., 5, pp. 235–409).

14   St J. Gould, *Ontogeny and Phylogeny* (Cambridge, Mass., 1977).

15   A. Jolly, *The Evolution of Primate Behaviour* (New York, 1972), p. 49.

16   A. Mitscherlich, *Auf dem Wege zur Vaterlosen Gesellschaft: Ideen zur Sozialpsychologie* (Munich, 1973), pp. 76ff., is worth reading on this point.

17   Mead perceived this, albeit only in a blurred interpretation. With neighbourly relationships in mind, he explains that it was 'a kind of generalization of the parental impulse or attitude and upon which all co-operative social behavior is more or less dependent' (*Mind*, pp. 228f.).

18   Cf. Mead, *Mind*, pp. 186ff. and 222ff.

19   On this point, cf. Dux, *Die Logik*, pp. 86ff. and 103ff.

20   Religious rites have nothing in common with the forms of ritualization that take place at the subhuman phase, e.g. among mallards, grey geese, etc. One has only to take a look at the formative process by means of which one or the other structures develop.

21   On the structure of expectation of interaction and, based on this, of norms, cf. Dux, *Rechtssoziologie* (Stuttgart, 1978), pp. 32ff.

22   Mead emphatically stressed that the fact that the social position taken by every

individual has been reflected on is the bond which actually engenders society; cf. *Mind*, p. 267, n. 12. Joas, 'George H. Mead' in D. Käsler (ed.), *Klassiker des soziologischen Denkens* (Munich, 1978), vol. II, p. 21, also refers to real cooperation as the process which actually forms the foundation of society in Mead's work.

23　Altruism can also be one reason that poses an obstacle to understanding moral problems – as shown by the answers of many of the women interviewed by Belenky and Gilligan. Cf. M. Belenky and C. Gilligan, 'Der Einfluß einer Abtreibungskrise auf die Moralentwicklung' in G. Lind et al. (eds), *Moralisches Urteilen und soziale Welt* (Weinheim and Basle, 1983).

24　The degree to which this question has still to be clarified is proved in an impressive manner by the so-called thesis of consonance between normative and psychological theory and, in other words, between philosophical pre-understanding and empirical development. Cf. Habermas, *Moral Consciousness*.

25　See, as representative of many, R. Lee and I. De Vere, 'Problems in the Study of Hunters and Gatherers' in *idem* (eds), *Man the Hunter* (New York, 1968 [1979]), p. 120.

26　Cf. for details, Dux, 'Egalität', pp. 174ff.

27　I hope to be able in the foreseeable future to submit an investigation of the process of the state's emergence and the formation of domination. An empirical case study which advances the current state of research a step further in essential respects has been made by Jürgen Biller with regard to the comparatively well documented emergence of the state in Orissa.

28　I am not able to discuss here the formation of the temple, the development of which is integrated into the formative process of domination and takes on various forms. It seems fairly certain that the formation of the temple is not the factor which actually advances the formation of domination, not even in Sumeria. In other contexts, it only played the role of stabilizing and securing domination. K. Eder, *Die Entstehung Staatlich organisierter Gesellschaften* (Frankfurt, 1976), holds a different view; cf. also Jürgen Biller, *Zur Entstehung von Herrschaft und Staat* (Freiburg, 1985).

29　Cf. T. Jacobson, 'Primitive Democracy in Ancient Mesopotamia', *Journal of Near Eastern Studies*, 2 (1943), p. 163.

30　It has often been noted that up to now morality referred to small interactive communities; K.-O. Apel, *Transformation der Philosophie* (Frankfurt, 1976), vol. II, p. 360.

31　Put explicitly by Eder, *Entstehung*; but precisely also Habermas, *TCA*, vol. II, pp. 172f.

NOTES TO CHAPTER 6

1　For the foundational significance of the problems of action and social order, see especially Jeffrey Alexander, *Theoretical Logic in Sociology*, vol. I: *Positivism, Presuppositions, and Current Controversies* (Berkeley, 1982). (The independence of the two problems from one another is discussed on pp. 117ff.) My approval of Alexander's formulation of this problem should not be construed as an expression of substantive agreement with his theoretical solutions. Cf.

my discussion of vol. II of his work in 'The Antinomies of Neo-functionalism, *Inquiry*, 31 (1988), pp. 471–94.

2 Jürgen Habermas, 'Labor and Interaction: Remarks on Hegel's Jena Philosophy of Mind', in *Theory and Practice* (Boston, 1973), pp. 142–69.

3 Axel Honneth, 'Arbeit und instrumentales Handeln' in Axel Honneth and Urs Jaeggi (eds), *Arbeit, Handlung, Normativität: Theorien des Historischen Materialismus* 2 (Frankfurt, 1980), pp. 185–233. For the connection between communicative abilities and human commerce with objects from the standpoint of the theory of socialization, see the chapter entitled 'Constitution of the Physical Object and Role-taking' in Hans Joas, *G. H. Mead: A Contemporary Re-examination of his Thought*, tr. Raymond Meyer (Cambridge, Mass., 1985).

4 Jürgen Habermas, 'The Classical Doctrine of Politics in Relation to Social Philosophy' in *Theory and Practice*, pp. 41–81. Thomas McCarthy, *The Critical Theory of Jürgen Habermas* (Cambridge, Mass., 1978).

5 Hannah Arendt, *The Human Condition* (Chicago, 1970).

6 Rüdiger Bubner, *Handlung, Sprache und Vernunft: Grundbegriffe praktischer Philosophie* (Frankfurt, 1982), pp. 61ff.

7 Isaiah Berlin, *Against the Current: Essays in the History of Ideas*, edited by Henry Harding (New York, 1980). Charles Taylor, *Hegel* (Cambridge, 1975). Habermas rejects the significance of this concept of action, objecting to it on empirical grounds, which are as such also questionable, in his 'A Reply to my Critics', in J. B. Thompson and D. Held (eds), *Habermas: Critical Debates* (London, 1983), pp. 219–83.

8 On this point, cf. my definitions of the concept of role in 'Role theories and socialization research' in H. J. Helle and S. N. Eisenstadt (eds), *Microsciological Theory* (Berkeley, 1985), pp. 37–53.

9 As one example among many, cf. John Dewey, 'The Reflex Arc Concept in Psychology' in John Dewey, *The Early Works*, vol. 5 (Carbondale, 1972), pp. 96–109. From this viewpoint, cf. the excellent analysis in Eduard Baumgarten, *Die geistigen Grundlagen des amerikanischen Gemeinwesens*, vol. II (Frankfurt, 1938), pp. 282ff. One of the few sociologists who have taken up the critique of the teleological interpretation of action, although with a very different end in mind than the one pursued here, is Niklas Luhmann, *Zweckbegriff und Systemrationalität* (Frankfurt, 1973), pp. 18ff.

10 This is, in my opinion, the *theoretically* interesting theme of Ulrich Oevermann's repeated critique of Habermas.

11 Cf. Harald Wenzel, 'Mead und Parsons' in Hans Joas (ed.), *Das Problem der Intersubjektivität* (Frankfurt, 1985), pp. 26–59.

12 Emile Durkheim, *The Elementary Forms of the Religious Life*, tr. J. W. Swain (London, 1976).

13 Emile Durkheim, *Pragmatisme et sociologie* (Paris, 1955).

14 Emile Durkheim and Marcel Mauss, 'De quelques formes primitives de classification' in Emile Durkheim, *Journal sociologique* (Paris, 1969), pp. 395–461.

15 I have treated this question in detail in 'Durkheim et le pragmatisme. La psychologie de la conscience et la constitution sociale des catégories' *Revue française de sociologie*, 25 (1984), pp. 560–81.

16 Johannes Berger, 'Die Versprachlichung des Sakralen und die Entsprachlichung

der Ökonomie', *Zeitschrift für Soziologie*, 2 (1982), pp. 353–65, reprinted in
this volume, pp. 165–80: Veit-Michael Bader, 'Schmerzlose Entkoppelung von
System und Lebenswelt? Engpässe der Theorie des kommunikativen Handelns
von Jürgen Habermas,' *Kennis en Methode* 7 (1983), pp. 329–355; Axel Honneth, *Kritik der Macht: Reflexionsstufen einer kritischen Gesellschaftstheorie*
(Frankfurt, 1985).

17 Using the theory of action, it can be shown that human symbolizing operations make it possible for human beings to cooperate and to communicate
without being present together in the same place at the same time.

18 This seems to me to be the point correctly made in the article by Alfred
Bohnen, 'Handlung, Lebenswelt und System in der soziologischen Theorie-
bildung: Zur Kritik der Theorie des kommunikativen Handelns von Jürgen
Habermas', *Zeitschrift für Soziologie*, 13 (1984), pp. 191–203.

19 Robert K. Merton, *Societal Theory and Social Structure* (London, 1964); Talcott Parsons, *The Social System* (London, 1951), p. 30, n. 5.

20 John Dewey, *The Public and Its Problems* (New York, 1927); and *Reconstruction in Philosophy* (New York, 1950).

21 See also Wolfgang van den Daele, 'Unbeabsichtigte Folgen' sozialen Handelns:
Anmerkungen zur Karriere des Themas' (and the other contributions on this
topic) in Joachim Matthes (ed.), *Lebenswelt und soziale Probleme: Verhand-
lungen des 20. Deutschen Soziologentages zu Bremen 1980* (Frankfurt, 1981),
pp. 237ff.

22 Max Weber, 'Über einige Kategorien der verstehenden Soziologie' in *Gesammelte Aufsätze zur Wissenschaftslehre* (Tübingen, 1973), 4th edition, pp. 427–
74. Donald N. Levine has written an interesting essay from the standpoint of
the rationality of types of order in Weber's theory, namely 'Rationality and
Freedom: Weber and Beyond', *Sociological Inquiry*, 51 (1981), pp. 5–25.

23 Niklas Luhmann, 'Zweck–Herrschaft–System: Grundbegriffe und Prämissen
Max Webers' in Renate Mayntz (ed.), *Bürokratische Organisation* (Cologne,
1968), pp. 36–55, and Luhmann's *Zweckbegriff und Systemrationalität* (Frankfurt, 1973).

24 In that case, Husserl would be an action theorist and utilitarianism or the
subjective theory of value a theory of order in economics.

25 I go into Habermas's interpretation of Mead in more detail in my introduction
to *Das Problem der Intersubjektivität*, pp. 7–25.

26 George Herbert Mead, *Gesammelte Aufsätze*, vol. 2 (Frankfurt 1983), pp. 361–
482.

27 Talcott Parsons, *The Structure of Social Action* [1937] (New York, 1968), here
pp. 250ff.

28 In his late essay on Cooley, Parsons explains that the concept of action is to be
introduced on an analytical level which presupposes neither the individual nor
an acting collective as a reference. Talcott Parsons, 'Cooley and the Problem of
Internalization' in Albert Reiss (ed.), *Cooley and Sociological Analysis* (Ann
Arbor, 1968), pp. 48–67.

29 Richard Münch, 'Von der Rationalisierung zur Verdinglichung der Lebenswelt?', *Soziologische Revue*, 5 (1982), pp. 390–7. Cf. also Münch, *Theorie des
Handelns* (Frankfurt, 1982) and my discussion of this book, 'Handlungstheorie

und das Problem sozialer Ordnung', *Kölner Zeitschrift für Soziologie und Sozialpsychologie*, 36 (1984), pp. 165–72.

30 This is true, for example, of Parsons's emphasis on the difference between professionalization and bureaucratization.

31 At this point, reflections about the consequences of discourse ethics for the judgement of the rationality of types of social order are called for.

32 David Lockwood, 'Social Integration and System Integration', in G. Zollschan and W. Hirsch (eds), *Explorations in Social Change* (Boston, 1964), pp. 244–57; Nicos Mouzelis, 'Social and System Integration: Some Reflections on a Fundamental Distinction', *British Journal of Sociology*, 15 (1974), pp. 395–409; Ramesh Mishra, 'System Integration, Social Action and Change: Some Problems in Sociological Analysis', in *Sociological Review*, 30 (1982), pp. 5–22.

33 Habermas himself uses such an argumentation against Horkheimer and Adorno (*TCA*, vol. II, p. 490).

34 Jürgen Habermas, *On the Logic of the Social Sciences*, tr. Shierry Weber Nicholsen and Jerry A. Stark (Cambridge, Mass., 1989).

35 Anthony Giddens, 'Functionalism: Après la lutte', *Social Research*, 43 (1976), pp. 352–66. Extremely interesting from this standpoint is the controversy about Jon Elster's critique of functionalism in *Theory and Society*, 11 (1982), pp. 453–539, with contributions from Jon Elster, G. A. Cohen, P. van Parijs, John E. Roemer, Johannes Berger and Claus Offe, and Anthony Giddens.

36 An exemplary presentation of the theory of 'negotiated order' can be found in Anselm Strauss et al., 'The Hospital and Its Negotiated Order' in Eliot Freidson (ed.), *The Hospital in Modern Society* (New York, 1963), pp. 147–69. For a review of the relevant literature, see David Maines, 'Social Organization and Social Structure in Symbolic Interactionist Thought', *Annual Review of Sociology*, 3 (1977), pp. 235–59. Also relevant to this topic are the political philosophy of Antonio Gramsci and the interesting attempt by Amitai Etzioni, *The Active Society* (New York, 1971).

37 Jürgen Habermas, 'Können komplexe Gesellschaften eine vernünftige Identität ausbilden?', in Habermas and Dieter Henrich, *Zwei Reden* (Frankfurt, 1974), pp. 23–84, above all, pp. 57ff.

38 Perhaps I should make it clear that I am not condemning social-scientific functionalism entirely. However, the relative success of its models can also be accounted for and appropriated within a different theoretical framework.

39 George Herbert Mead, *The Philosophy of the Act* (Chicago, 1938), pp. 26ff.; Georg Lukács, *Die Eigenart des Ästhetischen*, 2 vols (Neuwied, 1963); Agnes Heller, *Everyday Life*, translated by George Campbell (Boston, 1984). (See also my introduction to the German edition of Heller's work (Frankfurt, 1978), pp. 7–23).

40 Talcott Parsons and Edward A. Shils (eds), *Toward a General Theory of Action* (New York, 1962); Talcott Parsons, *The Social System* (London, 1951).

41 Interesting objections to Habermas's introduction of the concept of the life-world into his argumentation can be found in Herbert Schnädelbach, 'Transformation der kritischen Theorie', *Philosophische Rundschau* 29 (1982), pp. 161–178, reprinted pp. 7–22 above.

276   *Notes*

42 See note.[16] Also worth reading is Otto Kallscheuer, 'Auf der Suche nach einer politischen Theorie bei Jürgen Habermas', in *Ästhetik und Kommunikation*, 12 (1981), no. 45/6, pp. 171–82.
43 With regard to Habermas's interpretation of Marx, I should at least like to point out that, as a rule, Marx is not criticized for his lack of understanding of capitalism's civilizing role, as he is by Habermas, but rather for exaggerating that role.

NOTES TO CHAPTER 7

1 J. Habermas, 'Technology and Science as "Ideology",' in *Toward a Rational Society* (Boston, 1970), pp. 81–122. Here p. 106.
2 J. Habermas, N. Luhmann, *Theorie der Gesellschaft oder Sozialtechnologie?* (Frankfurt, 1971), hereafter cited as *TGST*.
3 *Legitimation Crisis*, tr. Thomas McCarthy (Boston, 1975), pp. 117ff.; hereafter cited as *LC*.
4 'Können komplexe Gesellschaften eine vernünftige Identität ausbilden?' in J. Habermas and D. Henrich, *Zwei Reden* (Frankfurt, 1974), pp. 23–84; partially translated into English as 'On Social Identity', Telos, 19 (1974), pp. 91–103.
5 Two vols (Boston, 1984 and 1987), cited as *TCA*. Page numbers in parentheses in the text will refer to volume II. The translations in this chapter do not correspond exactly to the published version.
6 *The Differentiation of Society* (New York, 1982), p. 78.
7 *Zwei Reden*, p. 60.
8 *LC*, p. 8.
9 *TGST*, pp. 149ff.
10 Ibid., p. 151.
11 Ibid., p. 164.
12 Ibid., pp. 165–66.
13 W. Buckley, 'Society as a Complex Adaptive System' in W. Buckley (ed.), *Modern Systems Research for the Behavioral Scientist* (Chicago, 1968), p. 497. Buckley, like Habermas, seeks to combine the two levels of analysis.
14 Ibid., p. 504.
15 Ibid., pp. 504–5. The study, by Anselm Strauss and others, appeared in E. Freidson (ed.), *The Hospital in Modern Society* (New York, 1963). One might also think here of Foucault's studies of the asylum, the clinic, and the prison, of Goffman's study of asylums, of the numerous studies by ethnomethodologists of practical reasoning in organizational settings of all sorts, and so on.
16 Egon Bittner, 'The Concept of Organization', *Social Research*, 32 (1965), pp. 239–55; reprinted in R. Turner (ed.), *Ethnomethodology* (Harmondsworth, 1974), pp. 69–81, here pp. 76–8.
17 'On the Concept of Political Power' in *Sociological Theory and Modern Society* (New York, 1967), pp. 297–354, here p. 308.
18 T. Parsons, '"Voting" and the Equilibrium of the American Political System' in *Sociological Theory and Modern Society*, pp. 223–63, here pp. 227ff.
19 Cf. *The Differentiation of Society*, pp. 150ff.
20 Ibid., p. 153.
21 Ibid., p. 154.
22 *LC*, pp. 134ff.

23 *LC*, pp. 33ff.

24 The two traditions have been brought together with great effect by Claus Offe, with whom Habermas shares many basic ideas on the nature and functioning of the modern state. See for instance Offe's *Contradictions of the Welfare State* (Cambridge, Mass., 1984).

25 Habermas classifies the latter as 'empirical' rather than 'rational' motivations. But they are no less a matter of orientations and not of results.

26 Thus Thomas Luckmann's remark, cited by Habermas on p. 311, to the effect that the objective meaning of action in specialized institutional domains typically does not coincide with its subjective meaning for the individual actor, could apply as well to actions whose point was known only to superiors.

27 As the unending flow of studies on the social psychology, politics (in the usual sense), human relations etc., of large organizations testifies. There is no obvious reason for drawing a sharp line between 'the communicative engendering of power' and its 'acquisition and maintenance', on the one hand, and 'rule or the exercise of power', on the other, such that the first two are to be studied by means of action theory, the last by systems theory – as Habermas does in 'Hannah Arendt: On the Concept of Power' in *Philosophical-Political Profiles*; tr. Frederick Lawrence (Cambridge, Mass., 1983), pp. 180–1.

28 *TGST*, p. 161.

29 Ibid., p. 231.

30 Ibid., pp. 144–5.

31 *LC*, pp. 123–4.

32 Cf. C. B. Macpherson, *The Life and Times of Liberal Democracy* (Oxford, 1977).

33 *LC*, pp. 130ff.

34 *LC*, p. 138.

35 Cf. *TGST*, p. 274; *LC*, p. 139.

36 J. Habermas, *Communication and the Evolution of Society* (Boston, 1978), p. 174. It is obvious that the same holds true for social organization.

37 *LC*, p. 130.

38 *TGST*, pp. 144–5.

39 *On the Logic of the Social Sciences*, pp. 77–8.

40 Thus in his introduction to organization theory, *Organizations: Structure and Process* (Englewood Cliffs, 1977), Richard Hall notes that: 'Few researchers have the tools or the ability to take into account all the various components that must be included in even a relatively simple open systems model' (p. 59). A problem he mentions shortly thereafter suggests, however, that this is more than just a question of tools and ability. He notes that the behaviour of organizations usually changes when they are threatened: 'The power of the external pressures and threats is the key variable' (p. 63). 'Unfortunately', he adds, 'there are no available systematic measures of the power of such threats' (ibid.). (I have not been able to learn whether one has been discovered in the meantime.)

41 In their summary of the different perspectives on organization theory, J. E. Haas and T. E. Drabek, *Complex Organizations: A Sociological Perspective* (New York, 1973), write of the open systems approach: 'Terms like "boundary", "adaptation", "feedback", and the like are useful as organizing concepts,

but difficult to use operationally. Predictive statements are hard to make ... Empirical studies that would sharpen the concepts and test some of the hypothesized relationships are almost totally absent' (pp. 92–3). On viewing organizations as natural (adaptive) systems, they quote George E. Homans as saying: 'We have a "language without any sentences" ' (p. 53). And they add: 'The "words" in that language remain very vague – perhaps impossible to make operational' (ibid.).

42 Haas and Drabek, *Complex Organizations*, pp. 52–3. Though Habermas wants to combine the inside and outside perspectives *in general*, he seems to consign formal organizations to a systems analysis in which neither formal structures nor informal relationships play much of a role.

43 D. Silverman, *The Theory of Organizations* (London, 1970), p. 68. He cites R. Mayntz, 'The Study of Organizations', *Current Sociology*, 13 (1964), in support of this view.

44 *The Rules of Sociological Method* (Chicago, 1938), p. 90, quoted in St. Mennell, *Sociological Theory: Uses and Unities* (New York, 1974), p. 156.

45 Mennell, *Sociological Theory*, p. 89.

46 *Zwei Reden*, pp. 66ff.

47 For instance, in his discussion of new social movements on pp. 395–6.

48 'The New Obscurity: The Crisis of the Welfare State and the Exhaustion of Utopian Energies' in Habermas, *The New Conservatism* (Cambridge, Mass., 1989), pp. 48–70, here pp. 64 and 67. Compare the essay by Claus Offe, 'Competitive Party Democracy and the Keynesian Welfare State' in *Contradictions of the Welfare State*, pp. 179–206, esp. 188ff.

49 I have focused on the political system. Similar considerations could be developed with regard to the economy. For example: Are interactions within large-scale economic organizations coordinated solely by administrative power? By power and money? Should they be? Are market relations steered solely by money? By money and administrative (government) power? Should they be?

50 *Knowledge and Human Interests* (Boston, 1971), pp. 254ff.; *Logic* pp. 182ff.

51 *Logic*, p. 1.

52 Ibid., pp. 77–9.

53 See the essays collected in *Theory and Practice* (Boston, 1973).

NOTES TO CHAPTER 8

1 See J. Habermas, *The Theory of Communicative Action* (*TCA*), vol. I, pp. 144f., 150f., 327ff., 332–7, 341ff., 357f., vol. II, pp. 119–23, 137–145, 148, 151–5, 173, 179–87, 202f., 260–85, 313–8, 374–8.

2 See ibid., vol. I, pp. 144f., 341–4, 397f., vol. II, pp. 166–9, 173, 185f., 202f., 301–5, 313–7, 332–43, 359–62, 374–8, 401ff. Referring to earlier writings by Habermas, H. Holzer 'accepted (his conception) as a research programme rich in perspectives' and despite his basic objections to Habermas's attempt at a reconstruction of historical materialism, noted that coming to terms with his work would be helpful in 'rendering more precise the developmental theory of historical materialism' (H. Holzer, *Evolution oder Geschichte?* (Berlin (GDR), 1979), pp. 130 and 190).

3   On (a) as a whole, see *TCA*, vol. I, pp. 8–42, 67–74, 178–85, 236–42 and the 'First Intermediate Reflections'.

4   On (b) as a whole, *TCA*, vol. II, pp. 23–7, 107–11, 113–52.

5   On (c) as a whole, ibid., pp. 153–97, 263–81, 301–31.

6   On (d) as a whole, ibid., pp. 283–7, 301–31.

7   Cf. ibid., pp. 343–57, 374–8, 389–403.

8   Subsequent (brief) references to *TCA* will be given in the text.

9   Cf. S. Toulmin, *Kritik der kollektiven Vernunft* (Frankfurt, 1978), pp. 568–82; *Knowing and Acting* (New York and London, 1976), pp. 285–95.

10 Cf. T. Kesselring, *Piagets genetische Erkenntnistheorie und Hegels Dialektik* (Frankfurt, 1979); P. Damerow, 'Handlung und Erkenntnis in der genetischen Erkenntnistheorie Piagets und in der Hegelschen Logik', in W. R. Beyer (ed.), *Hegel-Jahrbuch 1977/1978* (Cologne, 1979).

11 Cf. M. Theunissen in H. F. Fulda, R.-P. Horstmann and M. Theunissen, *Kritische Darstellung der Metaphysik* (Frankfurt, 1980), p. 90.

12 L. M. Batkin, *Die historische Gesamtheit der italienischen Renaissance* (Dresden, 1979), p. 88.

13 J. Habermas, *Moral Consciousness and Communicative Action*, tr. S. Nicholsen Weber and C. Lenhardt (Cambridge, Mass., 1990) p. 178.

14 In the sense of the 'substance of form' as used by G. W. F. Hegel, *Wissenschaft der Logik* II (Frankfurt, 1972), pp. 265–7. Cf. W. Krohn, ' "Wissen ist Macht": Zur Soziogenese eines neuzeitlichen wissenschaftlichen Geltungsanspruches' in K. Bayerts (ed.), *Wissenschaftsgeschichte und wissenchaftliche Revolution* (Cologne, 1981).

15 J. Piaget, *Structuralism*, (London, 1971).

16 H. J. Sandkühler, *Praxis und Geschichtsbewußtsein* (Frankfurt, 1973).

17 Cf. Habermas's reply to the critique of his conception in philosophical praxis by A. Heller in J. B. Thompson and D. Held (eds), *Habermas: Critical Debates* (London, 1982), pp. 220f.

18 P. Weiss, *Ästhetik des Widerstands* (Berlin (GDR), 1983).

19 W. Motsch and D. Viehweger (eds), *Richtungen der modernen Semantikforschung* (Berlin (GDR), 1983); W. Heinemann, *Negation und Negierung, Handlungstheoretische Aspekte einer linguistischen Kategorie* (Leipzig, 1983); W. Stelzner, *Epistemische Logik* (Berlin (GDR), 1984).

20 M. Bierwisch, 'Psychologische Aspekte der Semantik natürlicher Sprachen' in: Motsch and Viehweger, *Richtungen* pp. 38ff.

21 Ibid., p. 51.

22 See W. Hartung, 'Gesellschaftlichkeit der Sprache' in *Deutsche Zeitschrift für Philosophie*, 11 (1981), pp. 1308–10; W. Hartung and H. Schönfeld, *Kommunikation und Sprachvariation* (Berlin, 1981).

23 See, J. Berger, 'The Linguistification of the Sacred and the Delinguistification of the Economy', in this volume, pp. 165–80.

24 M. Theunissen, *Sein und Schein* (Frankfurt, 1978).

25 V. A. Vazjulin, *Logika 'Kapitala' K. Marx* (Moscow, 1968); J. Zeleny, *Die Wisschaftslogik bei Marx und 'Das Kapital'* (Berlin (GDR), 1968); E. Angehrn, *Freiheit und System bei Hegel* (Berlin, 1977). H. H. Holz, *Natur und Gehalt spekulativer Sätze* (Cologne, 1980), and *Dialektik und Widerspiegelung* (Cologne, 1983).

26   U. Eco, *A Theory of Semiotics* (Bloomington, 1976).

27   K. Marx, *Theorien über den Mehrwert* in Marx and Engels, *Werke* (*MEW*), vol. XXVI, Parts I–III (Berlin (GDR), 1965).

28   Marx, *Economic and Philosophic Manuscripts of 1844*, tr. Martin Milligan (Moscow, 1959); Marx, *Grundrisse*, tr. M. Nicolaus (Harmondsworth, 1973).

29   Marx's correspondence from 1862 to 1866, especially with Kugelmann, indicates that his research plan was drastically cut down to a part that could be put into practice in his lifetime (*MEW*, vols XXX and XXXI, Berlin (GDR), 1972).

30   Marx, *Capital*, vol. III, tr. David Fernbach (Harmondsworth, 1981).

31   Ibid. and vol. I, tr. B. Fowkes' (Harmondsworth, 1976).

32   Marx, *Grundrisse*, pp. 682–704; *Capital*, vol. I, pp. 617f.

33   See A. K. Pokrytan, *Das Historische und das Logische* (Berlin (GDR), 1981).

34   See G. Stiehler, *Gesellschaft und Geschichte* (Berlin (GDR), 1974), and *Widerspruchsdialektik und Gesellschaftsanalyse* (Berlin (GDR), 1977); E. Engelberg and W. Küttler (eds), *Formationstheorie und Geschichte* (Berlin (GDR), 1978).

35   See *inter alia* L. Kühne, 'Zum Begriff und zur Methode der Erforschung der Lebensweise' in *Weimarer Beiträge*, 8 (1978); I. Dölling, 'Zur Vermittlung von gesellschaftlichem und inviduellem Lebensprozeß' in *Weimarer Beiträge*, 10 (1981).

36   G. Lukács, *History and Class Consciousness*, tr. Rodney Livingstone (London, 1971).

37   Engelberg and Küttler, *Formationstheorie und Geschichte*, chs 3 and 4.

38   See *inter alia* Marx's own description of himself in his letter to J. Weydemeyer in *MEW*, vol. XXVIII, p. 508.

39   Marx and Engels, *Communist Manifesto*, tr. D. A. Drennen (Woodbury, N.Y., 1972), p. 176; Marx, *Theorien über den Mehrwert*, Part II, p. 111, and *Grundrisse*, pp. 145f.; Engels, *Anti-Dühring* in *MEW*, vol. XX, pp. 262–4; *Dialektik der Natur* in *MEW*, vol. XX, pp. 323f.

40   Engelberg and Küttler, *Formationstheorie und Geschichte*, chapter 5; Engels, Introduction written for the single-volume edition of Marx's *The Class Struggles in France 1848–1850* in *MEW*, vol. XXI. See also Engels's late letters in *MEW*, vols XXXVIII and XXXIX.

41   See A. A. Leontyev in A. N. Leontyev, A. A. Leontyev and E. G. Judin, *Grundfragen einer Theorie der sprachlichen Tätigkeit* (Berlin (GDR), 1984), pp. 61–72.

42   Although Habermas mentions L. S. Vygotsky in a marginal reference note, he does not work with his conception and school. L. S. Vygotsky, *Thought and Language*, tr. E. Hanfmann and G. Vakar (Boston, 1965).

43   See *inter alia* A. N. Leontyev, *Tätigkeit–Bewußtsein–Persönlichkeit* (Berlin (GDR), 1979); P. Ja. Galperin, *Zu Grundfragen der Psychologie* (Berlin (GDR), 1980); J. Lompscher (ed.), *Probleme der Ausbildung geistiger Handlungen. Neuere Untersuchungen zur Anwendung der Lerntheorie Galperins* (Berlin (GDR), 1972). A. Luria, *Language and Cognition* (London, 1982); D. Elkonin, *Psychologie des Spiels* (Berlin (GDR), 1980); A. N. Leontyev, et al., *Grundfragen*; B. F. Lomov, *Problema obschtschenija v psichologii* (Moscow, 1981), and *Meshlitschnoje wosprijatije v gruppe* (Moscow, 1981).

44   Cf. I. Prigogine, *Vom Sein zum Werden* (Munich, 1979); I. Prigogine and I.

Stengers, *Dialog mit der Natur* (Munich, 1981).

45 Cf. G. Tembrock, *Biokommunikation I und II* (Berlin, Oxford and Brunswick, 1971), and *Grundriß der Verhaltenswissenschaften* (Berlin (GDR), 1980).

46 G. Tembrock, 'Verhaltenswissenschaften in Theorie und Praxis' in *Sitzungsberichte der AdW der DDR*, no. 7/N (Berlin, 1983), p. 13.

47 On the problem of the degree of coupling of evolutionary mechanisms, without recognizing that this problem would have to be put in terms of communication theory, see the articles by R. Harré and S. Toulmin in H. H. Holz and H. J. Sandkühler (eds), *Dialektik*, no. 5: *Darwin und die Evollutionstheorie* (Cologne, 1982), pp. 68–78, 94–104. Determining the measure of coupling of evolutionary mechanisms would make it possible to answer the question as to the evolution of evolutionary criteria. Cf. on the problem of the evolution of evolutionary criteria K. M. Zavadsky and E. I. Kolchinsky, *Evoluzija Evoluziij* (Leningrad, 1977). This, in turn, would also permit an 'ecological' access, in Toulmin's sense (*Kritik der kollektiven Vernunft*, Frankfurt, 1978), to the specification of 'rationality', supplementing the access in terms of argumentation theory inaugurated by Toulmin, cf. S. Toulmin, *The Uses of Argument* (Cambridge, 1948); A. Janik, R. Rieke, S. Toulmin, *An Introduction to Reasoning* (London and New York, 1979).

48 Marx, *A Contribution to the Critique of Political Economy*, tr. S. W. Ryazanskaya (Moscow, 1981), p. 22.

49 Ibid., p. 213; cf. also Marx and Engels, *The German Ideology*, tr. S. W. Ryazanskaya (London, 1965), pp. 80ff.; Marx, *Grundrisse*, pp. 471, 473.

50 Marx, *Capital*, vol. I, p. 439.

51 See Marx, *Grundrisse*, pp. 304–5, 516–26, 682–7, 690–704; *Theorien über den Mehrwert*, Part I in *MEW*, vol. XXVI. 1, pp. 367–70; Part III in *MEW*, vol. XXVI. 3, pp. 252–6, cf. also H. Laitko, *Wissenschaft als allgemeine Arbeit* (Berlin (GDR), 1979).

52 Cf. also Marx, *Grundrisse*, pp. 682–704.

53 Ibid., pp. 397–8. Cf. Marx, *Capital*, vol. III, pp. 352–64, 614, 965–70; Marx, *Theory of Surplus Value*, tr. G. A. Bonner and E. Burns (London, 1951), pp. 368–71.

54 Marx, *Grundrisse*, pp. 398ff.; cf. pp. 474ff.

55 Marx, *Capital*, vol. I, pp. 287, 297.

56 Cf. ibid., vol. III, p. 164; ibid., vol. I, pp. 505–6; vol. II, tr. D. Fernbach (Harmondsworth, 1978), pp. 327f.

57 Within the context of his analysis of capital Marx rejects concepts of money that do not conceive of the money form as emerging from the value form, but outside this context also refers to the character of money as a sign. Cf. on these distinctions Marx, *Grundrisse* (Berlin, 1953), pp. 903, 908; *Capital*, vol. I, pp. 143, 167, 179, 182–7, 198, 207.

58 Cf. Marx, *Grundrisse*, pp. 532–3, 693–704; *Capital*, vol. I, p. 617.

59 Marx, *Theorien über den Mehrwert*, Part I, pp. 385f.

60 Ibid., pp. 379ff. Cf. Marx, *Capital*, vol. III, p. 414.

61 Cf. Marx, *Grundrisse*, pp. 90, 278f., 694f.; *Capital*, vol. I, p. 617; *Theorien über den Mehrwert*, Part III, pp. 511f.

62 Cf. Marx and Engels, *The German Ideology*, pp. 32ff., 43ff., 64ff., 91ff., 396, 415, 483; *Capital*, vol. I, pp. 470–89; vol. II, pp. 120ff.

63   Marx, *Capital*, vol. III, p. 182; cf. ibid., pp. 985ff., *Theorien über den Mehr-wert*, Part II, p. 11; *Grundrisse*, pp. 144–5.
64   Marx, *Grundrisse*, pp. 532–3; cf. ibid., p. 704.
65   Marx and Engels, *The German Ideology*, pp. 39, 41.
66   A. N. Leontyev et al., *Grundfragen*, pp. 62–70.
67   See H. H. Holz, *Dialektik und Widerspiegelung* (Cologne, 1983), and *Natur und Gehalt spekulativer Sätze* (Cologne, 1983).
68   Marx, *Grundrisse*, p. 483.
69   Cf. ibid., p. 80.
70   See Hartung, *Gesellschaftlichkeit der Sprache*, Hartung and Schönfeld, *Kommunikation und Sprachvariation*.
71   Cf. J. M. Lotman, 'Kultur–Information–Sprache' in his *Kunst als Sprache* (Leipzig, 1981), pp. 27ff.
72   Cf. Leontyev, *Tätigkeit*, pp. 102–9, 140–51; Luria, *Sprache und Bewußtsein*, pp. 129ff., 156ff., 172f., 282–90 (*Language and Cognition*, London, 1982); Elkonin, *Psychologie des Spiels*, pp. 335–66.
73   K. Holzkamp, *Gesellscháftlichkeit des Individuums* (Cologne, 1978), p. 156.
74   Cf. Kühne, *Zum Begriff und zur Methode*, p. 31.
75   See Leontyev, *Tätigkeit*, pp. 154, 220.
76   K. Holzkamp, *Gesellschaftlichkeit des Individuums*, p. 156, Cf. Dölling, 'Zur Vermittlung'.
77   Cf. Luria, *Sprache und Bewußtsein*, pp. 129ff., 156ff., 288ff.
78   See Leontyev et al., *Grundfragen*, pp. 112f., 117ff., 263ff.
79   Cf. Lotman, *Kunst als Sprache*, pp. 16, 113ff.
80   'Humanities' as distinct from the contrast between natural and social sciences; cf. J. Piaget, *Erkenntnistheorie der Wissenschaften vom Menschen* (Frankfurt, Berlin and Vienna, 1973).
81   Cf. on the structuring of an 'informatics' that covers this aspect of the theory of social communication K. Fuchs-Kitowsky, 'Wechselbeziehungen zwischen Automat und Gesellschaft: Zu Strategien des Einsatzes der automatisierten Informationsverarbeitung', *Zeitschrift der Humboldt-Universität zu Berlin*, *Math.-Naturwiss. R.*, 5 (1979); K. Fuchs-Kittowsky, H. Kaiser, R. Tschirshvitz and B. Wenzlaff, *Informatik und Automatisierung*, vol. I (Berlin, 1976).
82   V. I. Lenin, 'Konspekt zu Hegels "Wissenschaft der Logik"' in V. I. Lenin, *Werke*, vol. XXXVIII, Philosophische Hefte (Berlin (GDR), 1971), pp. 182, 189.

NOTES TO CHAPTER 9

1   The differentiation of structural components of the lifeworld (person, society and culture), following Mead; the differentiation of the value spheres of truth, goodness and beauty, following Weber; the decentring of the understanding of world, following Piaget; the genesis of post-conventional notions of morality, following Kohlberg; the linguistification of the sacred, following Durkheim; the institutionalization of individualism and value generalization, following Parsons.
2   Niklas Luhmann, 'Autopoiesis: Handlung und kommunikative Verständigung', *Zeitschrift für Soziologie*, 2 (1982), pp. 366–79.
3   'Even practices apparently related strictly to functions of communication for its

own sake ... or communication for the purpose of knowledge and cognition, such as holidays and ceremonies, ritual exchange-relations or, on another level, the circulation of scientific information, are always more or less overtly oriented toward political and economic functions.' Cf. P. Bourdieu, *Outline of a Theory of Practice*, tr. R. Nice (Cambridge, 1977). Bourdieu calls for the dichotomy between economic and non-economic spheres to be jettisoned because it prevents 'the science of economic practices from being grasped as a particular case of the economy of practical actions which is above all capable of grasing all actions, even those that are understood as disinterested or unmotivated or freed from the economy, as economic actions directed toward the maximalization of material or symbolic profit' (ibid., pp. 356f.).

4 Max Weber, *Wirtschaft und Gesellschaft* (Tübingen, 1972), p. 13.

5 Samuel Bowles and Herbert Gintis, 'Structure and Practice in the Labor Theory of Value', *The Review of Radical Political Economy* (1981), p. 12; cf. also Anthony Giddens, *New Rules of Sociological Method* (London, 1976), on the concept of structuration, as well as Bourdieu, *Outline*, on the concept of praxeological cognition.

6 O. E. Williamson, *Markets and Hierarchies: Analysis and Antitrust Implications* (New York, 1975).

7 R. Edwards, *Herrschaft im modernen Produktionsprozess* (Frankfurt, 1981).

8 Johannes Berger, 'Wandlungen von Krisisursachen im wohlfahrtsstaatlichen Kapitalismus' in *Monetäre Restriktionen: Die Inflationsbekämpfung* (*Argument*, Sonderband no. 68).

9 Samuel Bowles and Herbert Gintis, *The Crisis of Liberal Democractic Capitalism* (Amherst, 1980).

NOTES TO CHAPTER 10

1 Jürgen Habermas, *The Theory of Communicative Action*, (Boston, 1987), vol. II, p. 400 (hereafter cited as *TCA*).

2 Ibid., p. 399.

3 Cf. with regard to this thesis, which can draw on the results of Lévi-Strauss's analysis of mythical thought, Antje Linkenbach, *Opake Gestalten des Denkens: Jürgen Habermas und die Rationalität fremder Lebensformen* (Munich, 1986).

4 Jürgen Habermas, *Vorstudien und Ergänzungen zur Theorie des Kommunikativen Handelns* (Frankfurt, 1984), pp. 506–7 (hereafter cited as *VE*).

5 Such ideas are to be found, for example, in some of the more recent works of Ferenc Feher and Agnes Heller. They interpret capitalism, democracy and industrialization as three autonomous 'logics of modernity'. Cornelius Castoriadis, by contrast, emphasizes two constitutive elements of modernity which, in the final instance, are based on imaginary significations and thus cannot be reduced to any unambiguous structural or developmental patterns. In this view the specifically capitalist project of an unlimited expansion of rational mastery – which makes possible an unleashing of the productive forces, but can also take on other forms – is linked in a complex and contradictory manner with the more or less explicit idea of an autonomous society, i.e. one oriented toward a maximum of self-determination. After a first attempt in the shape of

the Greek polis and following its revival in the urban movements of the Middle Ages, this project has in its later stages – not only through the practice of the workers' movement, but also through the agency of other social forces – come to play an important role in determining the shape of the modern world. Finally, some of the French theorists who have discussed this topic use a concept of modernity almost diametrically opposed to the above. Two representative studies in this context are Henri Lefebvre's *Introduction à la modernité* (Paris, 1967) and Jean Chesneaux's *De la modernité* (Paris, 1983). Their approach focuses on the specifically modern dynamics of real abstraction, which does not fully come into force until a relatively late stage of capitalist development; this stage is characterized by the absorption or marginalization of revolutionary tendencies as well as by an accelerated process of internationalization. The basic underlying pattern of modernity would accordingly be a generalized strategy of subsumption, which promotes a more rapid destruction of precapitalist traditions and cuts away the ground under anticapitalist aspirations. Chesneaux writes in this vein (p. 21) that 'the more "modern" an activity becomes, the more it is separated from its natural and social environment.' It goes without saying that this thesis amounts in the final instance to an equation of modernization with the destruction of meaning; such prospects prompted Michel Leiris to coin an untranslatable play on words: 'La modernité s'est muée en merdonité.'

6   *TCA*, vol. II, p. 312.

7   Ibid., p. 345.

8   It would seem advisable to speak of 'non-capitalist' rather than 'state capitalist' or 'bureaucratic-socialist' societies. the term 'socialist' is, even when used in a derogatory context, an unnecessary concession to an official ideology which has proclaimed the identification of post-revolutionary societies with socialism as a dogma. On the other hand, the designation 'non-capitalist' is not intended to suggest that the societies concerned have definitively severed all ties to the 'historical universe' (Castoriadis) of capitalism. The development of the Soviet model has to a great degree been co-determined by a dependence – partly direct in nature and partly taking the indirect form by subaltern competition – on the capitalist world system.

9   *VE*, p. 480.

10 Ibid., p. 568.

11 In his 'Critical Sociology and Authoritarian State Socialism' in John B. Thompson and David Held (eds), *Habermas: Critical Debates* (London, 1982), pp. 196–218, Andrew Arato lists three ideological complexes which either compete with Marxism-Leninism or enter into conjunctural or long-term combinations with it: firstly, a reformism bereft of clear political contours which takes the historical model of the NEP as its point of orientation; secondly an authoritarian-technocratic trend; and finally a traditionalist-nationalist current.

12 Habermas's aversion to the theory of totalitarianism leads him – among other things – to interpret its best-known literary version in the spirit of a very different diagnosis of the times. He speaks of an 'Orwellian state ... in which all integrative operations have been converted from the ... sociative mechanism of reaching understanding in language over to systemic mechanisms'

(*TCA*, vol. II, p. 312). But it seems extremely far-fetched to describe Big Brother and Newspeak as systemic mechanisms; they are, rather, paradigmatic examples of the pseudo-concrete (Kosik).

13 Immanuel Wallerstein, *The Modern World System*, vols I–III (New York, 1974, 1978 and 1988); *Essays on the Capitalist World Economy* (New York, 1979); *Historical Capitalism* (London, 1989). Cf. also the essay 'The Modern World System as a Civilization', *Thesis Eleven* no. 20, pp. 70–86.

14 Wallerstein, *Historical Capitalism*, p. 56.

15 Cf. Fernard Braudel, *Civilization and Capitalism, 15th–18th Century*, vols I–III (Glasgow, 1981, 1982 and 1984).

16 Wallerstein also emphasizes that monopolistic strategies do not represent symptoms of decay or of the approaching demise of capitalism. 'Thus monopolistic practice and competitive motivation have been a paired reality of historical capitalism' (*Historical Capitalism*, p. 34).

17 A classic example of this line of argument is Schumpeter's essay 'Zur Soziologie der Imperialismen' first published in 1919 in *Archiv fur Sozialwissenschaft und Sozialpolitik*. Among recent contributions, Arno J. Mayer's *The Persistence of the Old Regime* (London, 1981) is particularly noteworthy.

18 For an example of the neo-Marxist reception of Hegel's theory of the state see Henri Lefebvre's *De l'Etat*, vols I–IX (Paris, 1976–8). Cf. in particular his conclusion: 'Having overcome various trials and tribulations – liberal democracy, progressive conservatism etc. – the state returns to its Hegelian prototype. The state and its logic, the products of a revolution, turn against their history (and in this sense against all history) in the course of a worldwide process, the analysis of which calls for the introduction of new concepts' (vol. IV, p. 402).

19 Recent sociology of development has focused on the developmental potential of the different traditions and the numerous hybrid forms of tradition and modernity; in this context, the writings of S. N. Eisenstadt are particularly revealing. But his analyses also show the limits of such an approach; as long as one conceives of modernity as a closed and unified civilizational model, tradition can, in principle, only be regarded as either a limiting or a predisposing factor (or, from another point of view, as a retarding or accelerating one). Cf. S. N. Eisenstadt, 'European Expansion and the Civilization of Modernity' in H. Wesseling (ed.), *Expansion and Reaction* (Leiden, 1978), pp. 167–86. But if modernity is understood as an open and ambivalent constellation, the traditions capable of further development can play a genuinely co-determining role.

20 Cf. Niklas Luhmann, 'Einleitende Bemerkungen zu einer Theorie symbolisch generalisierter Kommunikationsmedien' in his *Soziologische Aufklärung*, vol. II (Opladen, 1975), pp. 170–192.

21 *TCA*, vol. I, p. 95.

22 Ibid., p. 287.

23 Ibid., vol. II, p. 138. We can ignore the third component of the lifeworld at this juncture; the culturalistic – more precisely cognitivistic – thrust becomes apparent from the fact that Habermas defines personality as the embodiment of those competences which enable the subject to participate in language and action.

24 Georges Sorel, *Über die Gewalt* (Frankfurt, 1969), p. 208.

25   *TCA*, vol. II, p. 337f.

26   I have analysed the internal conflict of paradigms in the theory of value in my *Zwischen Natur und Gesellschaft* (Cologne, 1976), pp. 192–289.

27   Hannah Arendt, *The Origins of Totalitarianism* (London, 1986).

28   Leszek Nowak, *Property and Power: Towards a Non-Marxian Historical Materialism* (Dordrecht, 1983).

29   In his rejoinder to Giddens's objections (*VE*, p. 548), Habermas mentions three concepts of power which he proposes to integrate in his theory: in addition to the media-theoretic concept, the communications-theoretic concept of power used by Arendt, and the Weberian concept of domination. However, Habermas combines the three perspectives in a manner which excludes any power-theoretic synthesis. He raises the two latter concepts only in the context of legitmation problems; the actual power-theoretic issues are reserved for media theory.

30   For a good example, cf. Ernest Gellner, *Nationalism* (Oxford, 1985), pp. 18–22; similar thoughts are to be found in the works of other theorists.

31   Cornelius Castoriadis, 'Reflections on Development and Rationality', *Thesis Eleven* no. 10/11, pp. 18–36; cf. also his *The Imaginary Institution of Society* (Cambridge, 1987).

32   Norbert Elias, *Was ist Soziologie?* (Munich, 1970), p. 99.

33   *TCA*, vol. I, p. 397.

34   Karl Marx, *Grundrisse* (Harmondsworth, 1977), p. 109.

35   *VE*, p. 489.

36   Cf. Jürgen Habermas, *Zur Rekonstruktion des Historischen Materialismus* (Frankfurt, 1976), pp. 171–3.

37   *TCA*, vol. II, p. 353.

38   Ibid., p. 354.

39   Cf. ibid., p. 398.

40   Cf. Jürgen Habermas, *The Philosophical Discourse of Modernity*, tr. Frederick Lawrence (Cambridge, 1987).

41   *TCA*, vol. II, p. 196.

42   H. A. Korff's essay 'Das Wesen der Romantik', first published in 1929, is still very relevant to this issue; it was republished in *Begriffsbestimmung der Romantik* (Darnstadt, 1968). Among recent contributions, Georges Gusdorf's works are particularly noteworthy: *Naissance de la conscience romantique au XVIIIème siècle* (Paris, 1976); *Fondements du savoir romantique* (Paris, 1982); *Dieu et le néant dans le savoir romantique* (Paris, 1983) and *L'homme romantique* (Paris, 1984).

43   Marx, *Grundrisse*, p. 162.

44   Hans Blumenberg, *Arbeit am Mythos* (Frankfurt, 1979), pp. 68–126. At another point in his *Die Lesbarkeit der Welt* (Frankfurt, 1981), p. 233, he speaks of an 'immanent tendency open to mad delusion, of the species' which supposedly manifests itself in the more extreme forms of Romantic consciousness. But as the historical experience of our century has shown, this 'openness to mad delusion' can also make use of absolutized figures of Enlightenment thought. A case in point is the phantasm of a complete mastery over nature, but also such aberrant visions as that of a closed and definitive scientific *Weltanschauung* of revolutionary action.

45 Max Weber, *The Methodology of the Social Sciences* (New York, 1949), p. 81.

46 Cf. Ben Anderson, *Imagined Communities* (London, 1983). The concept of modernity which Habermas uses in *The Theory of Communicative Action* and later writings occludes the specific problematic of the nation and nationalism. But in an earlier text (*Zur Rekonstruktion*, p. 29), we come across the following reference: 'The nation is a modern form of identity which blunts the contradiction between the infra-state universalism of bourgeois law and morality on the one hand and the particularism of the single state on the other, making both of them subjectively bearable.' This suggested interpretation could easily be generalized if we proceed from a concept of modernity as a field of tensions. We would then have to examine to what extent nationalism has also contributed to the blunting or preventive neutralization of other polarities.

47 There is, of course, another explanatory hypothesis which has been put forward by some analysts of Soviet affairs; Moshe Lewin's book, *The Gorbachev Phenomenon*, is perhaps the most representative example. On this view, the policies known as *glasnost* and *perestroika* are above all a response to the internal transformations of Soviet society. But the change of course was obviously not brought about by the pressure of social forces, and everything we know about the structure and the history of Soviet-type societies suggests that the adaptation of the state to the 'social system' should not be taken for granted. This is easier to understand if we analyse the state in terms of a transfunctional fusion of the sources of social power rather than the dysfunctional over-extension of a medium.

48 Cf. Cornelius Castoriadis, *Devant la guerre* (Paris, 1982).

NOTES TO CHAPTER 11

1 Cf. the essays in John B. Thompson and David Held (eds), *Habermas: Critical Debates* (London, 1982); R. J. Bernstein (ed.), *Habermas and Modernity* (Cambridge, 1985); further contributions are to be found in *New German Critique, Special Issue on Jürgen Habermas*, 35 (Summer 1985).

2 Jürgen Habermas, *Vorstudien und Ergänzungen zur Theorie des kommunikativen Handelns* (Frankfurt, 1984), pp. 11–126.

3 Jürgen Habermas, *Moral Consciousness and Communicative Action*.

4 Jürgen Habermas, *The Philosophical Discourse of Modernity*, tr. Frederick Lawrence (Cambridge, 1987); this discussion had in different ways already been 'called for' by American colleagues: Hubert L. Dreyfus and Paul Rabinow, *Michel Foucault: Beyond Structuralism and Hermeneutics* (Brighton, 1982); Martin Jay, *Marxism and Totality* (Berkeley, 1984) p. 509; on the challenge neo-structuralism poses for Critical Theory see also Albrecht Wellmer, *In Defence of Modernity*.

5 For a preparatory piece, see Habermas, 'Moral und Sittlichkeit. Hegels Kantkostik im Lichte der Diskursethik', *Merkur*, 442 (1985), p. 1041ff.

6 H. Gripp, *Jürgen Habermas, Und es gibt sie doch. Zur Kommunikationstheoretischen Begründung von Vernunft bei Jürgen Habermas* (Munich,

1984); St. K. White, *Habermas on Reason, Justice and Modernity* (Cambridge, 1988).

7 Cf. Wilhelm von Humboldt, 'Über den Nationalcharakter der Sprachen' in *Schriften zur Sprachphilosophie. Werke*, vol. III (Darmstadt, 1963), p. 81: 'A lively, engaged conversation in which the speakers truly exchange ideas and feelings is in itself the central point of language, as it were, the essence of which can only be conceived of as echo and re-echo, as speech and reply, and which, in its origins and its transformations never belonged to One but always to All, lies in the lonely depths of each person's Spirit and yet comes to the fore only in sociality.'

8 Von Humboldt, 'Über die Verschiedenheit des menschlichen Sprachbaus und ihren Einfluß auf die geistige Entwicklung des Menschengeschlechts', *Werke*, vol. III, p. 438: 'Language has an objective and independent effect precisely because it is subjectively effected and dependent ... Its dead part, so to speak, must always be generated anew in thought, become alive in speech or understanding and therefore completely merge with the subject ... In this manner it on each occasion experiences the full influence of the individual upon it; yet this influence is already in itself bound by what it [language as a system] effects and has effected.'

9 Ibid., p. 439.

10 Von Humboldt, 'Über den Dualis', *Werke*, vol. III, pp. 138f., 'An unalterable dualism resides in the original essence of language, and the possibility of speech is determined by someone speaking and someone replying. Thought itself is already substantially accompanied by a proclivity for social existence, and human beings long for ... a You that accords with the I, concepts appear to be determinate and certain for them only by being reflected back by a foreign capacity for thought ... The objectivity appears even more perfected if this division does not occur solely within the subject, but rather when the person imagining can truly perceive the thought outside him, which is possible only if perceived in an imagining and thinking Being other than himself. There is no agent other than language mediating between one capacity for thought and another.'

11 Von Humboldt, *Werke*, vol. III, pp. 80f.

12 Ibid., p. 208.

13 Ibid., 'Über den Dualis', pp. 113ff.; 'Über die Verschiedenheit des menschlichen Sprachbaus', ibid., pp. 191ff., in particular pp. 200ff.

14 Von Humboldt, 'Über die Verschiedenheit', p. 160.

15 Von Humboldt, *Werke*, vol. III, p. 150.

16 Ibid., p. 160.

17 Von Humboldt, 'Über den Nationalicharakter der Sprachen', *Werke*, vol. III, pp. 64ff.

18 Von Humboldt, *Werke*, vol. III, p. 20: 'The sum of the cognizable, as the field to be processed by the human Spirit, lies in the middle ... between all language.'

19 Ibid., p. 419.

20 Ibid., pp. 147–8: 'If there is an idea visible throughout all history which gained increasing validity ... then it is the drive to overcome the barriers

which prejudices and one-sided views of all sorts inimically erect between humans and to treat all humanity, without consideration of religion, nation and colour, as one great, almost fraternal tribe.'

21 Cf. Habermas, *Moral Consciousness*, p. 105f. and p. 175f.

22 Cf. the same argument as put forward by Rüdiger Bubner in 'Rationalität als Lebensform. Zu J. Habermas "Theorie des kommunikativen Handelns"' in *Handlung, Sprache und Vernunft* (Frankfurt, 1982), pp. 295ff., 312: 'It is precisely this which pragmatic philosophy has always regarded as a main problem, namely how activity logically follows from a correct insight ... Aristotle insists that the eudaemonia of a successful life is not the object of intersubjectively mediated knowledge but is rather that final horizon of meaningful practice given directly with the human disposition to act.' I have attempted to show why this position, which Bubner has since developed fully (in his *Geschichtsprozesse und Handlungsnormen* (Frankfurt, 1984) cannot be carried to its logical conclusions, in my essay in Herbert Schnädelbach (ed.), *Rationalität* (Frankfurt, 1983), pp. 218ff.

23 Habermas, *Discourse*, pp. 341ff.

24 Charles Taylor, 'Theories of Meaning' in his *'Human Agency and Language, Philosophical Papers*, vol. I (Cambridge 1985), pp. 215ff.

25 I have put forward this argument with respect to Heidegger, Derrida and Castoriadis in *Discourse*, pp. 153ff., 179ff. and 318ff. respectively.

26 I have elaborated on this controversy in moral theory in *Moralität und Sittlichkeit* (Frankfurt, 1985).

27 Thomas A. McCarthy, 'Rationality and Relativism: Habermas' Overcoming of Hermeneutics' in Thompson and Held, pp. 79ff., as well as my answer (to earlier objections) in ibid., pp. 238ff.; cf. also Thomas A. McCarthy, 'Rationalization in the Theory of Communicative Action' in Bernstein, *Hebermas*, pp. 177ff. as well as my reply in ibid., pp. 203ff.

28 Cf. Martin Jay, *Marxism*, pp. 510ff.; B. Waldenfels, *In den Netzen der Lebenswelt* (Frankfurt, 1985), and for my critique of Foucault and Derrida, Habermas, *Discourse* pp. 161ff. and 266ff.

29 Cf. on this Albrecht Wellmer, 'Reason, Utopia and the Dialectic of Enlightenment' in Bernstein, *Habermas*, pp. 35ff., in particular pp. 51ff., and Jürgen Habermas, *Discourse*, pp. 343ff.

30 Habermas, *Moral Consciousness*, p. 18f.

31 Habermas, *Discourse*, pp. 207ff.

32 Cf. fig. 22 in Habermas, *TCA*, vol. II, p. 143

33 Cf. the similar objection raised by G. Lohmann, 'Verdinglichung als empirische Frage' in *Philosophische Rundschau*, 30 (1983), pp. 267ff.

34 Habermas, *Vorstudien*, pp. 226ff., in particular pp. 244ff.

35 Cf. the excursus on the three roots of communicative action in Habermas, *TCA*, vol. II, pp. 62ff.

36 In his excellent doctoral thesis, James F. Bohmann used this thought in order to reformulate the Marxist concept of ideology: *Language and Social Criticism* (Boston University, 1985).

37 Cf. my reply to Martin Jay, which relies on Albrecht Wellmer's analysis, in Bernstein *Habermas*, pp. 199ff. I was not able to take Martin Seel's highly

instructive *Die Kunst der Entzweiung* (Frankfurt, 1985) into account in my answer.

38   In this volume, p. 22.

39   Habermas, *TCA*, vol. I, pp. 114ff.

40   On the virtual participation of the interpreter, cf. ibid., pp. 113ff.

41   Wolfgang Kuhlmann, 'Philosophie und rekonstruktive Wissenschaft', (MS, 1985), contribution to a symposium on the 'Theory of Communicative Action' held in the Centre for Interdisciplinary Studies in Bielefeld.

42   Cf. Jürgen Habermas, 'Rückkehr zur Metaphysik?', *Merkur* 438/9, (September/October 1985), pp. 898–905.

43   I have elaborated this for the relation between moral philosophy and moral developmental psychology, in *Moral Consciousness*.

44   However, Wellmer objects that 'unavoidable suppositions of this type are hypostatized by a discourse theory of truth just as the equally unavoidable suppositions that our words and meanings have a definite meaning are hypostatized by formal semantics' A. Wellmer, 'Zur Rekonstruktion der Diskursethik' in his *Ethik und Dialog: Elemente des moralistischen Urteils* (Frankfurt, 1986). I would counter that precisely these 'hypostatizations', if indeed they are such, *have* to be undertaken by the parties to the argument and the communicative actors themselves – and not by theorists who merely reconstruct these unavoidable presuppositions.

45   I shall return to the observations on truth theory in H. Scheit's *Wahrheit – Diskurs – Demokratie* (Munich, 1987) in a different context. The criticism voiced by L. Nagl, *Gesellschaft und Autonomie* (Vienna, 1983), pp. 29ff. also refers to this complex of issues.

46   R. Zimmermann, *Utopie, Rationalität, Politik* (Freiburg, 1985).

47   Cf. also M. Bartels, 'Sprache und soziales Handeln. Eine Auseinandersetzung mit Habermas' Sprachbegriff', *Zeitschrift für philosophische Forschung*, 36 (1982).

48   Cf. E. Tugendhat, 'J. Habermas on Communicative Action' in G. Seebass and R. Tuomela (eds), *Social Action* (Dordrecht, 1985), pp. 179ff.

49   I am using some of J. Bohman's thoughts; cf. the second chapter in his *Language*, pp. 139ff.

50   Davidson himself lists the categories of sentences which can initially not be analysed by means of the theory: 'Truth and Meaning' in *Synthese* (1967) p. 310.

51   John Searle's 'taxonomy of illocutionary acts' in his *Expression and Meaning* (Cambridge University Press, Cambridge, 1979); cf. also Searle and D. Vanderveken, *Foundations of Illocutionary Logic* (Cambridge, 1985).

52   Cf. my critique of Searle in *TCA*, vol. I, pp. 323ff.

53   R. Zimmermann, *Utopie*, p. 373: 'Habermas hereby expands the talk of the illocutionary sense of speech acts in such a manner that it includes an understanding of its social function.'

54   Cf. Tugendhat's example in Seebass and Tugendhat, *Social Action*, p. 184.

55   Zimmermann speaks of the 'social deployment' of the same illocutionary forces in different contexts. Here, the illocutionary meaning of a normative prescription is 'superimposed' on the illocutionary meaning of the demand.

56 That this second set of conditions belongs to the very meaning of the request expressed can be seen from the meaning that turning it down would have. The foreigner can, with a 'no', negate the presuppositions for the existence of the propositional component ('I have no money on me') or the sincerity of the speaker ('You are trying to con me'), i.e. the claim to truth or sincerity equally implied. Yet, only by saying 'no' so as to dispute the normative context ('Nowadays one does not beg') does the hearer dispute the explicitly raised validity claim.

57 *Inquiry*, 28 (1985), pp. 111ff.

58 Formal semantics is able all the more easily to stylize this borderline case as the norm because demands in the course of ontogeny are initially learned as simple imperatives reinforced by sanctions and only at a later date are acquired as normatively 'backed-up' imperatives.

59 Cf. Habermas, *TCA*, vol. I, pp. 292 and 329.

60 Misunderstandings may have resulted from the fact that, in earlier publications, I *first* presented action types in terms of the criteria for the action orientations ascribed to the actor – and not from the sociological standpoint of the combination of actor attitudes (orientation to success vs. orientation towards reaching understanding) and forms of coordinating different action plans (influence vs. consensus). The underlying teleological structure of all action, including social interactions, was thus lost from view.

61 For example, M. Baurmann, 'Understanding as an Aim and Aims of Understanding' in Seebass and Tuomela, *Social Action*, pp. 187ff. Cf. also Berger, above, p. 172.

62 Zimmermann, *Utopie*, p. 379 nevertheless justifiably objects that 'conversation' cannot be construed *from the same standpoint* as norm-guided or dramaturgical action. The interest in communication gradually becomes independent of the interest in pursuing action plans of one's own; this would suggest, by contrast, that conversation is a special case if studied functionally.

63 This does not exclude combinations such as those which Max Weber considered under the heading 'Social Action': in the case of economic action anchored in civil law, for example, the conflicting action orientations are situated at a different level from that of a normative consensus regarding the legal framework involved. It equally does not exclude hybrid forms such as a politician's rhetorical behaviour: this cannot be analysed point by point in terms of the model of latently strategic behaviour. One must as a whole take the hierarchization of levels of action into account, if both types of action are interwoven. Communicative action is always embedded in the teleological action contexts of the individuals respectively party to it. Admittedly, the situation of someone guilelessly pursuing a random action goal or one not declared explicitly owing to the circumstances must be distinguished from the case of the cunning pursuit of a deliberately concealed, i.e. non-declared action goal striven for strategically as the expected side-effect of a consensus reached communicatively. Conversely, the strategic use of communicative means may be subordinated to the goal of consensus formation if, for example, the situation permits only an indirect process of 'giving the other person to understand something'. I assume that the corresponding actorial attitudes

can also form a hierarchy; attitudes oriented toward success and those oriented toward reaching understanding are incompatible only with reference to one and the same level of action.

64 Johannes Weiss, 'Verständigungsorientierung und Kritik', *Kölner Zeitschrift für Soziologie und Sozialpsychologie* (1983), no. 1, pp. 108ff.

65 Weiss, 'Verständigungsorientierung', p. 113.

66 Cf. Habermas, *TCA*, vol. I, pp. 143–9. The ebullient and sharp-sighted defence of the concept of lifeworld used in social phenomenology which U. Matthiesen devises in order to parry my attempt to adopt this Husserlian heritage for a theory of communication (*Das Dickicht der Lebenswelt und die Theorie des kommunikativen Handelns* (Munich, 1983) suffers from an *over-hasty* linking of the formal-pragmatic analysis of the lifeworld and the sociological use of an empirical concept of lifeworld, which is first introduced into my argument immediately following this analysis. This change of pers-pective is not to be found in Husserl, who always retains the role of the phenomenologist; Schütz misunderstands this to constitute a transition to a regional ontology.

67 Axel Honneth, *Kritik der Macht* (Suhrkamp, Frankfurt, 1985), p. 330.

68 Ibid., p. 317.

69 I, incidentally, do indeed introduce the medium of power in an action-theoretic context, in *TCA*, vol. II. pp. 277f.

70 'Verständigungsorientierung', p. 112.

71 Jürgen Habermas and Niklas Luhmann, *Theorie der Gesellschaft oder Sozial-technologie* (Frankfurt, 1971) p. 254; see further Habermas, 'Hannah Arendt: On the Concept of Power', *Philosophical-Political Profiles*, pp. 171ff.

72 Habermas and Luhmann, *Theorie*, p. 254.

73 Ibid., p. 255: 'Normative systems of institutions which exercise power (and which are repressive in the sense that they prevent interests being realized) can be maintained with the aid of mechanisms which (a) convert the normatively-demanded renunciation of interest realization into an automati-cally functioning, intra-psychic denial of drives . . . ; and (b) secure inter-subjective recognition by norms despite their repressive character, i.e. legiti-mate the institutional order . . . I assume that both mechanisms are connected to the structure of ordinary-language communication and generate ideological distortions of communication.' The formation of ideology, which I at that time still explained with the help of psychoanalytical assumptions, can today, as has been shown in J. F. Bohmann's *Language*, be analysed using a theory of communication.

74 Dux does not pay any real attention to my treatment of anthropological materials; cf. the second chapter in Fred van Gelder's doctoral thesis, inspired by Alfred Schmidt, *Habermas' Begriff des Historischen Materialismus* (Frankfurt, 1985).

75 Richard Münch, *Die Struktur der Moderne* (Frankfurt, 1984).

76 Ibid., p. 96.

77 Münch himself comes to this counterintuitive conclusion, ibid., p. 93: 'When a community says "we hold the theory that the earth circles round the sun to be true" then this is not meant as a statement of fact, but as an expression of

the fact that "holding-this-statement-to-be-true" is socially binding. If an individual disagrees with this statement by the community, then this comprises ... deviation from the norm.'

78 Münch speaks in this context of 'affective binding (bonding) via ritual to tradition'.

79 Habermas, *Discourse*, pp. 199ff.

80 Habermas, *Vorstudien*, pp. 482ff., Habermas, *Discourse*, pp. 62ff., 75ff., 327ff.

81 E. Angehrn doubts this in his, 'Krise der Vernunft. Neuere Beiträge zur Diagnose und Kritik der Moderne', *Philosophische Rundschau* (1986). Admittedly he bases his doubts on the problematic assumption that the paradigm-forming figure of though – reflexion, i.e. the self-referentiality of the cognizing subject – can be *detached* from the objectified relation of the imagining subject to what it imagines, i.e. from the subject-object model.

82 Cf. Habermas, *Legitimation Crisis*, tr. Thomas McCarthy (Boston, 1975) pp. 1ff.

83 The term 'functional integration' (Habermas, *TCA*, vol. II, p. 232) led to misunderstandings – it is, as stated, a quote from Parsons and is equivalent to the label 'system integration' otherwise used.

84 To answer McCarthy and Honneth, let me point out that in the passage they refer to (Habermas, *TCA*, vol. II, p. 232) it is precisely this that I maintain.

85 This amends my position in Habermas, *Vorstudien*, p. 603.

86 One could, taking the example of Luhmann's sociology of law, show in detail that the redefinition of a lifeworldly action domain as a subsystem can be accomplished only at the cost of occluding the essential phenomena from the analysis – that is, at the cost of forfeiting the explanatory power of the theory. We must not forget in this context that the legal system is, owing to its position as agent mediating between system and lifeworld, a relatively favourable example.

87 Habermas, *TCA*, vol. II, pp. 264ff.

88 Honneth, *Kritik*, pp. 332ff.

89 Cf. my excursus on Luhmann in *Discourse*, pp. 368ff. The two-level constuction of my concept of society itself results in my having to distance myself from the most recent developments in Luhmann's systems theory, developments which have gone under the heading of 'authopoiesis'. The media-steered subsystem remain enracinated in the normative context of the lifeworld via the underlying foundations of civil and public law. Cultural action systems such as science cannot be exclusively defined in terms of only one function, however great the degree of their differentiation may be. Rather, they remain tied – via institutions (such as universities) which bundle functions together – to the lifeworldly functional linkage of cultural reproduction, social integration and socialization. One can show empirically that it is here that the 'system autonomy' of such domains of action comes up against its limits. Law has not become 'autonomous' of morality and politics to the extent that it can only describe within an autopoietic, self-referential system that is closed within itself. The result of forcibly doing so is an accesent that is inappropriate to, or a reinterpretation of essential aspects of law. I shall provide justifications for this claim.

90   My more far-reaching attempt to provide structural justifications for this state of affairs (because material reproduction would have to flow into the objective world via the results and consequences of goal-oriented interventions) is daring, perhaps wrong, and at any rate superfluous.

91   Habermas, *TCA*, vol. II, pp. 336ff.

92   Like Berger, F. Cerutti emphasizes in his 'Habermas und Marx' (*Leviathan*, 11 (1983), pp. 365ff.) that 'the system steered by exchange-values ... can equally be partially *or completely* modified by the resistances, struggles and alternative solutions that issue from the lifeworld'. I disagree only with respect to the possibility of the 'liquidation of the medium of exchange value' as a whole. Cerutti appears, as does Marx, to have in mind the possibility that the economy, steered by the flow of money, can switch without losses in differentiation from the medium of money over to the 'media of science and technology' (p. 363). The scepticism I harbour with regard to such a solution and my insistence on the intrinsic value for social evolution of systemically differentiated steering media should by no means be read to signify that I 'have to conceive of the gradual independence achieved by the capitalist economic system' (p. 368) as being irreversible.

93   Habermas, *TCA*, vol. II. pp. 185.

94   In Habermas, *The New Conservatism* tr. Shierry Nicholsen Weber (Cambridge, 1990), pp. 48–70.

95   Habermas, *Discourse*, pp. 357ff.

96   Klaus Eder, *Geschichte als Lernprozeß?* (Frankfurt, 1986).

97   Habermas, *TCA*, vol. II, pp. 166ff.; cf. my analysis of principles of societal organization in Habermas, *Zur Rekonstruktion des historischen Materialismus* (Frankfurt, 1976), pp. 167ff.

98   Cf. Habermas, *TCA*, vol. II, pp. 181ff. and 281f.

99   F. Cerutti, 'Habermas und Marx', p. 353.

100 I admittedly view the relation between communications theory and Lukács's early thesis on reification differently; cf. an interpretation which I find very plausible, undertaken by Hauke Brunkhorst using the tools of a postempiricist theory of science, 'Paradigmenkern und Theoriedynamik der Kritischen Theorie der Gesellschaft', *Soziale Welt*, 34 (1983), pp. 21ff.

101 For an opposing position see Hauke Brunkhorst on two variants of the reception of Romanticism: 'Romantik und Kulturkritik', *Merkur*, 346 (June, 1985), pp. 484ff.

102 Matthiesen, *Dickicht*, cf. the summarizing remarks on p. 133ff.

103 Herbert Scheit, *Wahrheit*, ch. 5: 'Die Konsenstheorie der Wahrheit als die Idee der Demokratie'.

Index